DARE to DISAPPOINT

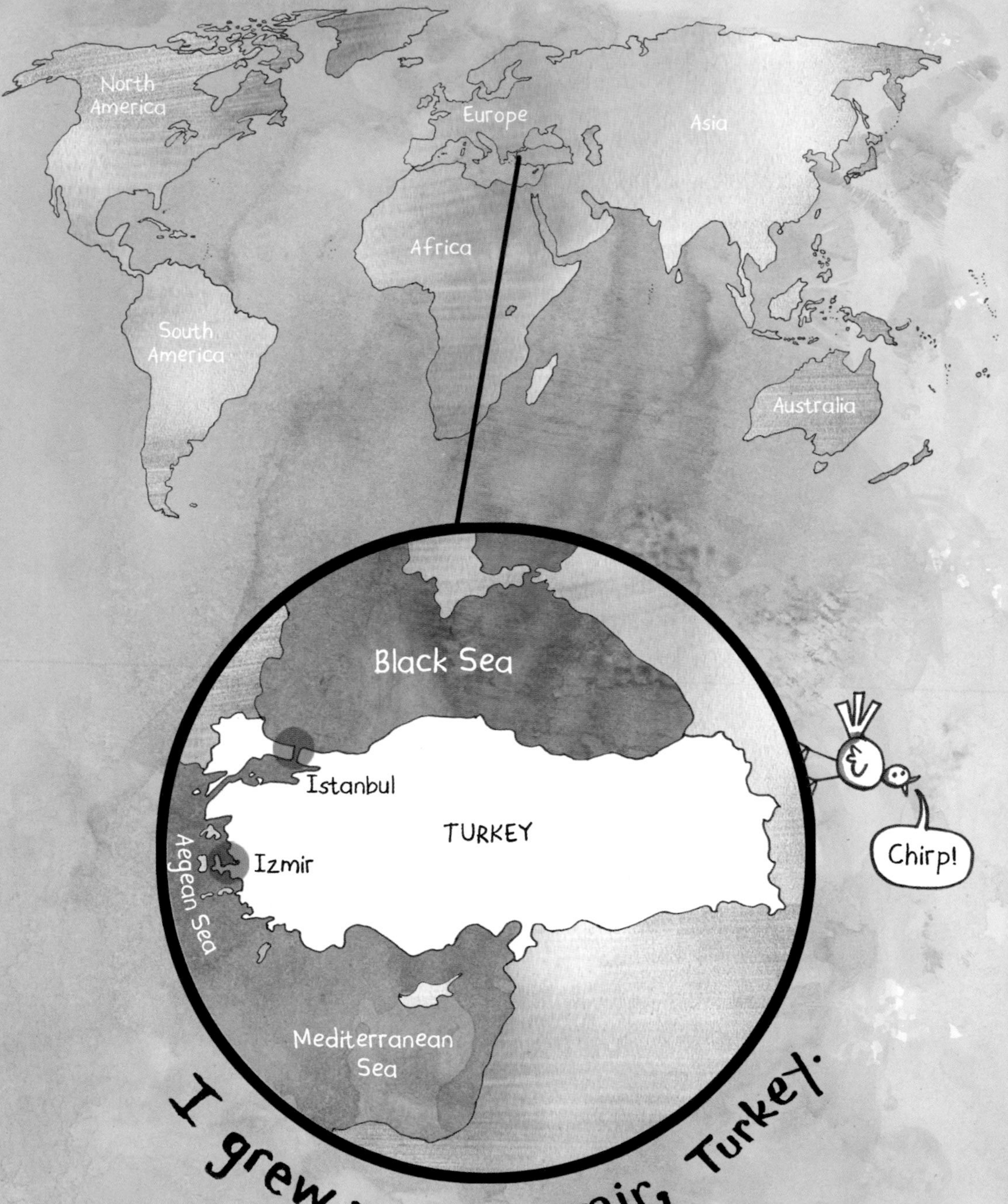
North America
Europe
Asia
Africa
South America
Australia
Black Sea
Istanbul
TURKEY
Izmir
Aegean Sea
Mediterranean Sea
Chirp!

I grew up in Izmir, Turkey.

DARE to DISAPPOINT

Growing Up in Turkey

Özge Samancı

Margaret Ferguson Books

FARRAR STRAUS GIROUX · NEW YORK

Farrar Straus Giroux Books for Young Readers
An imprint of Macmillan Publishing Group, LLC
175 Fifth Avenue, New York, NY 10010

Copyright © 2015 by Özge Samanci
Color separations by Embassy Graphics
Printed in China
Designed by Andrew Arnold
First edition, 2015
5 7 9 10 8 6 4

fiercereads.com

Library of Congress Cataloging-in-Publication Data
Samanci, Özge, 1975-
    Dare to disappoint : growing up in Turkey / Özge Samanci. — First edition.
      pages cm
    "Margaret Ferguson Books."
    ISBN 978-0-374-31698-3 (paperback)
    1. Samanci, Özge, 1975- —Juvenile literature. 2. Samanci, Özge, 1975- —Comic books,
strips, etc. 3. Artists—Turkey—Juvenile literature. 4. Artists—Turkey—Biography—
Comic books, strips, etc. 5. Turkey—History—1960- —Juvenile literature. 6. Turkey—
History—1960- —Comic books, strips, etc. I. Title.

NX565.Z9S26 2015
700.92—dc23
[B]
                                                                    2015000704

Our books may be purchased in bulk for promotional, educational, or business use. Please
contact your local bookseller or the Macmillan Corporate and Premium Sales Department
at (800) 221-7945 x5442 or by email at MacmillanSpecialMarkets@macmillan.com.

For Mom, Dad, Pelin, and Uncle Nihat

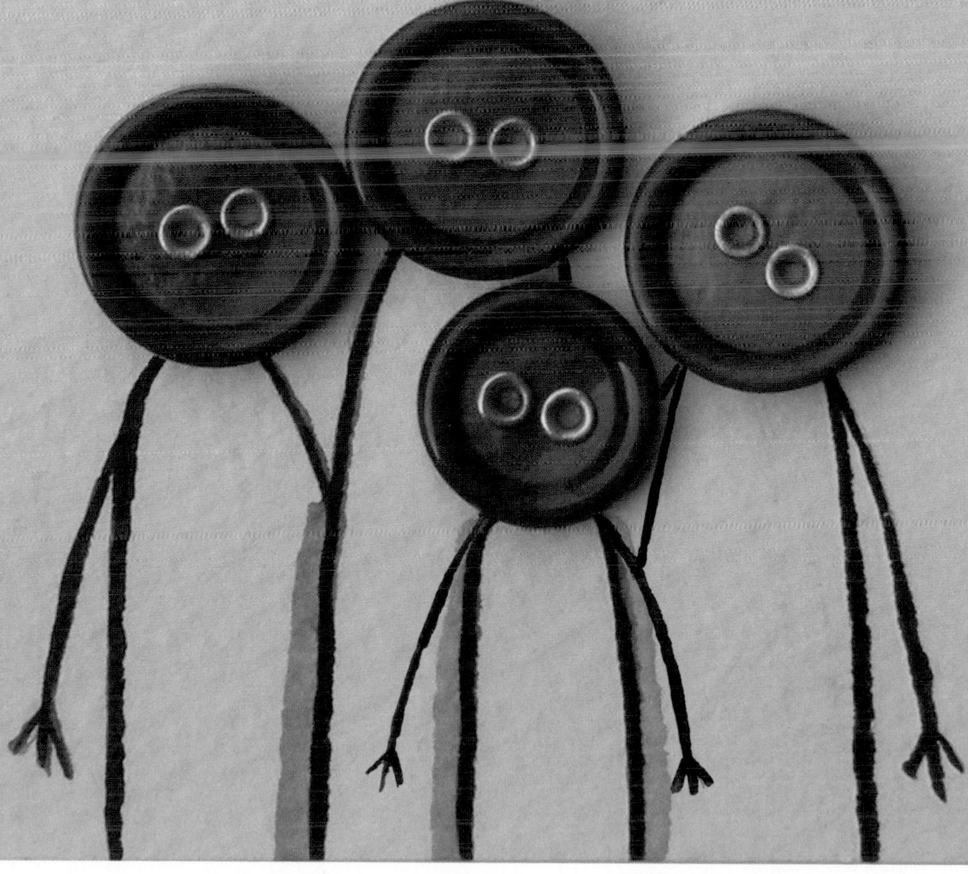

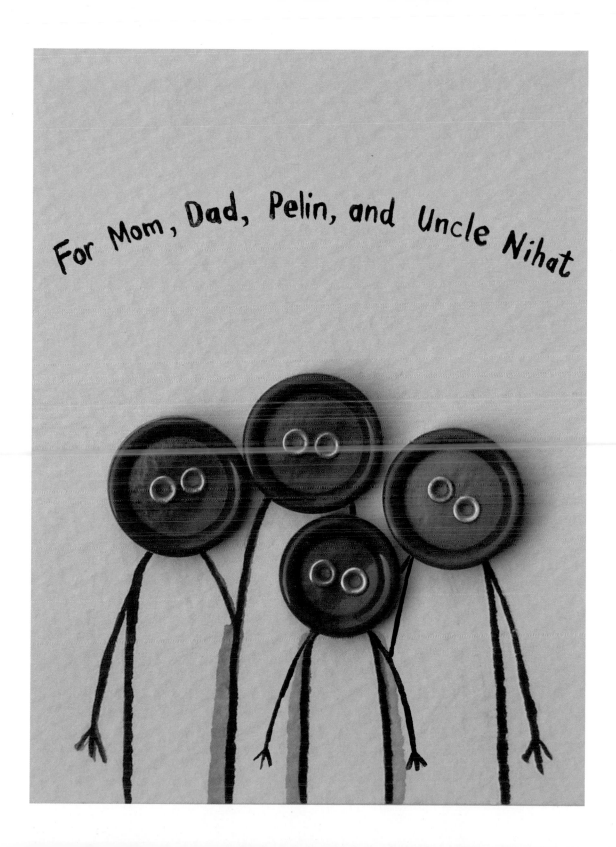

Table of Contents

DARE to DISAPPOINT

Chapter 1

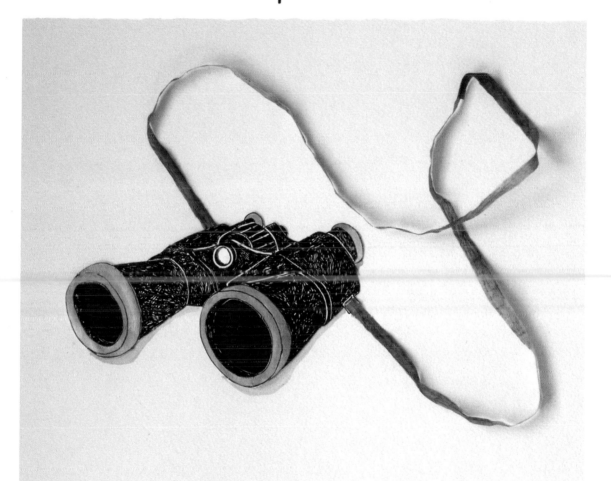

The Other Side

The primary school was across the street from our apartment. Sometimes during recess my sister, Pelin, would come to the edge of the school yard and Mom and I would look at her with binoculars.

Wave, Özge. And don't drop the binoculars.

My sister, Pelin, 8 years old

Hey Hello Hey!

6 years old

School was the place where you could wave to your mother and your sister, who were watching you with binoculars.

I wanted to be on the other side of the binoculars.

I wanted it so much.

When will I start school?

For example, when my cousin came to show her school uniform to my mom...

Auntie, look at my uniform.

Hmm... Flared skirt...

A uniform!

My mom taught sewing at a vocational women's high school.

I turned into a little monster.

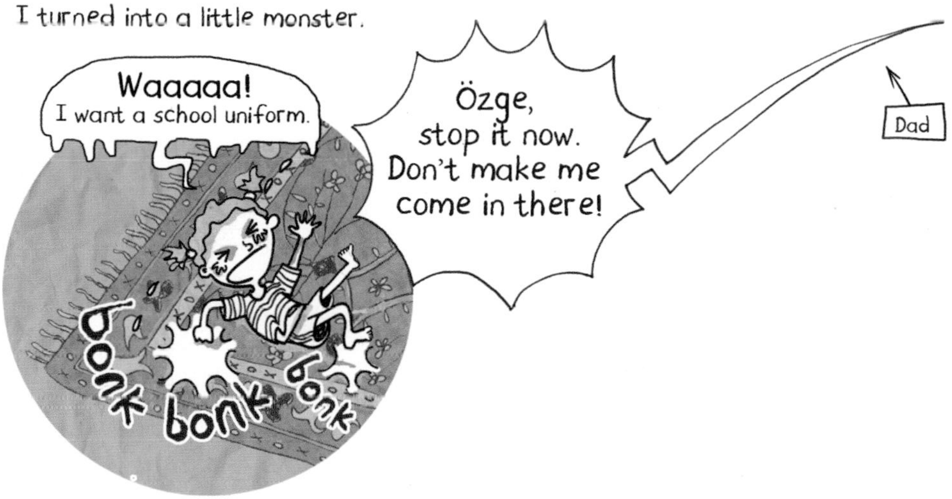
Waaaaa!
I want a school uniform.
Özge, stop it now. Don't make me come in there!
Dad
bonk bonk bonk

Dad was a teacher, too. He taught technical drawing at a vocational men's high school. It was not a good idea to scream or cry around him.

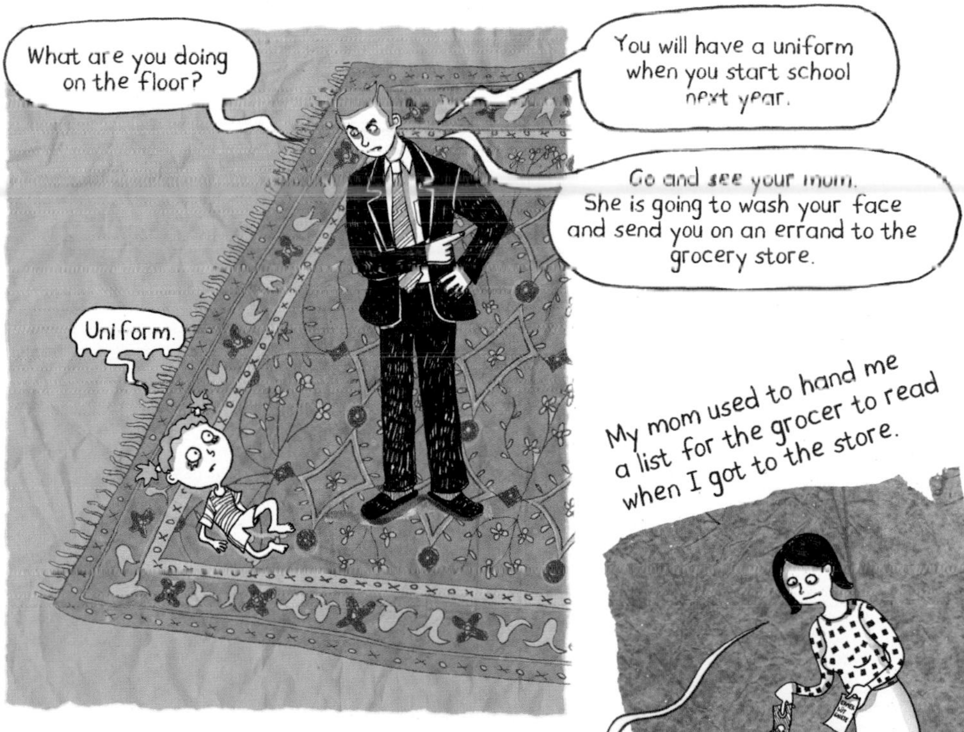
What are you doing on the floor?
You will have a uniform when you start school next year.
Go and see your mom. She is going to wash your face and send you on an errand to the grocery store.
Uniform.

My mom used to hand me a list for the grocer to read when I got to the store.

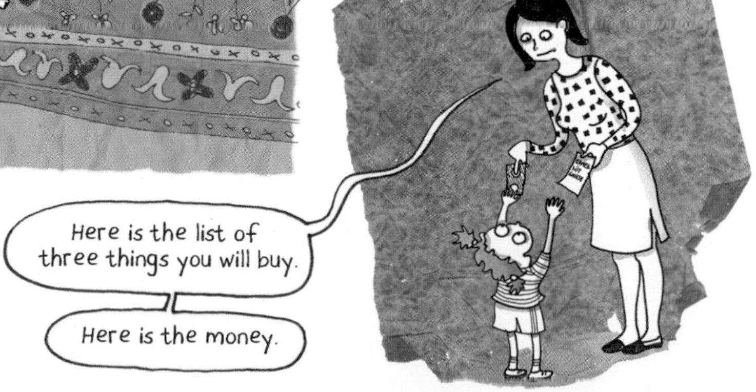
Here is the list of three things you will buy.
Here is the money.

Otherwise, on my way to the grocery store while looking at

kitty cats

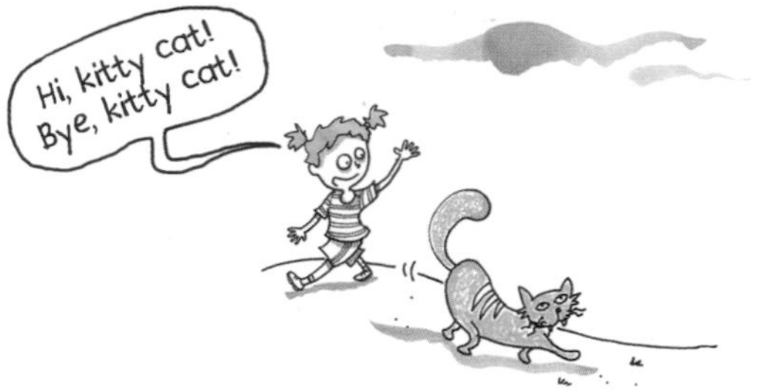
Hi, kitty cat! Bye, kitty cat!

cockleburs

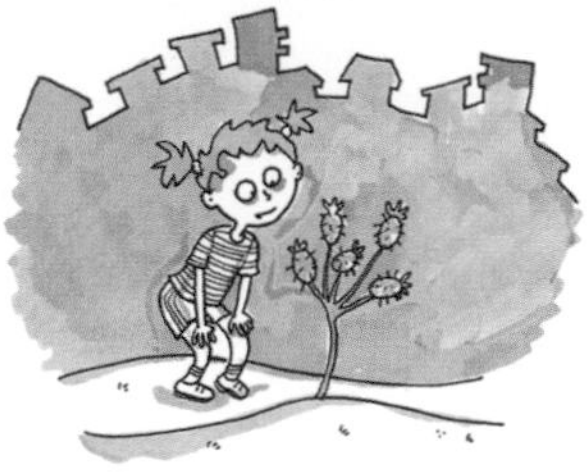

and slogans on the walls

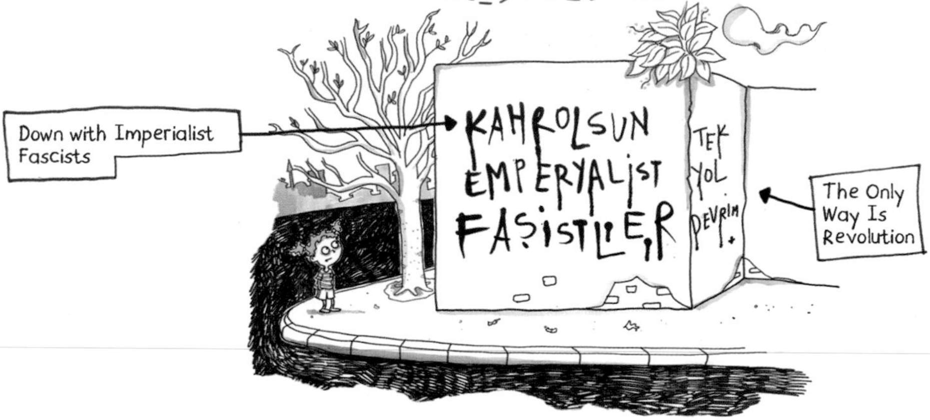
Down with Imperialist Fascists
KAHROLSUN EMPERYALİST FAŞİSTLER
TEK YOL DEVRİM
The Only Way Is Revolution

I would forget what I was supposed to buy

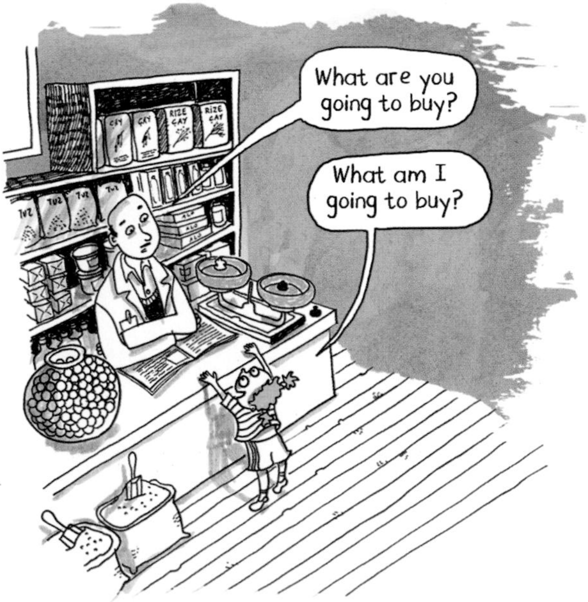
What are you going to buy?
What am I going to buy?

and have to run back home.

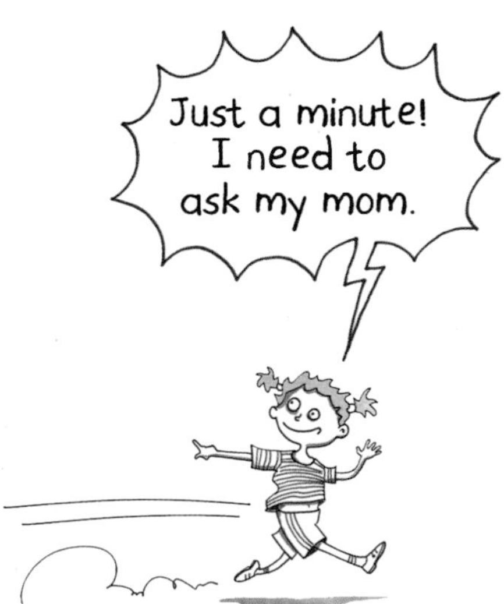
Just a minute! I need to ask my mom.

But one day,

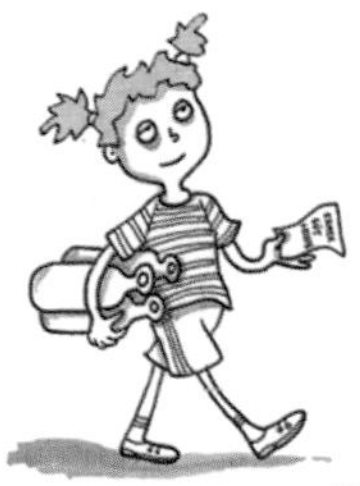

a list in one hand

empty milk bottles in my other hand

my feet took me to Pelin's school instead of the grocery store.

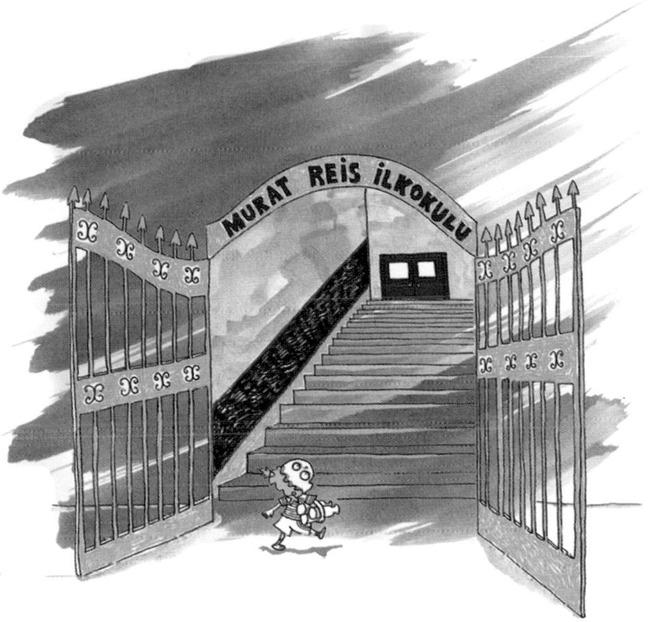
MURAT REIS İLKOKULU

I knew which was her classroom. I knocked on the door and ran in . . .

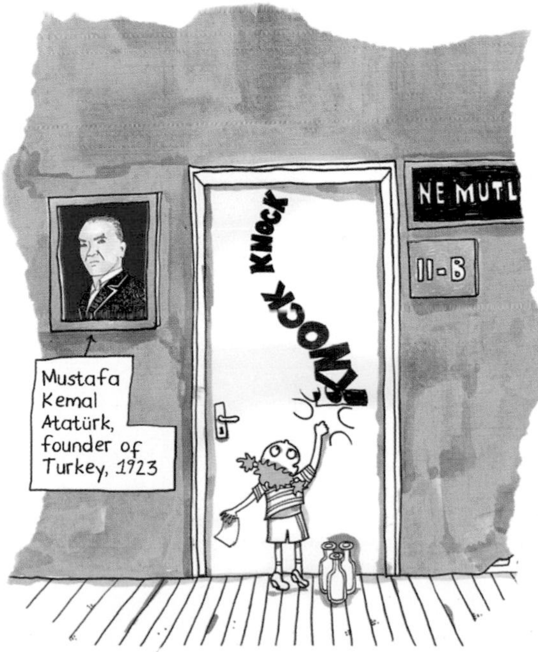
NE MUTL
II-B
KNOCK KNOCK KNOCK
Mustafa Kemal Atatürk, founder of Turkey, 1923

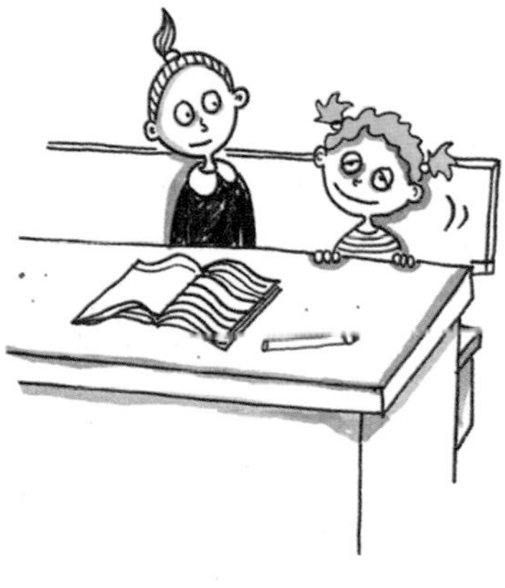

and sat next to Pelin.

Pelin's teacher was fond of children
and stopped teaching math
when he saw me.

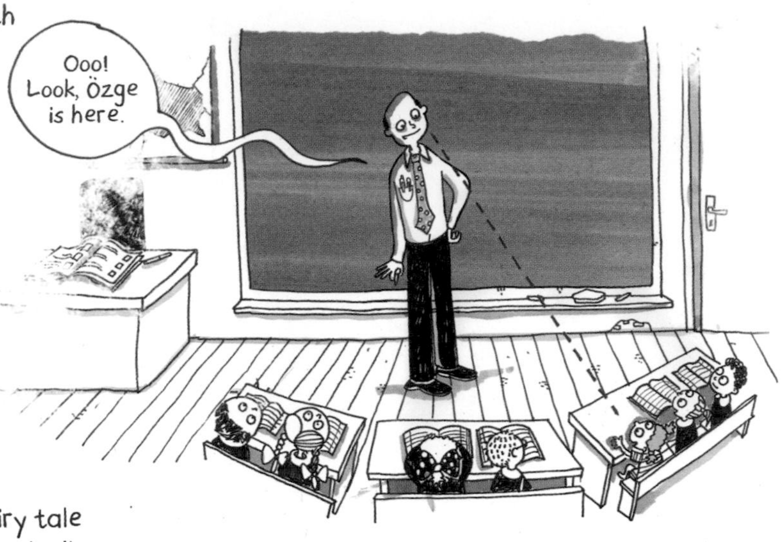
Ooo! Look, Özge is here.

He started to tell us a fairy tale
and drew pictures to illustrate it.
Pelin's classmates welcomed me because their lesson was canceled.
All forty children were thrilled with the impromptu story hour.

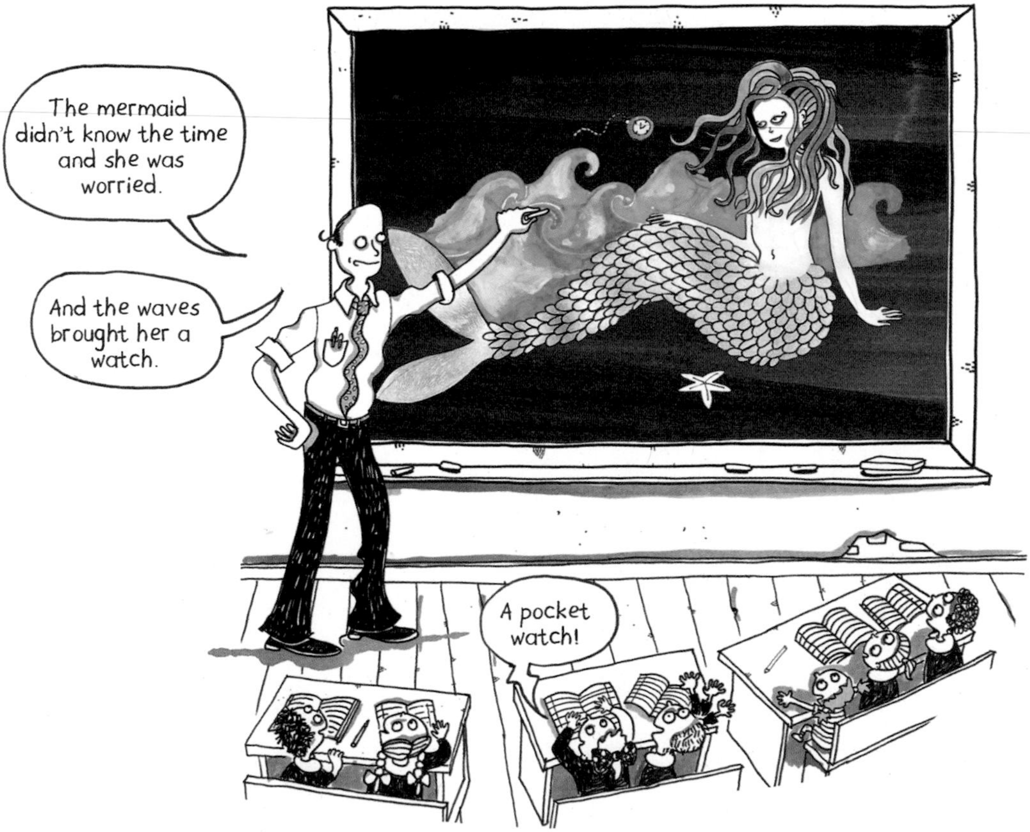
The mermaid didn't know the time and she was worried.
And the waves brought her a watch.
A pocket watch!

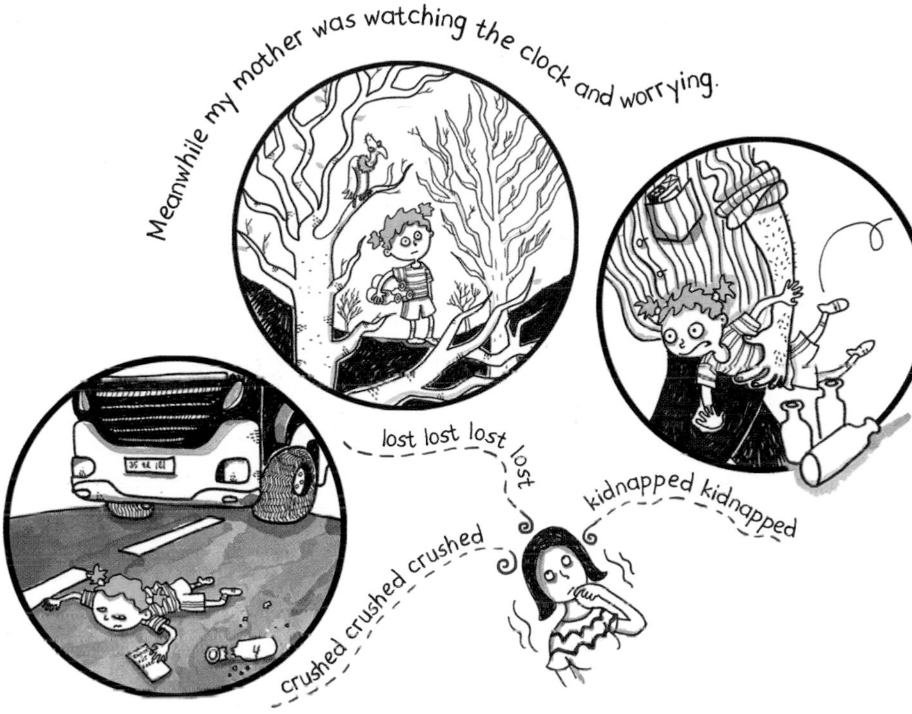
Meanwhile my mother was watching the clock and worrying.
lost lost lost lost
kidnapped kidnapped
crushed crushed crushed

First, she ran to the grocery store.

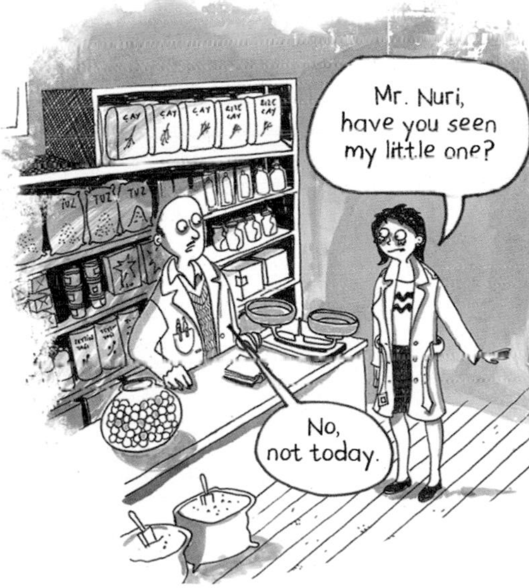
Mr. Nuri, have you seen my little one?
No, not today.

Then she asked some children who were playing on the street.

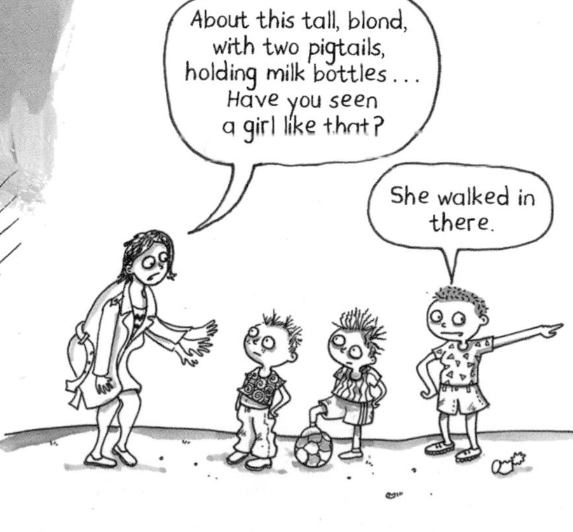
About this tall, blond, with two pigtails, holding milk bottles . . . Have you seen a girl like that?
She walked in there.

Mom rushed into the classroom
and saw this happy
scene . . .

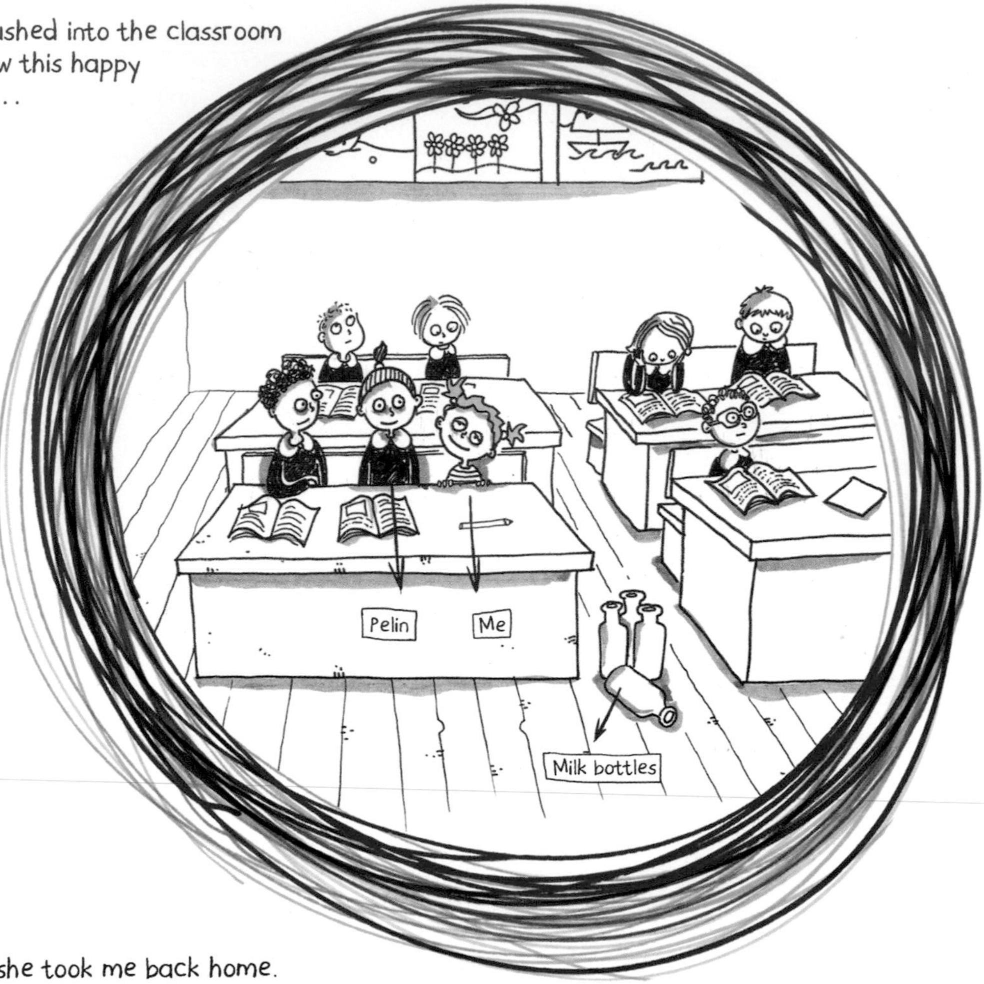
Pelin
Me
Milk bottles

and she took me back home.

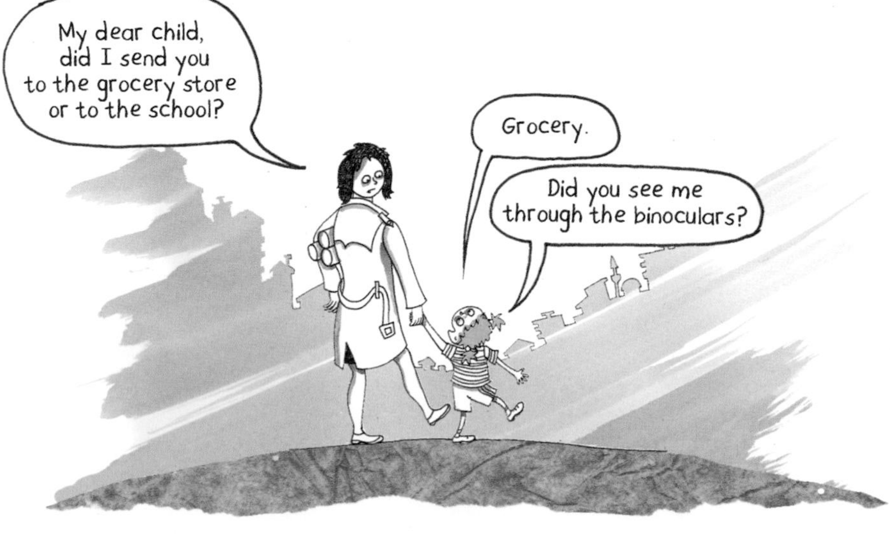
My dear child, did I send you to the grocery store or to the school?
Grocery.
Did you see me through the binoculars?

Chapter 2

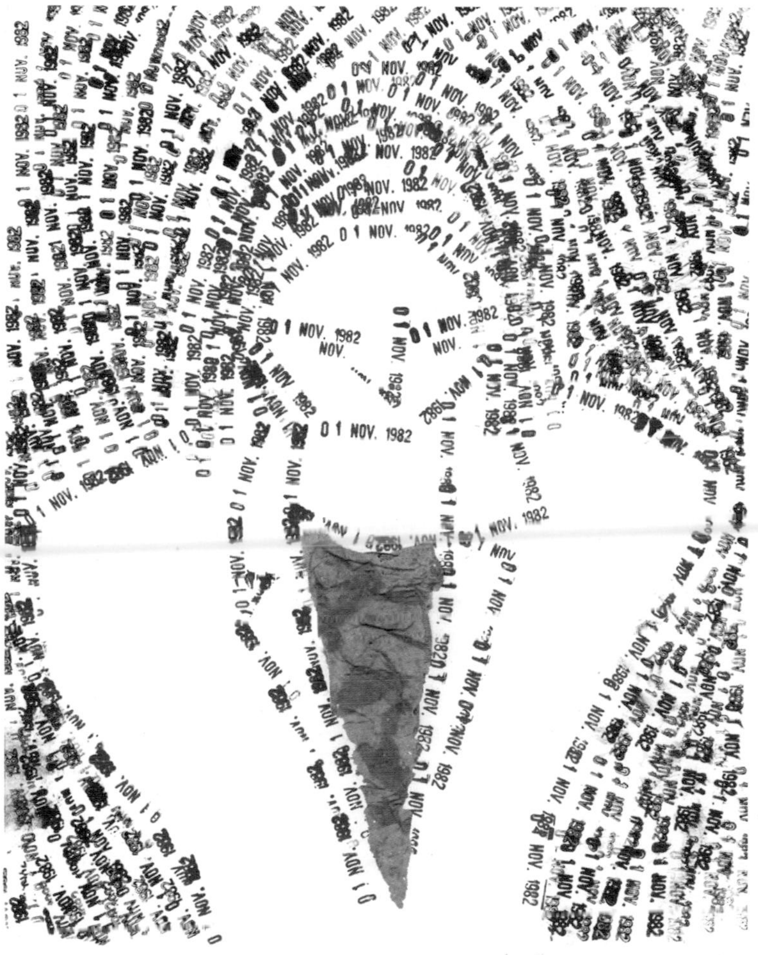
0 1 NOV. 1982

First-Grade Teacher

When I started primary school everybody was relieved.

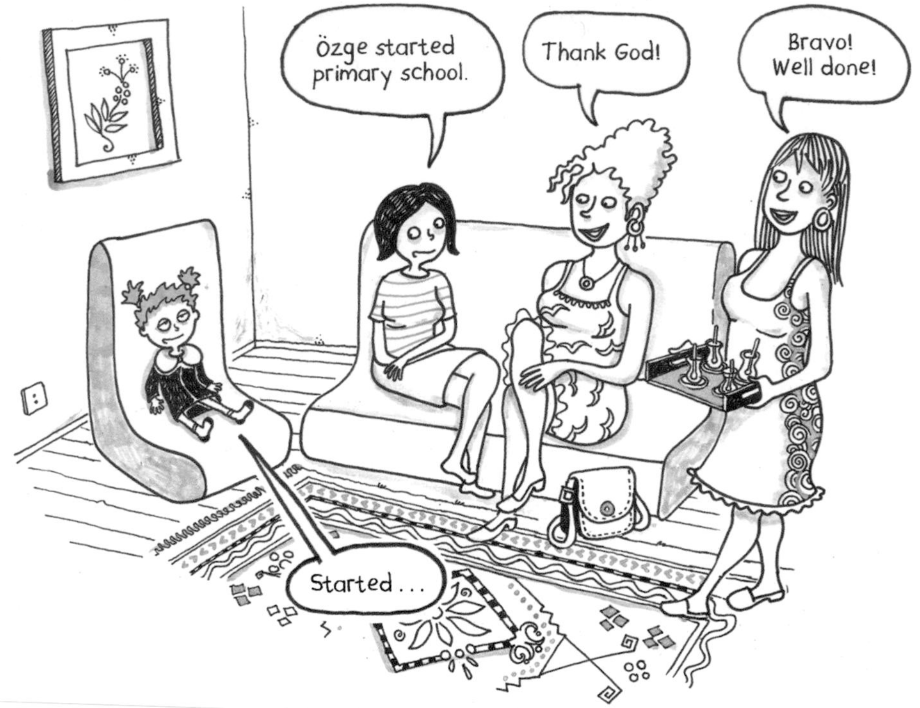
Özge started primary school.
Thank God!
Bravo! Well done!
Started . . .

Finally I found my identity.

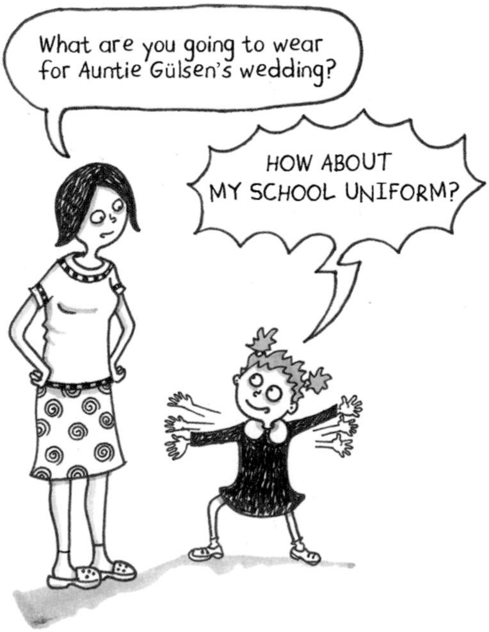
What are you going to wear for Auntie Gülsen's wedding?
HOW ABOUT MY SCHOOL UNIFORM?

But I was unaware of what was coming. Like many first graders, I immediately developed a crush on my teacher.

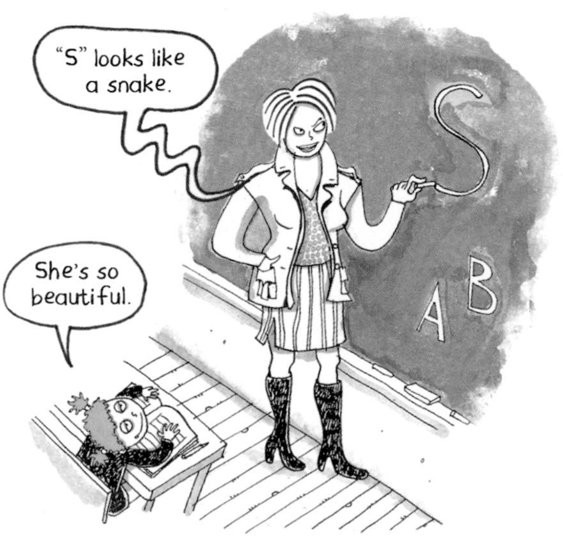
"S" looks like a snake.
She's so beautiful.
S
A
B

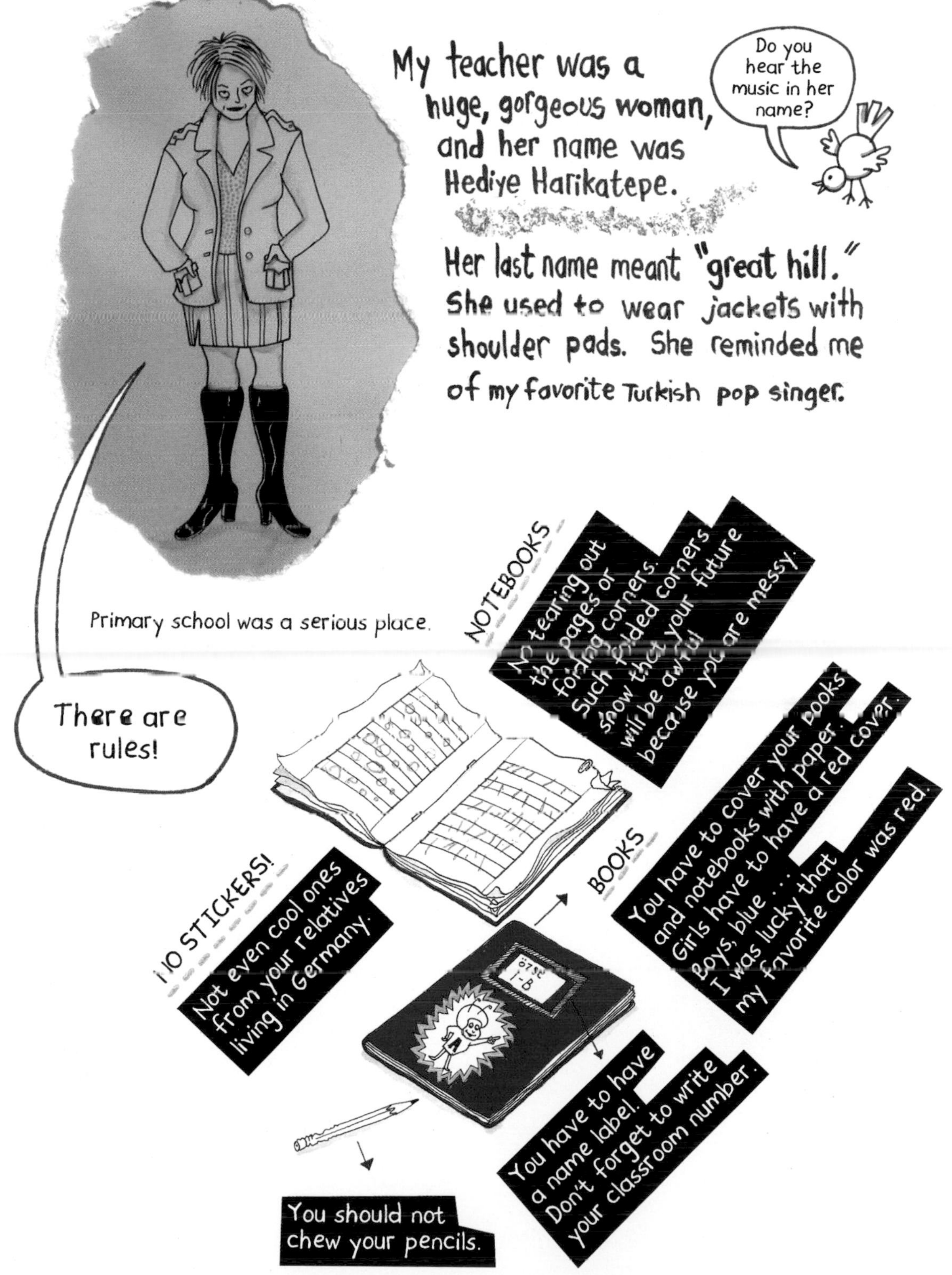

My teacher was a huge, gorgeous woman, and her name was Hediye Harikatepe.
Do you hear the music in her name?
Her last name meant "great hill." She used to wear jackets with shoulder pads. She reminded me of my favorite Turkish pop singer.
Primary school was a serious place.
There are rules!
NOTEBOOKS
No tearing out the pages or folding corners. Such folded corners show that your future will be awful because you are messy.
BOOKS
You have to cover your books and notebooks with paper. Girls have to have a red cover. Boys, blue . . . I was lucky that my favorite color was red.
NO STICKERS!
Not even cool ones from your relatives living in Germany.
You have to have a name label. Don't forget to write your classroom number.
You should not chew your pencils.

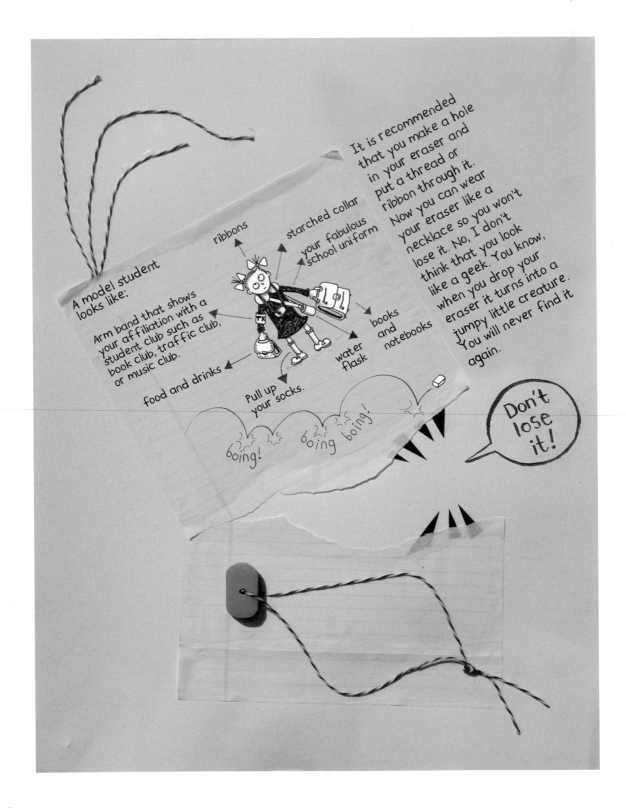

A model student looks like:

ribbons

starched collar

your fabulous school uniform

Arm band that shows your affiliation with a student club such as book club, traffic club, or music club.

food and drinks

Pull up your socks.

water flask

books and notebooks

It is recommended that you make a hole in your eraser and put a thread or ribbon through it. Now you can wear your eraser like a necklace so you won't lose it. No, I don't think that you look like a geek. You know, when you drop your eraser it turns into a jumpy little creature. You will never find it again.

boing!

boing! boing!

Don't lose it!

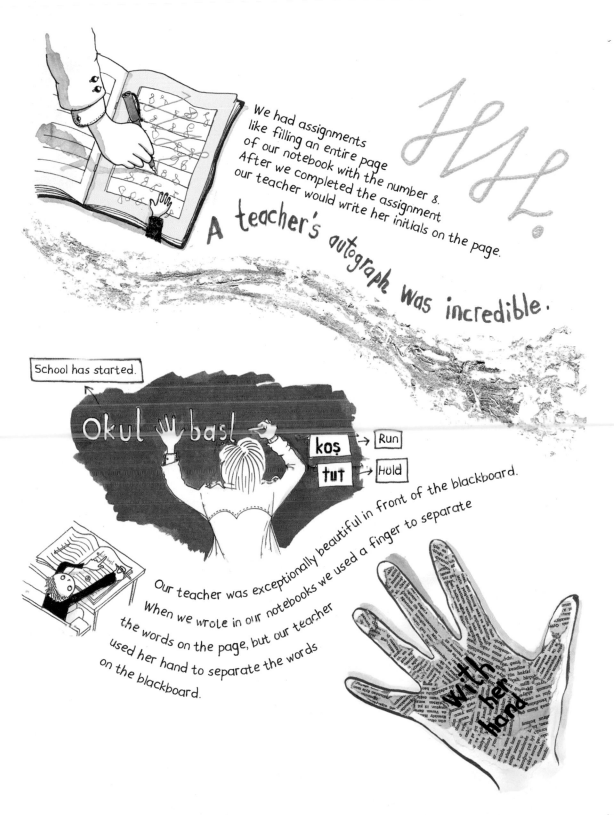

We had assignments like filling an entire page of our notebook with the number 8. After we completed the assignment our teacher would write her initials on the page.

A teacher's autograph was incredible.

School has started.

Okul başl

koş → Run

tut → Hold

Our teacher was exceptionally beautiful in front of the blackboard. When we wrote in our notebooks we used a finger to separate the words on the page, but our teacher used her hand to separate the words on the blackboard.

with her hand

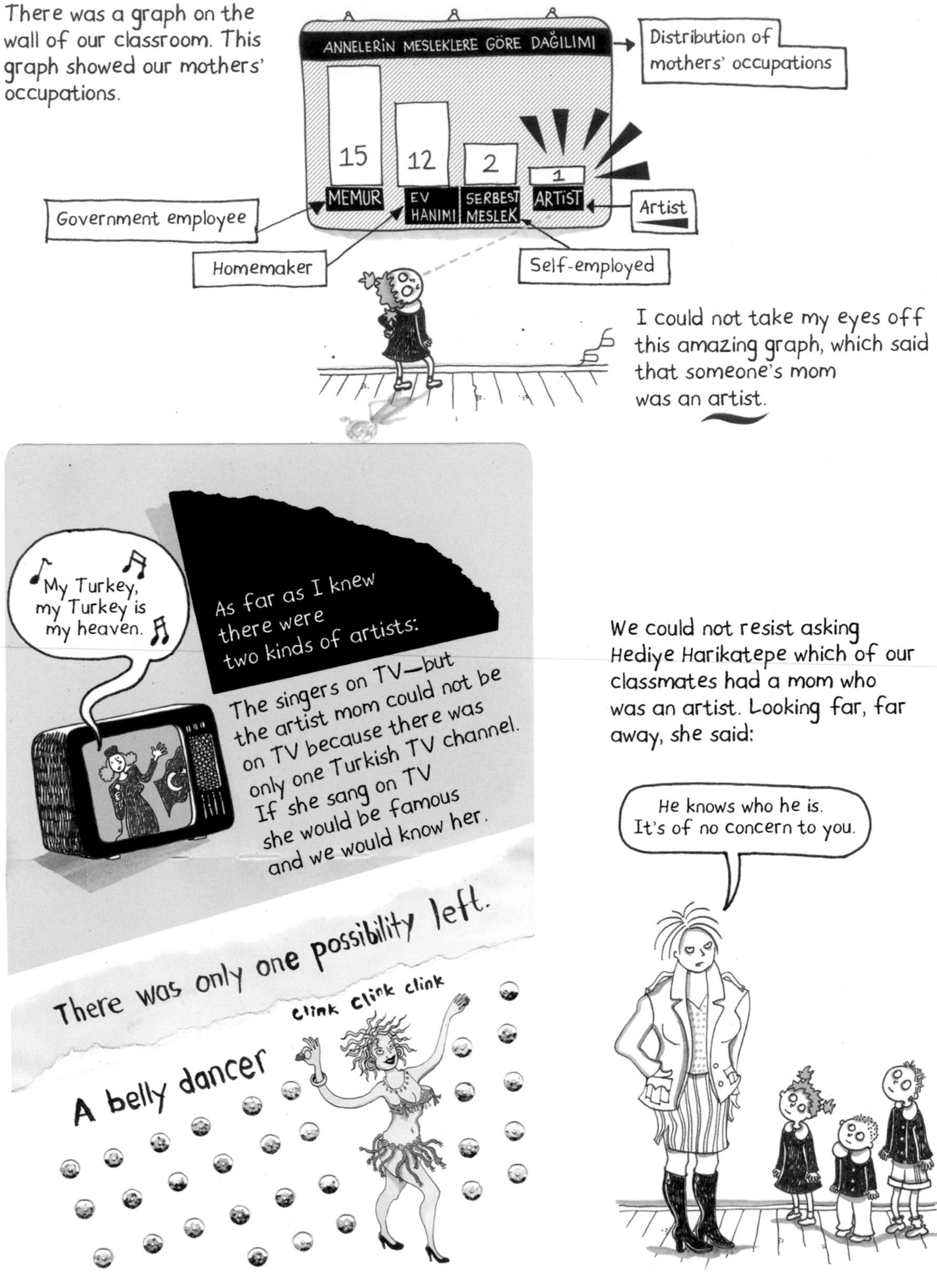
There was a graph on the wall of our classroom. This graph showed our mothers' occupations.
ANNELERİN MESLEKLERE GÖRE DAĞILIMI
Distribution of mothers' occupations
15
12
2
1
MEMUR
EV HANIMI
SERBEST MESLEK
ARTİST
Government employee
Homemaker
Self-employed
Artist
I could not take my eyes off this amazing graph, which said that someone's mom was an artist.
As far as I knew there were two kinds of artists:
My Turkey, my Turkey is my heaven.
The singers on TV—but the artist mom could not be on TV because there was only one Turkish TV channel. If she sang on TV she would be famous and we would know her.
There was only one possibility left.
clink clink clink
A belly dancer
We could not resist asking Hediye Harikatepe which of our classmates had a mom who was an artist. Looking far, far away, she said:
He knows who he is. It's of no concern to you.

Our teacher was very mysterious.
She knew so many more things than
we did.

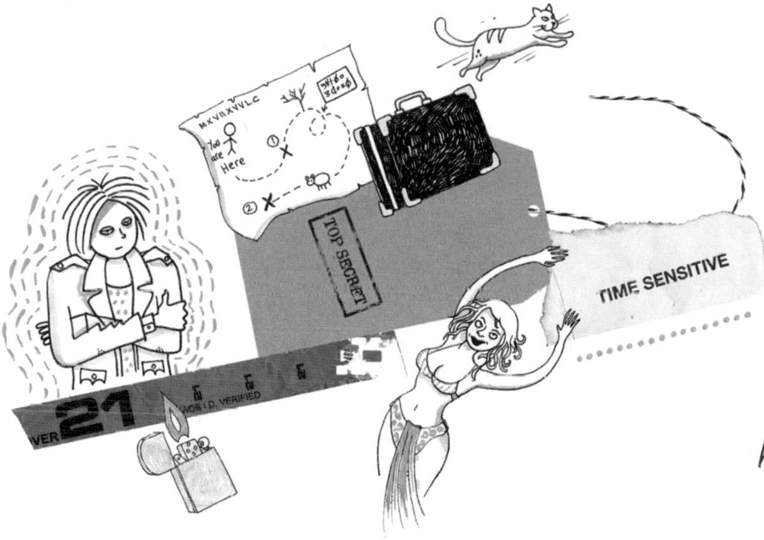
You are Here
TOP SECRET
TIME SENSITIVE
VER 21

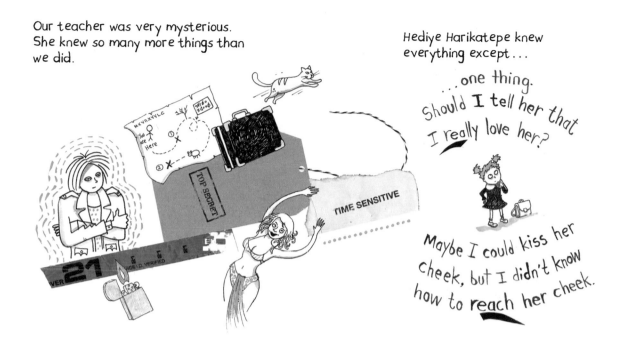

Hediye Harikatepe knew
everything except...

...one thing.
Should **I** tell her that
I really love her?

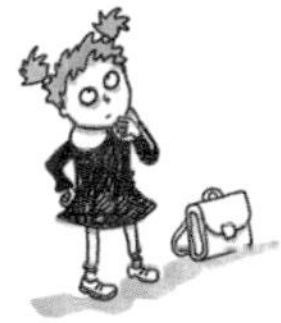

Maybe I could kiss her
cheek, but I didn't know
how to reach her cheek.

I talked to my cousin about it
and she said she had actually kissed
her teacher! She told me how to do it.

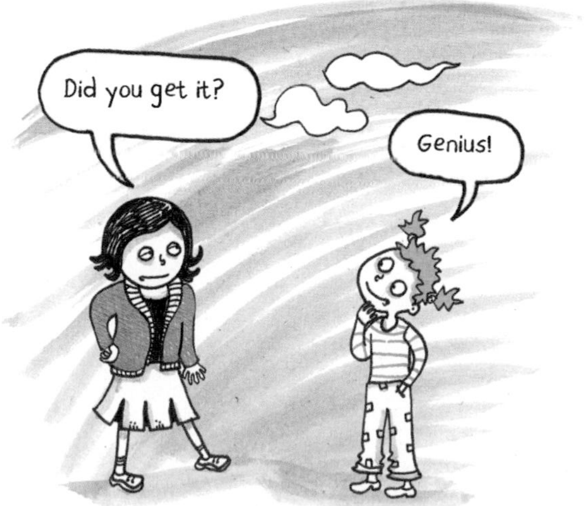
Did you get it?
Genius!

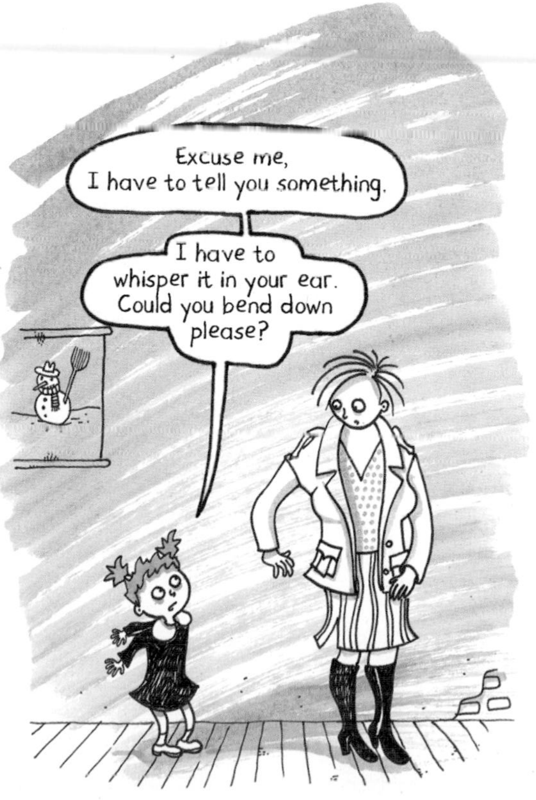
Excuse me,
I have to tell you something.
I have to whisper it in your ear. Could you bend down please?

Our teacher
kindly bent
down to me.

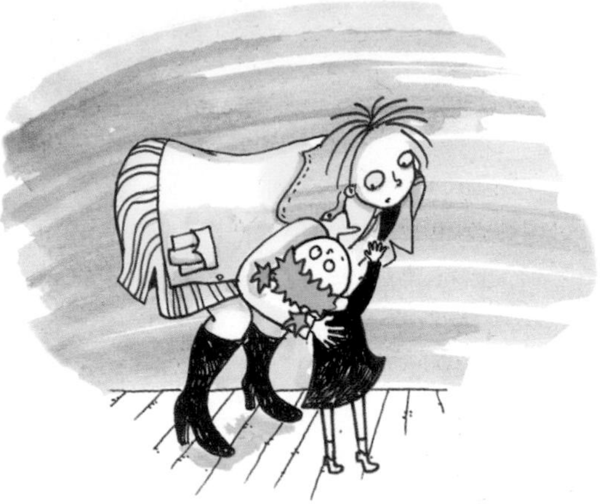

I was stunned. There were veins on her cheek.

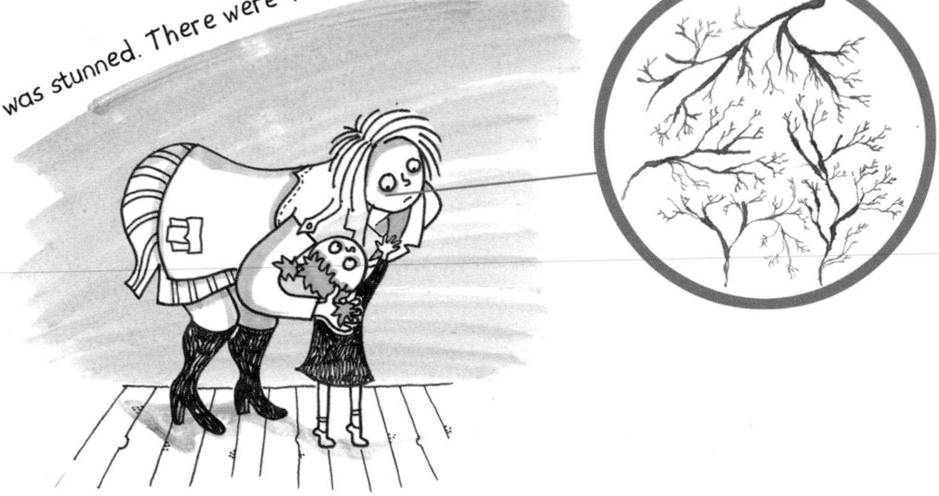

It was too late to step back, so I kissed her.

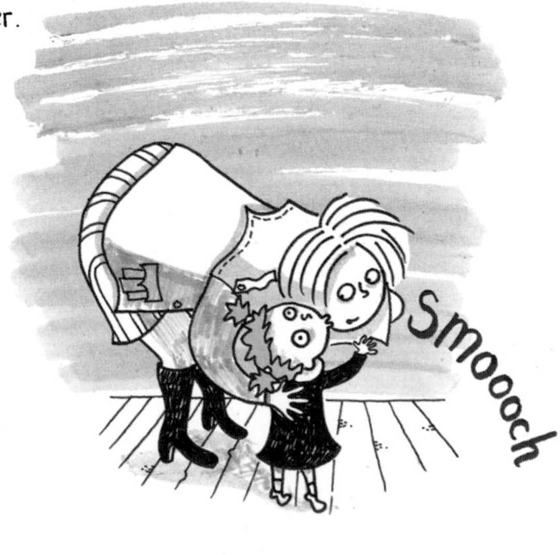
Smoooch

I think she liked it, but
I was in shock.

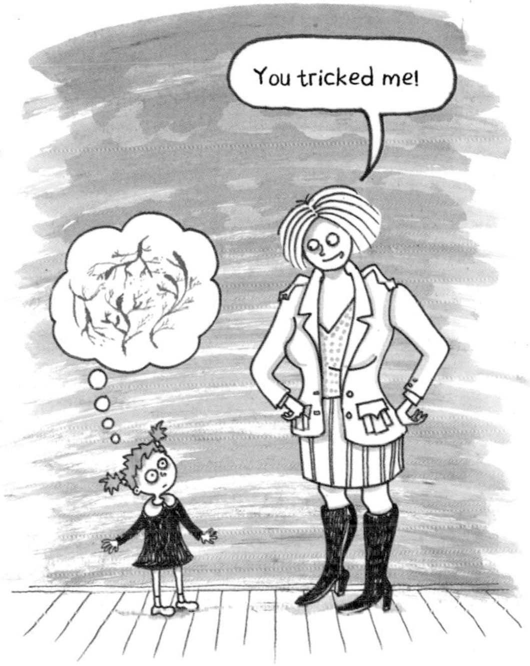
You tricked me!

At home Dad asked:

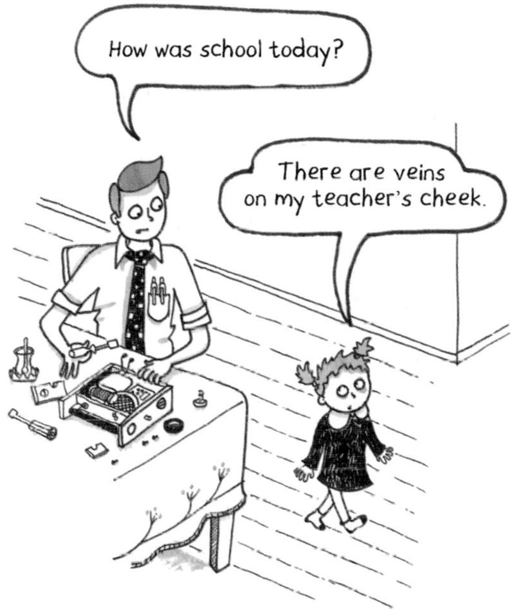
How was school today?
There are veins on my teacher's cheek.

I told my mom.

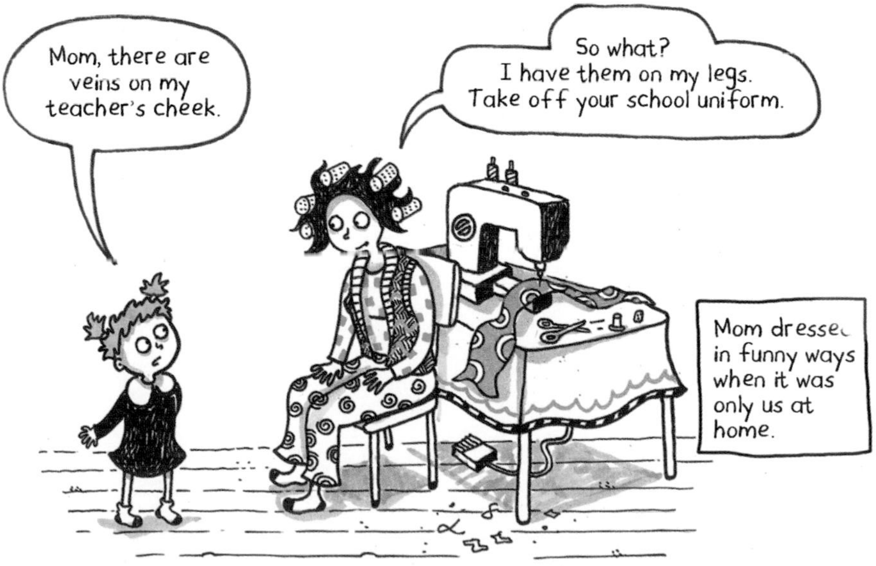
Mom, there are veins on my teacher's cheek.
So what? I have them on my legs. Take off your school uniform.
Mom dressed in funny ways when it was only us at home.

And Pelin:

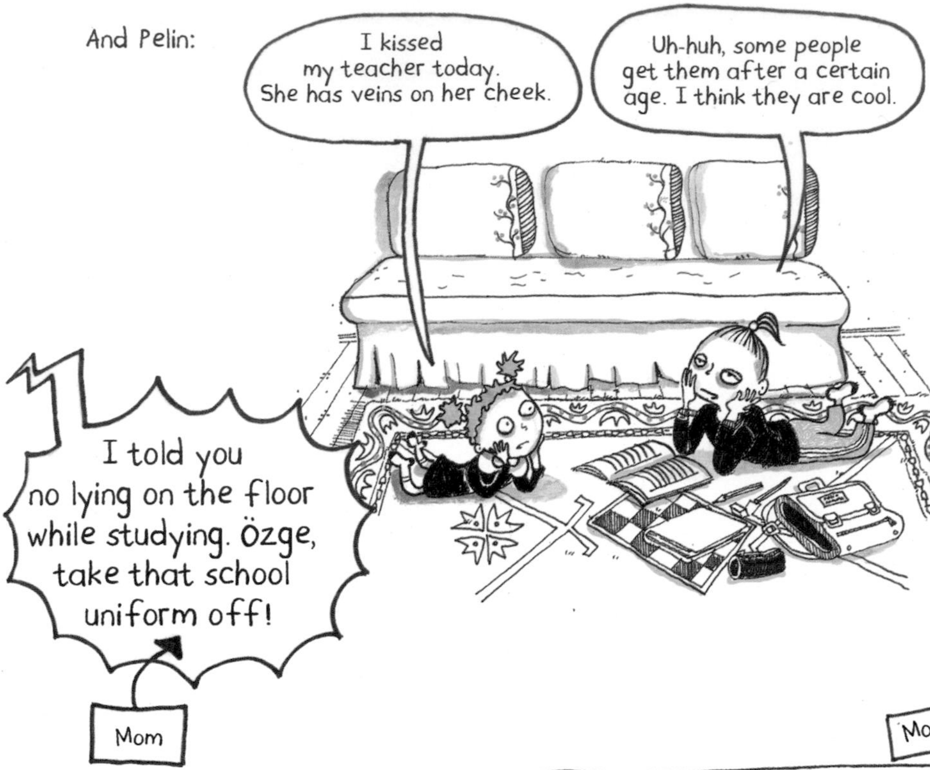

I kissed my teacher today. She has veins on her cheek.
Uh-huh, some people get them after a certain age. I think they are cool.
I told you no lying on the floor while studying. Özge, take that school uniform off!
Mom

I spent some time thinking.

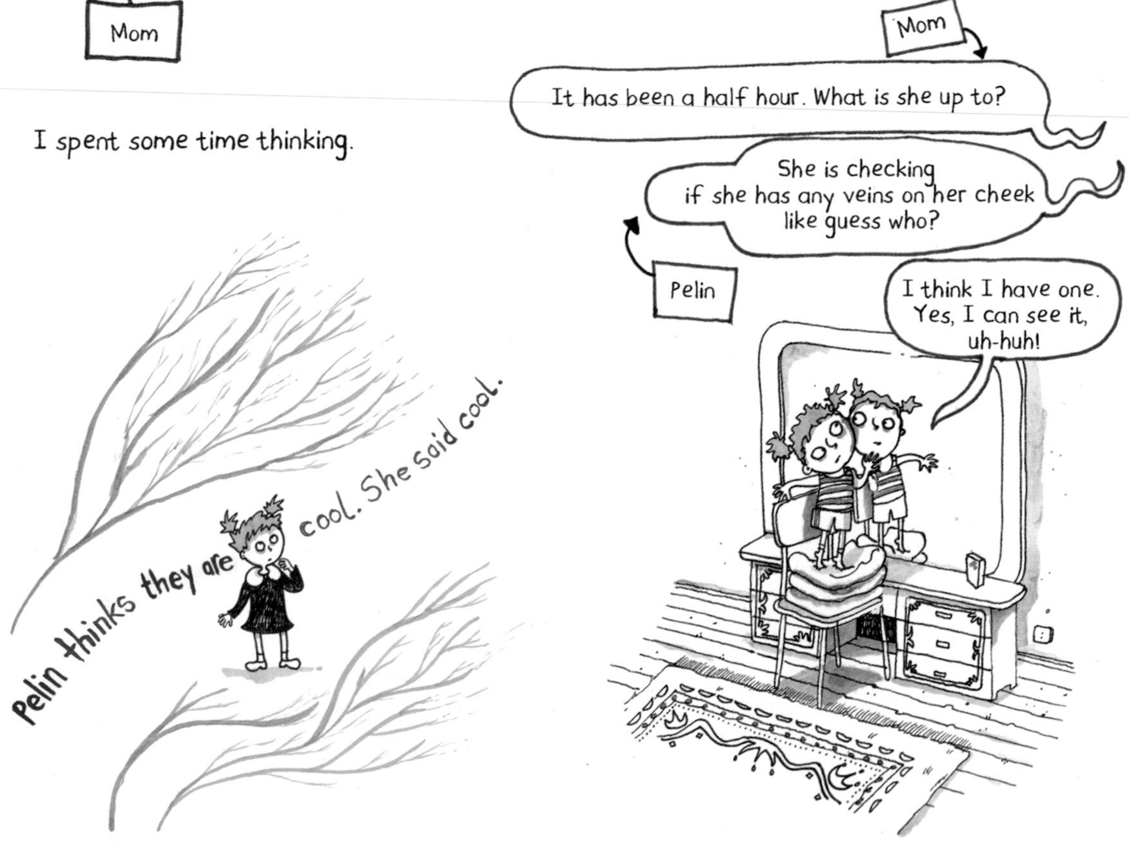

Mom
It has been a half hour. What is she up to?
She is checking if she has any veins on her cheek like guess who?
Pelin
I think I have one. Yes, I can see it, uh-huh!
Pelin thinks they are cool. She said cool.

Chapter 3

Atatürk

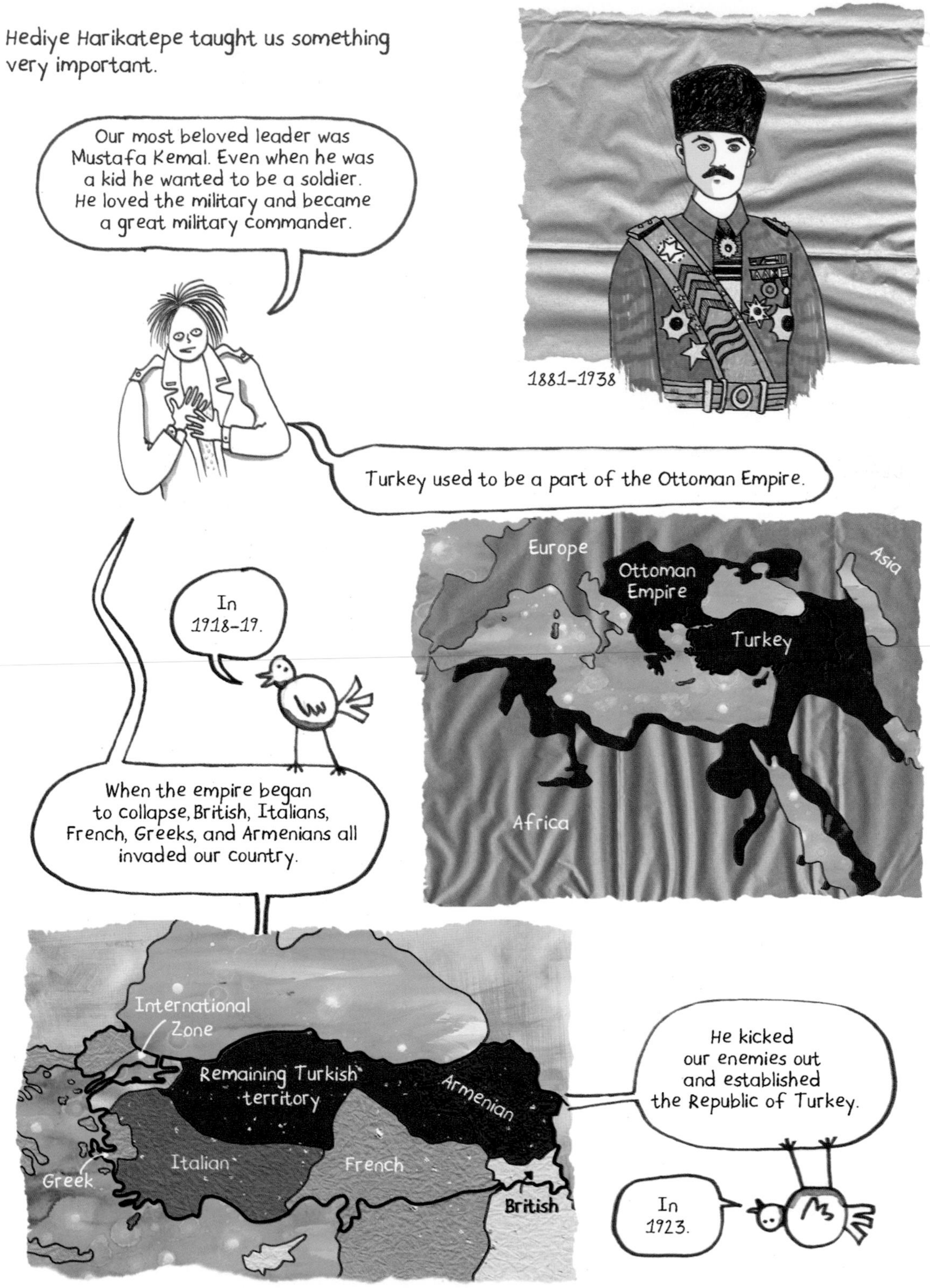
Hediye Harikatepe taught us something very important.
Our most beloved leader was Mustafa Kemal. Even when he was a kid he wanted to be a soldier. He loved the military and became a great military commander.
1881–1938
Turkey used to be a part of the Ottoman Empire.
Europe
Ottoman Empire
Asia
Turkey
Africa
In 1918–19.
When the empire began to collapse, British, Italians, French, Greeks, and Armenians all invaded our country.
International Zone
Remaining Turkish territory
Armenian
Italian
French
Greek
British
He kicked our enemies out and established the Republic of Turkey.
In 1923.

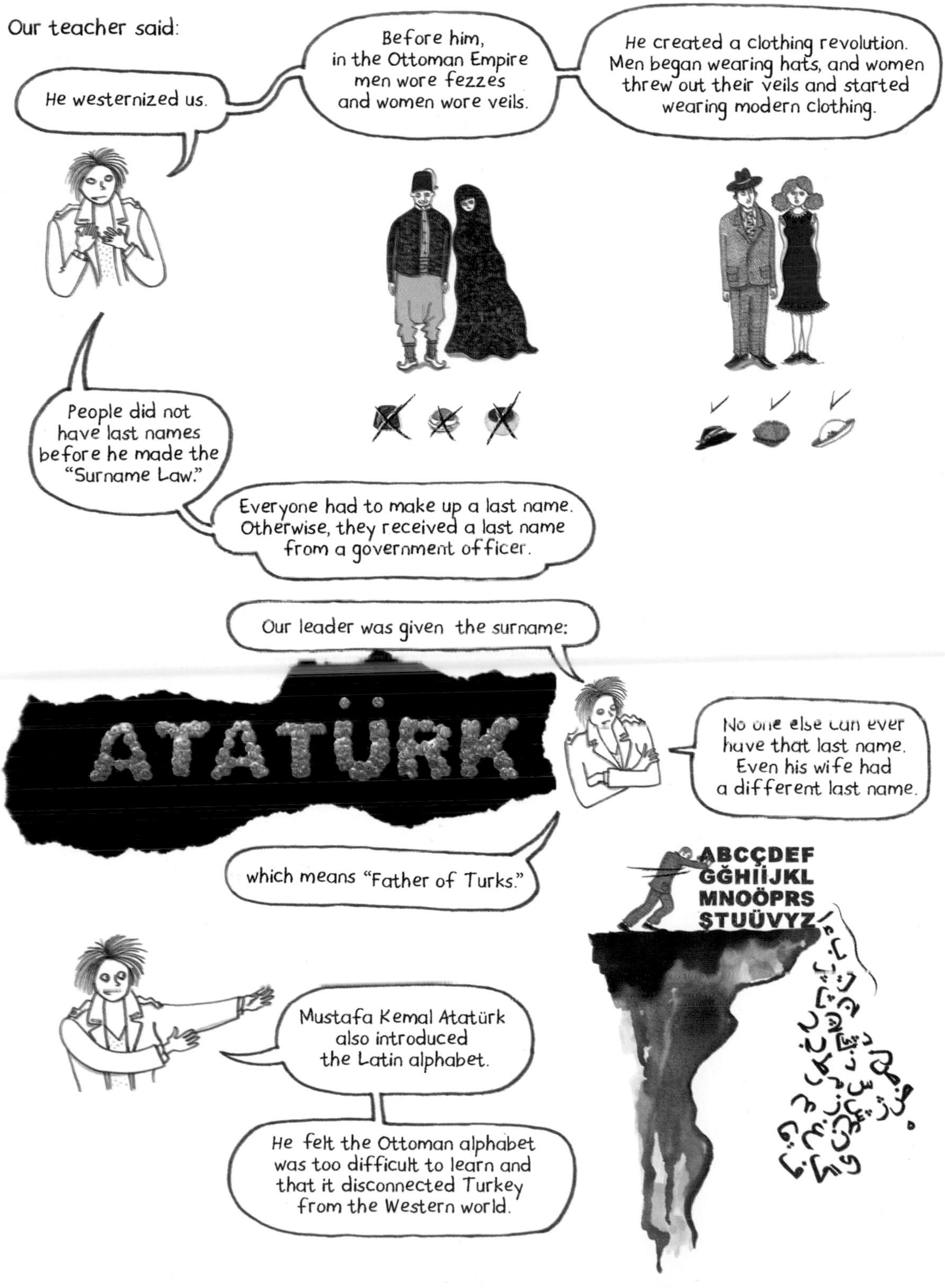
Our teacher said:
He westernized us.
Before him, in the Ottoman Empire men wore fezzes and women wore veils.
He created a clothing revolution. Men began wearing hats, and women threw out their veils and started wearing modern clothing.
People did not have last names before he made the "Surname Law."
Everyone had to make up a last name. Otherwise, they received a last name from a government officer.
Our leader was given the surname:
ATATÜRK
which means "Father of Turks."
No one else can ever have that last name. Even his wife had a different last name.
Mustafa Kemal Atatürk also introduced the Latin alphabet.
He felt the Ottoman alphabet was too difficult to learn and that it disconnected Turkey from the Western world.
ABCÇDEF
GĞHIİJKL
MNOÖPRS
ŞTUÜVYZ

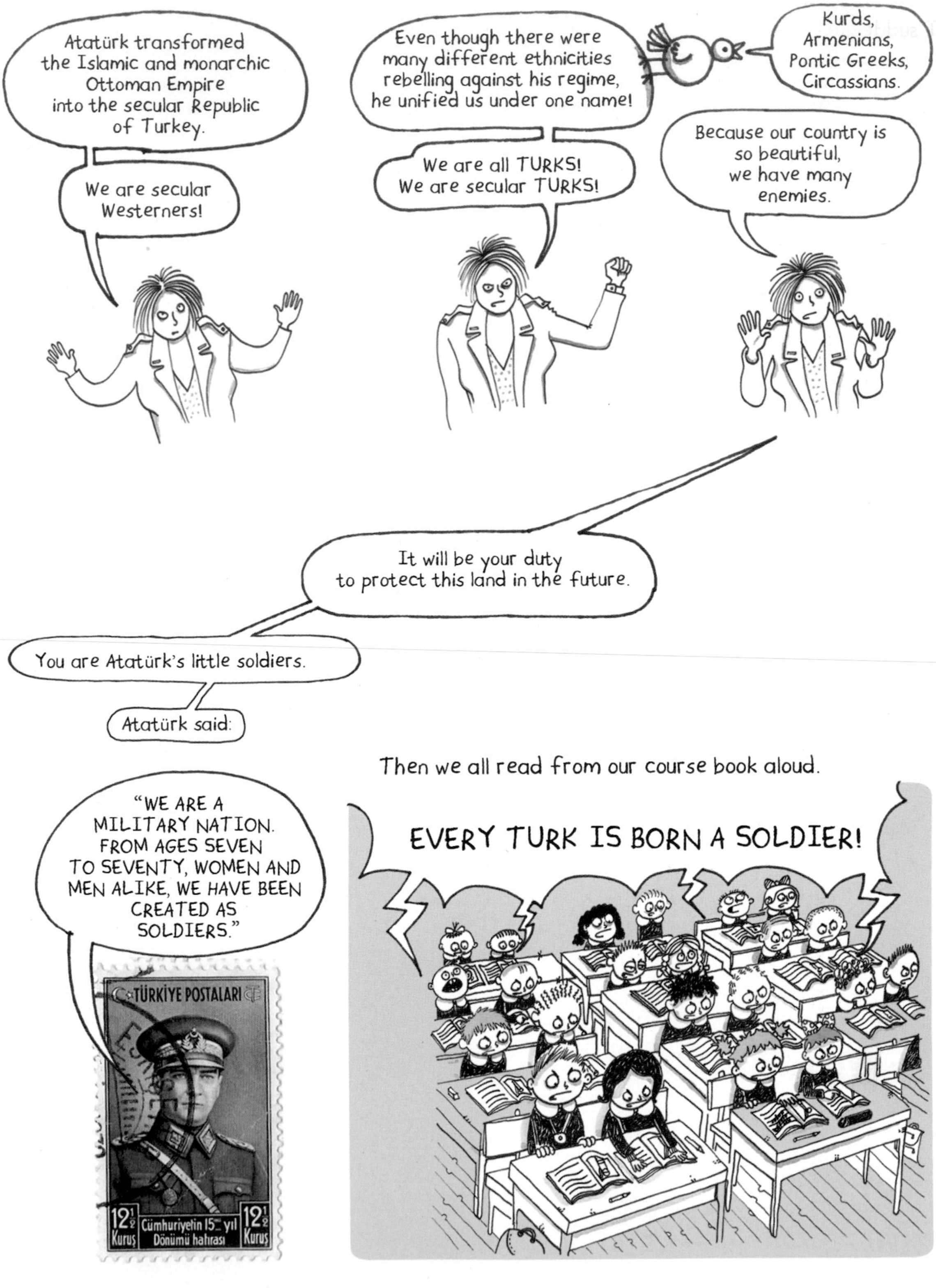
Atatürk transformed the Islamic and monarchic Ottoman Empire into the secular Republic of Turkey.
We are secular Westerners!
Even though there were many different ethnicities rebelling against his regime, he unified us under one name!
Kurds, Armenians, Pontic Greeks, Circassians.
We are all TURKS! We are secular TURKS!
Because our country is so beautiful, we have many enemies.
It will be your duty to protect this land in the future.
You are Atatürk's little soldiers.
Atatürk said:
"WE ARE A MILITARY NATION. FROM AGES SEVEN TO SEVENTY, WOMEN AND MEN ALIKE, WE HAVE BEEN CREATED AS SOLDIERS."
TÜRKIYE POSTALARI
12½ Kuruş
Cümhuriyetin 15_ yıl Dönümü hatırası
12½ Kuruş
Then we all read from our course book aloud.
EVERY TURK IS BORN A SOLDIER!

I suddenly understood why I saw Atatürk's image everywhere.

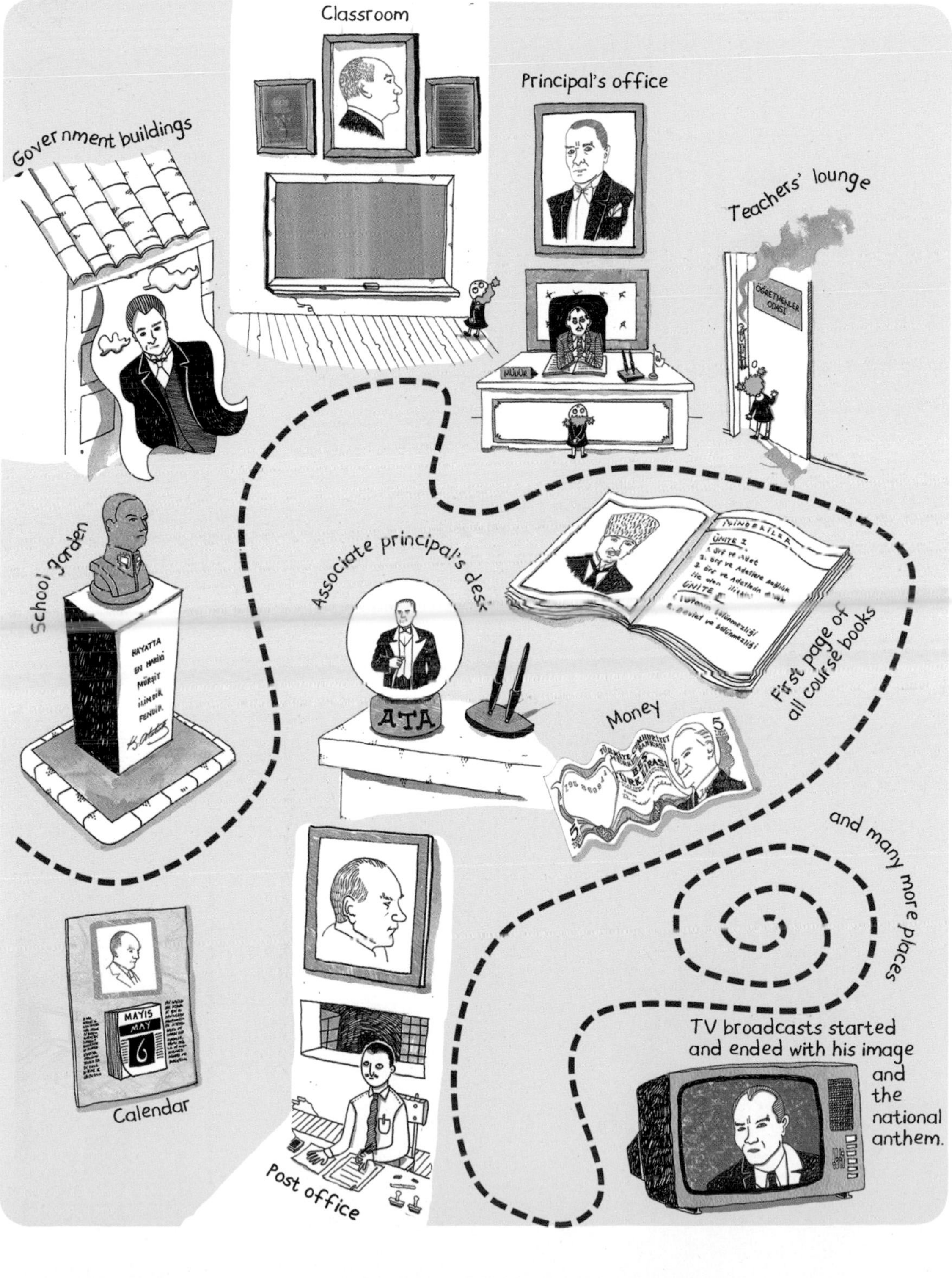

Classroom
Principal's office
Government buildings
Teachers' lounge
ÖĞRETMENLER ODASI
MÜDÜR
School garden
HAYATTA EN HAKİKİ MÜRŞİT İLİMDİR, FENDİR.
Associate principal's desk
ATA
First page of all course books
Money
and many more places
TV broadcasts started and ended with his image and the national anthem.
MAYIS
MAY
6
Calendar
Post office

We even had a picture of Atatürk in our dining room.

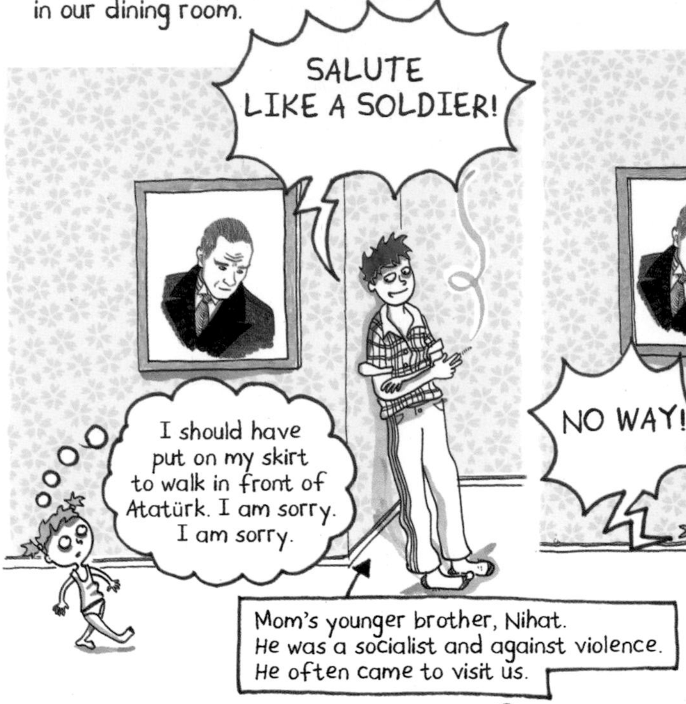
SALUTE LIKE A SOLDIER!
I should have put on my skirt to walk in front of Atatürk. I am sorry. I am sorry.
Mom's younger brother, Nihat. He was a socialist and against violence. He often came to visit us.

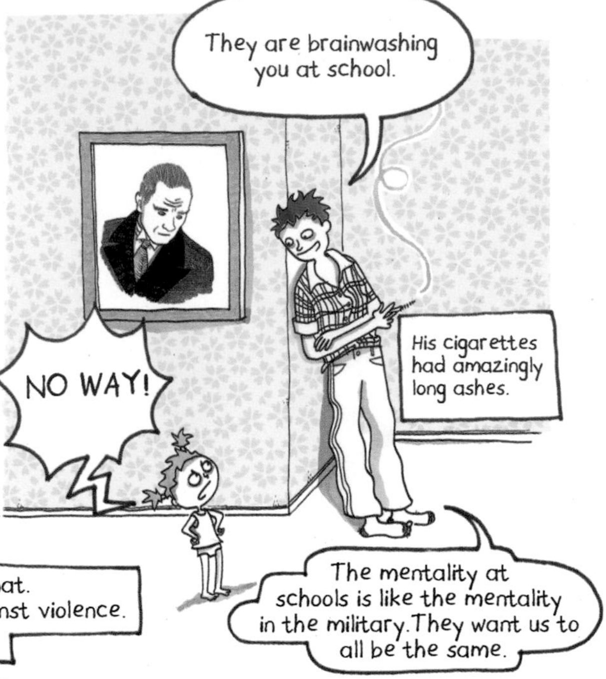
They are brainwashing you at school.
NO WAY!
His cigarettes had amazingly long ashes.
The mentality at schools is like the mentality in the military. They want us to all be the same.

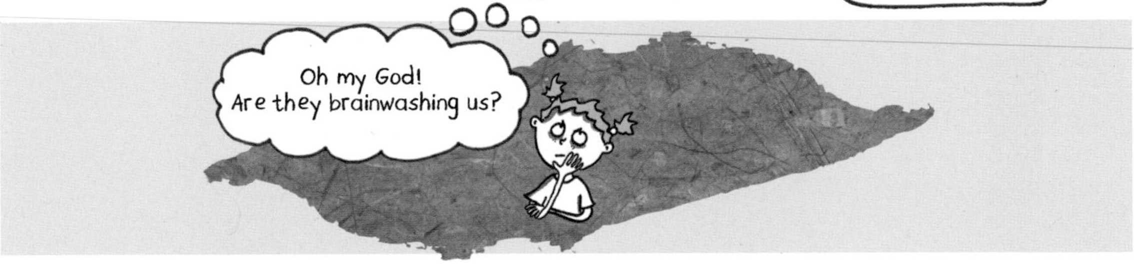
Oh my God! Are they brainwashing us?

In order to organize us in the school yard for the daily morning assembly . . .

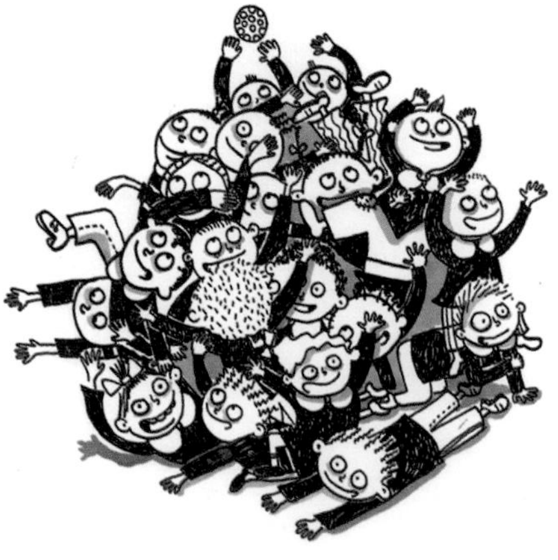

. . . teachers taught us basic military poses.

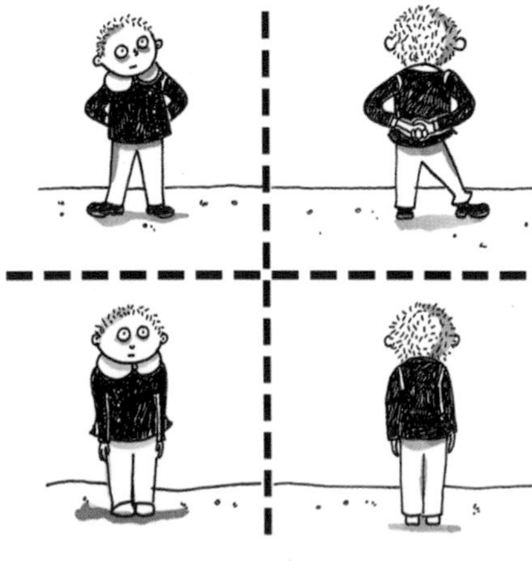

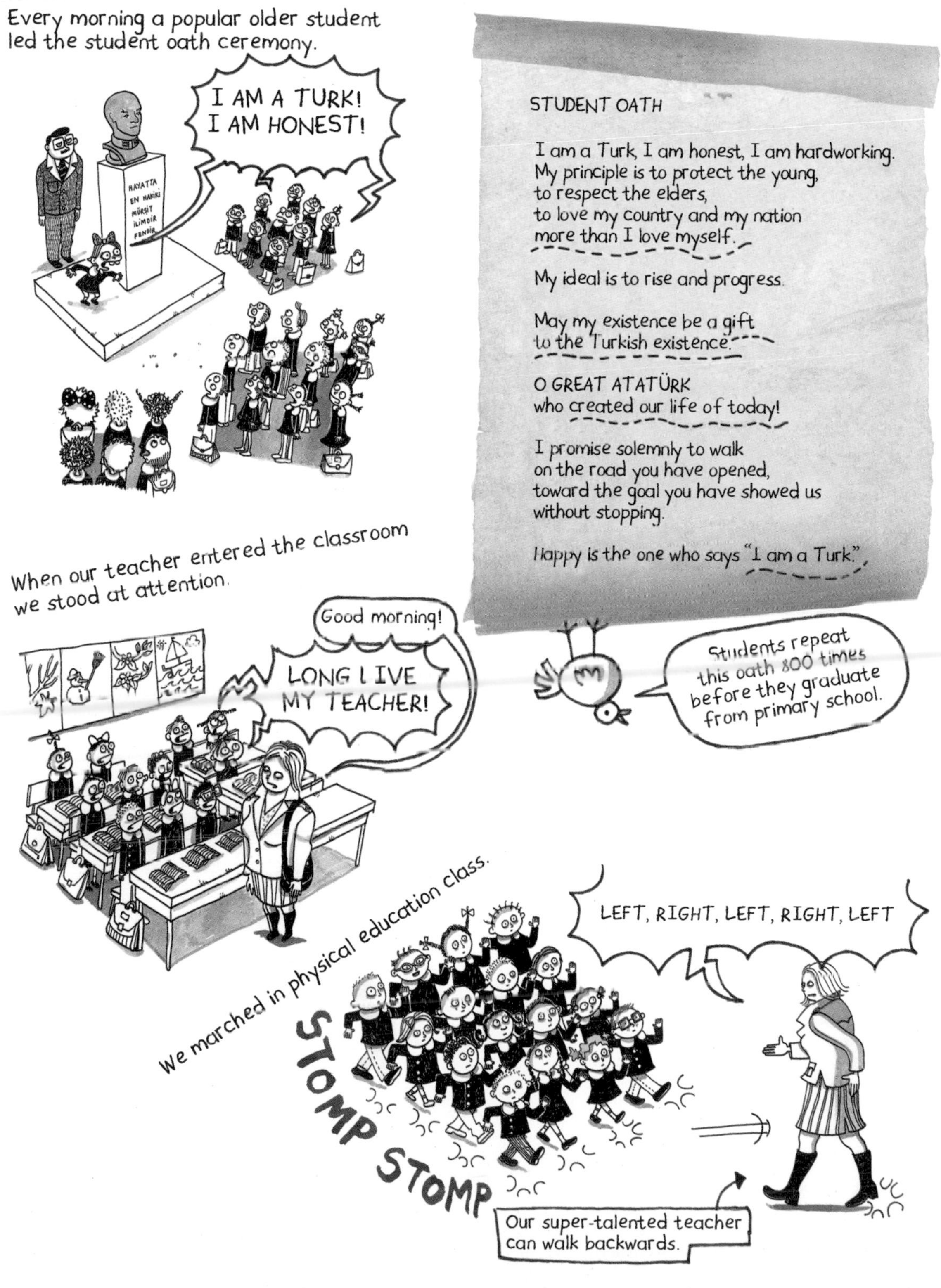

Every morning a popular older student led the student oath ceremony.
HAYATTA EN HAKİKİ MÜRŞİT İLİMDİR FENDİR
I AM A TURK! I AM HONEST!
STUDENT OATH
I am a Turk, I am honest, I am hardworking.
My principle is to protect the young,
to respect the elders,
to love my country and my nation
more than I love myself.
My ideal is to rise and progress.
May my existence be a gift
to the Turkish existence.
O GREAT ATATÜRK
who created our life of today!
I promise solemnly to walk
on the road you have opened,
toward the goal you have showed us
without stopping.
Happy is the one who says "I am a Turk."
Students repeat this oath 800 times before they graduate from primary school.
When our teacher entered the classroom we stood at attention.
Good morning!
LONG LIVE MY TEACHER!
We marched in physical education class.
LEFT, RIGHT, LEFT, RIGHT, LEFT
STOMP STOMP STOMP
Our super-talented teacher can walk backwards.

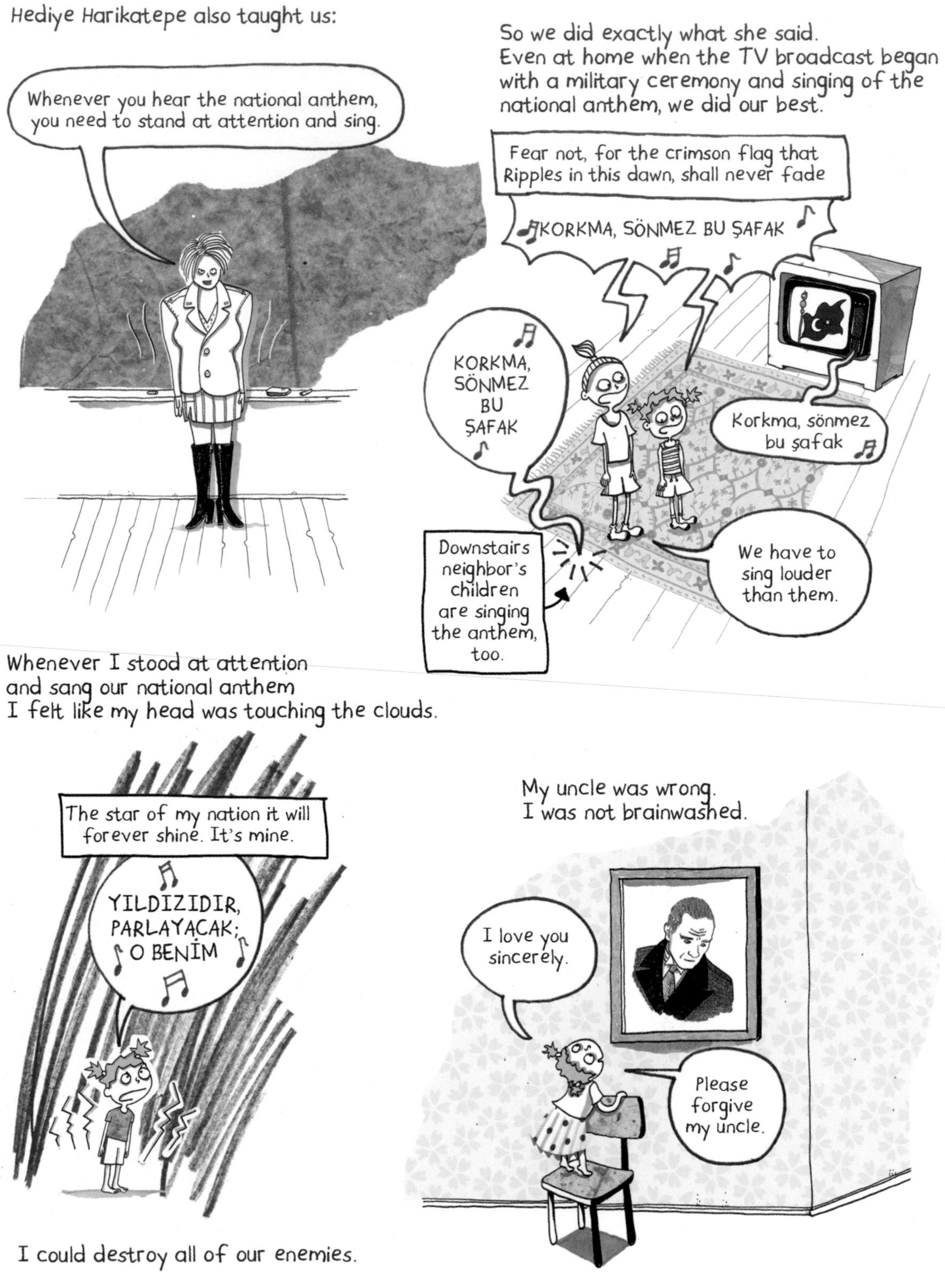
Hediye Harikatepe also taught us:
Whenever you hear the national anthem, you need to stand at attention and sing.
So we did exactly what she said.
Even at home when the TV broadcast began with a military ceremony and singing of the national anthem, we did our best.
Fear not, for the crimson flag that Ripples in this dawn, shall never fade
KORKMA, SÖNMEZ BU ŞAFAK
KORKMA, SÖNMEZ BU ŞAFAK
Korkma, sönmez bu şafak
Downstairs neighbor's children are singing the anthem, too.
We have to sing louder than them.
Whenever I stood at attention and sang our national anthem I felt like my head was touching the clouds.
The star of my nation it will forever shine. It's mine.
YILDIZIDIR, PARLAYACAK; O BENİM
I could destroy all of our enemies.
My uncle was wrong. I was not brainwashed.
I love you sincerely.
Please forgive my uncle.

Chapter 4

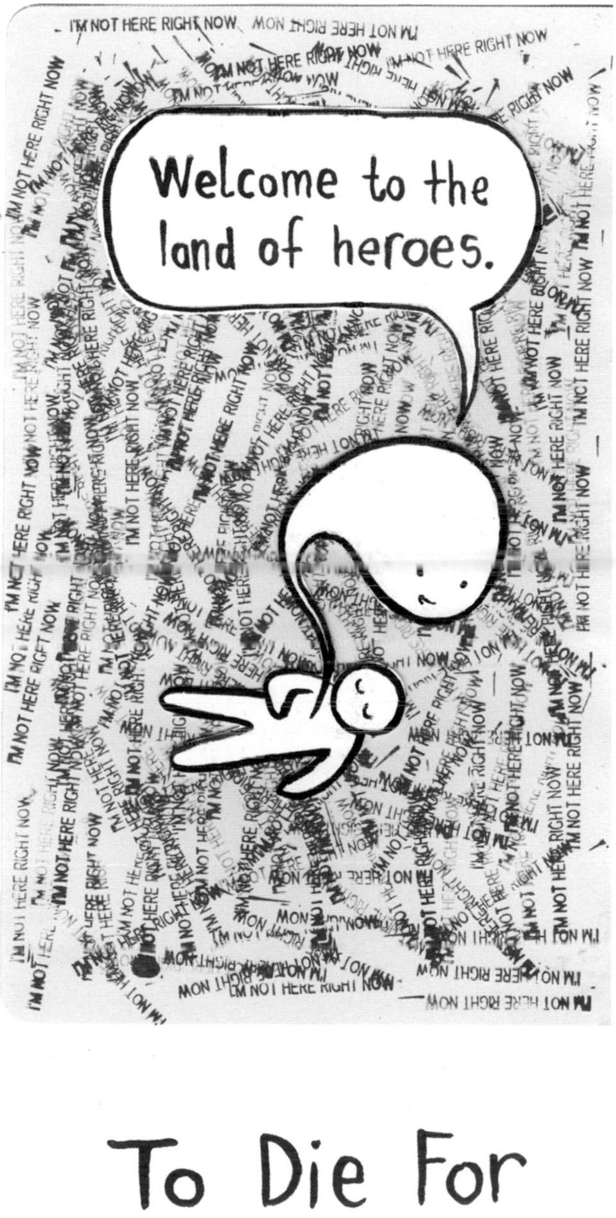
Welcome to the land of heroes.
I'M NOT HERE RIGHT NOW

To Die For

Curtains are wonderful playthings.

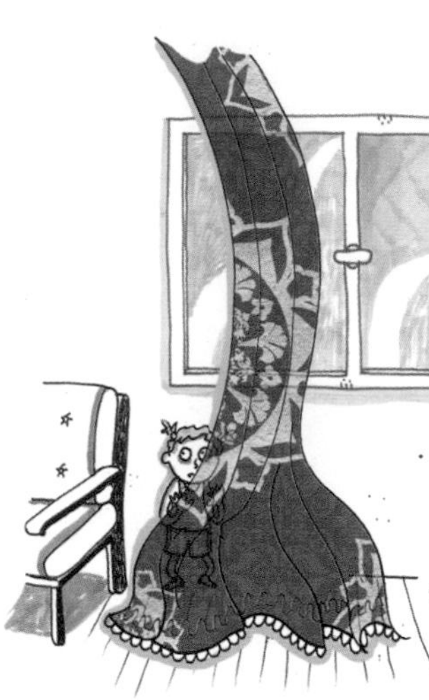

You can hide...

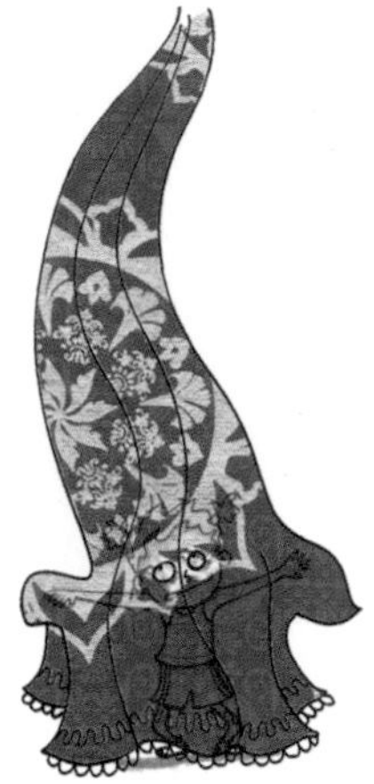

be a ghost...

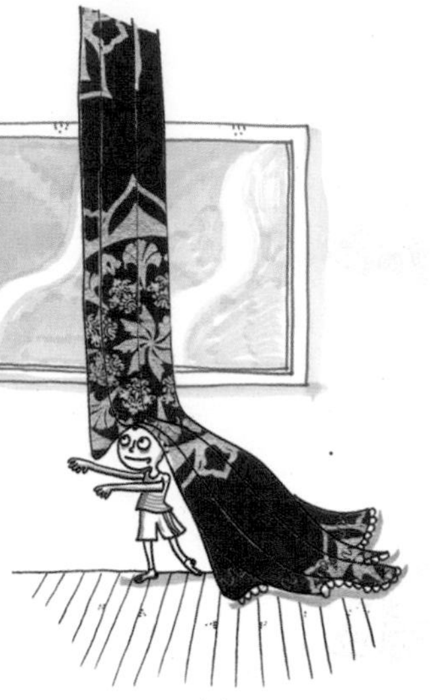

make a wedding gown...

shake them and
watch dust particles
float in the air.

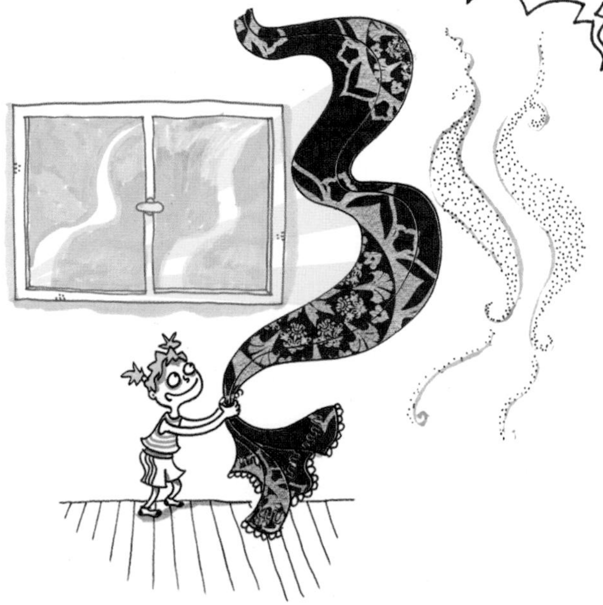

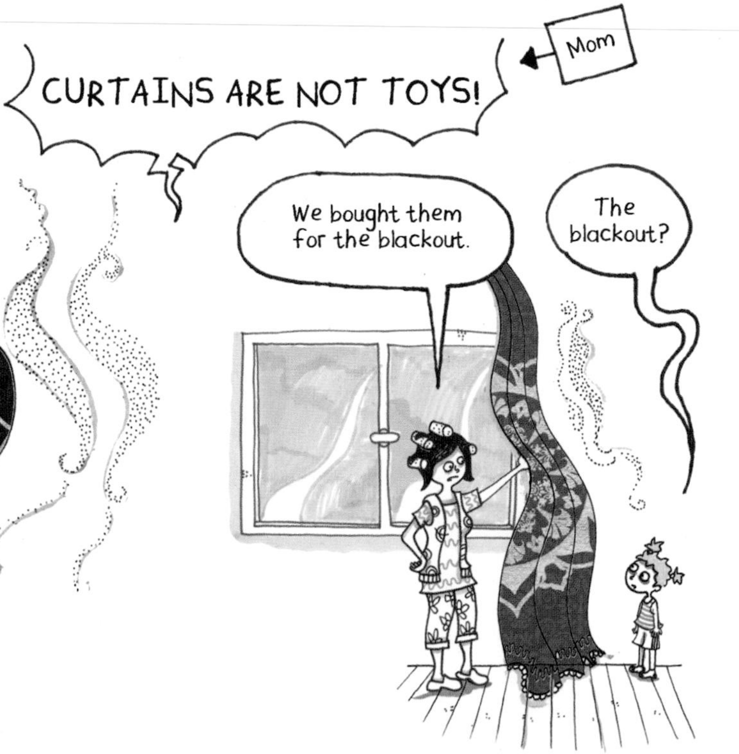
CURTAINS ARE NOT TOYS!
Mom
We bought them for the blackout.
The blackout?

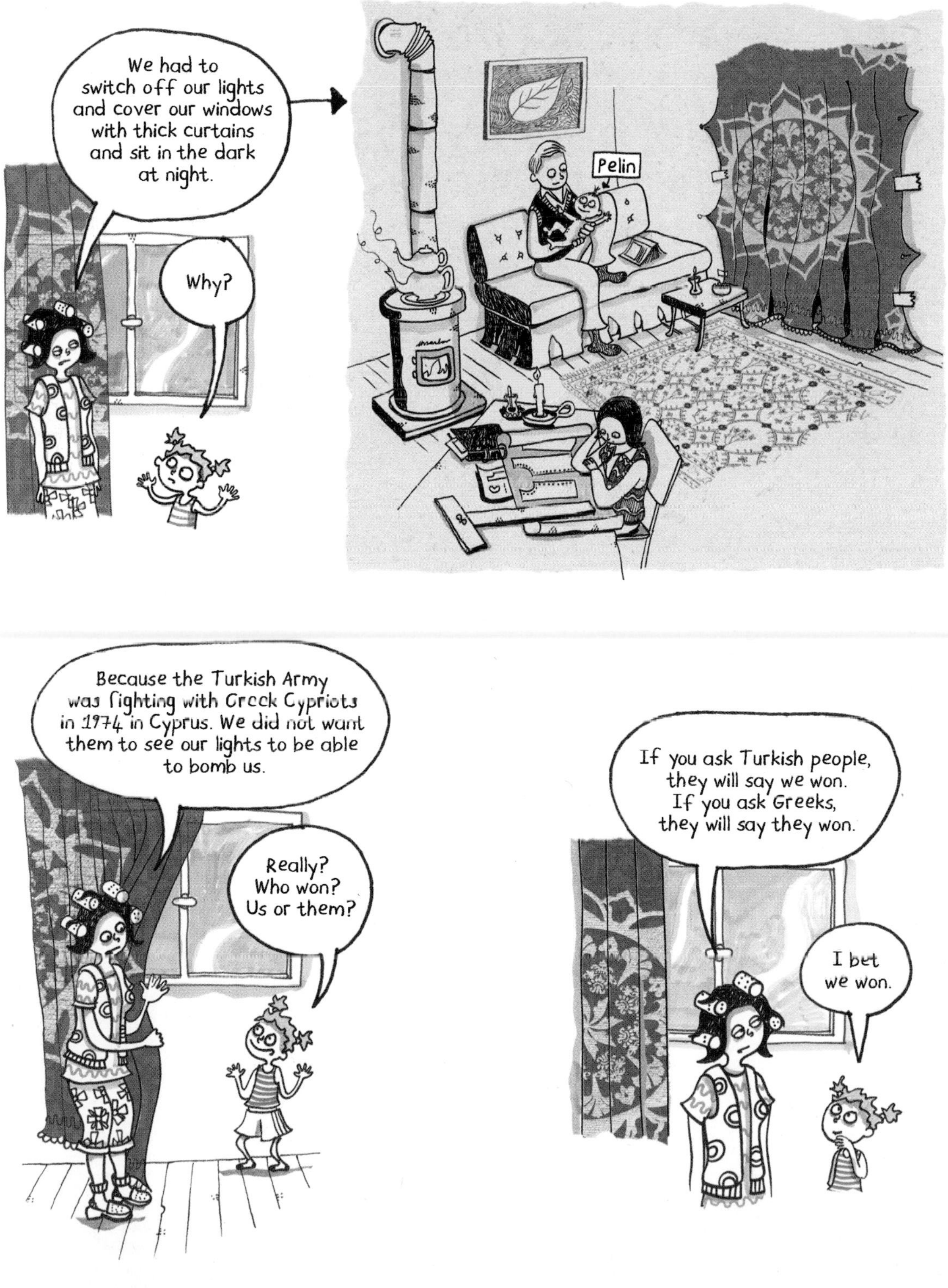
We had to switch off our lights and cover our windows with thick curtains and sit in the dark at night.
Why?
Pelin
Because the Turkish Army was fighting with Greek Cypriots in 1974 in Cyprus. We did not want them to see our lights to be able to bomb us.
Really? Who won? Us or them?
If you ask Turkish people, they will say we won. If you ask Greeks, they will say they won.
I bet we won.

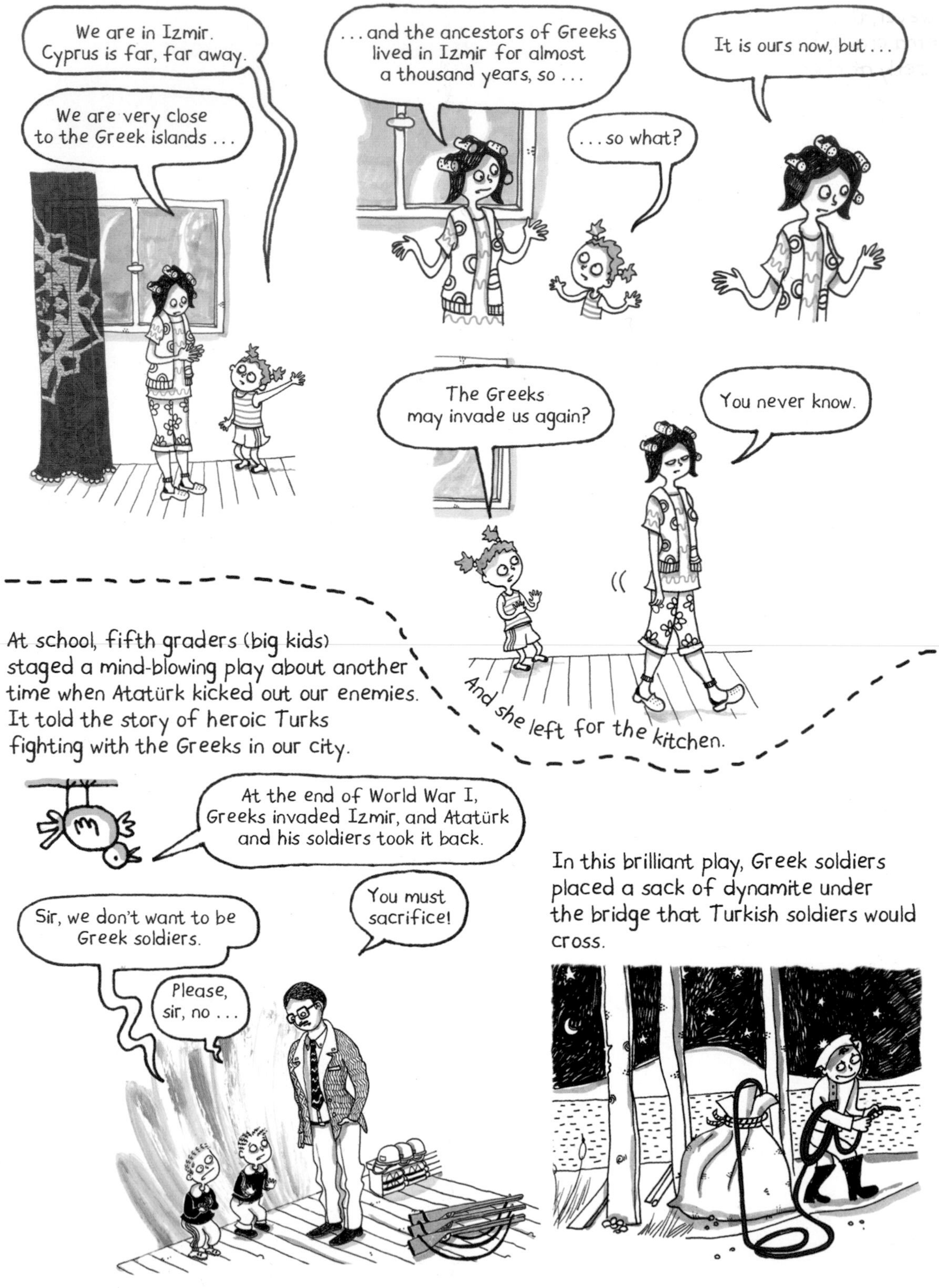
We are in Izmir. Cyprus is far, far away.
We are very close to the Greek islands . . .
. . . and the ancestors of Greeks lived in Izmir for almost a thousand years, so . . .
. . . so what?
It is ours now, but . . .
The Greeks may invade us again?
You never know.
And she left for the kitchen.
At school, fifth graders (big kids) staged a mind-blowing play about another time when Atatürk kicked out our enemies. It told the story of heroic Turks fighting with the Greeks in our city.
At the end of World War I, Greeks invaded Izmir, and Atatürk and his soldiers took it back.
Sir, we don't want to be Greek soldiers.
You must sacrifice!
Please, sir, no . . .
In this brilliant play, Greek soldiers placed a sack of dynamite under the bridge that Turkish soldiers would cross.

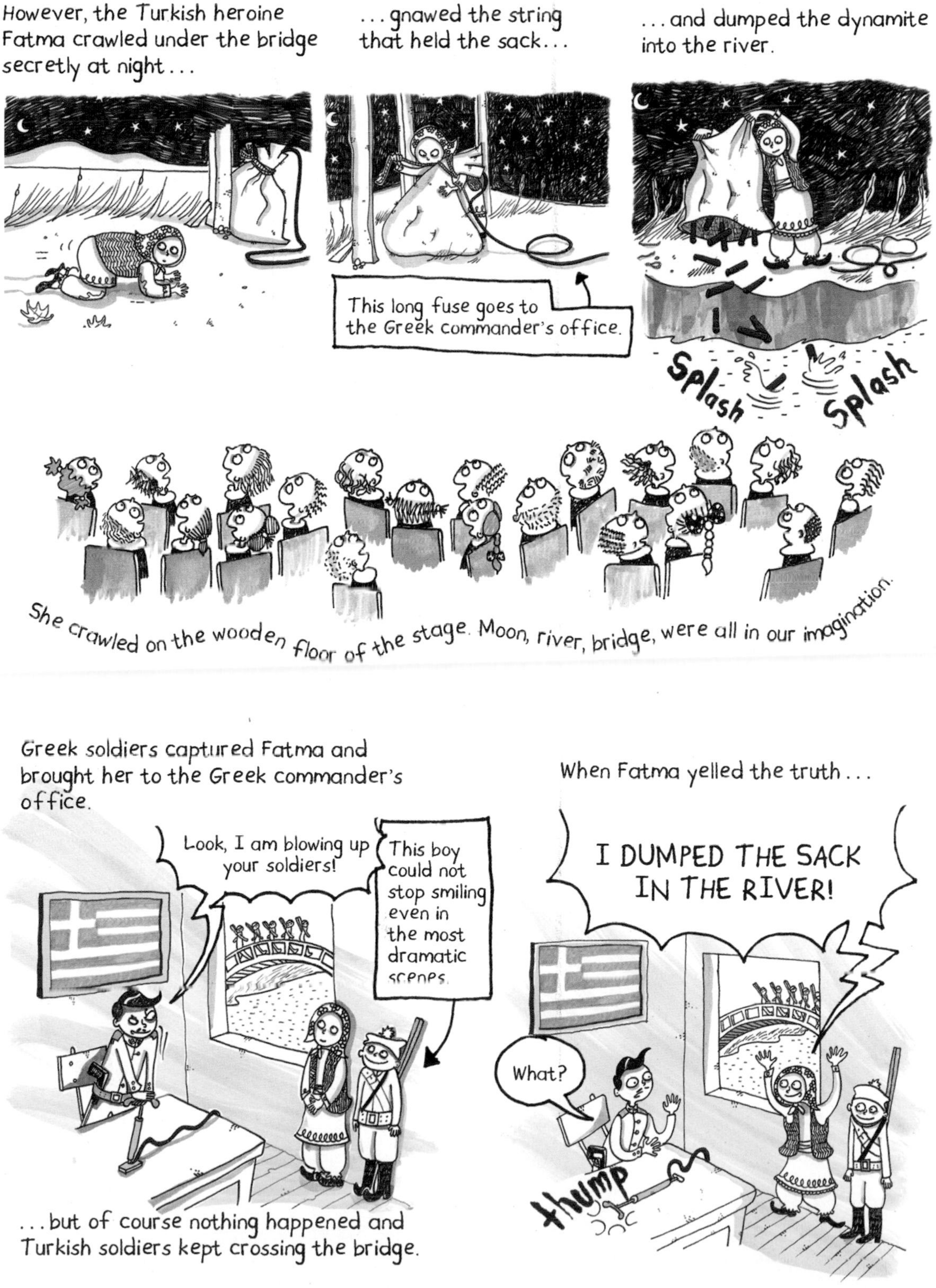
However, the Turkish heroine Fatma crawled under the bridge secretly at night . . .
. . . gnawed the string that held the sack . . .
This long fuse goes to the Greek commander's office.
. . . and dumped the dynamite into the river.
Splash
Splash
She crawled on the wooden floor of the stage. Moon, river, bridge, were all in our imagination.
Greek soldiers captured Fatma and brought her to the Greek commander's office.
Look, I am blowing up your soldiers!
This boy could not stop smiling even in the most dramatic scenes.
. . . but of course nothing happened and Turkish soldiers kept crossing the bridge.
When Fatma yelled the truth . . .
I DUMPED THE SACK IN THE RIVER!
What?
thump

. . . the commander killed her . . .

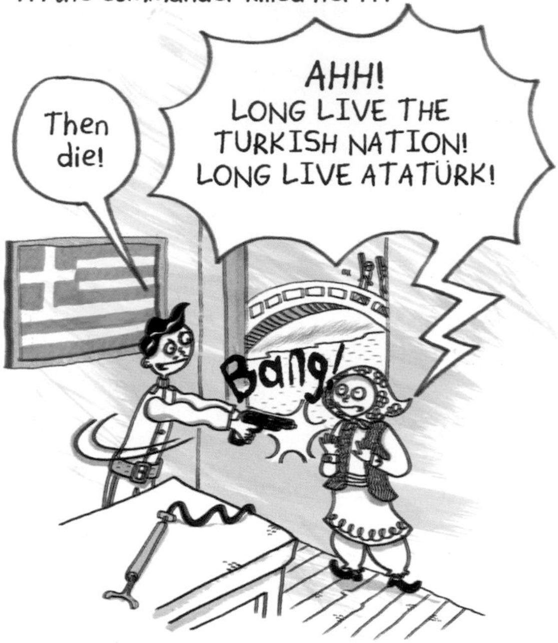

Then die!
AHH!
LONG LIVE THE TURKISH NATION!
LONG LIVE ATATÜRK!
Bang!

. . . and then Turkish soldiers ran in and killed the Greek commander.

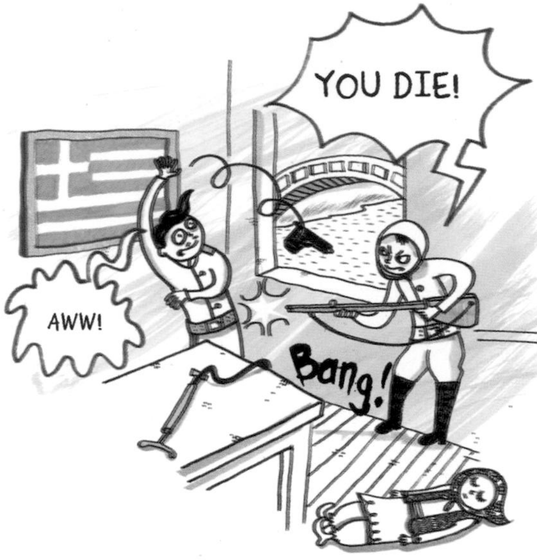

YOU DIE!
AWW!
Bang!

When the performers came out to bow, the girl who played Fatma was draped in a Turkish Flag.

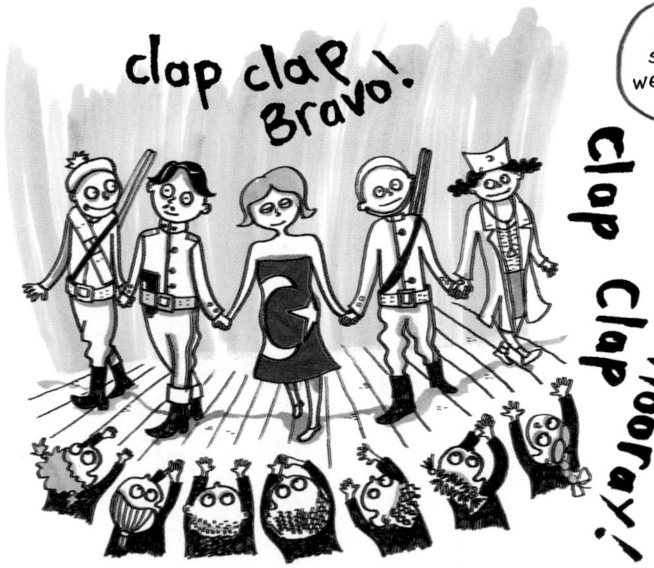

clap clap
Bravo!
clap Clap
Hooray!

After the play, emotions were bursting inside of me. I went home and immediately shared my feelings.

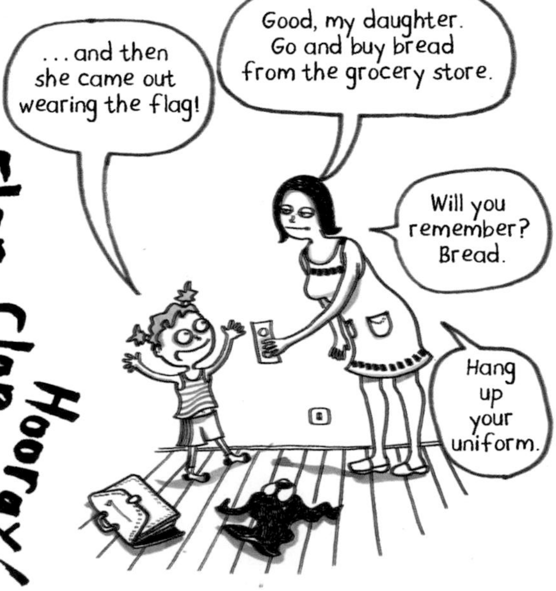

. . . and then she came out wearing the flag!
Good, my daughter. Go and buy bread from the grocery store.
Will you remember? Bread.
Hang up your uniform.

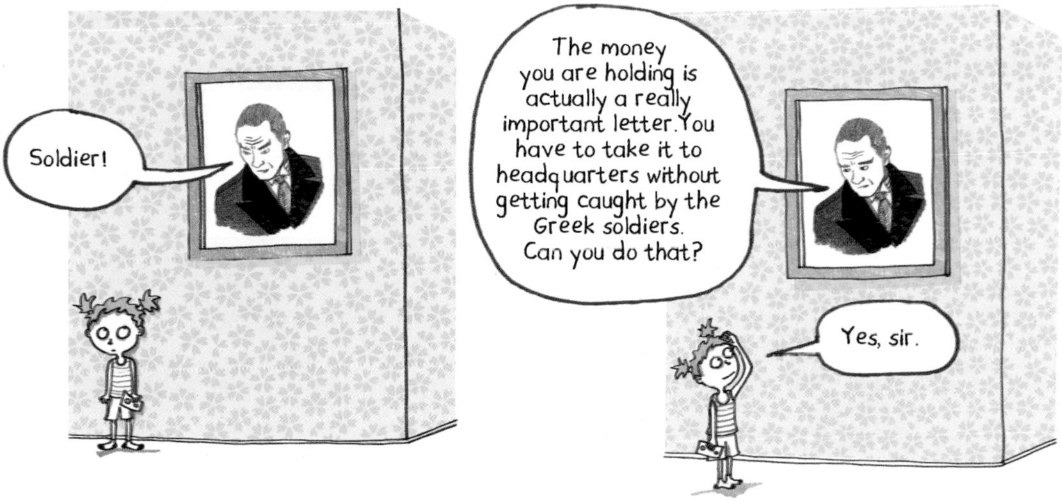
Soldier!
The money you are holding is actually a really important letter. You have to take it to headquarters without getting caught by the Greek soldiers. Can you do that?
Yes, sir.

On my way to headquarters . . .

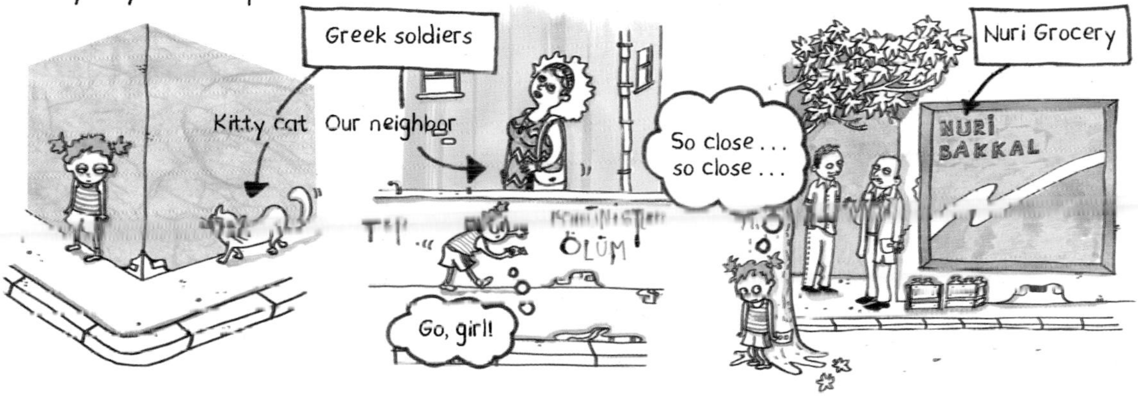
Greek soldiers
Kitty cat
Our neighbor
ÖLÜM
Go, girl!
So close . . . so close . . .
Nuri Grocery
NURİ BAKKAL

Finally, I gave the letter to the commander.

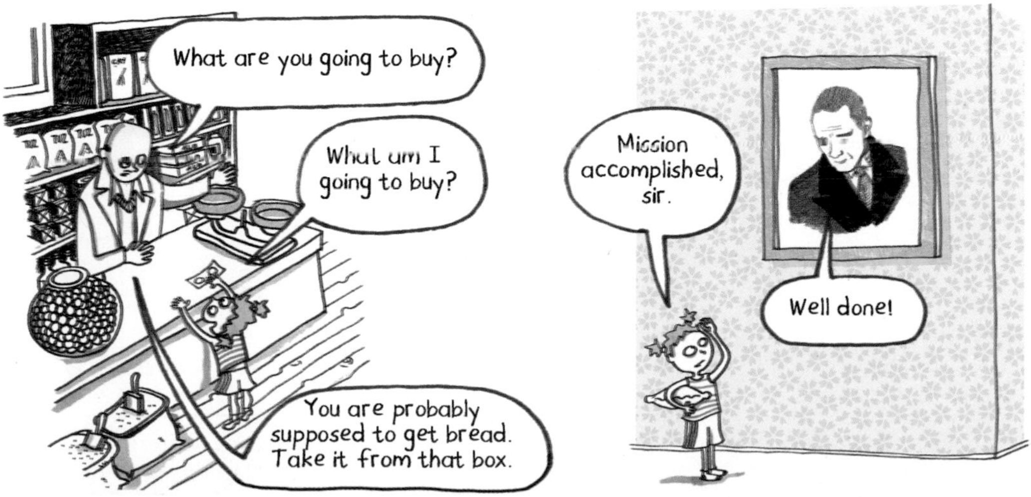
What are you going to buy?
What am I going to buy?
You are probably supposed to get bread. Take it from that box.
Mission accomplished, sir.
Well done!

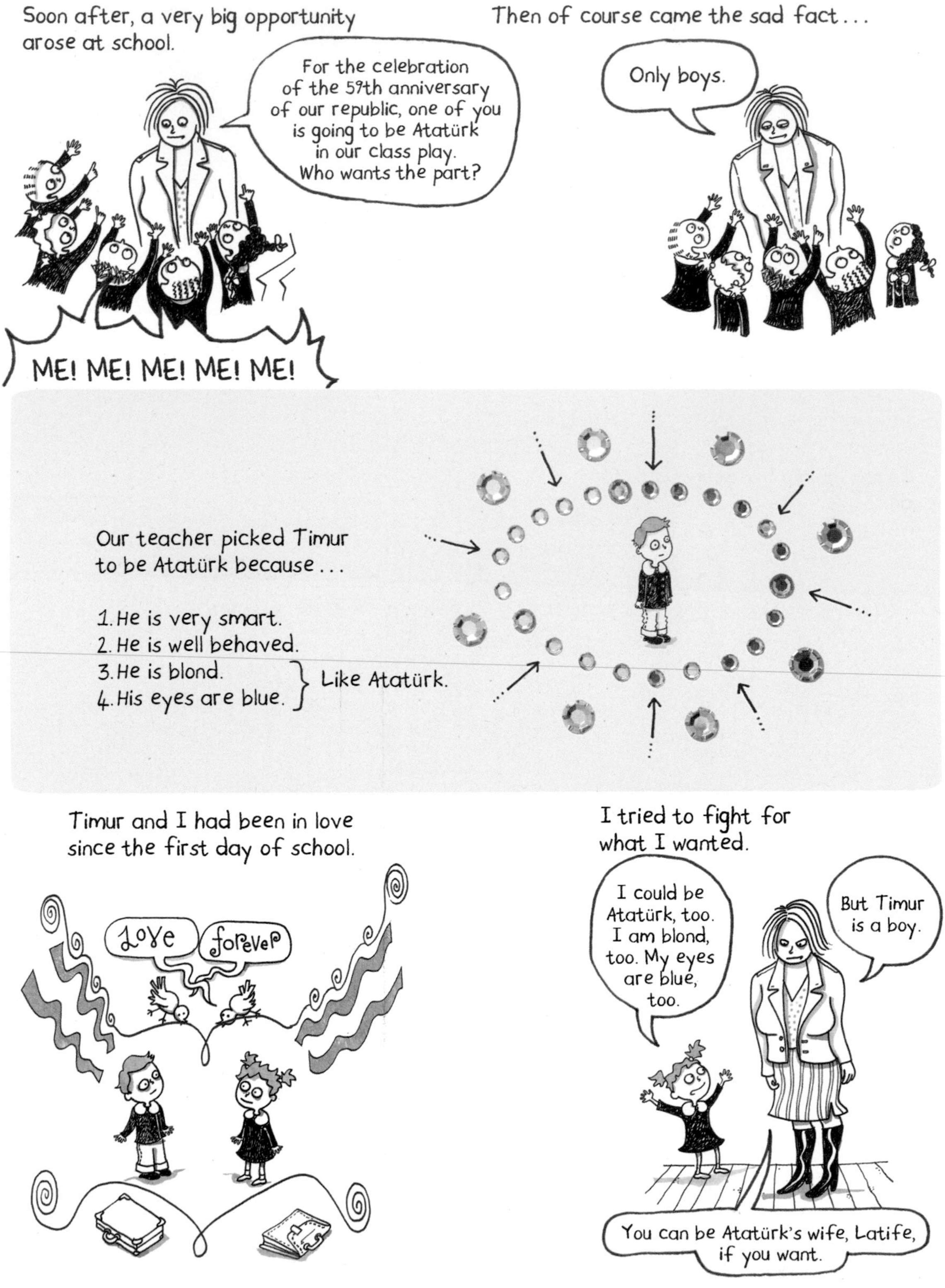
Soon after, a very big opportunity arose at school.
For the celebration of the 57th anniversary of our republic, one of you is going to be Atatürk in our class play. Who wants the part?
ME! ME! ME! ME! ME!
Then of course came the sad fact...
Only boys.
Our teacher picked Timur to be Atatürk because...
1. He is very smart.
2. He is well behaved.
3. He is blond.
4. His eyes are blue.
Like Atatürk.
Timur and I had been in love since the first day of school.
Love
forever
I tried to fight for what I wanted.
I could be Atatürk, too. I am blond, too. My eyes are blue, too.
But Timur is a boy.
You can be Atatürk's wife, Latife, if you want.

Despite my feelings for Timur, the role of Atatürk's wife was unacceptable.

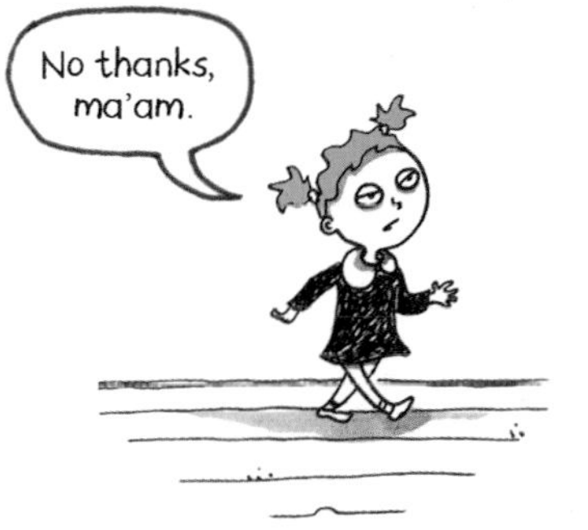
No thanks, ma'am.

Atatürk was now between Timur and me.

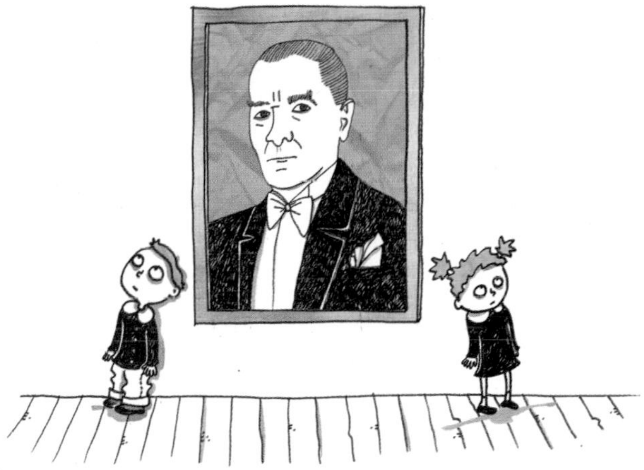

I was upset and when I got home from school I wanted to talk to Pelin about this, but Pelin and our neighbor Engin were already outside playing. They had made up a trick to look older and taller to people passing by.

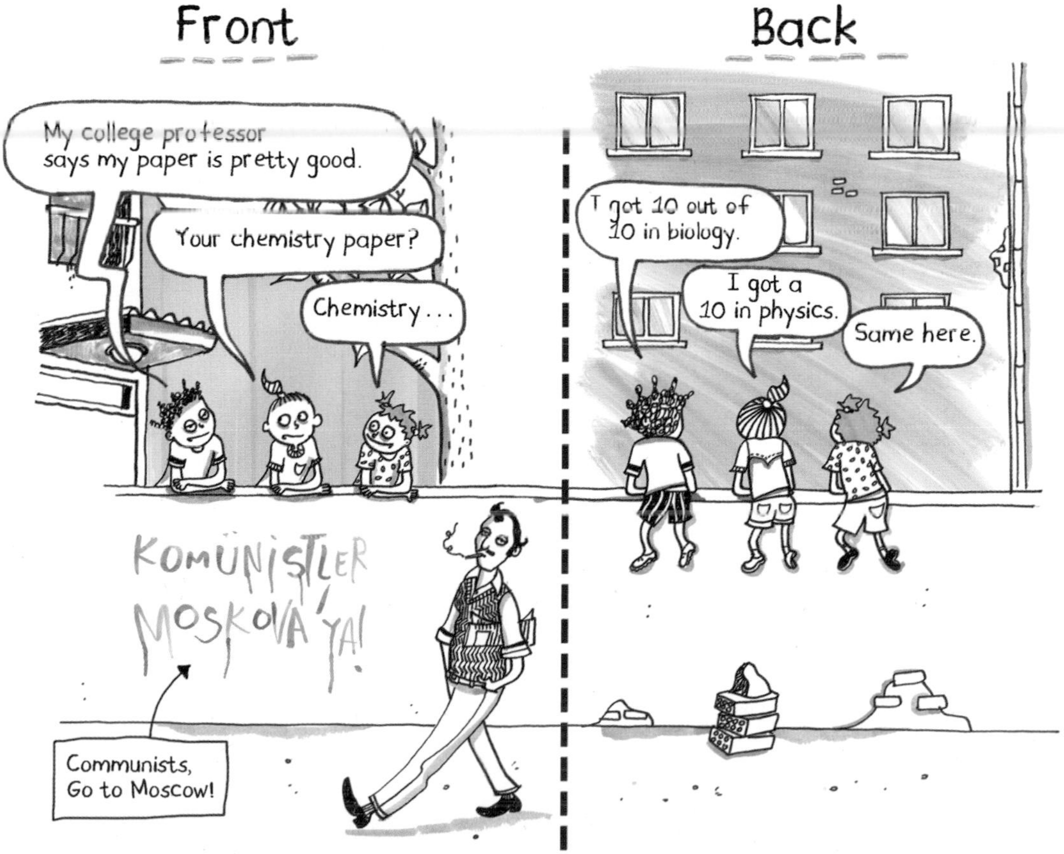
Front
Back
My college professor says my paper is pretty good.
Your chemistry paper?
Chemistry . . .
I got 10 out of 10 in biology.
I got a 10 in physics.
Same here.
KOMÜNISTLER MOSKOVA'YA!
Communists, Go to Moscow!

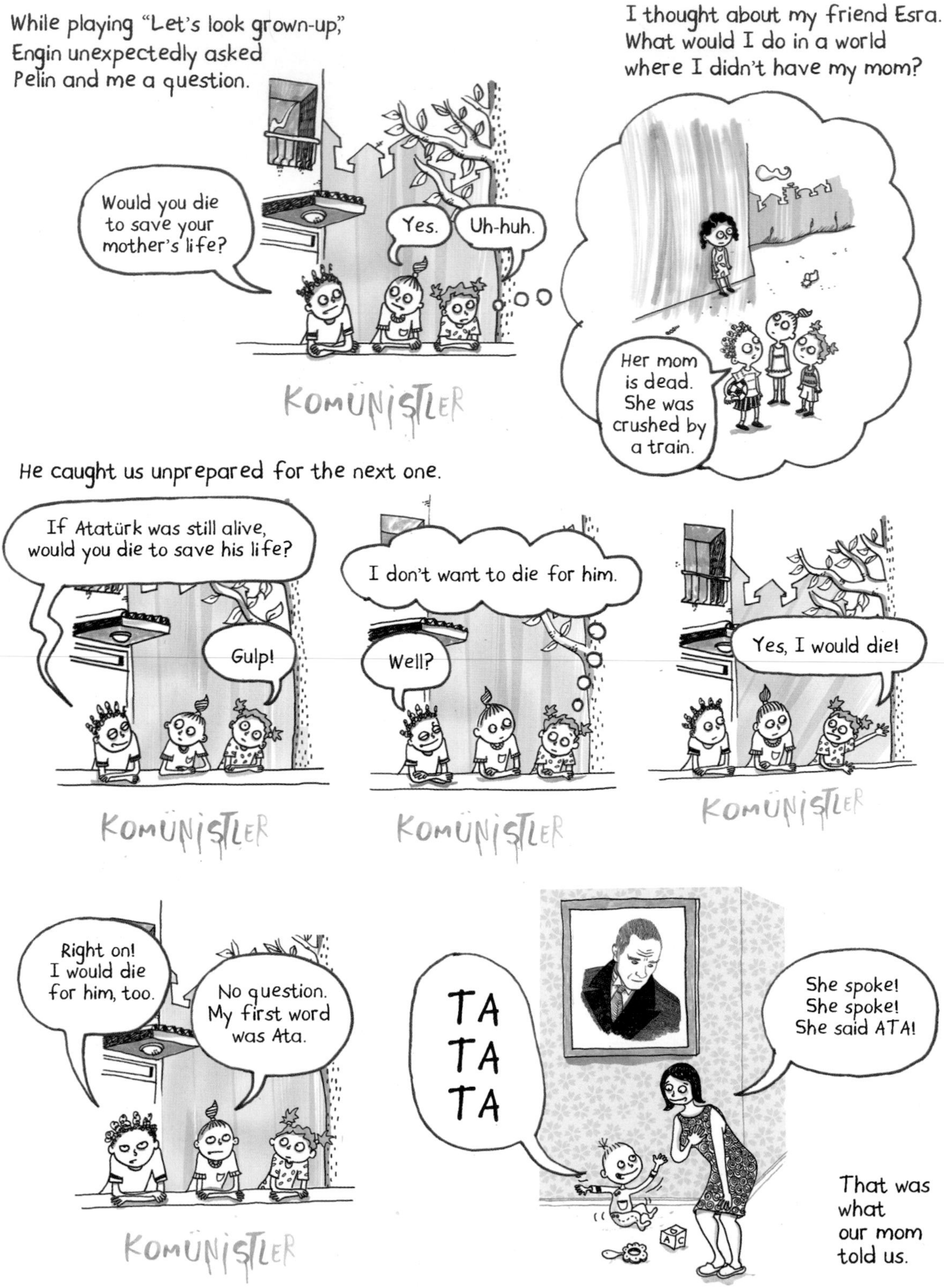

While playing "Let's look grown-up," Engin unexpectedly asked Pelin and me a question.
Would you die to save your mother's life?
Yes.
Uh-huh.
KOMÜNISTLER
I thought about my friend Esra. What would I do in a world where I didn't have my mom?
Her mom is dead. She was crushed by a train.
He caught us unprepared for the next one.
If Atatürk was still alive, would you die to save his life?
Gulp!
KOMÜNISTLER
I don't want to die for him.
Well?
KOMÜNISTLER
Yes, I would die!
KOMÜNISTLER
Right on! I would die for him, too.
No question. My first word was Ata.
KOMÜNISTLER
TA TA TA
She spoke! She spoke! She said ATA!
That was what our mom told us.

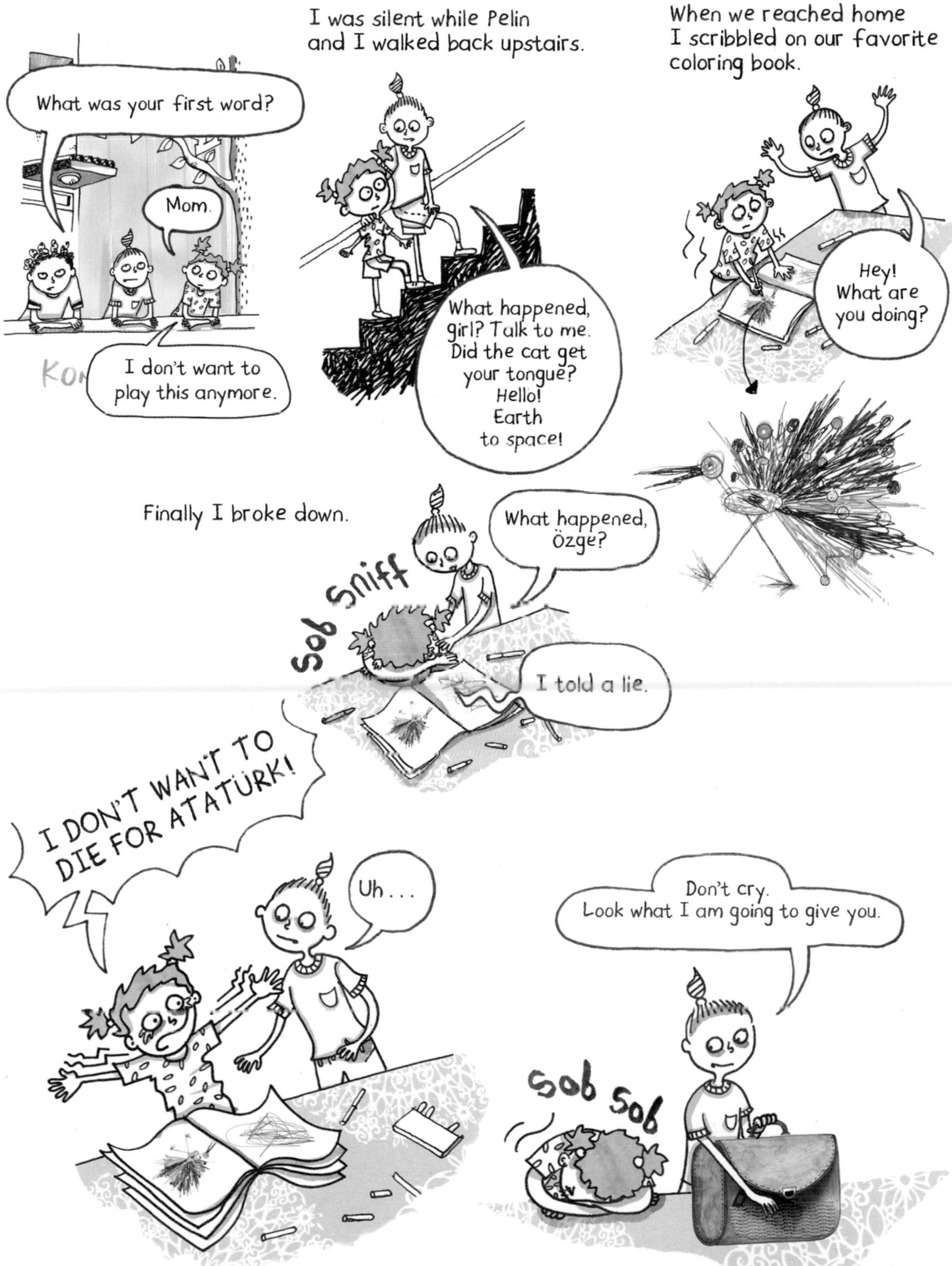
What was your first word?
Mom.
I don't want to play this anymore.
I was silent while Pelin and I walked back upstairs.
What happened, girl? Talk to me. Did the cat get your tongue? Hello! Earth to space!
When we reached home I scribbled on our favorite coloring book.
Hey! What are you doing?
Finally I broke down.
What happened, Özge?
Sob Sniff
I told a lie.
I DON'T WANT TO DIE FOR ATATÜRK!
Uh . . .
Don't cry. Look what I am going to give you.
Sob Sob

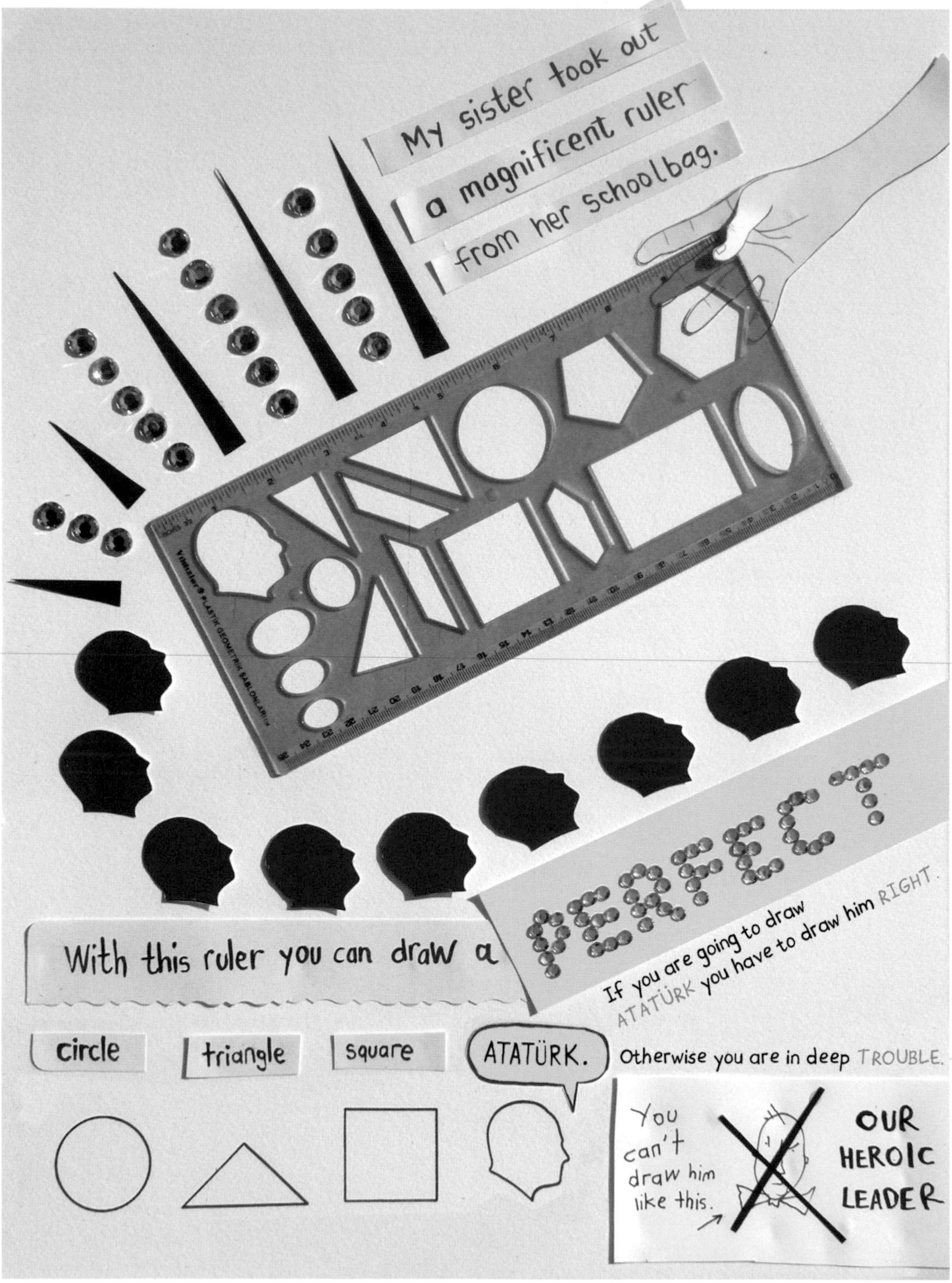
My sister took out
a magnificent ruler
from her schoolbag.
With this ruler you can draw a
PERFECT
If you are going to draw ATATÜRK you have to draw him RIGHT.
circle
triangle
square
ATATÜRK.
Otherwise you are in deep TROUBLE.
You can't draw him like this.
OUR HEROIC LEADER

Chapter 5

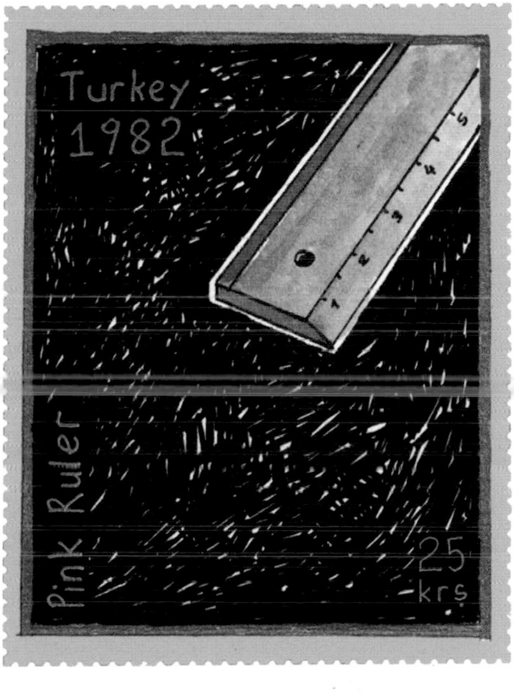
Turkey
1982
Pink Ruler
25
krs

Pink Ruler

My parents had a bunch of cool rulers because of the subjects they taught.

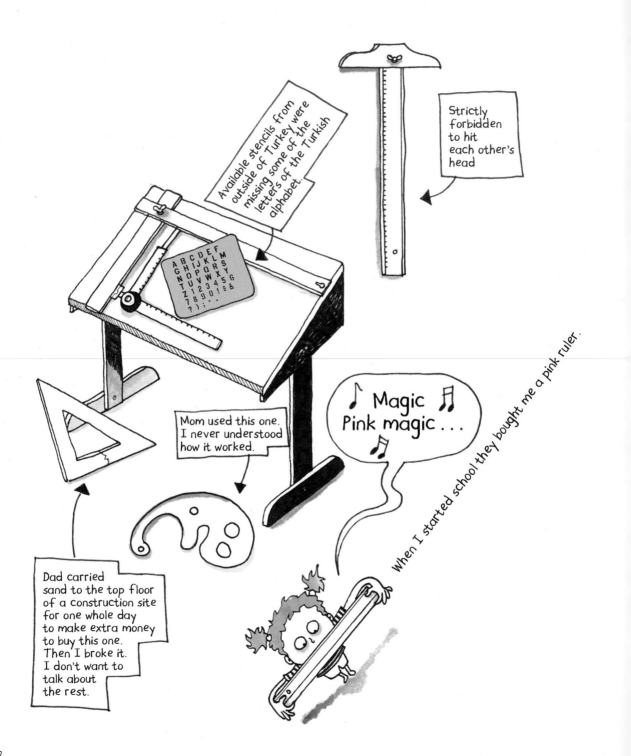

Available stencils from outside of Turkey were missing some of the letters of the Turkish alphabet.

Strictly forbidden to hit each other's head

Mom used this one. I never understood how it worked.

♪ Magic ♫ Pink magic . . .

When I started school they bought me a pink ruler.

Dad carried sand to the top floor of a construction site for one whole day to make extra money to buy this one. Then I broke it. I don't want to talk about the rest.

A pink ruler can be used for many things.

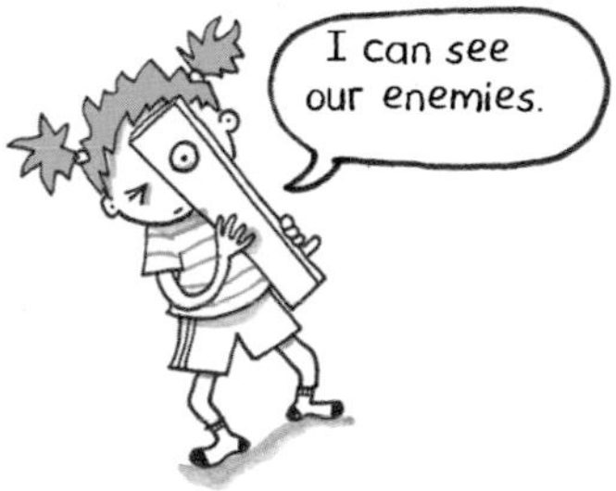
I can see our enemies.

A Binocular

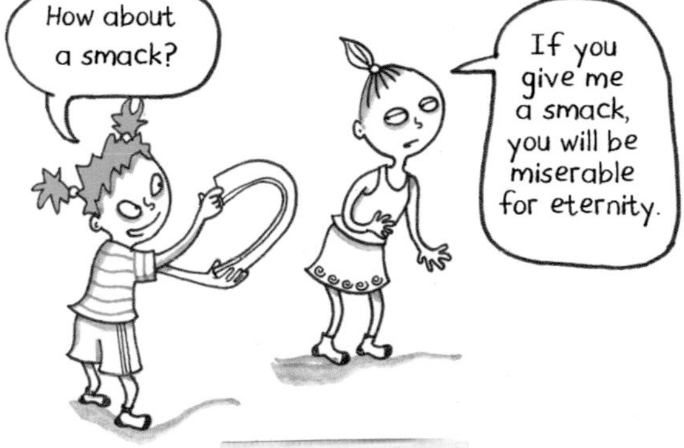
How about a smack?
If you give me a smack, you will be miserable for eternity.

A Smacker

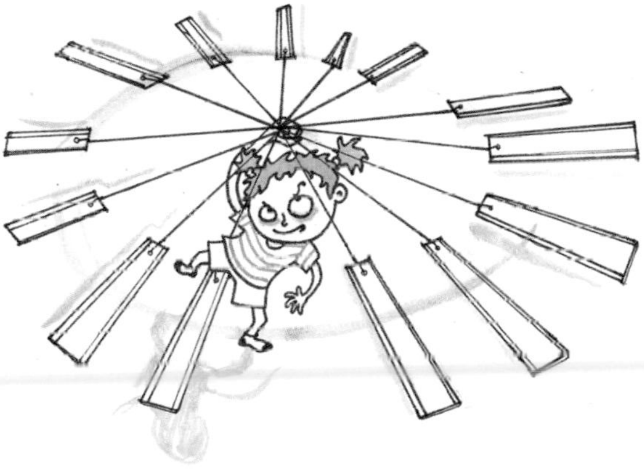

Add a string— A Propeller

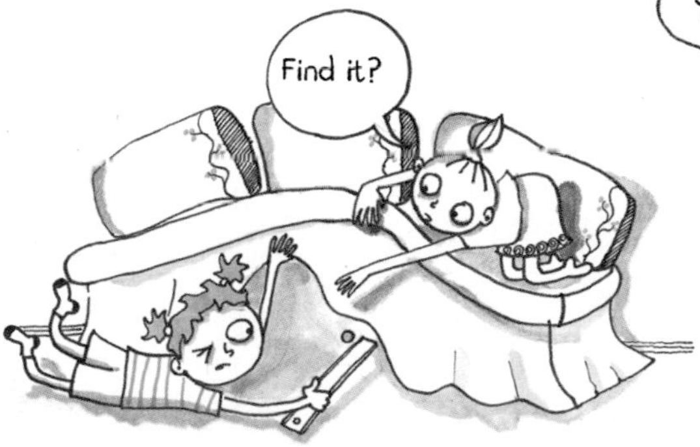
Find it?

A Rescue Device

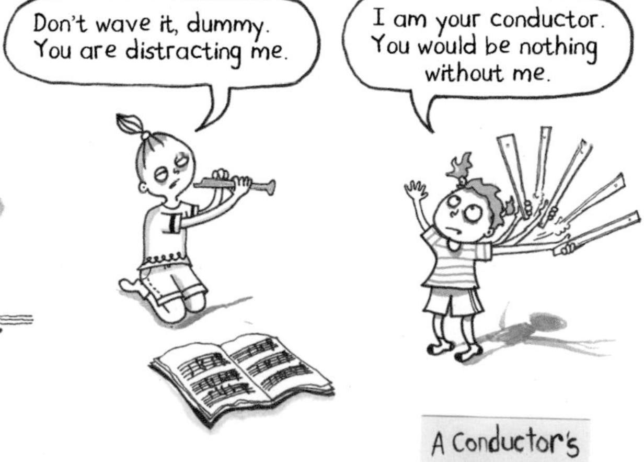
Don't wave it, dummy. You are distracting me.
I am your conductor. You would be nothing without me.

A Conductor's Baton

Oddly enough, my pink ruler was also once used to deliver a message.

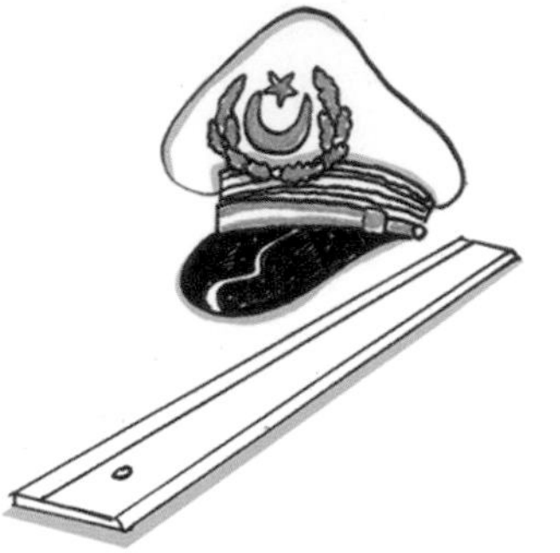

During the late 1970s people divided into two groups—left wing and right wing. They fought in a civil war.

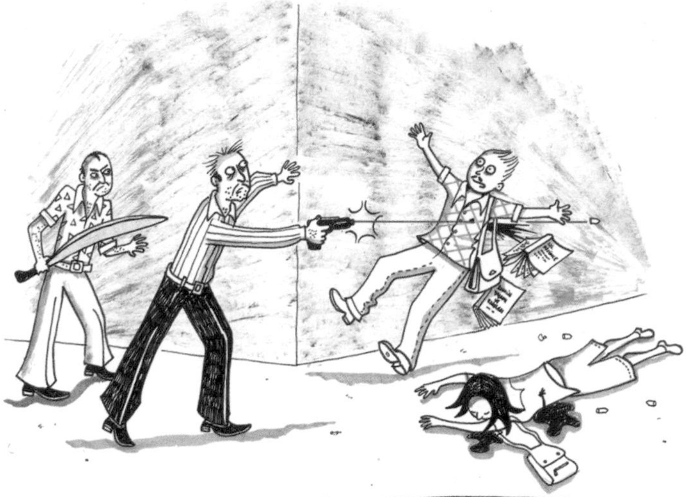

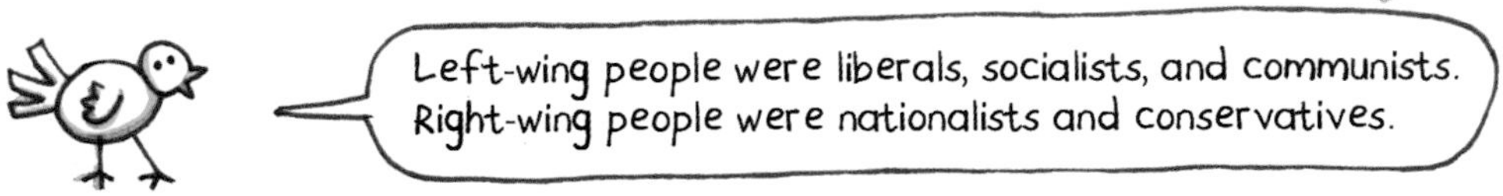
Left-wing people were liberals, socialists, and communists. Right-wing people were nationalists and conservatives.

Then in 1980, General Kenan Evren led a military coup and took over the government. That was the end of the civil war and the start of new restrictions.

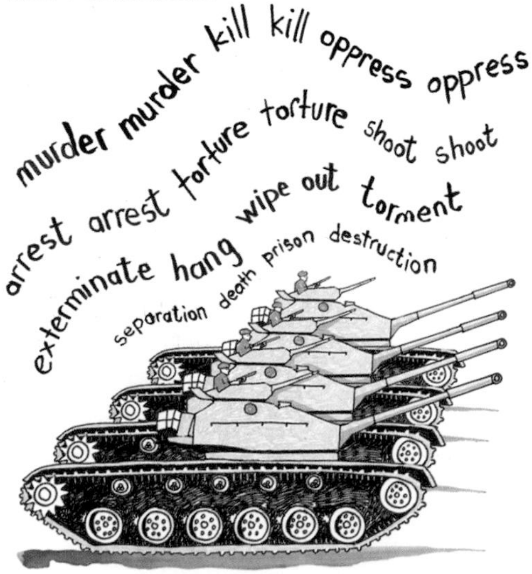
murder murder kill kill oppress oppress
arrest arrest torture torture shoot shoot
wipe out torment
exterminate hang prison destruction
separation death

It was forbidden to be on the streets after 11 p.m.

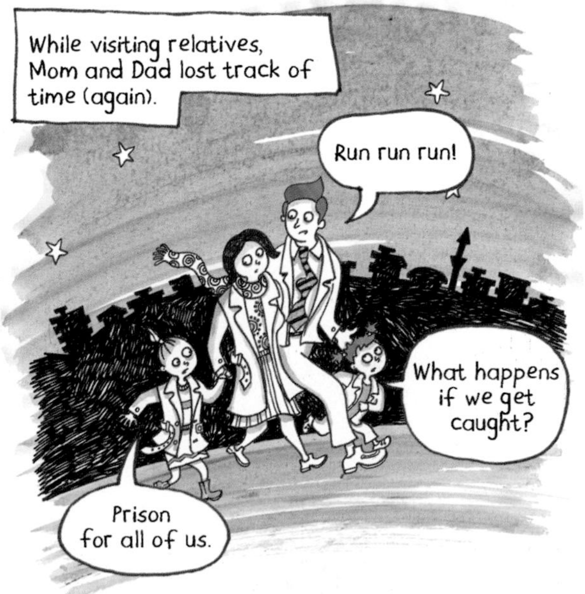
While visiting relatives, Mom and Dad lost track of time (again).
Run run run!
What happens if we get caught?
Prison for all of us.

The one channel on Turkish TV was broadcast by the government. I mostly saw generals and soldiers on TV. Belly dancers and singers who sang about anything other than the great nation of Turks were banned.

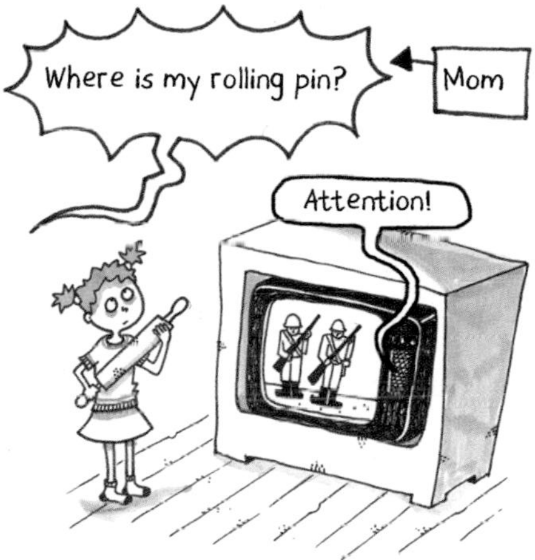

Where is my rolling pin?
Mom
Attention!

If a newspaper wrote something against the military, it was temporarily shut down.

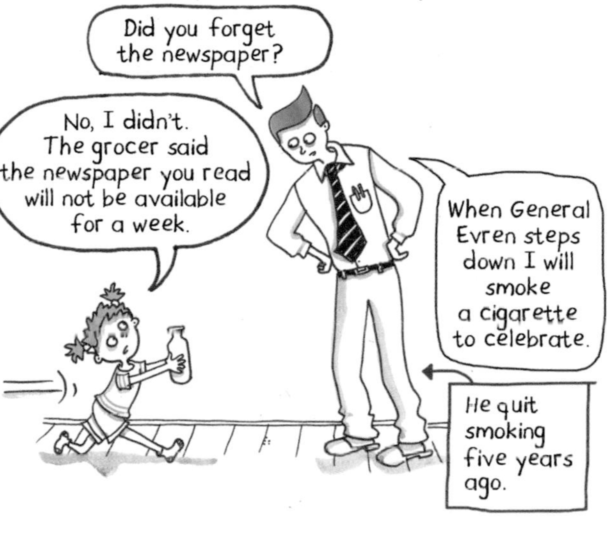

Did you forget the newspaper?
No, I didn't. The grocer said the newspaper you read will not be available for a week.
When General Evren steps down I will smoke a cigarette to celebrate.
He quit smoking five years ago.

Books and magazines that mentioned any left-wing ideas were banned.

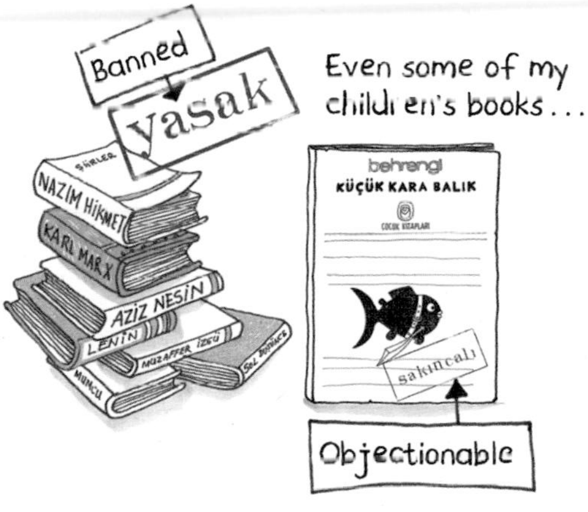

Banned
yasak
NAZIM HİKMET
KARL MARX
AZİZ NESİN
LENİN
Even some of my children's books . . .
behrengi
KÜÇÜK KARA BALIK
sakıncalı
Objectionable

Policemen could burst into anyone's home anytime without a search warrant. If they found anything banned, they arrested everyone at home, imprisoned them, and tortured them.

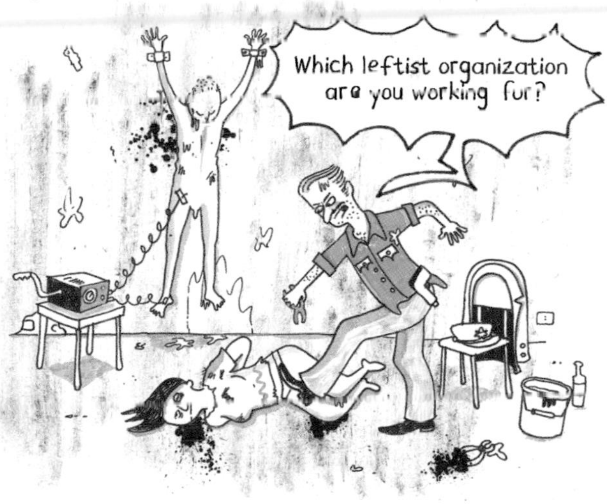

Which leftist organization are you working for?

After the coup, the military executed fifteen people in two years. One of the victims, Erdal Eren, was 17 years old.

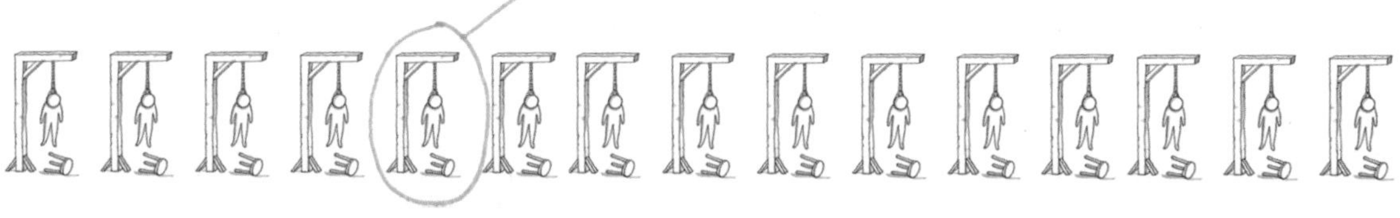

When a journalist asked about the execution of a 17-year-old, General Evren said:

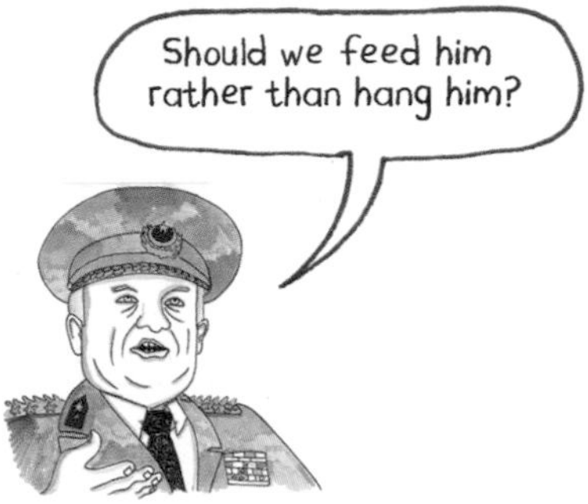

Should we feed him rather than hang him?

In 1982, there was a nationwide vote on a new constitution written by soldiers who had led the coup.

You could accept or reject this new constitution.

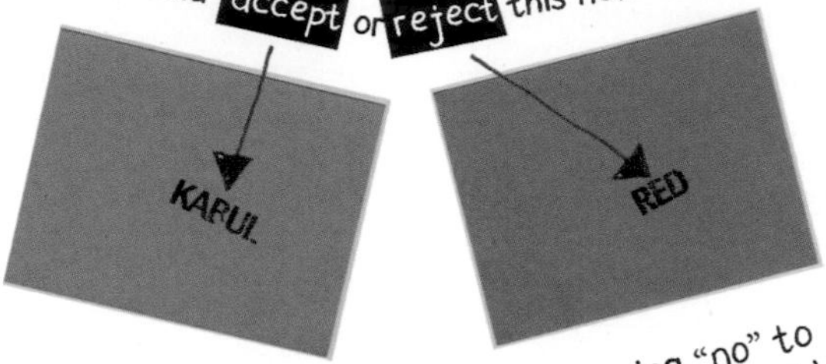

KABUL
RED

But saying "no" to the military could be dangerous.

General Evren wanted everyone to say "yes" to the constitution. Then he could be recognized as the president and the military could stay in power.

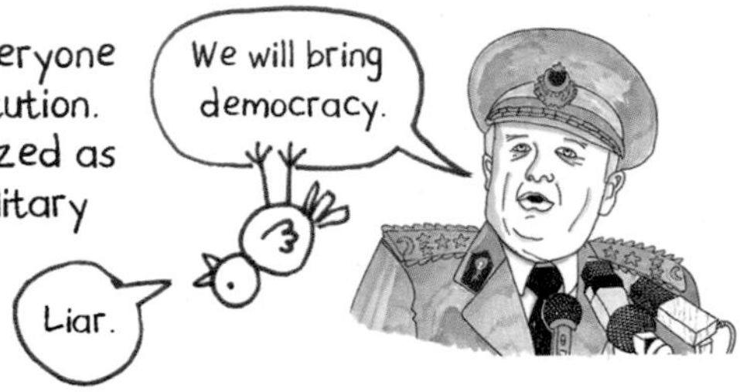

We will bring democracy.
Liar.

There was a rumor that the envelopes people were going to put their votes in would be slightly transparent.

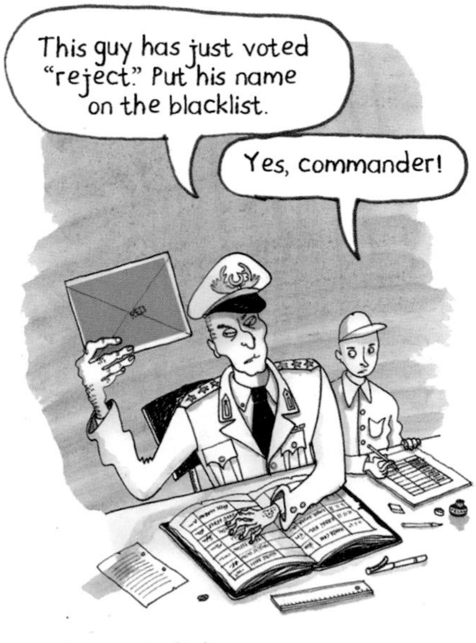

This guy has just voted "reject." Put his name on the blacklist.
Yes, commander!

A military-led democracy was a paradox.

One night on TV, before the election, two guys who opposed the government jumped on the soccer field during a game and held up a sign.

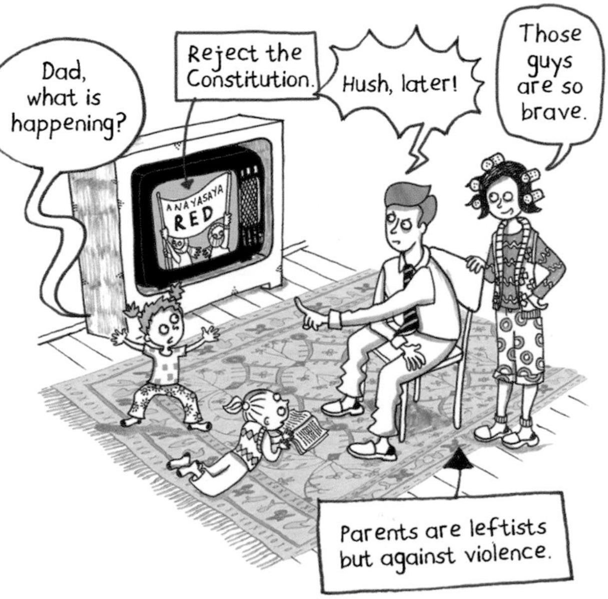

Dad, what is happening?
Reject the Constitution.
ANAYASAYA RED
Hush, later!
Those guys are so brave.
Parents are leftists but against violence.

Suddenly, the game was replaced by a historic vase. The vase appeared whenever things got out of control. I saw it almost every day.

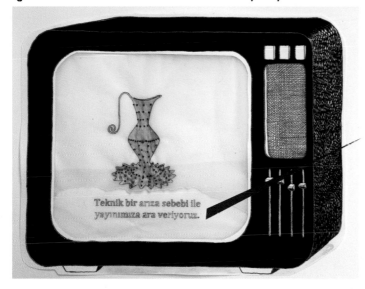

Teknik bir arıza sebebi ile yayınımıza ara veriyoruz.

Due to technical difficulties our broadcast has been suspended.

My memory is in color ■ ■ ■ ■ ■
but the vase and lettering
were black-and-white. ■□■□■

The next day at school I was telling my deskmate, Damla, what happened on TV.

THEN THEY CUT THE BROADCAST AND THE VASE CAME!

Suddenly
Hediye Harikatepe's
hand came over . . .

Was this really happening?

Hediye Harikatepe was
borrowing my pink ruler.

My pink ruler was being
blessed by her hands.

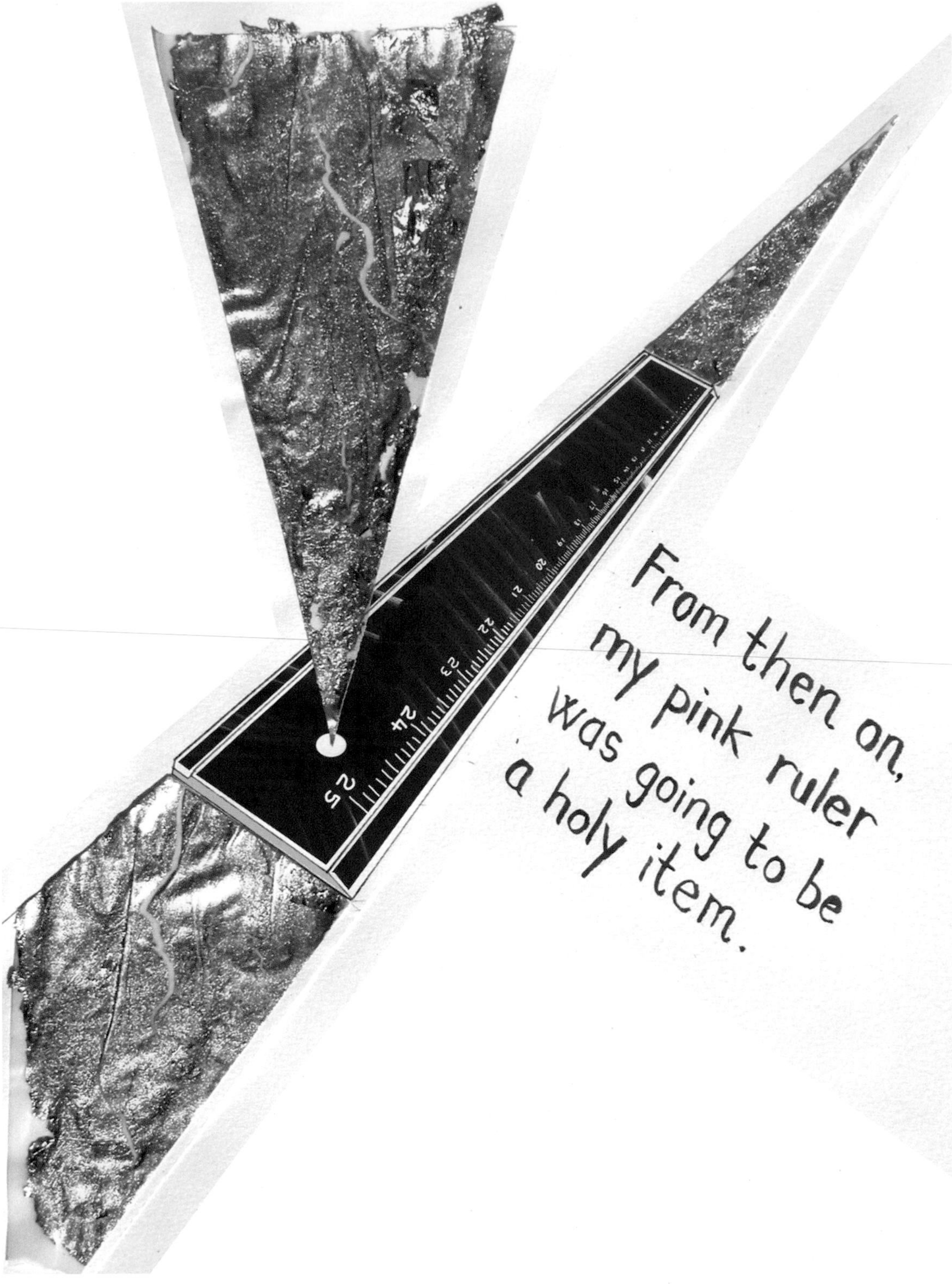
20
21
22
23
24
25

From then on,
my pink ruler
was going to be
a holy item.

She took my ruler and said:

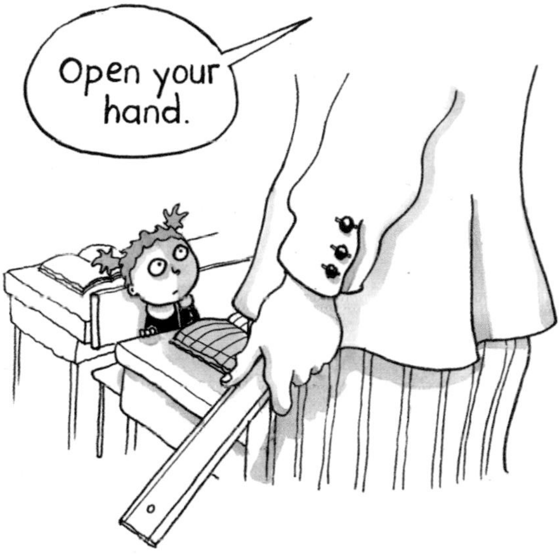
Open your hand.

I opened my hand.

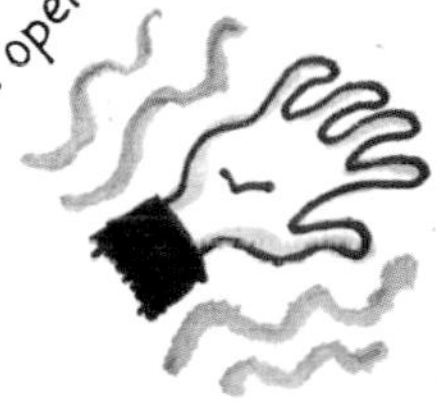

The entire classroom went silent.

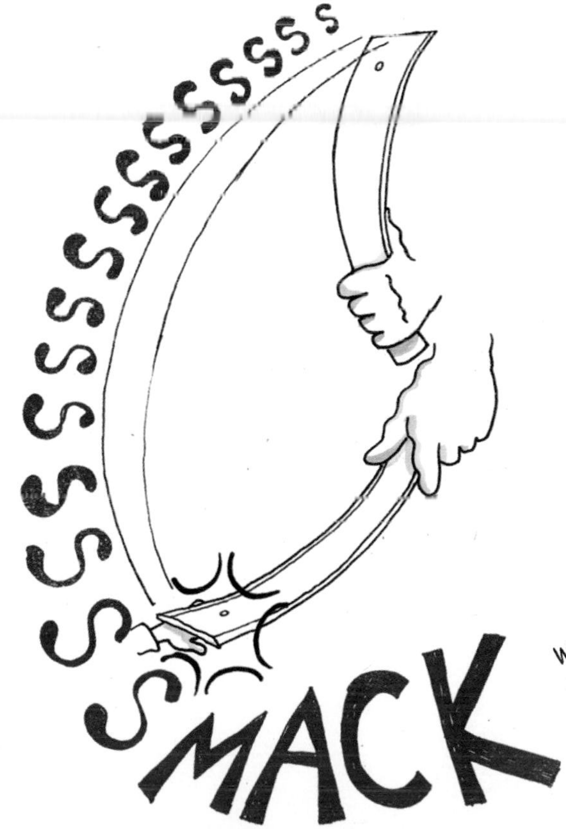
SSSSSSSSSSSSSSSSSMACK

Was I talking about something forbidden?
What did I do?

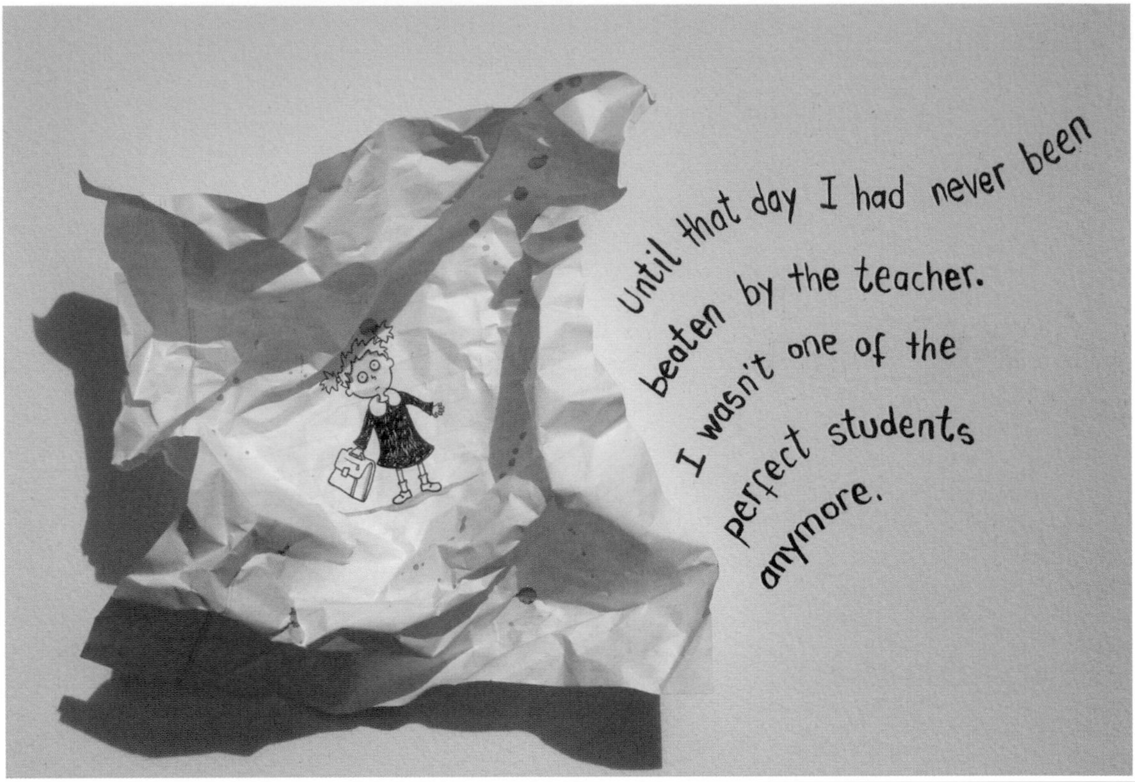
Until that day I had never been
beaten by the teacher.
I wasn't one of the
perfect students
anymore.

Right at that moment
Hediye Harikatepe told Damla . . .

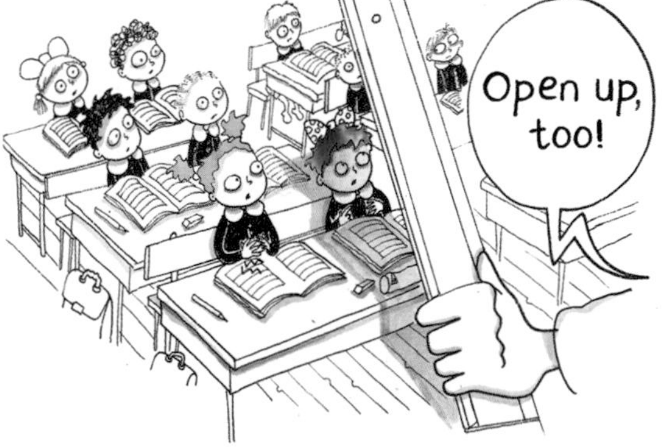
Open up,
too!

. . . and she hit her.

Then she moved on to the desk
behind us, and things got even stranger.

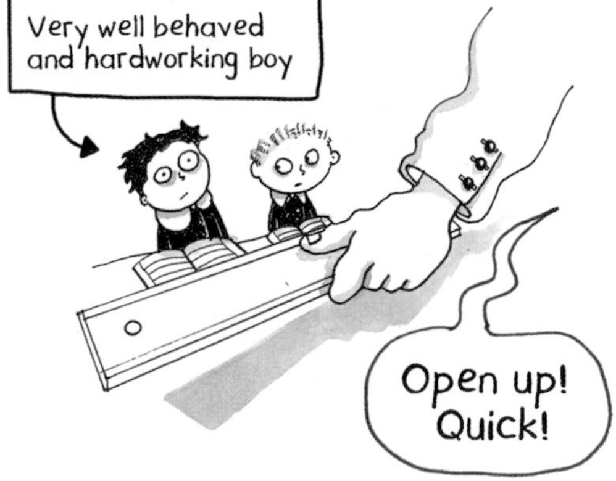
Very well behaved
and hardworking boy
Open up!
Quick!

Was it because Hediye Harikatepe had had a bad night? Did Hediye Harikatepe herself know what this was about? I was the one talking. How was Damla responsible, too?
She beat every student in the class with my pink ruler!
Embarrassing but true, I felt a sigh of relief.

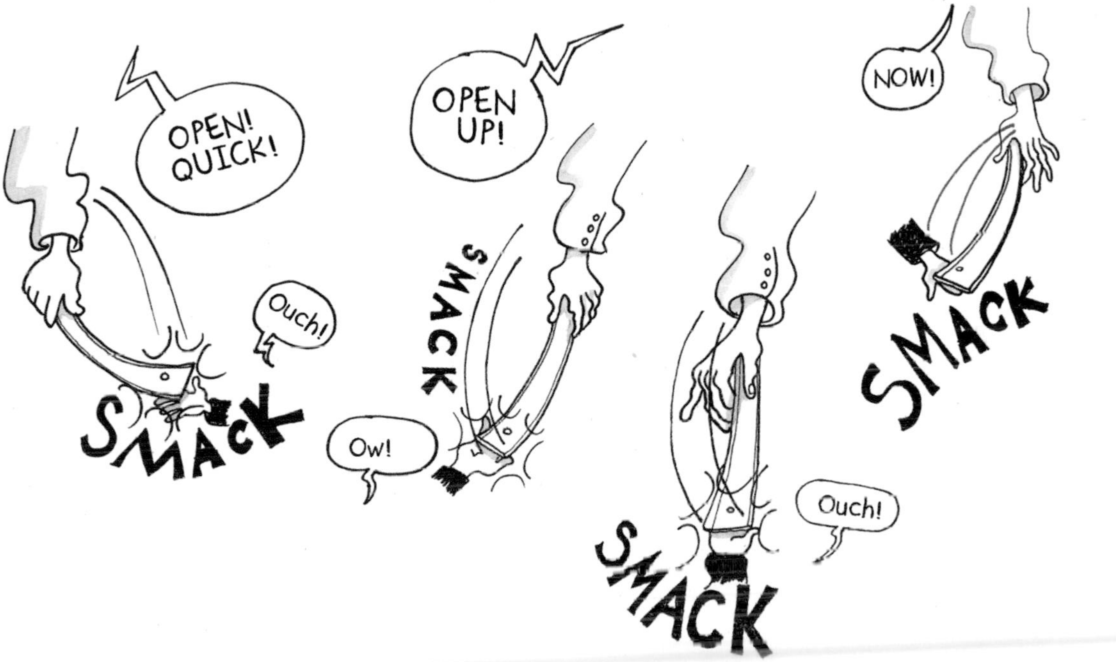
OPEN! QUICK!
Ouch!
SMACK
OPEN UP!
SMACK
Ow!
SMACK
Ouch!
NOW!
SMACK

When she was done all you could hear was the sound of our pencils, the sound of her chalk, and the squeaking of the old hardwood floor.

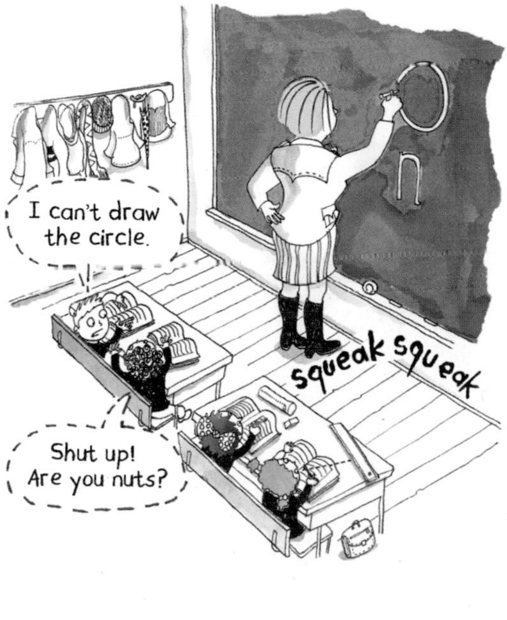
I can't draw the circle.
Shut up! Are you nuts?
squeak squeak

Since there was no way I was going to tell Dad about this, I had to at least tell Mom that I got a beating at school.

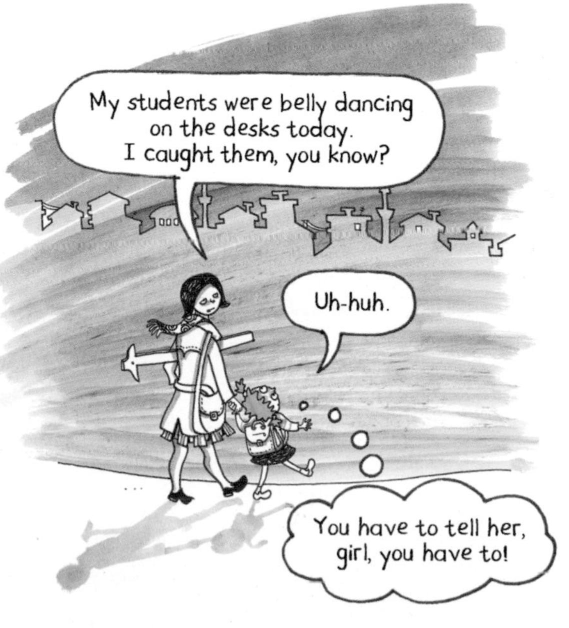
My students were belly dancing on the desks today. I caught them, you know?
Uh-huh.
You have to tell her, girl, you have to!

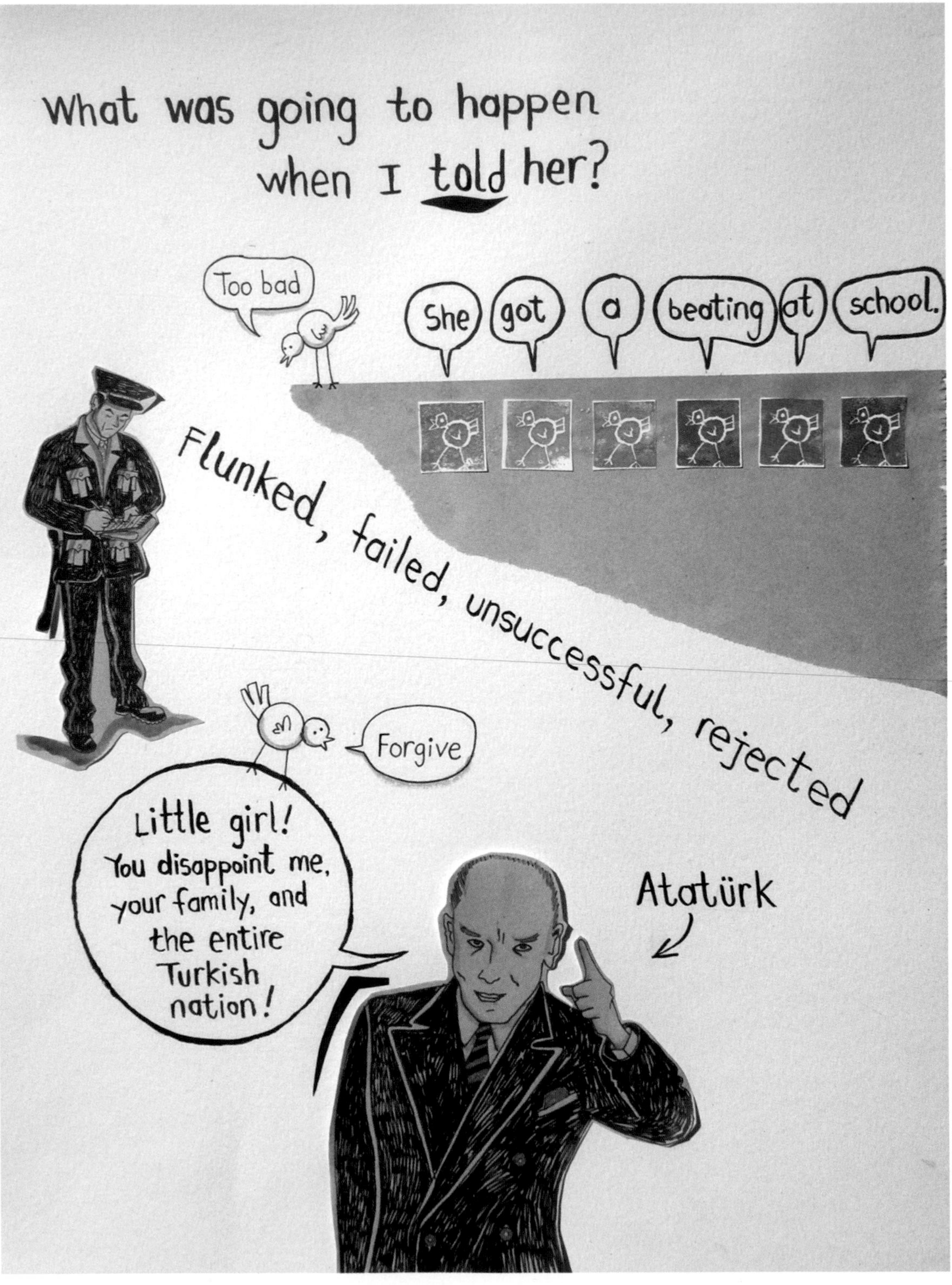

What was going to happen when I told her?
Too bad
She got a beating at school.
Flunked, failed, unsuccessful, rejected
Forgive
Little girl! You disappoint me, your family, and the entire Turkish nation!
Atatürk

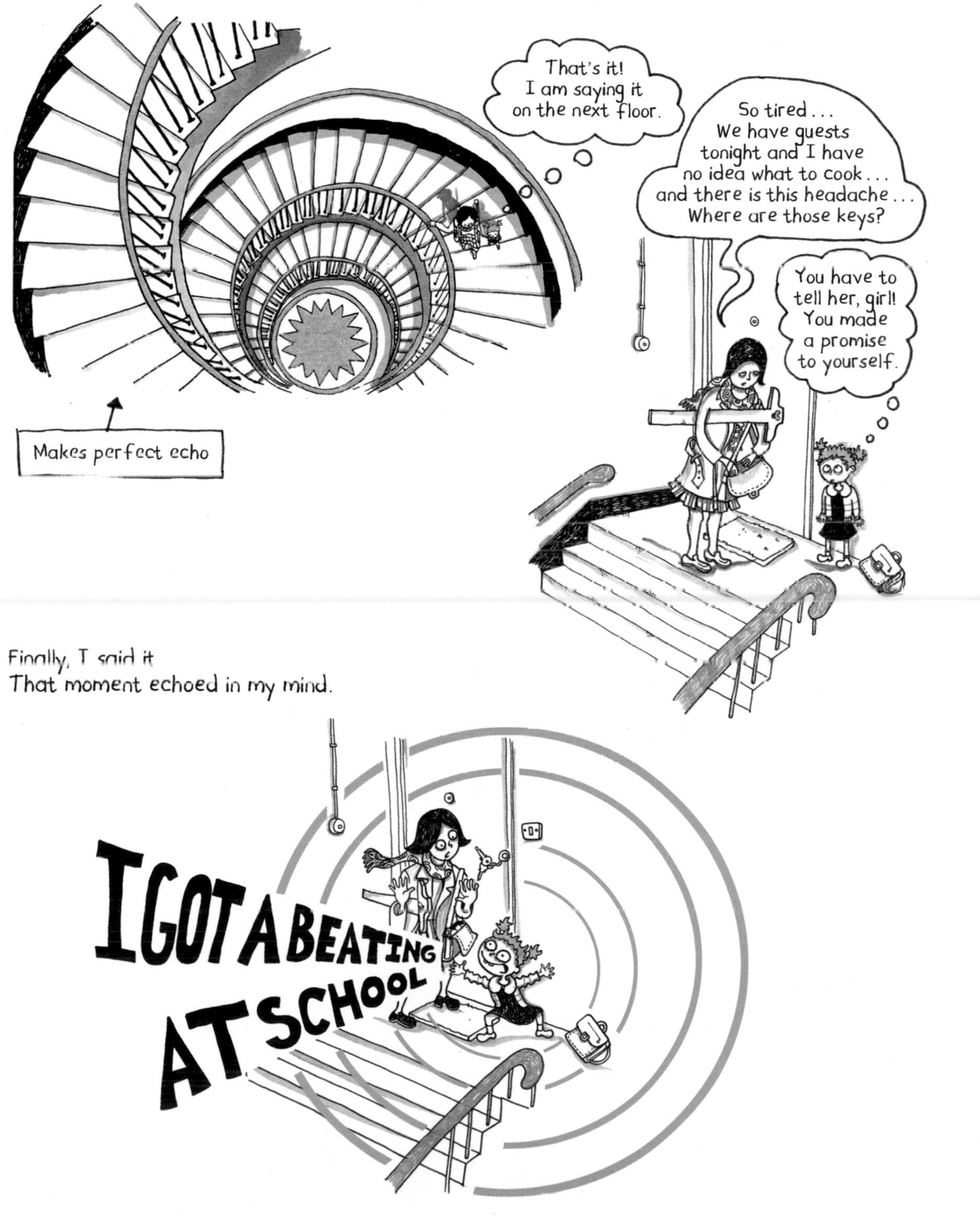

Makes perfect echo
That's it! I am saying it on the next floor.
So tired . . . We have guests tonight and I have no idea what to cook . . . and there is this headache . . . Where are those keys?
You have to tell her, girl! You made a promise to yourself.
Finally, I said it
That moment echoed in my mind.
I GOT A BEATING AT SCHOOL

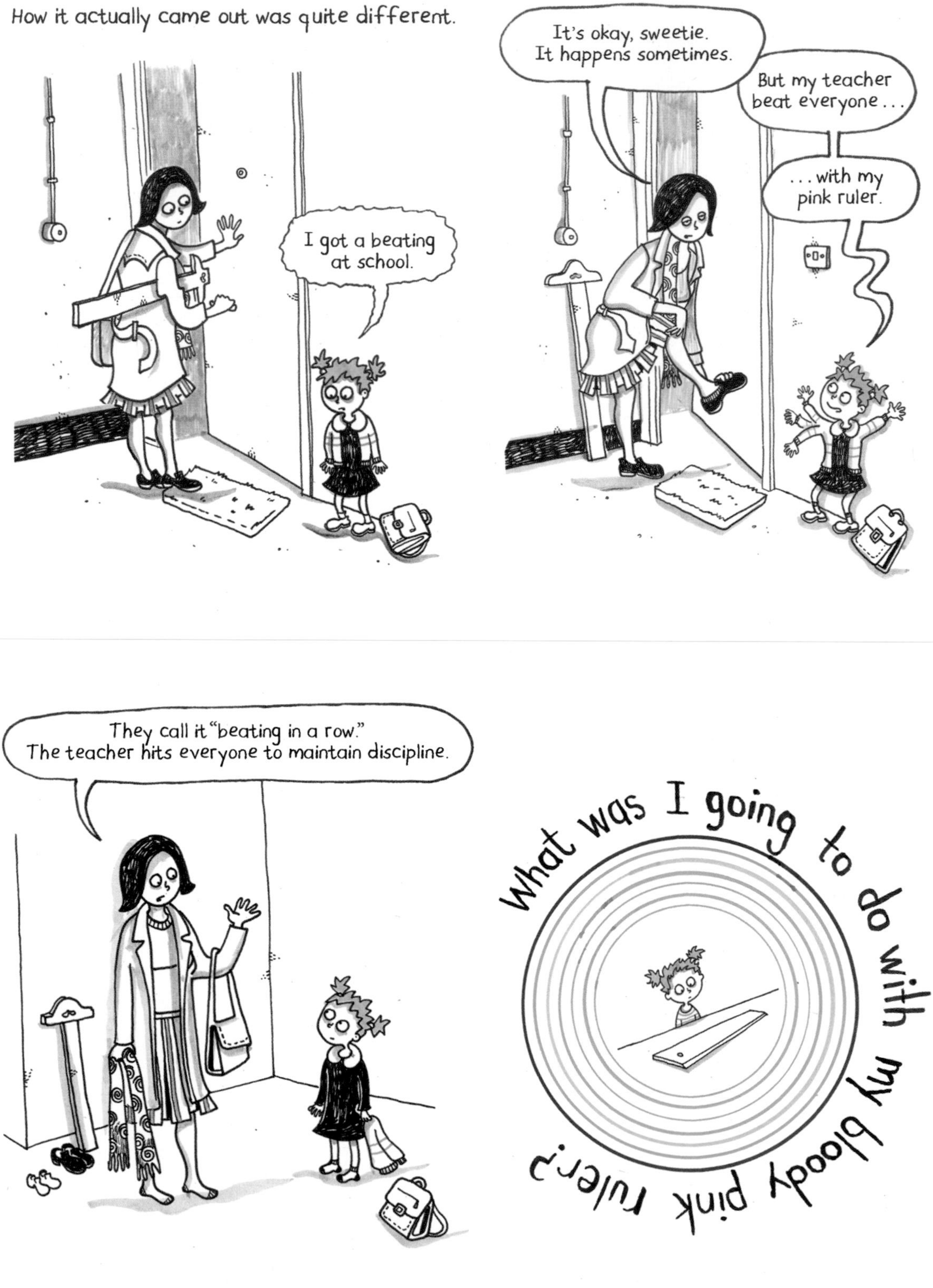
How it actually came out was quite different.
I got a beating at school.
It's okay, sweetie. It happens sometimes.
But my teacher beat everyone . . .
. . . with my pink ruler.
They call it "beating in a row." The teacher hits everyone to maintain discipline.
What was I going to do with my bloody pink ruler?

There were four options.

Break it.

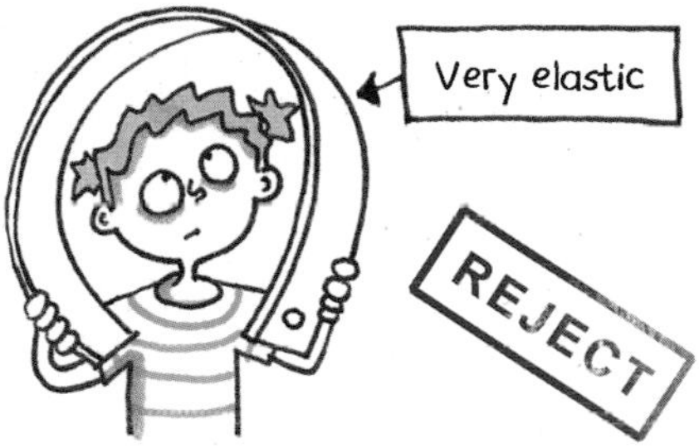
Very elastic
REJECT

Burn it.

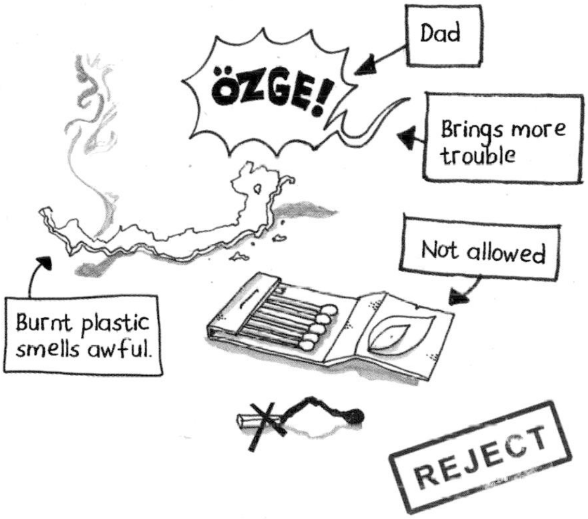
Dad
ÖZGE!
Brings more trouble
Not allowed
Burnt plastic smells awful.
REJECT

Purposefully lose it.

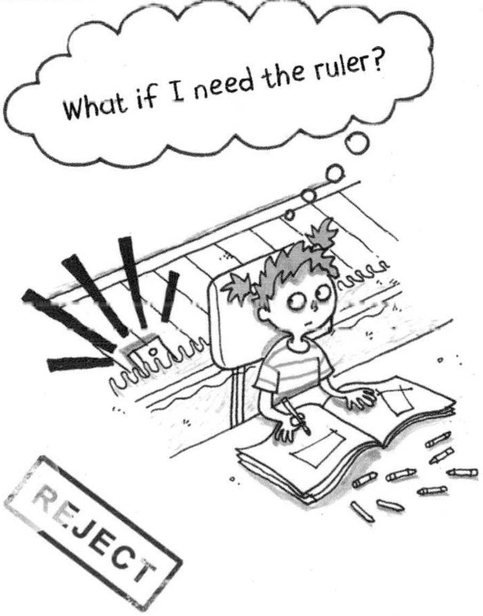
What if I need the ruler?
REJECT

Learn how to live with it.

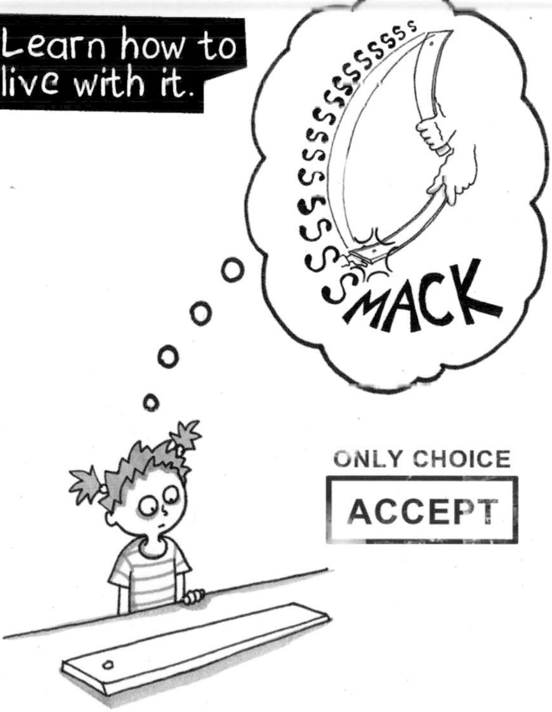
SSSSSSSSSSSSSSSSSSSSMACK
ONLY CHOICE
ACCEPT

When things are hard to deal with, why can't that historic vase appear in real life?

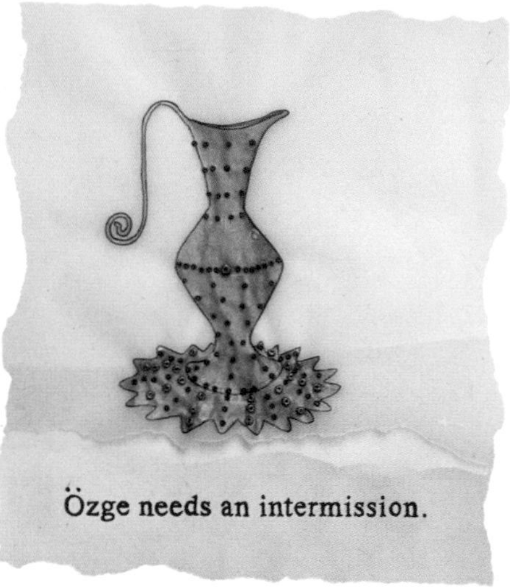
Özge needs an intermission.

Does learning to live with cruelty mean that I have to be the same way?

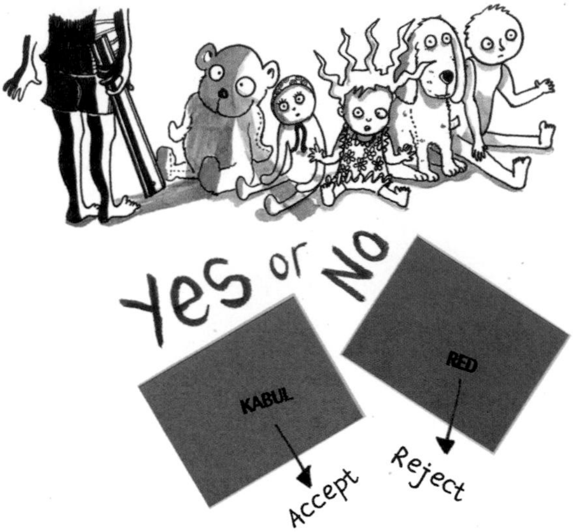
Yes or No
KABUL
Accept
RED
Reject

Here is my vote.

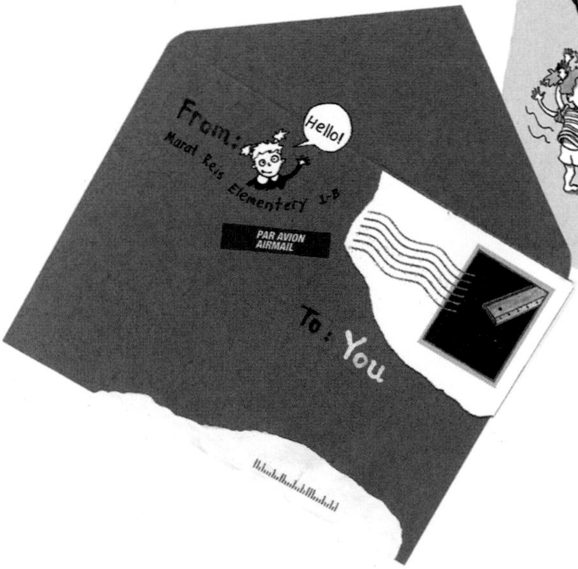
From:
Marat Reis Elementery 1-B
Hello!
PAR AVION
AIRMAIL
To: You

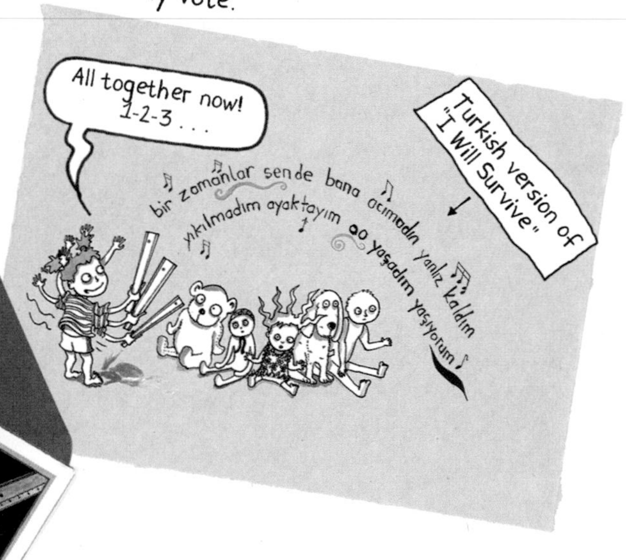
All together now! 1-2-3 . . .
Turkish version of "I Will Survive"
bir zamanlar sende bana acımadın yanlız kaldım
yıkılmadım ayaktayım oo yaşadım yaşıyorum

Chapter 6

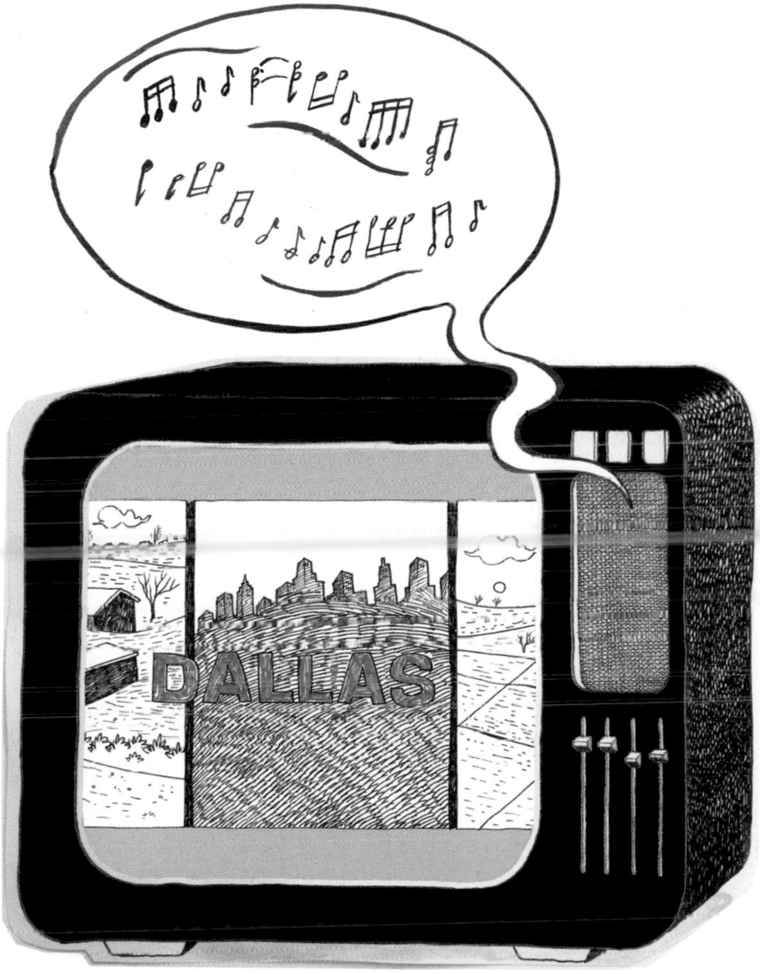
DALLAS

Single Channel

In the early 1980s most products were available in only one or two brands.

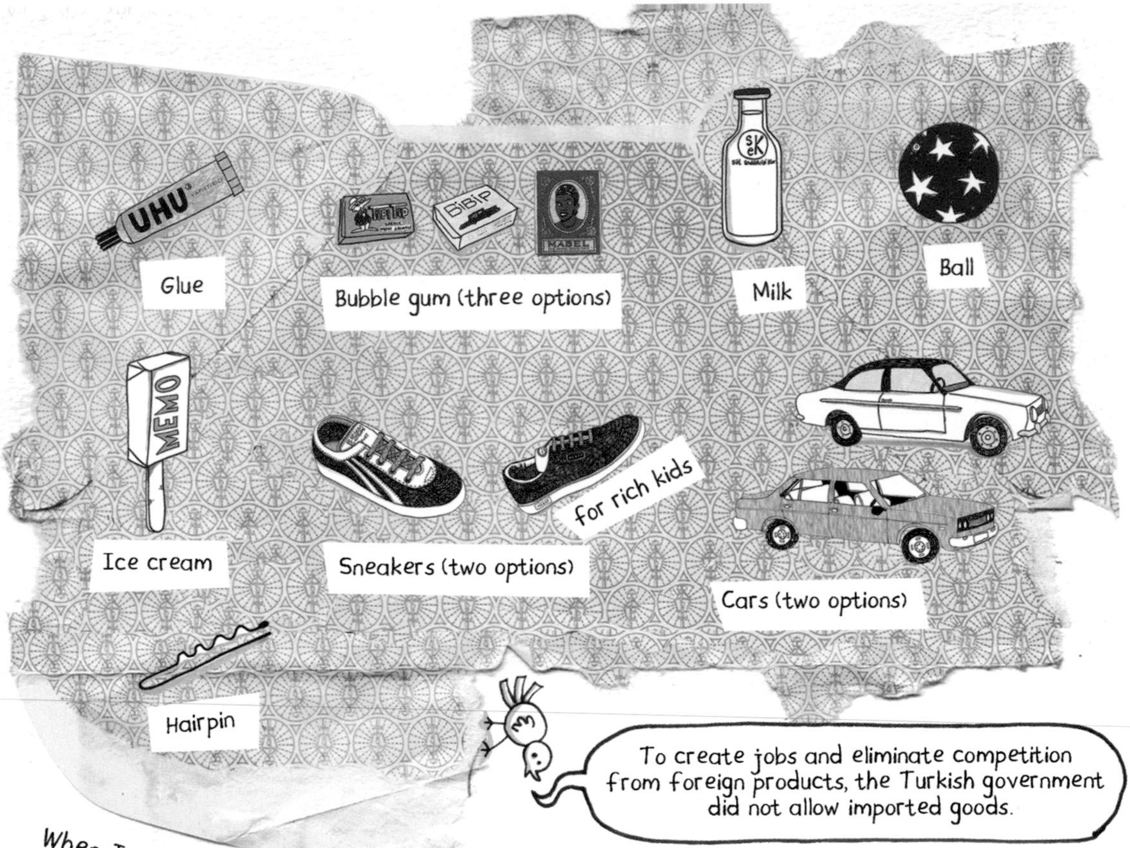
UHU
Glue
BiBiP
MABEL
Bubble gum (three options)
Milk
Ball
MEMO
Ice cream
Sneakers (two options)
for rich kids
Cars (two options)
Hairpin
To create jobs and eliminate competition from foreign products, the Turkish government did not allow imported goods.

When I went to the grocery store I asked for what I wanted without using a brand name.

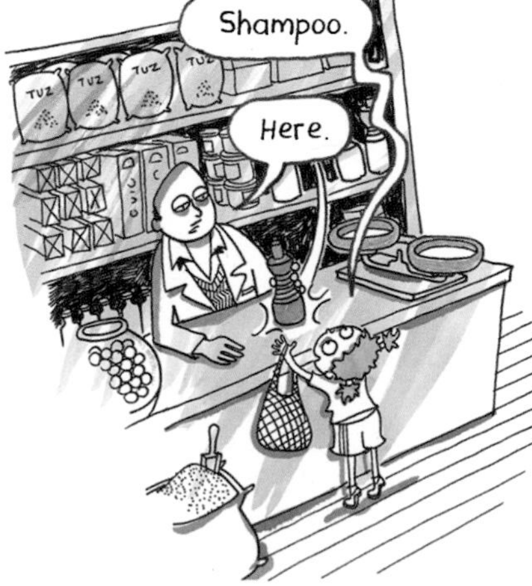
Shampoo.
Here.
TUZ

Early one morning someone knocked on our door. This was very unusual.

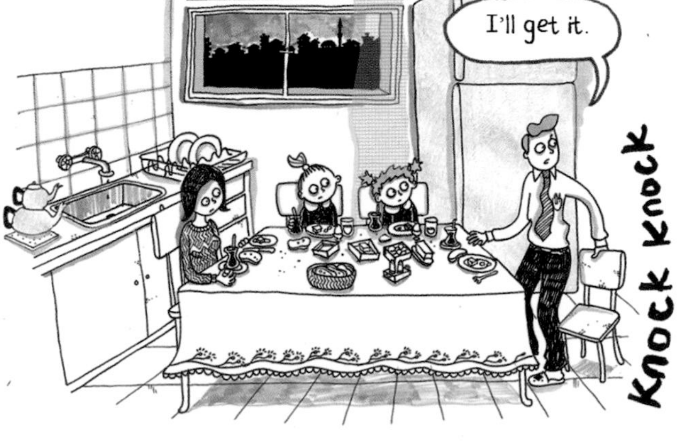
I'll get it.
Knock knock

Dad talked to a peddler in a whisper.
Pelin and I could only hear a few words.

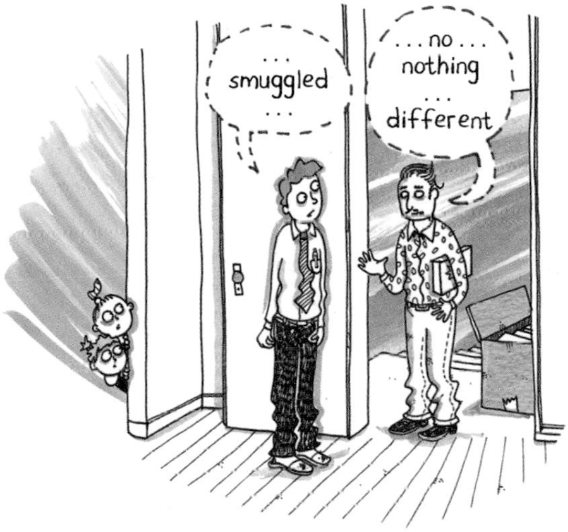
... smuggled ...
... no ... nothing ... different

Then he called Mom.

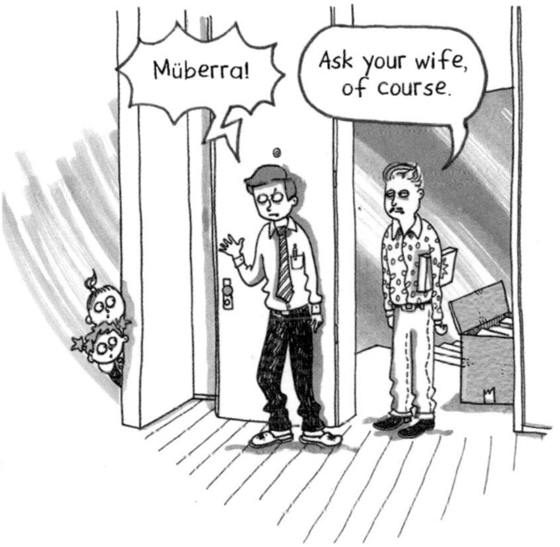
Müberra!
Ask your wife, of course.

They whispered and pointed at us.

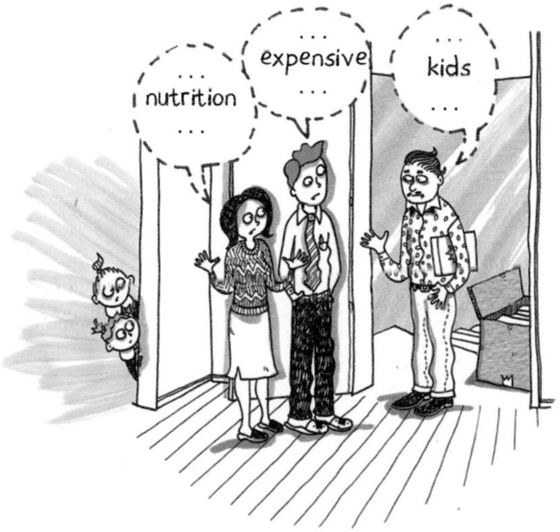
... nutrition ...
... expensive ...
... kids ...

Finally, they came back with a box.
There were big smiles on their faces.

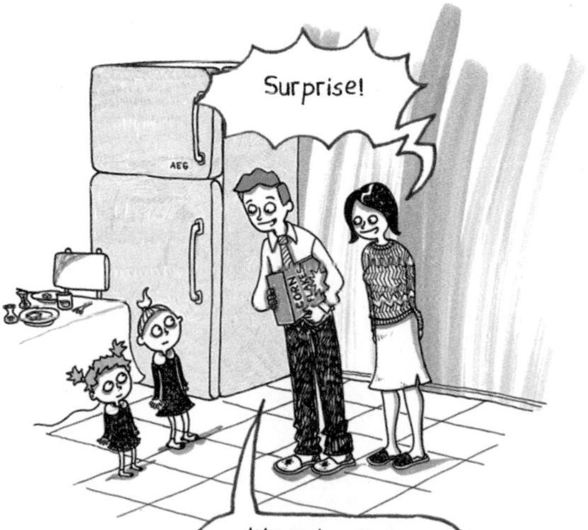
AEG
Surprise!
We got you a box of Corn Flakes!

This smuggled food was so expensive that it was kept up high in a cabinet. Sometimes after our breakfast we had a little bowl of Corn Flakes as a treat.

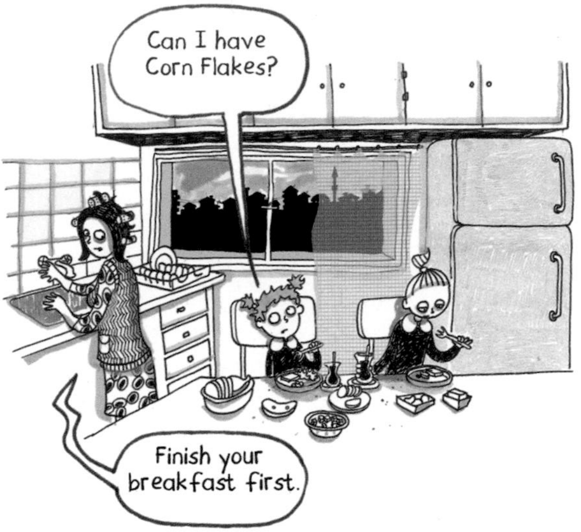
Can I have Corn Flakes?
Finish your breakfast first.

At school . . .

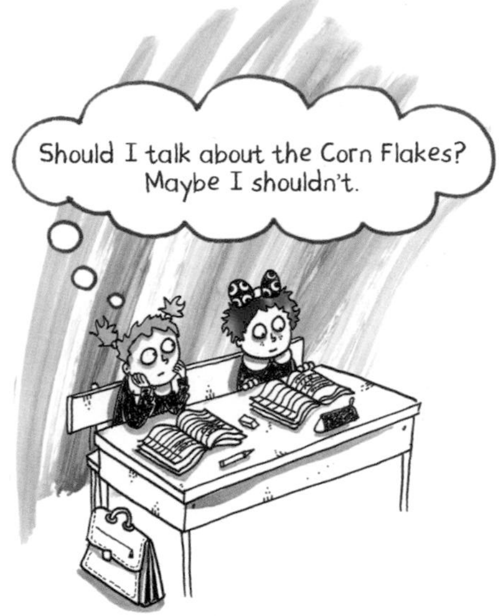
Should I talk about the Corn Flakes? Maybe I shouldn't.

Although the government did not allow imported goods, they did allow some foreign TV shows. The best part of having only one channel was that everyone watched the same programs.

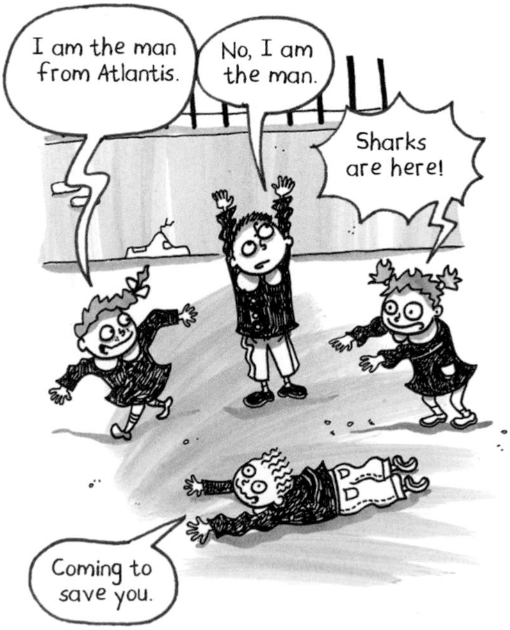
I am the man from Atlantis.
No, I am the man.
Sharks are here!
Coming to save you.

There were only one or two shows just for kids during an entire week. While we were playing on the street someone would suddenly shout:

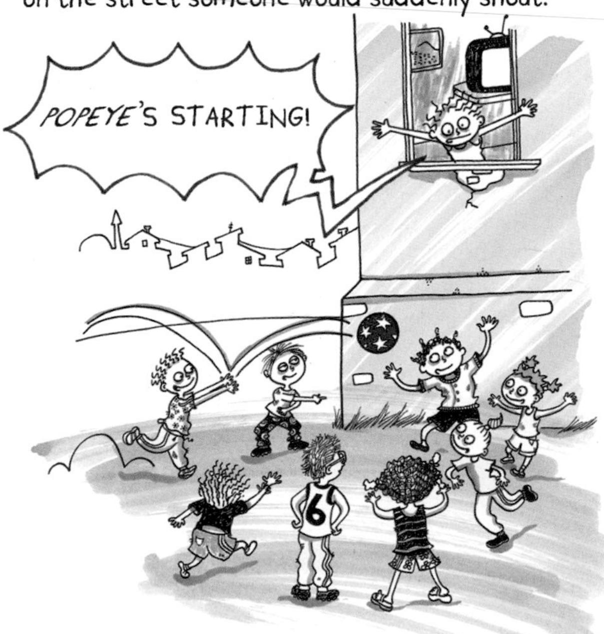
POPEYE'S STARTING!

. . . and we would run home.

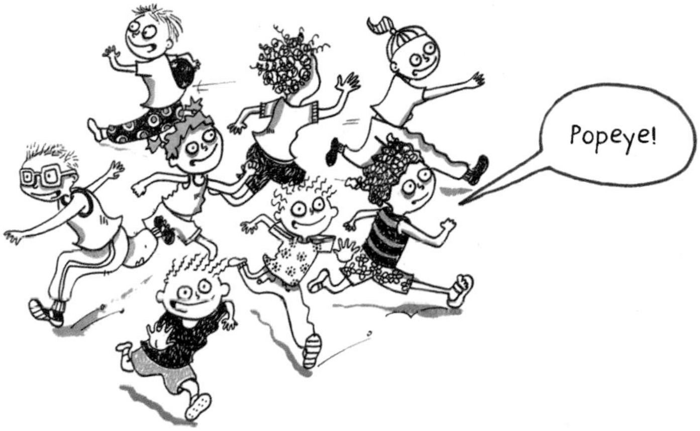
Popeye!

There was another way of accessing cartoons, but it only worked for people living along the coast. From Izmir we could see the Greek Islands. We were also able to receive their broadcasts.

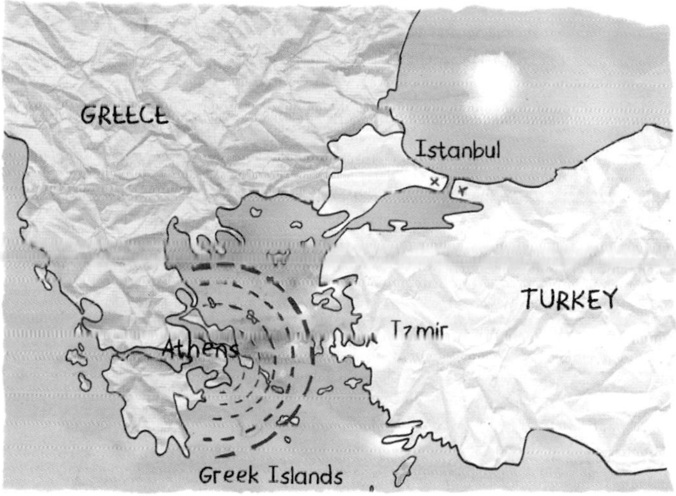
GREECE
Istanbul
TURKEY
Athens
Izmir
Greek Islands

Greek television had two channels, and they used to show more cartoons than Turkish TV.

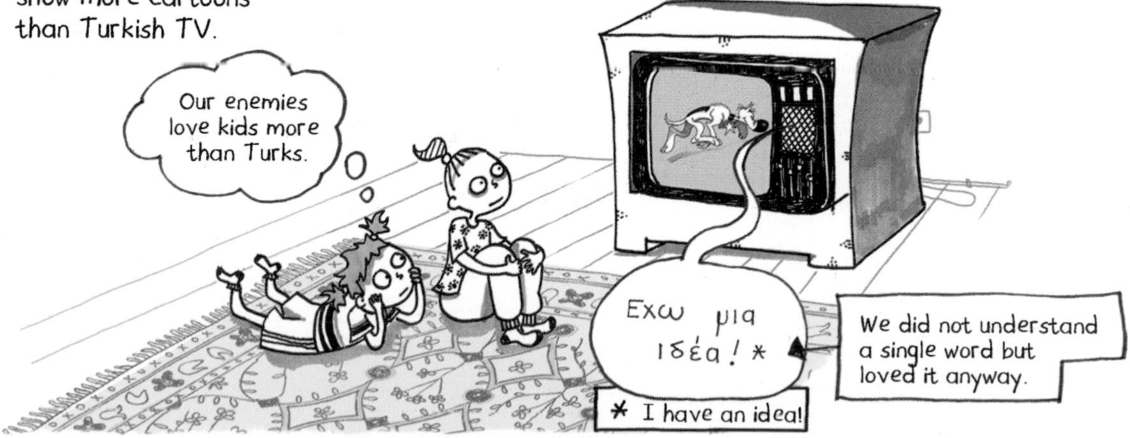
Our enemies love kids more than Turks.
Εχω μια ιδέα! *
* I have an idea!
We did not understand a single word but loved it anyway.

There was one show the government allowed that attracted people like a magnet.

Dallas was a soap opera from the U.S. As soon as *Dallas* started, life stopped.

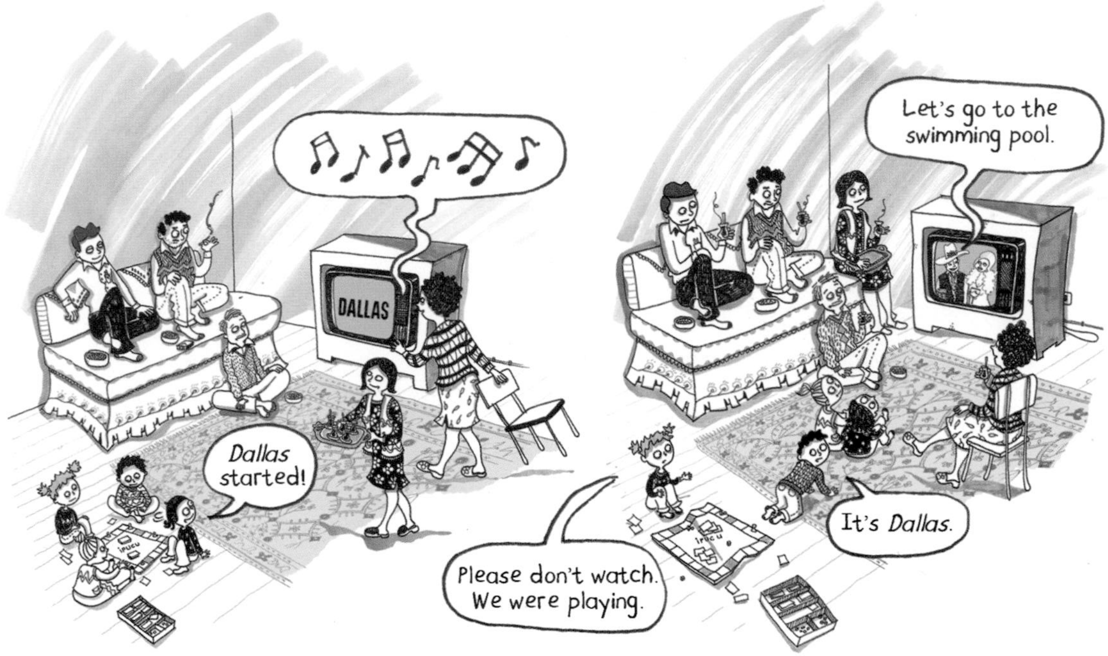
DALLAS
Dallas started!
Please don't watch. We were playing.
Let's go to the swimming pool.
It's *Dallas*.

All the streets were empty.

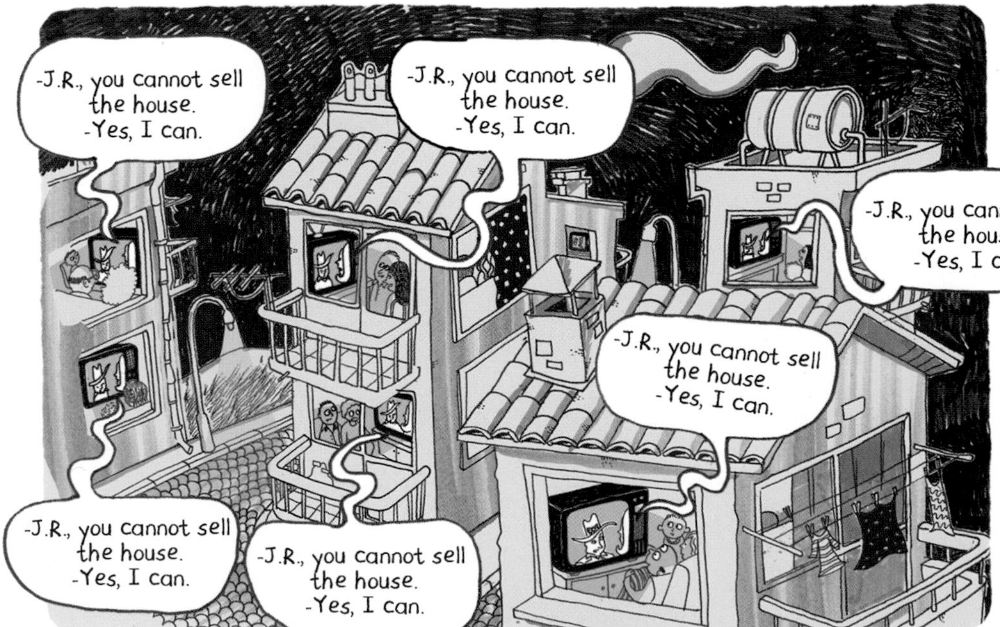
-J.R., you cannot sell the house. -Yes, I can.
-J.R., you cannot sell the house. -Yes, I can.
-J.R., you cannot sell the house. -Yes, I can.
-J.R., you cannot sell the house. -Yes, I can.
-J.R., you cannot sell the house. -Yes, I can.
-J.R., you cannot sell the house. -Yes, I can.

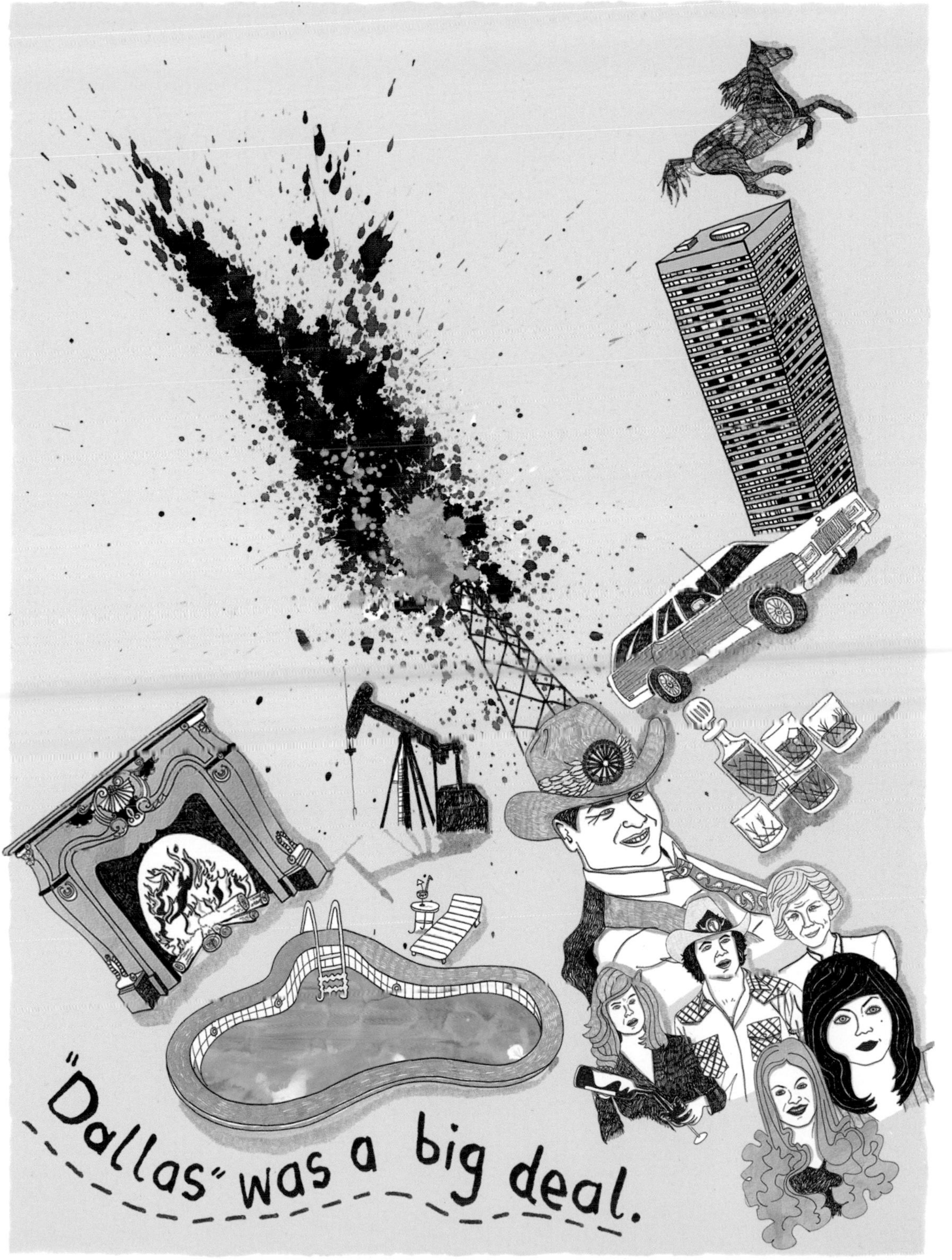
"Dallas" was a big deal.

I even used to pretend I was an Olympic swimmer and our carpet was the pool in *Dallas*.
Then one day Dad announced to Pelin and me:

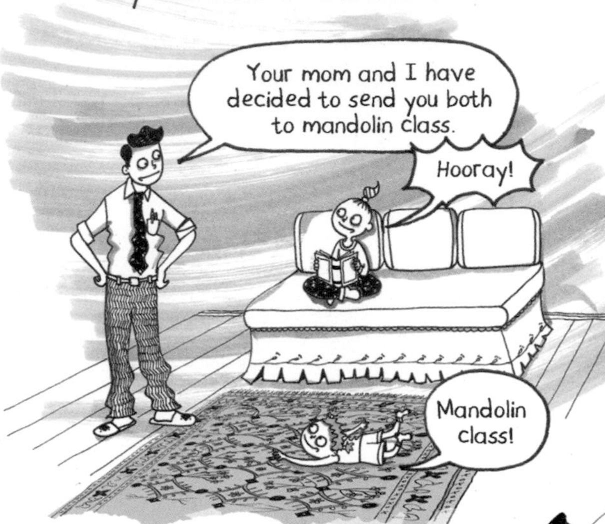
Your mom and I have decided to send you both to mandolin class.
Hooray!
Mandolin class!

He had brought home one mandolin for us to share.

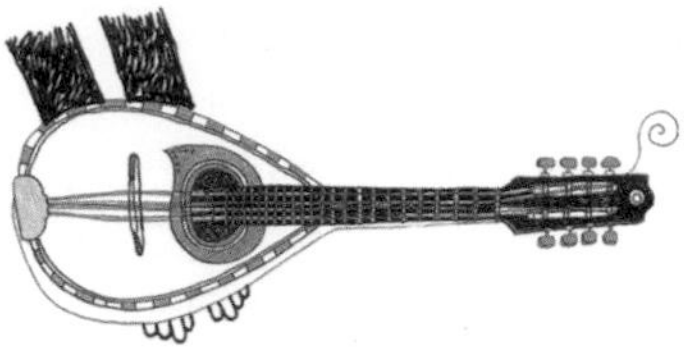

My mom immediately sewed a special cover for it.

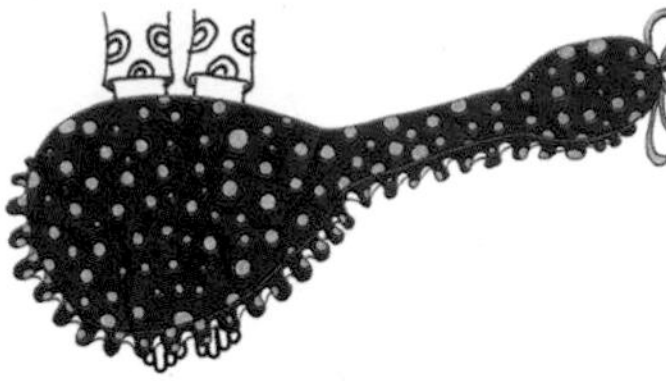

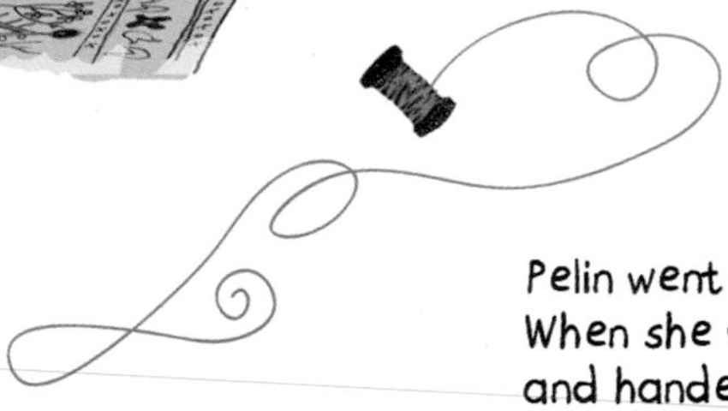

When I held the mandolin under my arm, I turned into the most important person in the world.

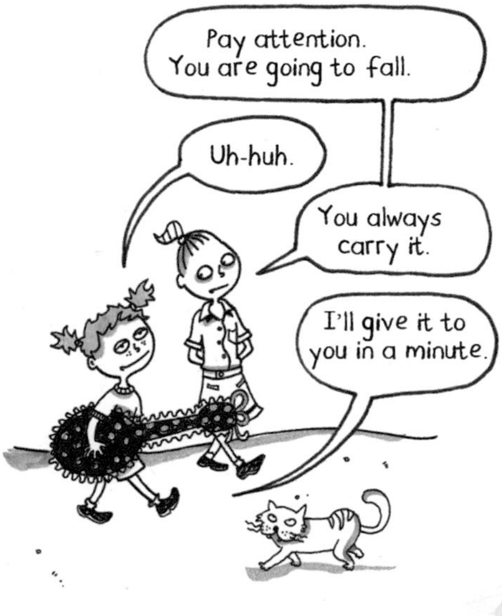
Pay attention. You are going to fall.
Uh-huh.
You always carry it.
I'll give it to you in a minute.

Pelin went to the class in the morning.
When she was done she met me outside and handed me the mandolin so I could take the same class at noon.

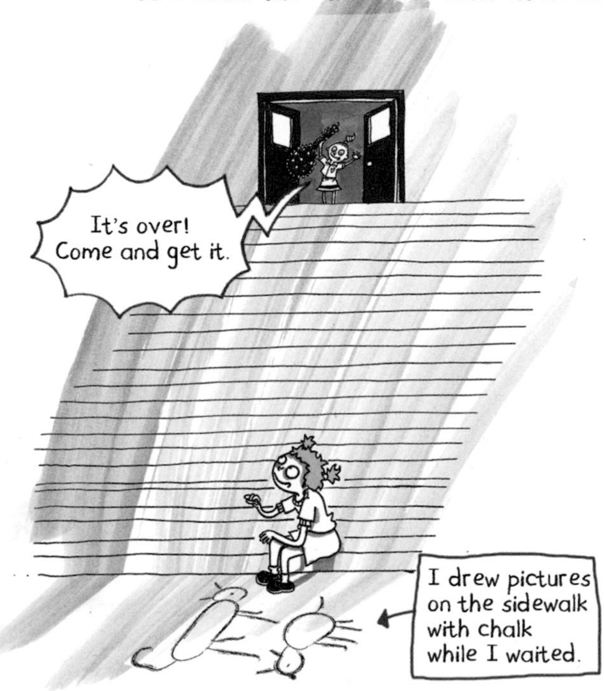
It's over! Come and get it.
I drew pictures on the sidewalk with chalk while I waited.

Once, she handed the mandolin to me and whispered:

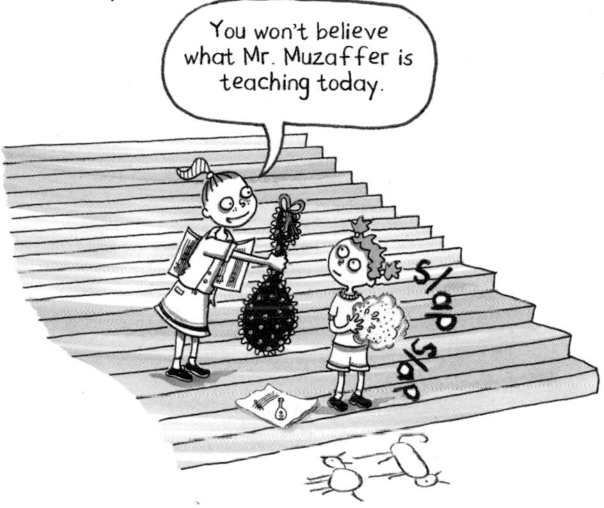
You won't believe what Mr. Muzaffer is teaching today.
slap
slap

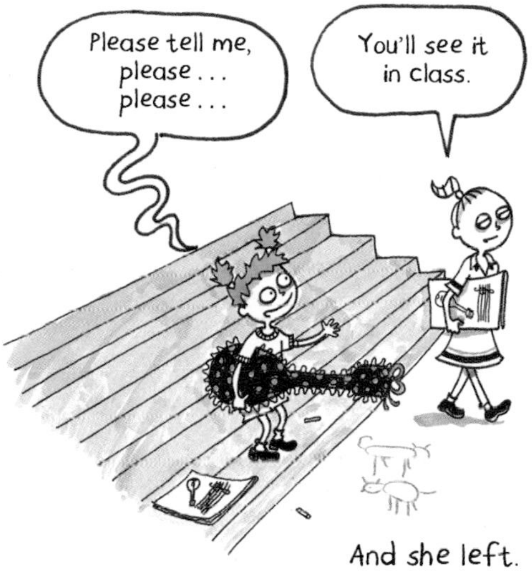
Please tell me, please . . . please . . .
You'll see it in class.

And she left.

Thirty kids with mandolins waited for the teacher.

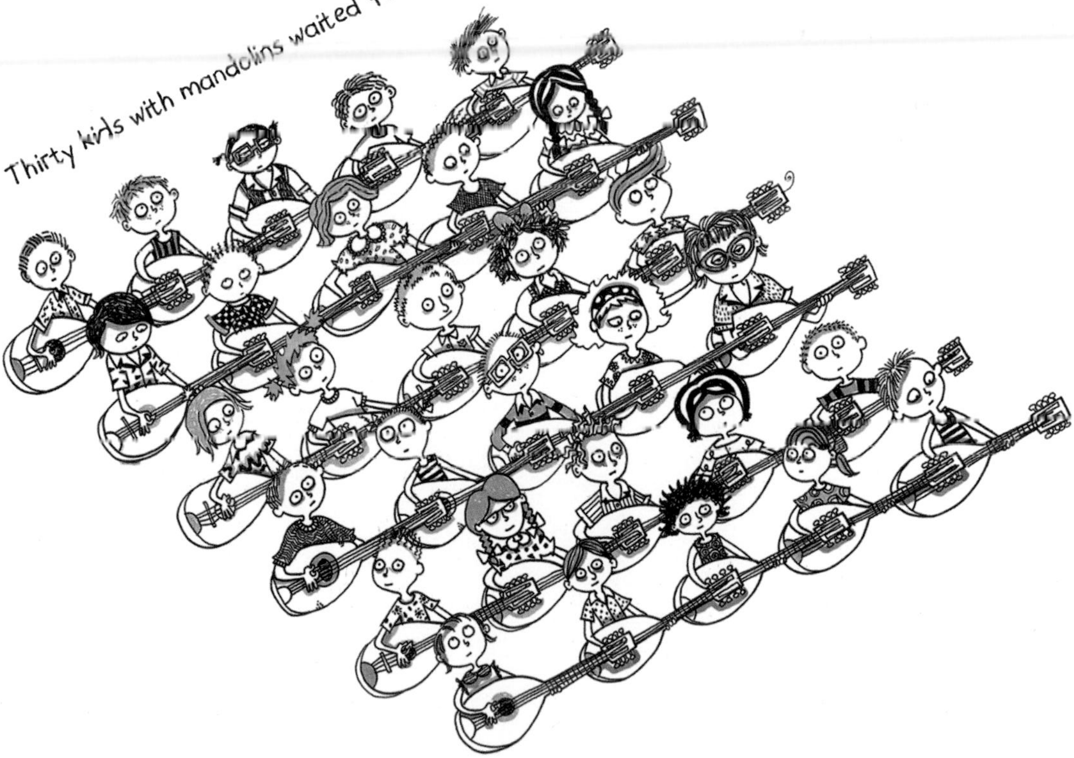

Mr. Muzaffer drew the musical staff and treble clef and wrote the title of the song we would be playing that week.

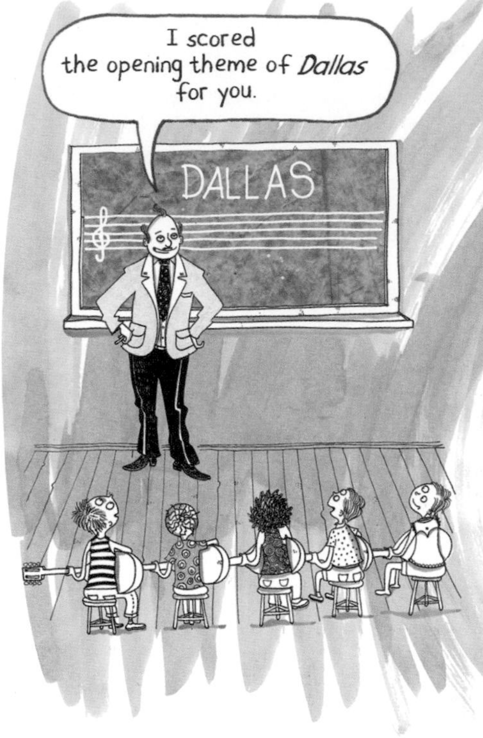
I scored the opening theme of *Dallas* for you.
DALLAS

Our teacher said "Play," and we played and sang the notes of *Dallas* with love and excitement.

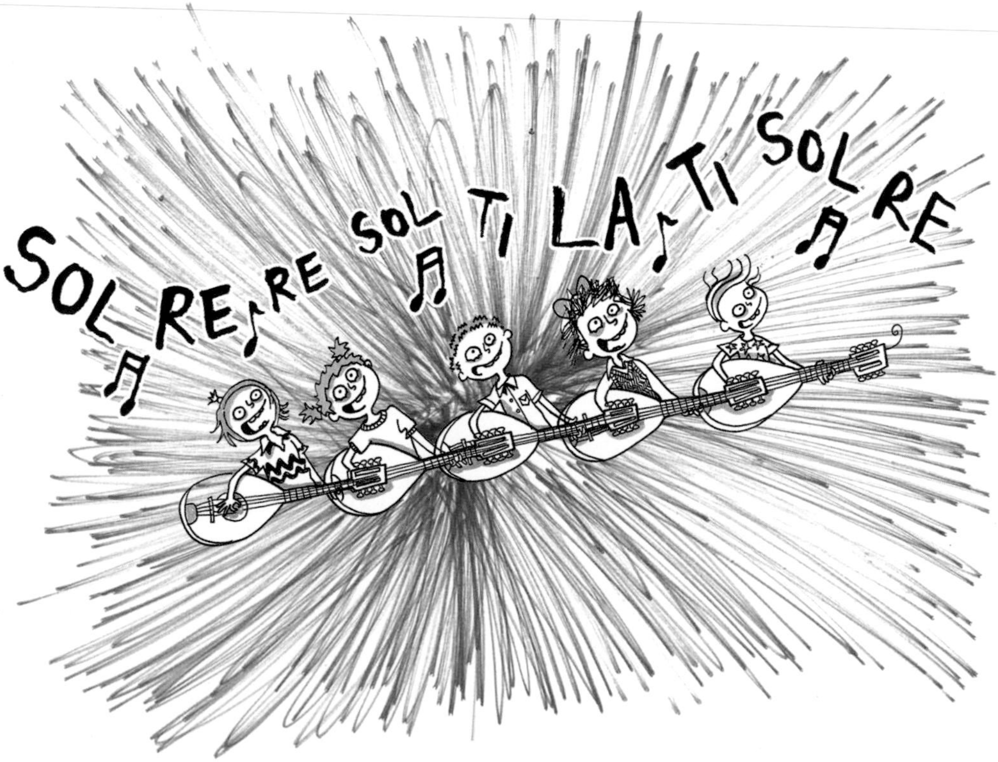
SOL RE RE SOL TI LA TI SOL RE

Chapter 7

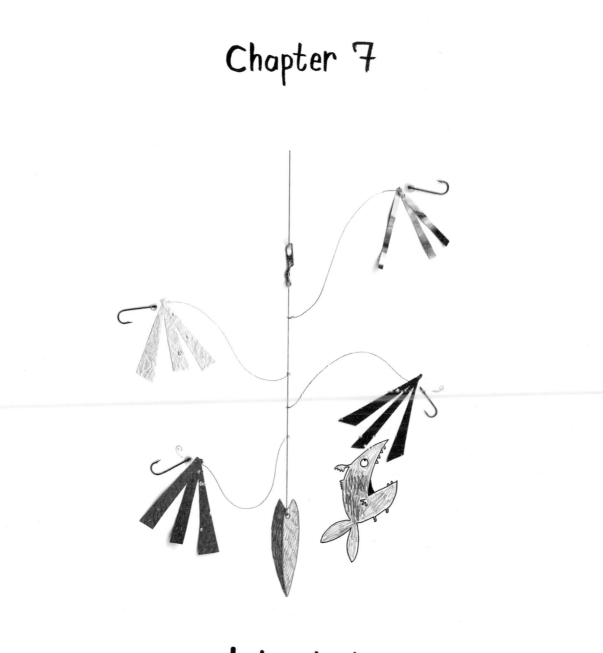

Istanbul

Like most people in Turkey
at this time, we did not have a phone.

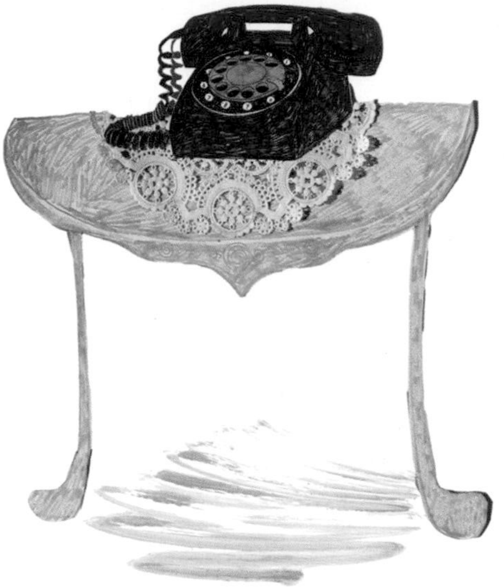

The best part of this was
that the door turned into a place
for surprises.

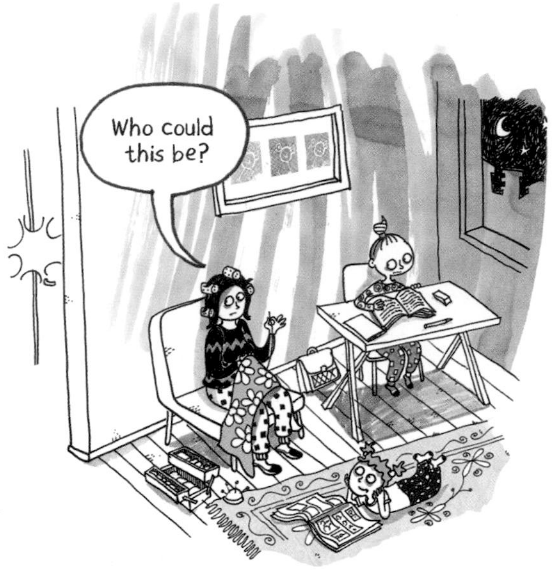
Who could this be?

It was Uncle Nihat.

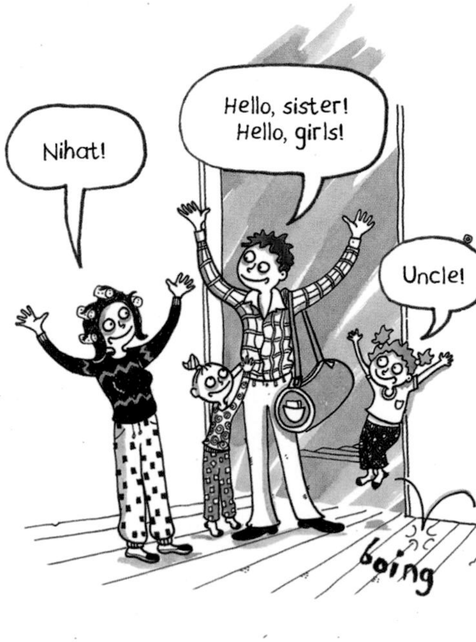
Nihat!
Hello, sister! Hello, girls!
Uncle!
boing

Uncle Nihat lived with his friends in Istanbul.
He liked to travel and sometimes he visited us
for a few days. He always packed a tiny bag.

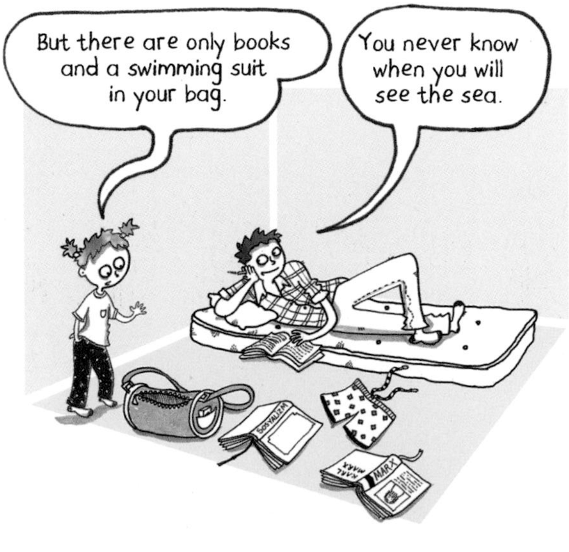
But there are only books and a swimming suit in your bag.
You never know when you will see the sea.

He was a storyteller. Kids in our building came to our apartment to listen to him.

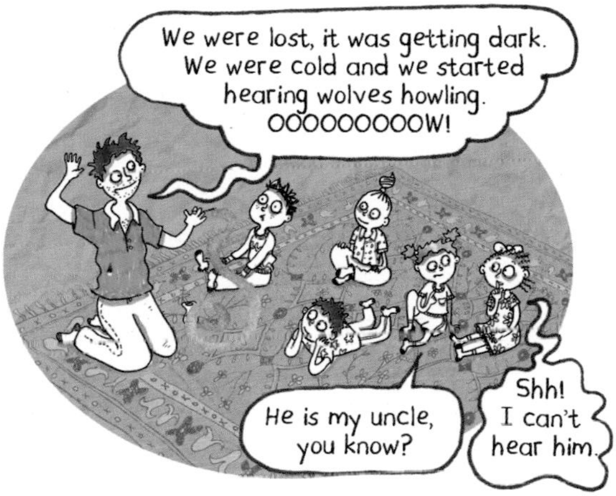
We were lost, it was getting dark. We were cold and we started hearing wolves howling. OOOOOOOOOW!
He is my uncle, you know?
Shh! I can't hear him.

Uncle Nihat was the complete opposite of my safety-oriented parents.

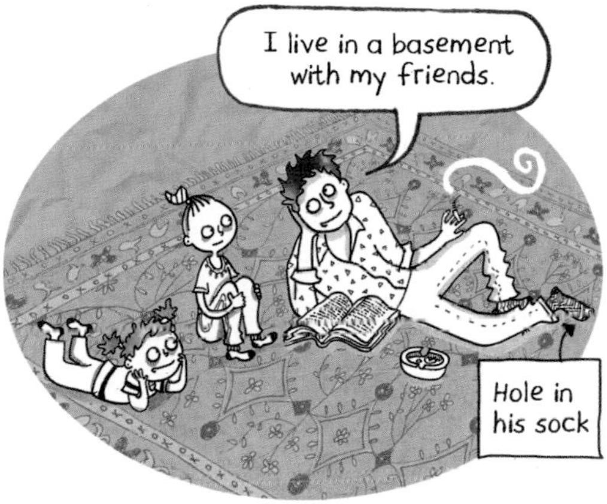
I live in a basement with my friends.
Hole in his sock

Uncle Nihat told us that at his place when he switched on the lights he could see lots of bugs running in all directions. These bugs were so big that he could hear their footsteps.

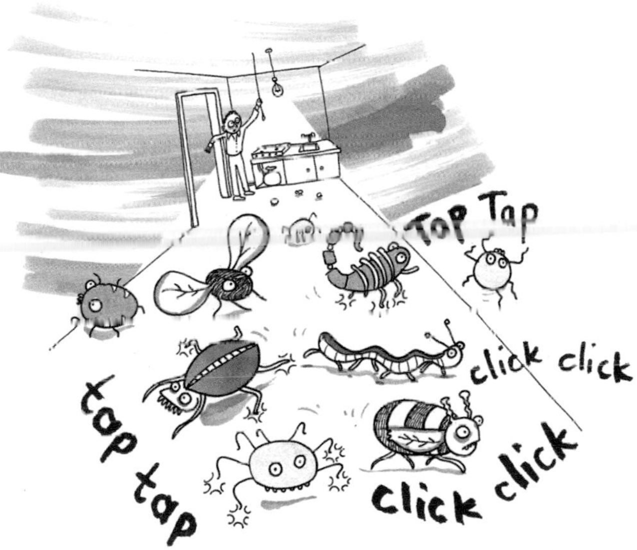
Tap Tap
click click
tap tap
click click

Istanbul gets cold in the winter, and the basement did not have any heat . . .

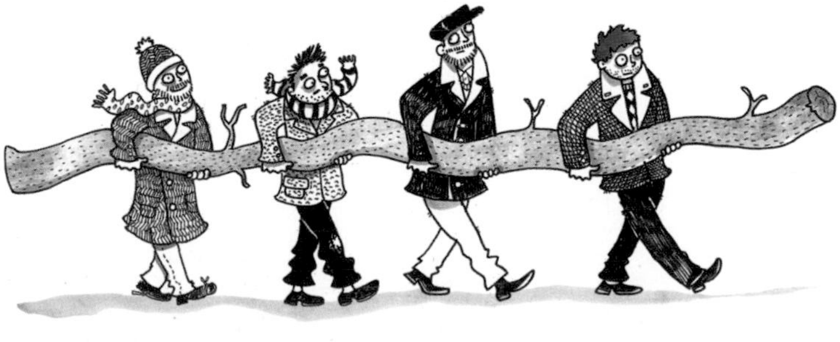

. . . so they stole a log from a construction site.

The log was very long and it did not fit into the tiny basement apartment, so they stuck one end out the window . . .

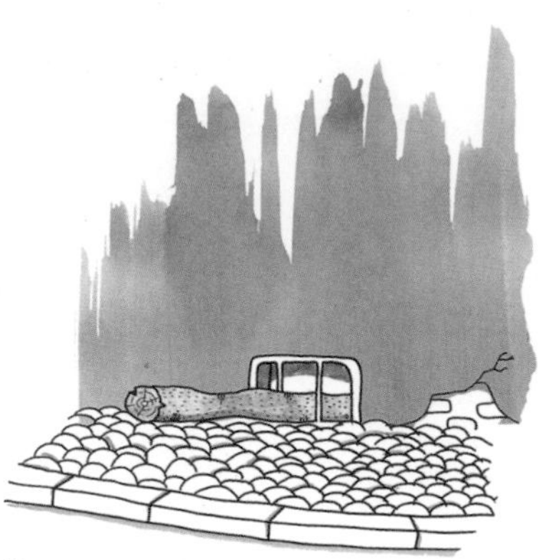

. . . and they put the other end into the stove to burn it.

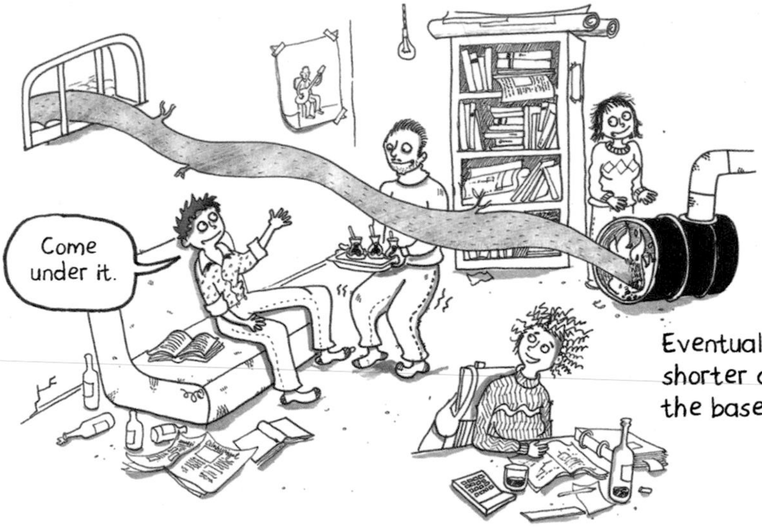
Come under it.

Eventually the log got shorter and fit into the basement.

What they called a stove was really a barrel that they had taken from that same construction site. Since they did not want to carry it they rolled it down a hill at midnight.

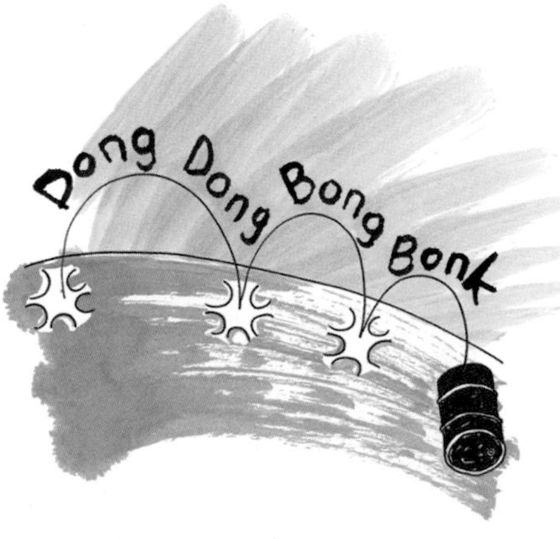
Dong Dong Bong Bonk

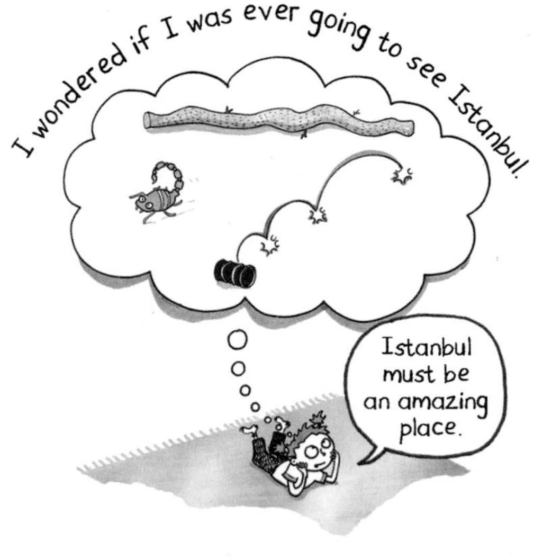
I wondered if I was ever going to see Istanbul.
Istanbul must be an amazing place.

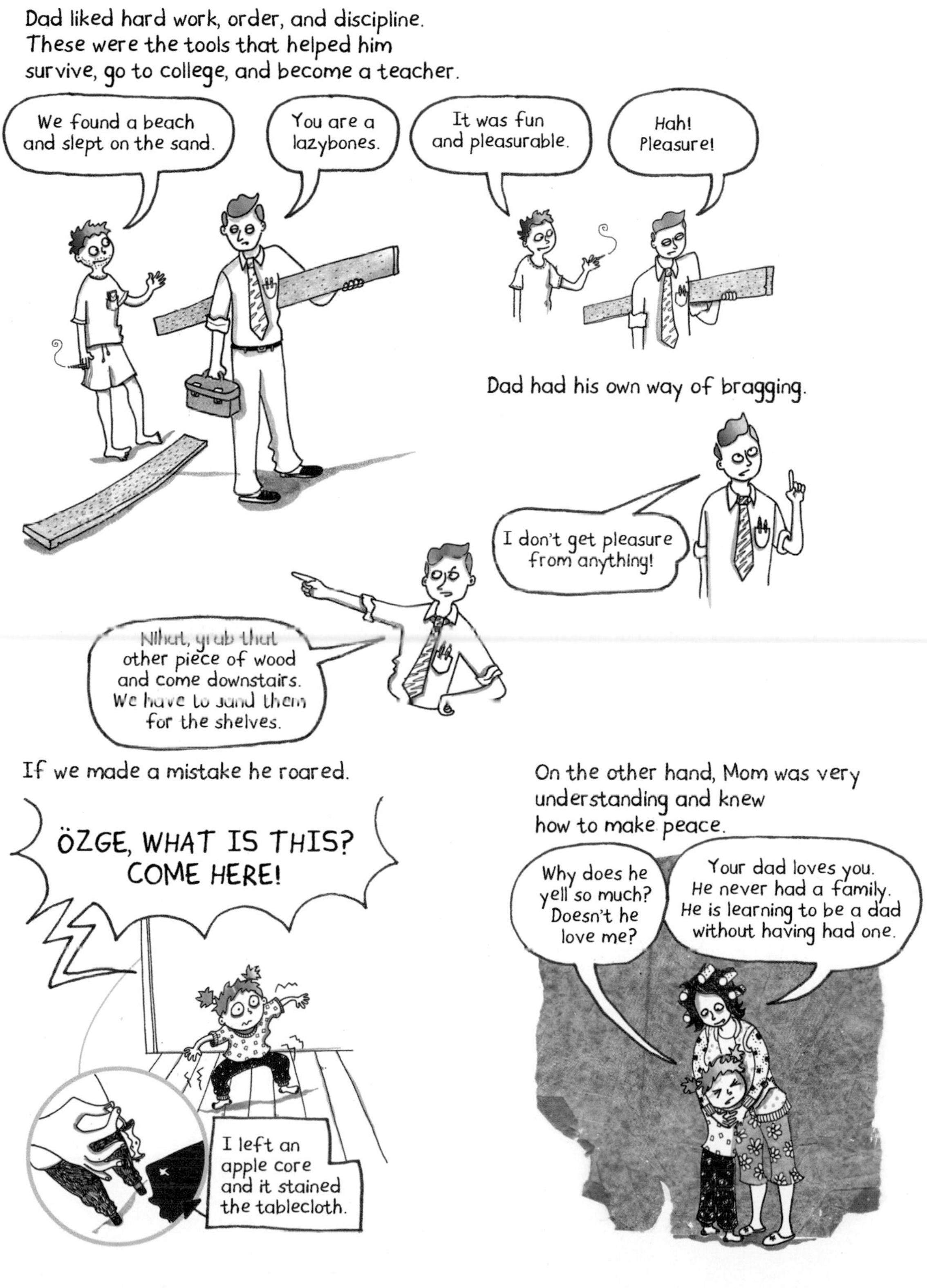
Dad liked hard work, order, and discipline. These were the tools that helped him survive, go to college, and become a teacher.
We found a beach and slept on the sand.
You are a lazybones.
It was fun and pleasurable.
Hah! Pleasure!
Dad had his own way of bragging.
I don't get pleasure from anything!
Nihat, grab that other piece of wood and come downstairs. We have to sand them for the shelves.
If we made a mistake he roared.
ÖZGE, WHAT IS THIS? COME HERE!
I left an apple core and it stained the tablecloth.
On the other hand, Mom was very understanding and knew how to make peace.
Why does he yell so much? Doesn't he love me?
Your dad loves you. He never had a family. He is learning to be a dad without having had one.

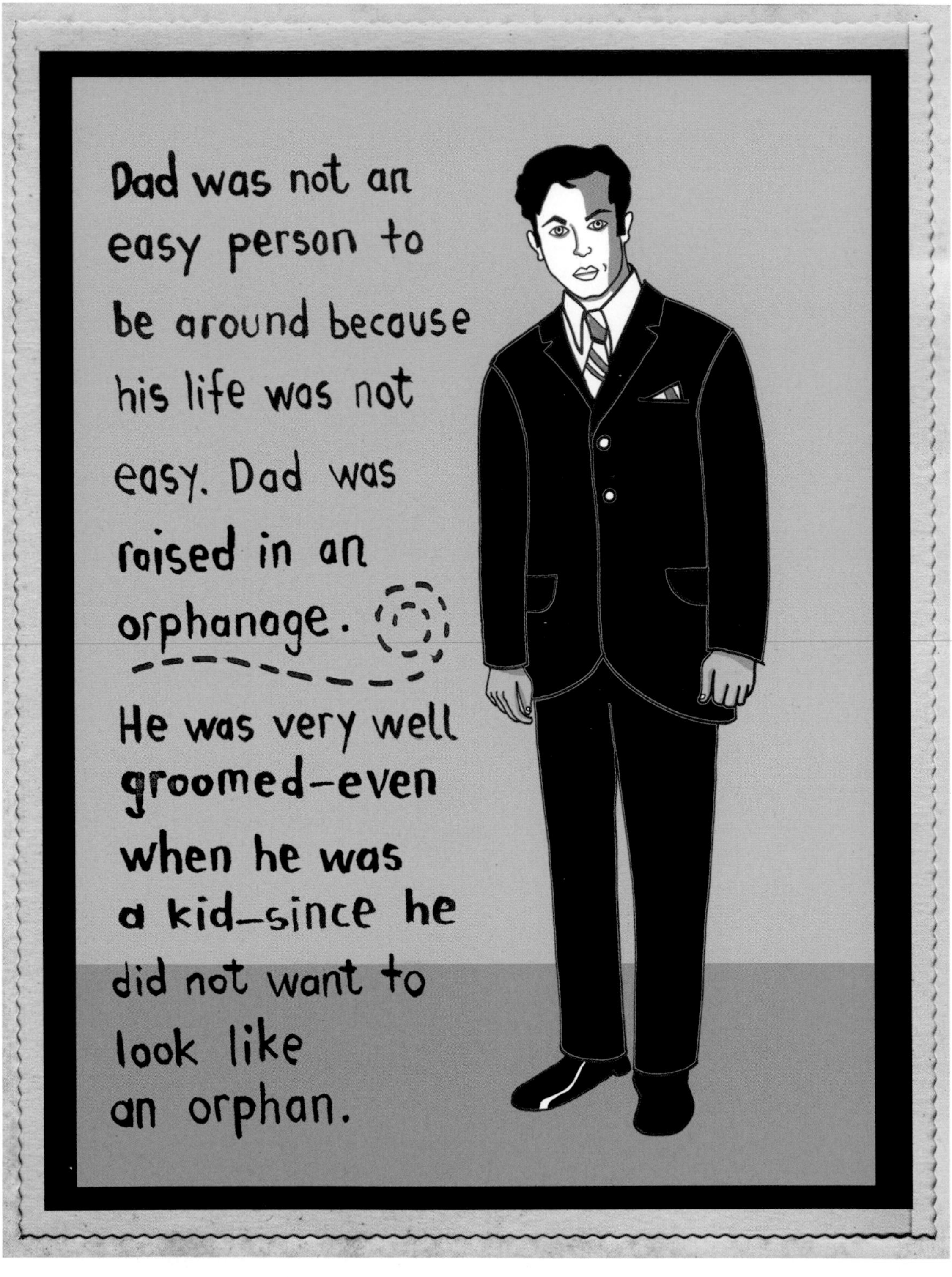
Dad was not an easy person to be around because his life was not easy. Dad was raised in an orphanage.
He was very well groomed—even when he was a kid—since he did not want to look like an orphan.

We had no grandparents.
Mom and Uncle Nihat's parents died in a car accident.
Uncle Nihat was 13 years old when it happened.

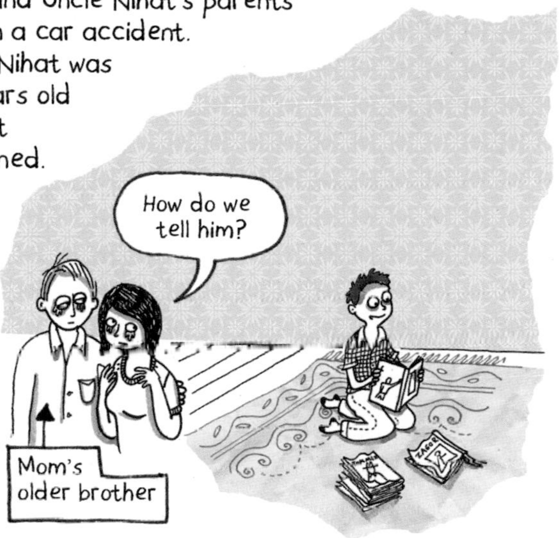
How do we tell him?
Mom's older brother

Even though Dad and Uncle Nihat were different, Dad was very protective of Uncle Nihat, maybe because they both lost their parents when they were young.

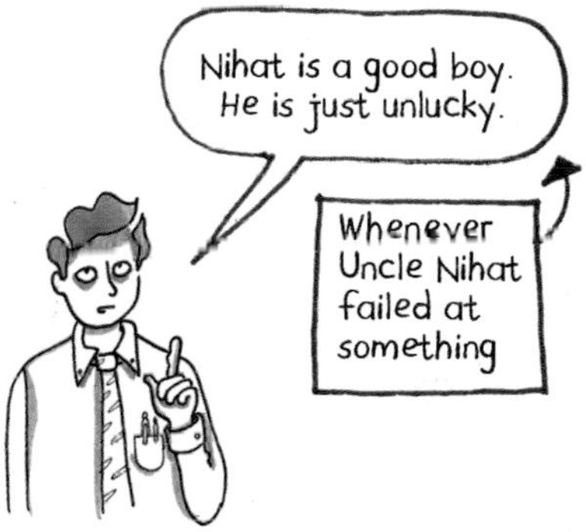
Nihat is a good boy. He is just unlucky.
Whenever Uncle Nihat failed at something

What was it like growing up with no parents?

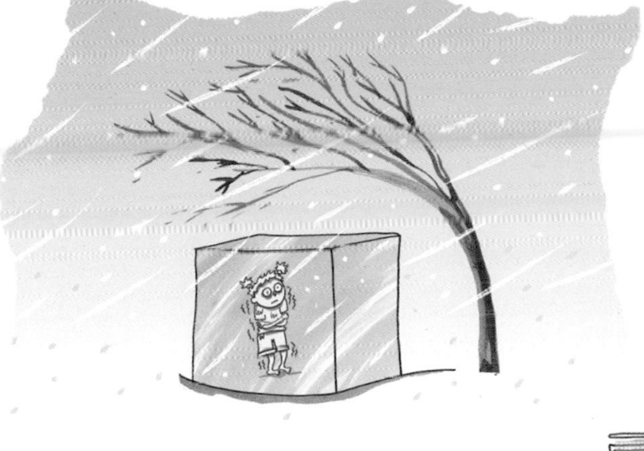

One night shortly after Uncle Nihat's visit, Mom pulled a letter from her bag and read it to us at dinner. The letter was from the Ministry of Education.

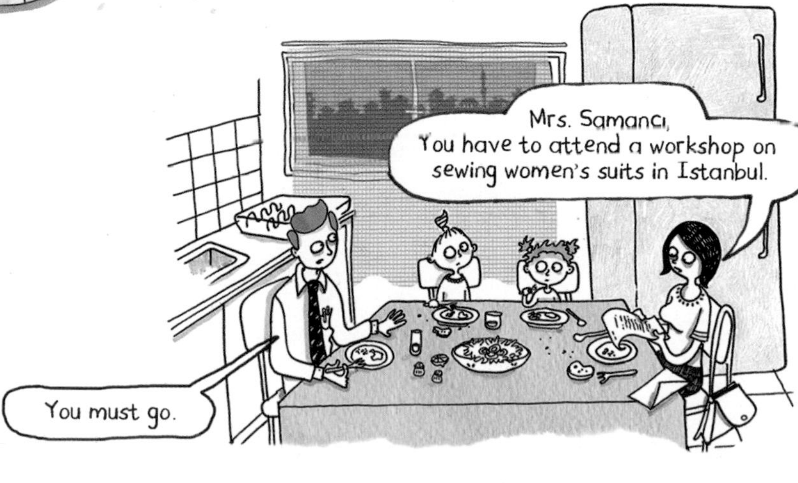
Mrs. Samancı,
You have to attend a workshop on sewing women's suits in Istanbul.
You must go.

I was devastated.
I had never been away from my mom.

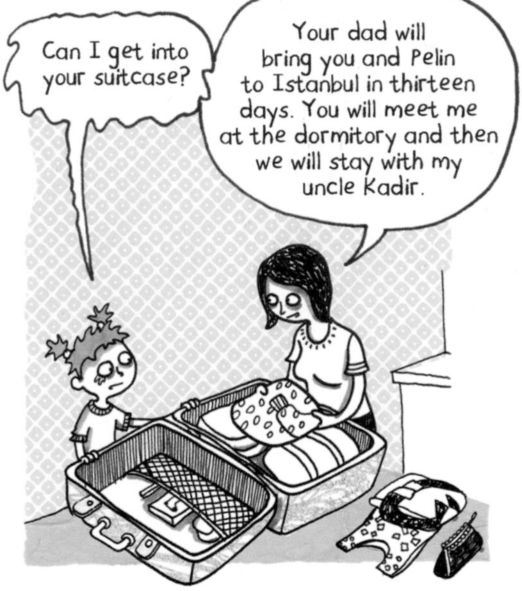
Can I get into your suitcase?
Your dad will bring you and Pelin to Istanbul in thirteen days. You will meet me at the dormitory and then we will stay with my uncle Kadir.

To be able to connect with Dad, I needed Mom. But she was gone. I didn't know how to hold on until I would see her again. Pelin gave me a splendid idea.

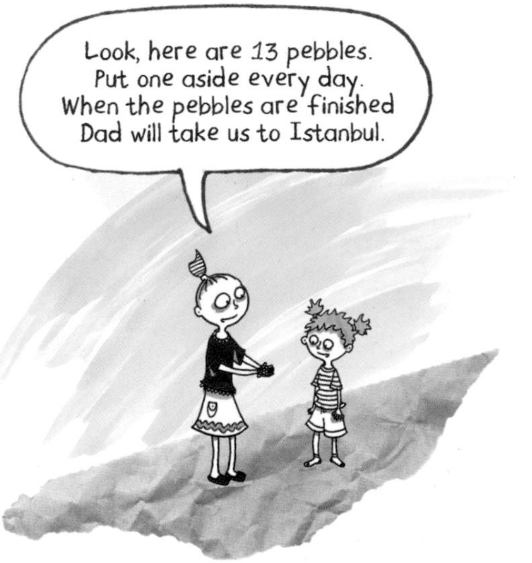
Look, here are 13 pebbles. Put one aside every day. When the pebbles are finished Dad will take us to Istanbul.

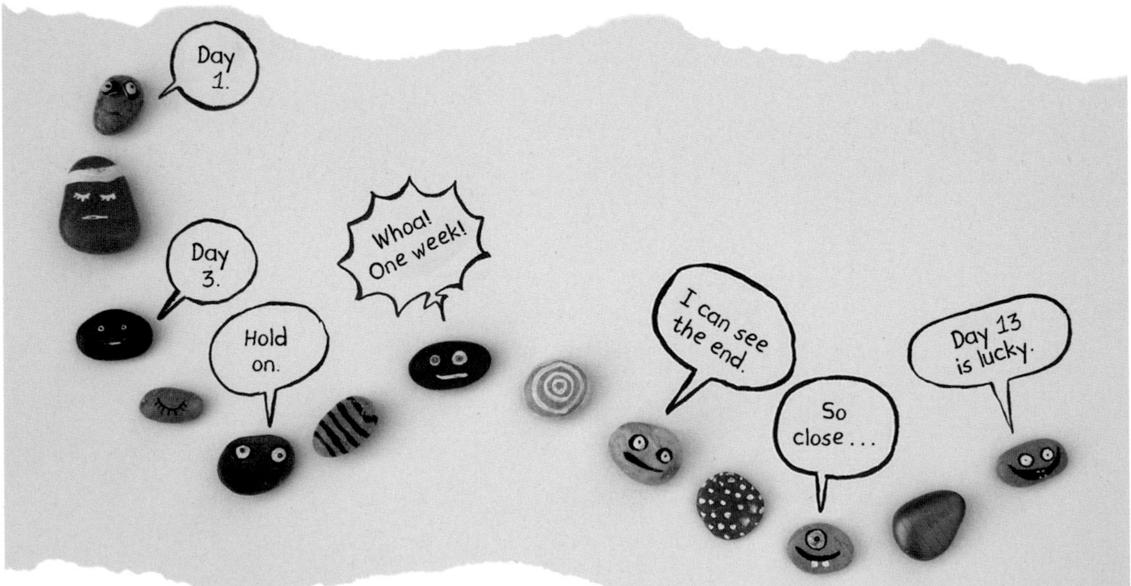
Day 1.
Day 3.
Hold on.
Whoa! One week!
I can see the end.
So close...
Day 13 is lucky.

The pebbles helped me through the time until Pelin, Dad, and I took the long bus ride to Istanbul.

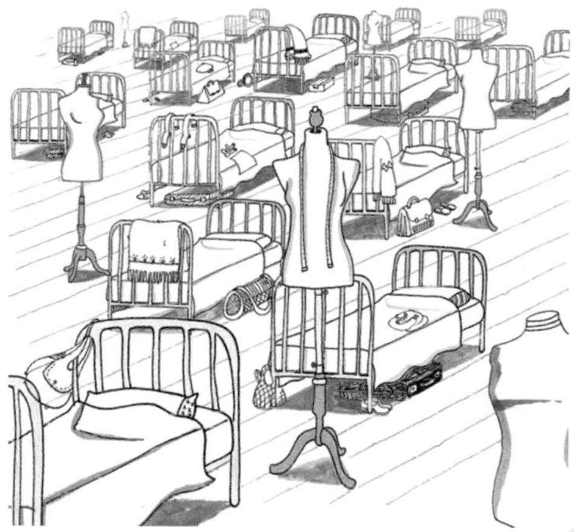

It was Mom's last day at the workshop. Dad left us and went to see his friends, and Pelin and I stayed with Mom.

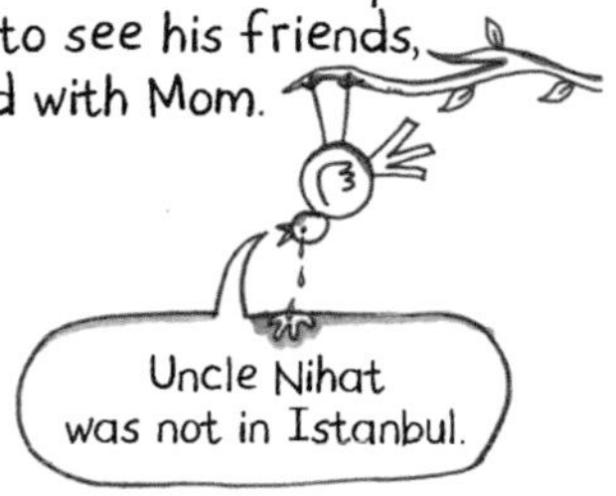
Uncle Nihat
was not in Istanbul.

There were forty other sewing teachers attending the workshop. The women, Pelin, and I took a bus trip to see famous palaces. My mom's friends were belly dancing on the bus

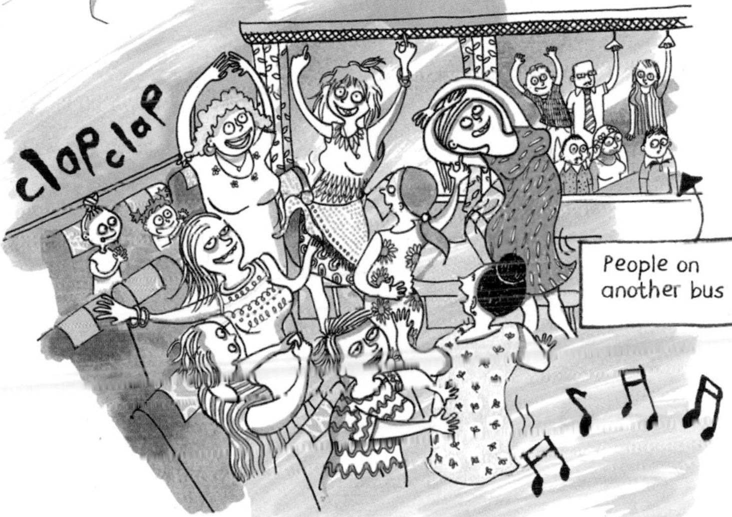
clap clap
People on
another bus

One of my mom's colleagues asked me:

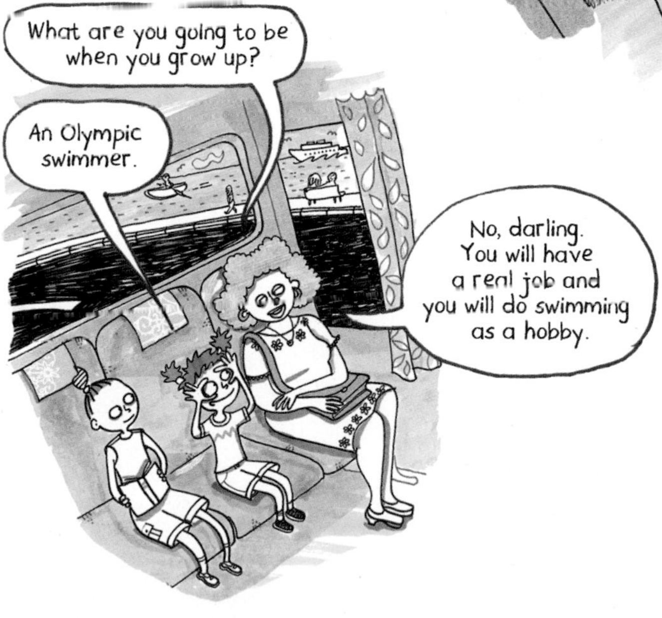
What are you going to be when you grow up?
An Olympic swimmer.
No, darling. You will have a real job and you will do swimming as a hobby.

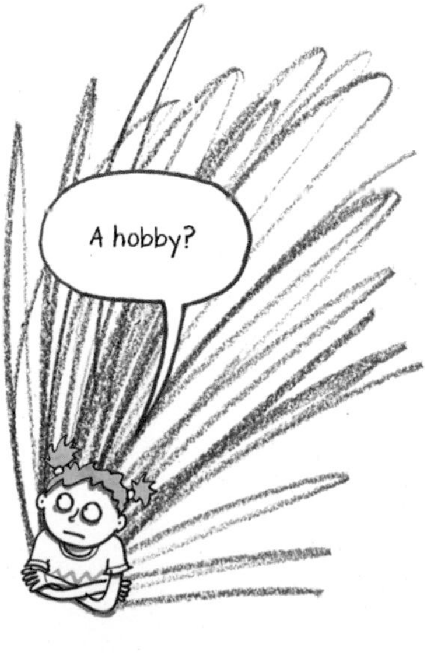
A hobby?

I was not talking about a hobby. I was talking about a passion. I immediately took action.

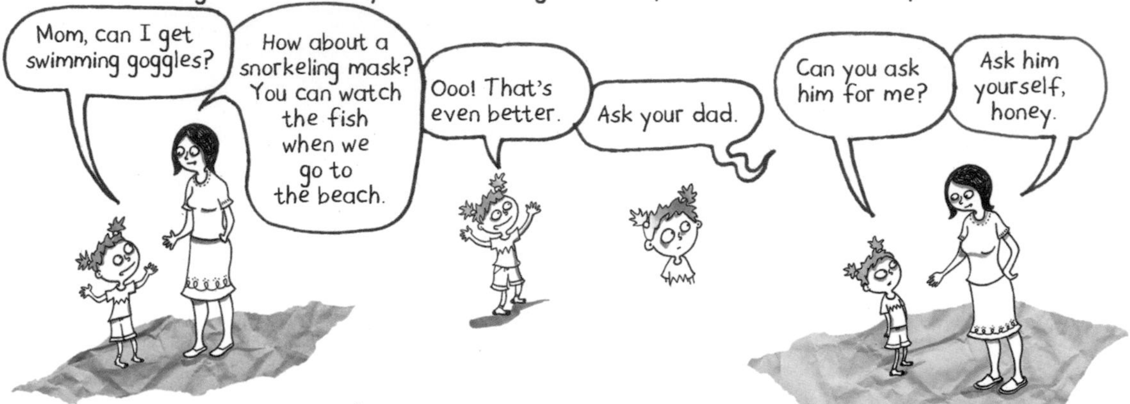

Mom, can I get swimming goggles?
How about a snorkeling mask? You can watch the fish when we go to the beach.
Ooo! That's even better.
Ask your dad.
Can you ask him for me?
Ask him yourself, honey.

That night I approached Dad.

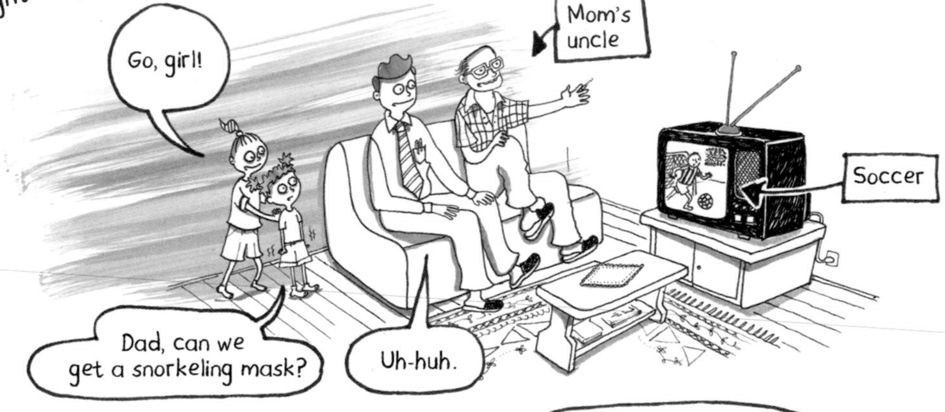

Go, girl!
Mom's uncle
Soccer
Dad, can we get a snorkeling mask?
Uh-huh.

It was easier than I thought. The next day we walked through the labyrinth-like streets around the Grand Bazaar. Pelin and Mom went to fabric stores while Dad and I took a different direction.

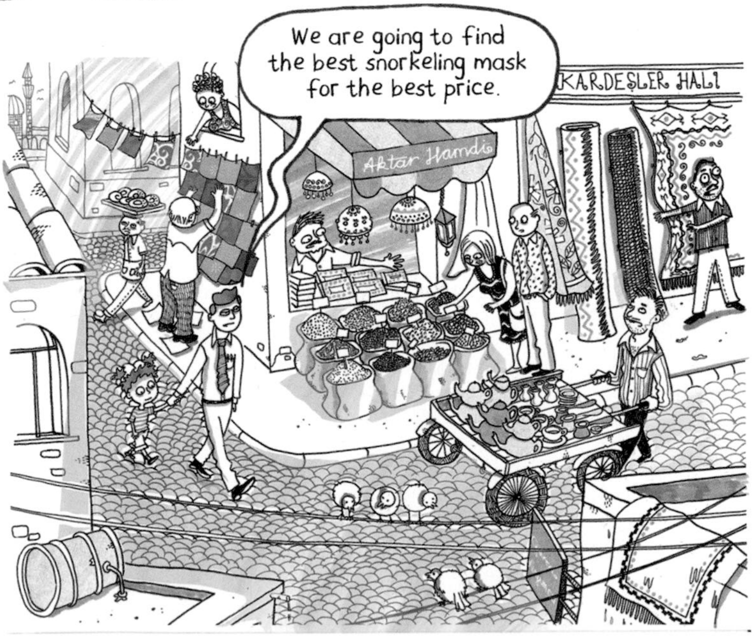

We are going to find the best snorkeling mask for the best price.
KARDEŞLER HALI
Aktar Hamdi

Dad and I went to an amazing store.

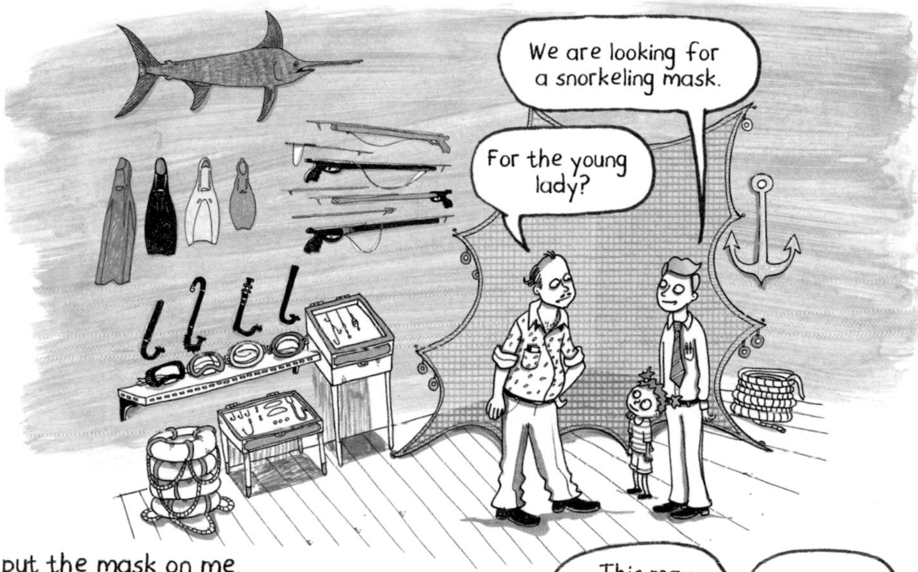
We are looking for a snorkeling mask.
For the young lady?

They put the mask on me.

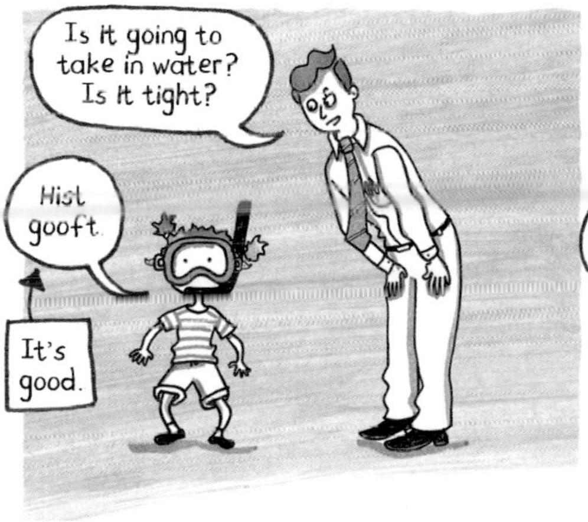
Is it going to take in water? Is it tight?
Hist gooft.
It's good.

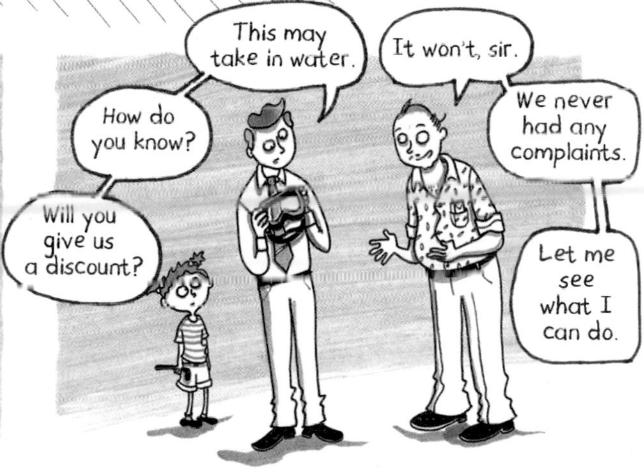
This may take in water.
It won't, sir.
How do you know?
We never had any complaints.
Will you give us a discount?
Let me see what I can do.

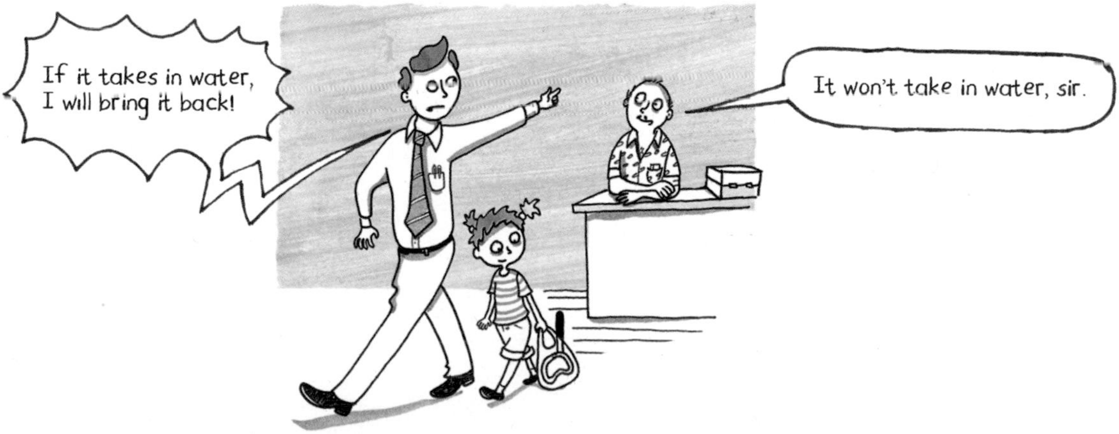
If it takes in water, I will bring it back!
It won't take in water, sir.

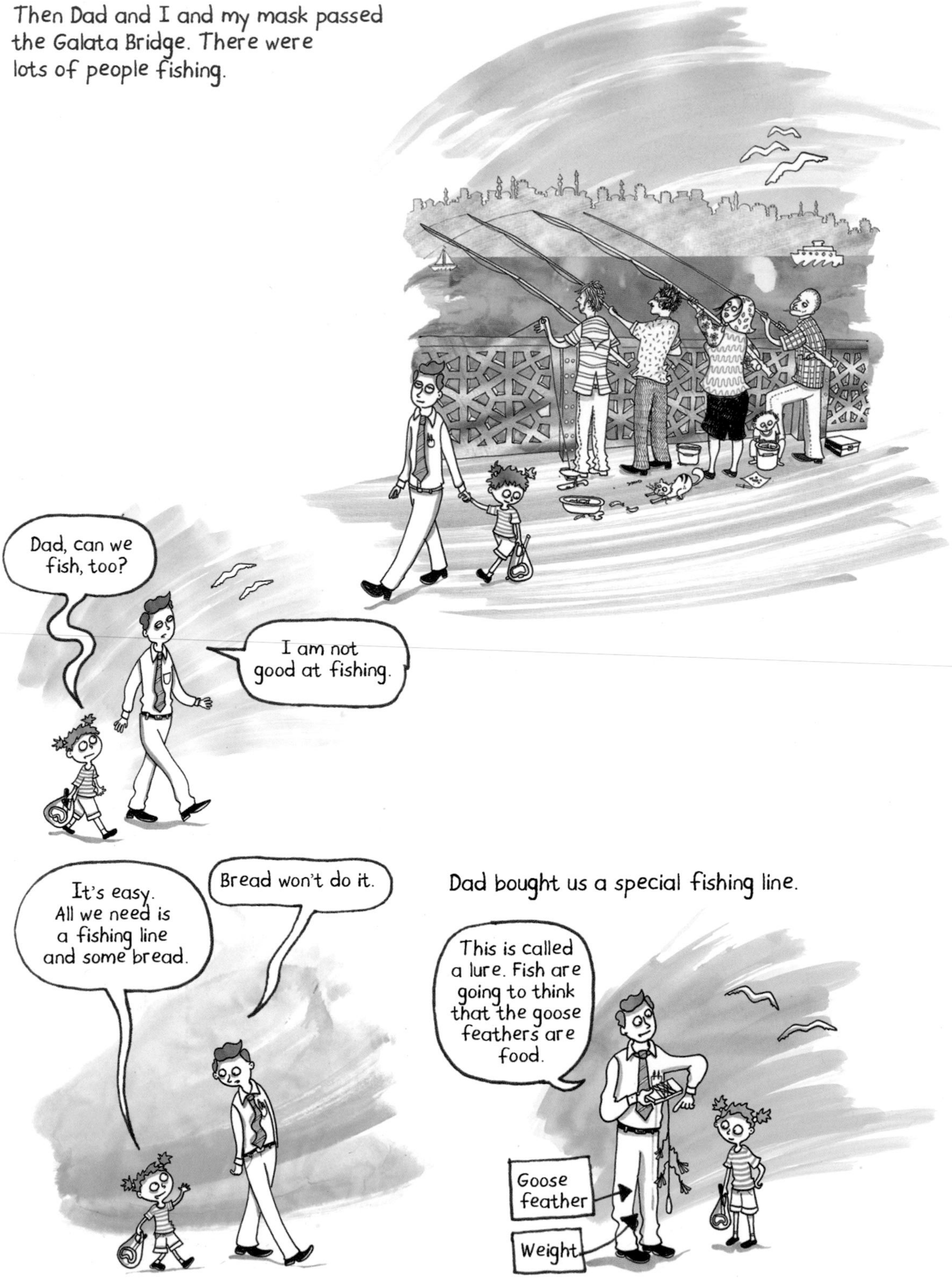
Then Dad and I and my mask passed the Galata Bridge. There were lots of people fishing.
Dad, can we fish, too?
I am not good at fishing.
It's easy. All we need is a fishing line and some bread.
Bread won't do it.
Dad bought us a special fishing line.
This is called a lure. Fish are going to think that the goose feathers are food.
Goose feather
Weight

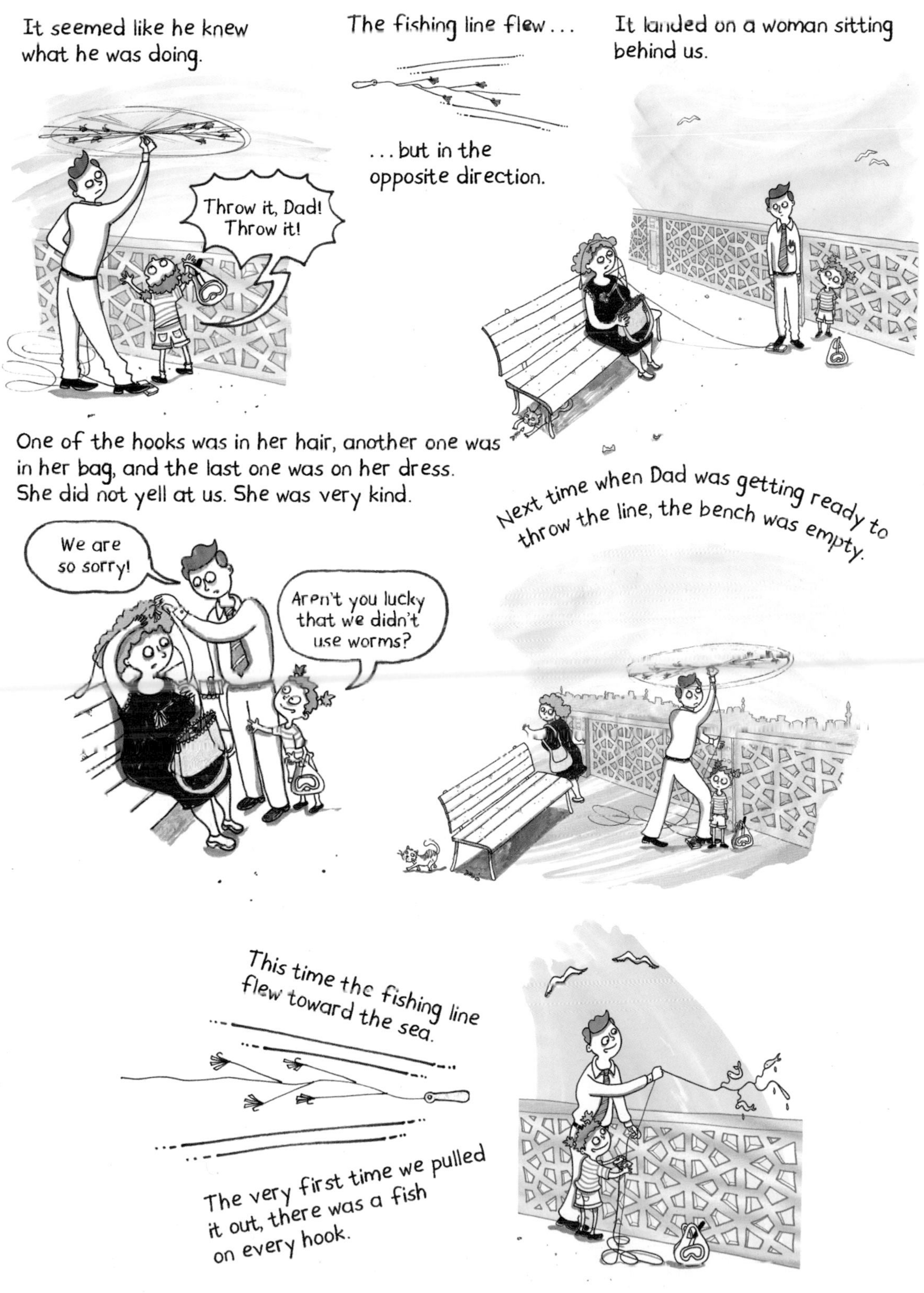
It seemed like he knew what he was doing.
Throw it, Dad! Throw it!
The fishing line flew...
...but in the opposite direction.
It landed on a woman sitting behind us.
One of the hooks was in her hair, another one was in her bag, and the last one was on her dress. She did not yell at us. She was very kind.
We are so sorry!
Aren't you lucky that we didn't use worms?
Next time when Dad was getting ready to throw the line, the bench was empty.
This time the fishing line flew toward the sea.
The very first time we pulled it out, there was a fish on every hook.

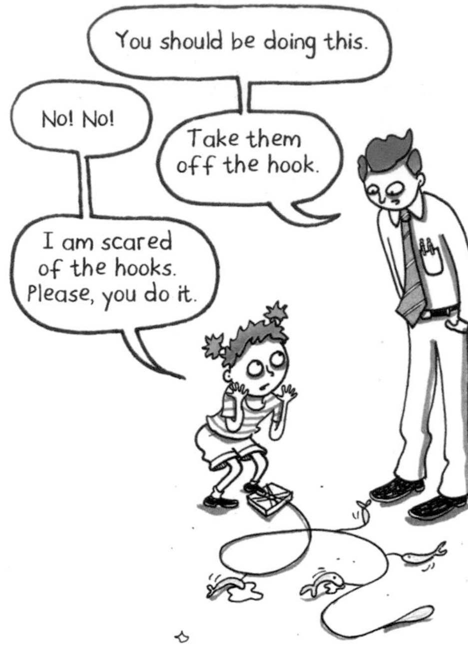
Take them off the hook.
You should be doing this.
I am scared of the hooks. Please, you do it.
No! No!

Dad had empathy with suffering animals.

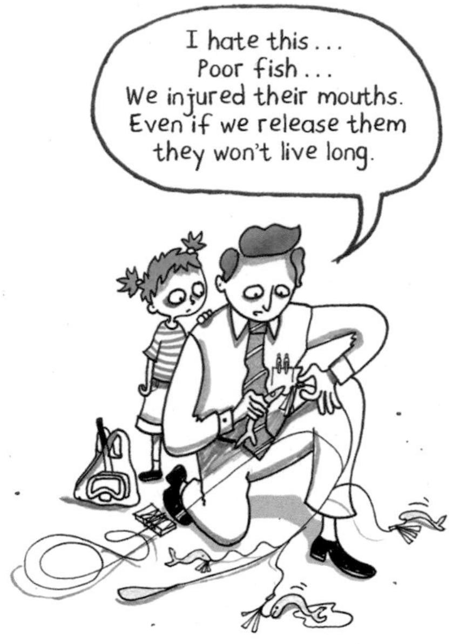
I hate this . . .
Poor fish . . .
We injured their mouths.
Even if we release them they won't live long.

We caught eight little fish and took them with us. I was feeling like a very successful hunter. Dad knew everything. How to get around Istanbul, where to buy a snorkeling mask, how to take the fish off the hook.

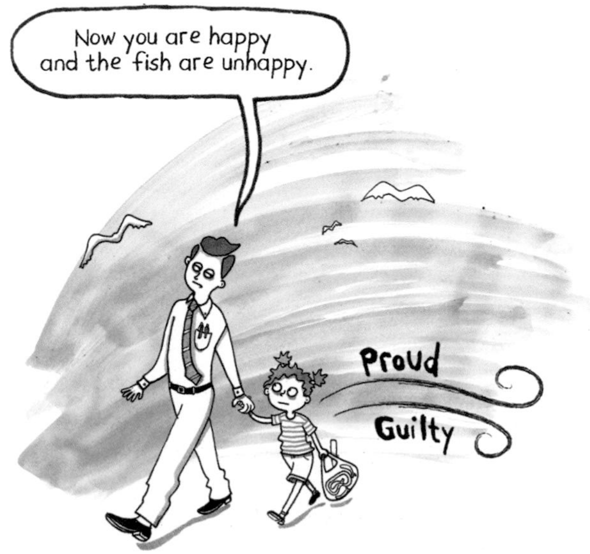
Now you are happy and the fish are unhappy.
Proud
Guilty

When we got to Mom's uncle's house Dad filled a plastic bucket with water.

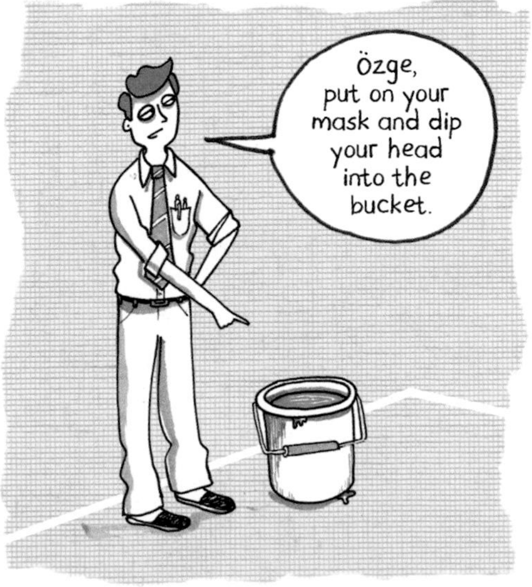
Özge, put on your mask and dip your head into the bucket.

I put on the mask and dived into the bucket.

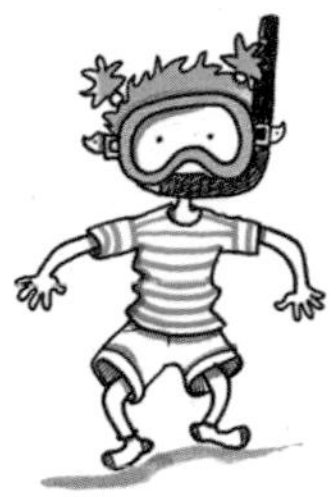

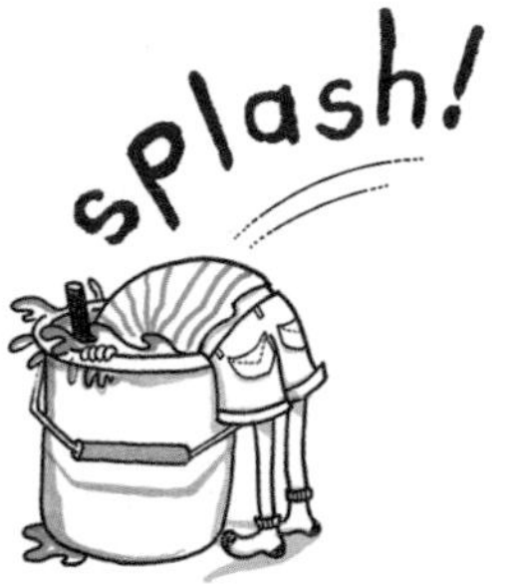
splash!

I saw something like this:

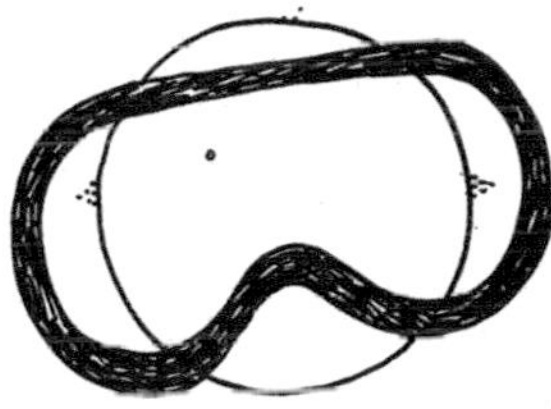

A very clear view of the bottom of the bucket.

I heard Dad's voice from outside.

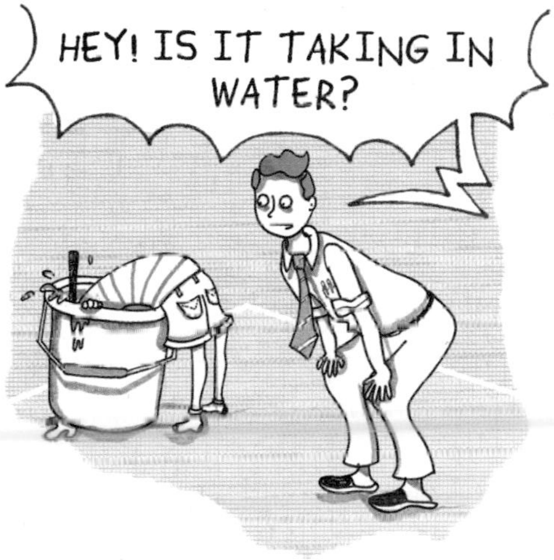
HEY! IS IT TAKING IN WATER?

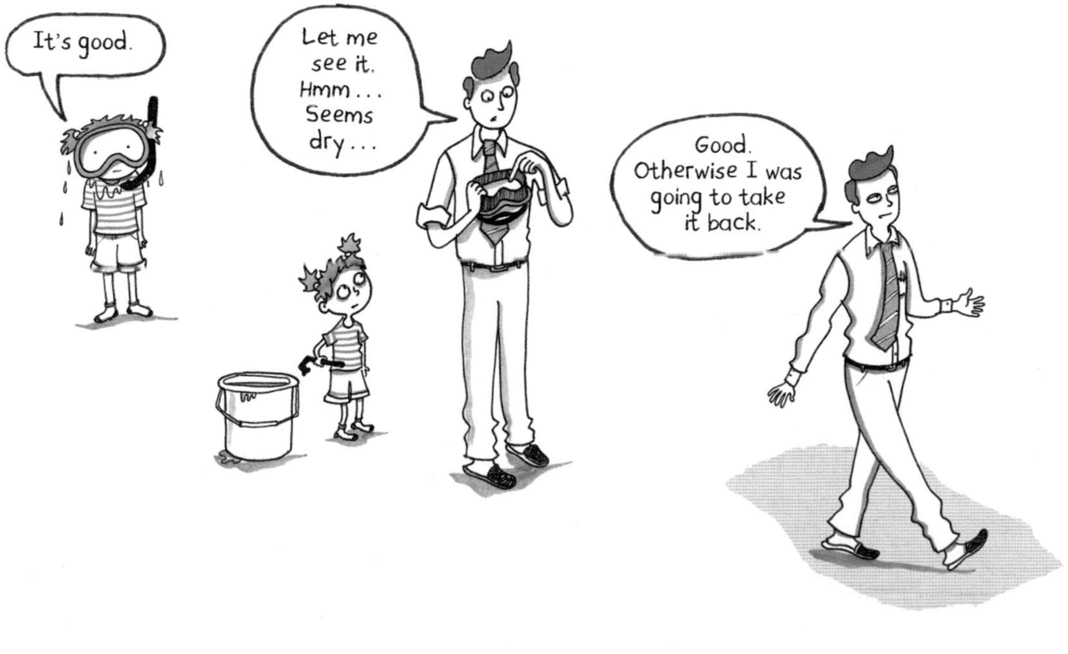
It's good.
Let me see it. Hmm . . . Seems dry . . .
Good. Otherwise I was going to take it back.

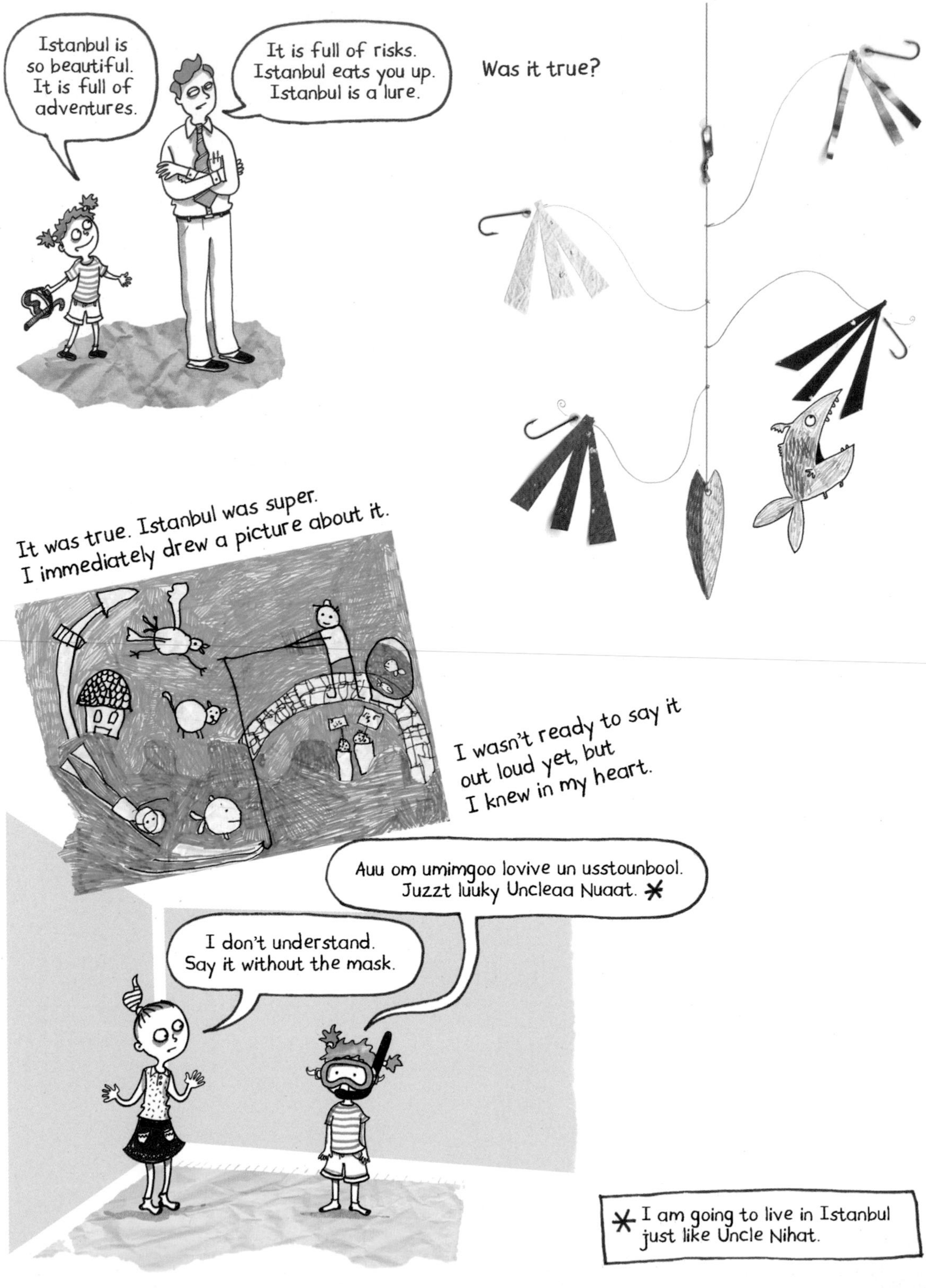
Istanbul is so beautiful. It is full of adventures.
It is full of risks. Istanbul eats you up. Istanbul is a lure.
Was it true?
It was true. Istanbul was super. I immediately drew a picture about it.
I wasn't ready to say it out loud yet, but I knew in my heart.
Auu om umimgoo lovive un usstounbool. Juzzt luuky Uncleaa Nuaat. *
I don't understand. Say it without the mask.
* I am going to live in Istanbul just like Uncle Nihat.

Chapter 8

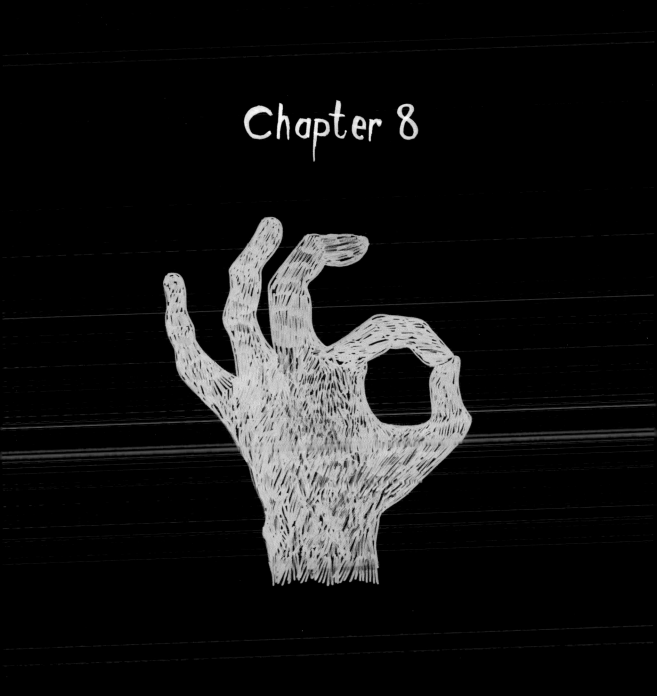

Zero

We had a lot of zeros on Turkish money.

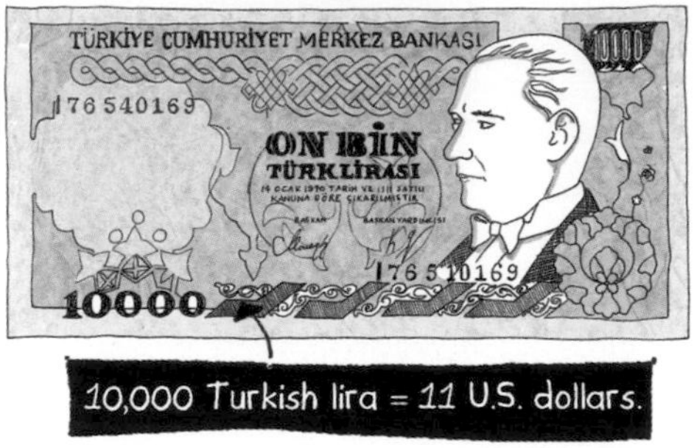
TÜRKİYE CUMHURİYET MERKEZ BANKASI
ON BİN
TÜRK LİRASI
10000
10,000 Turkish lira = 11 U.S. dollars.

While people were fascinated with the lifestyle in *Dallas* they elected a new prime minister, Turgut Özal, whose dream was to transform Turkey into a little U.S.

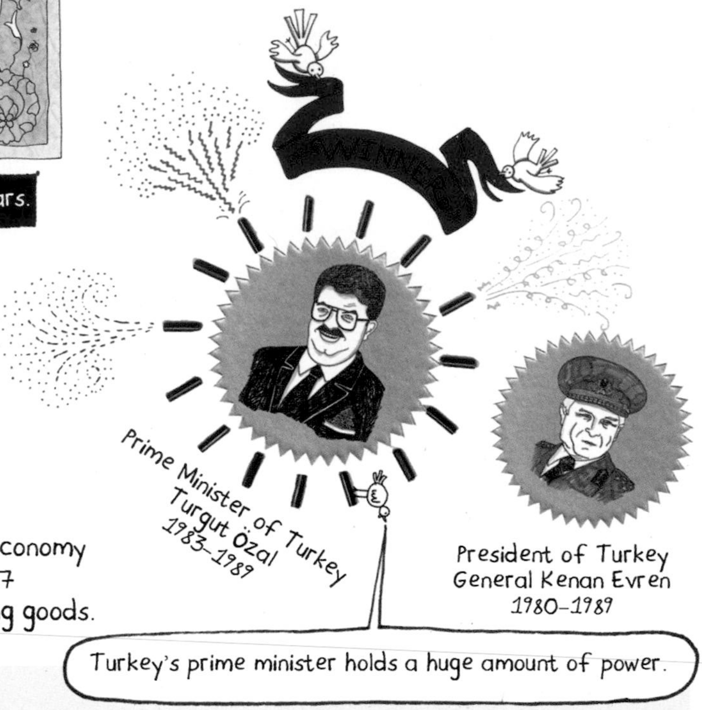
WINNER
Prime Minister of Turkey
Turgut Özal
1983–1989
President of Turkey
General Kenan Evren
1980–1989
Turkey's prime minister holds a huge amount of power.

Özal started directing the Turkish economy toward the free market, and by 1987 we were both importing and exporting goods.

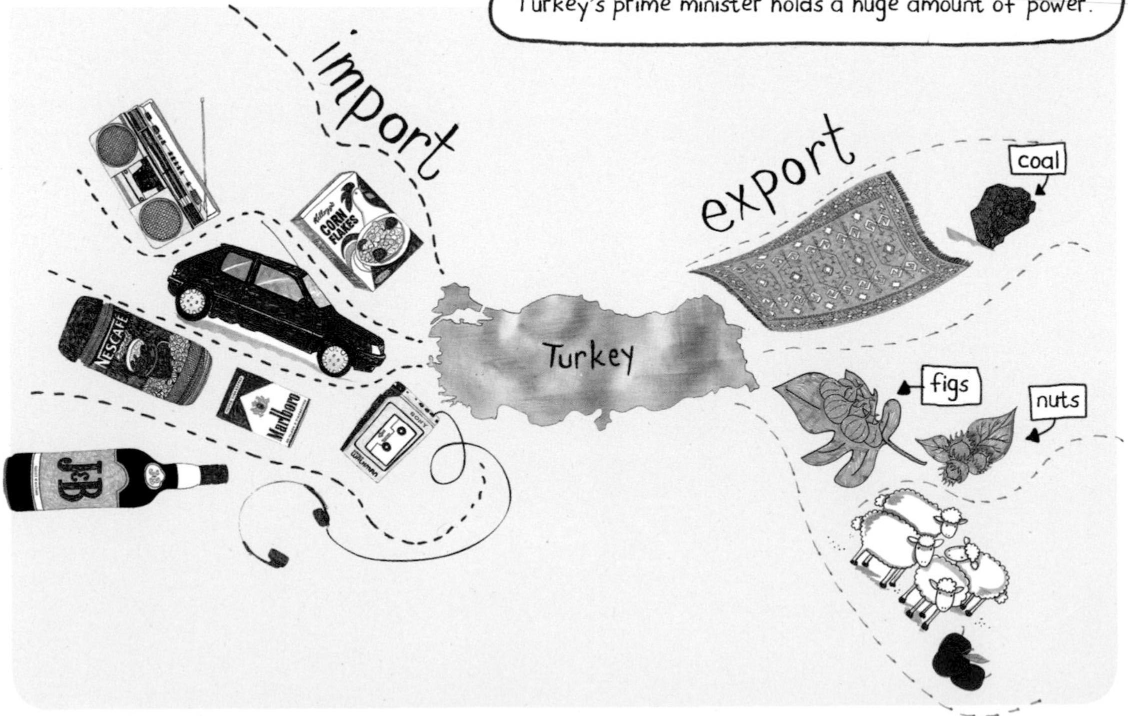
import
export
coal
Turkey
figs
nuts

Some people became immensely rich very quickly, and others got poorer. Mom's and Dad's salaries were paid by the government. Even though prices were going up every month, they still earned the same amount of money.

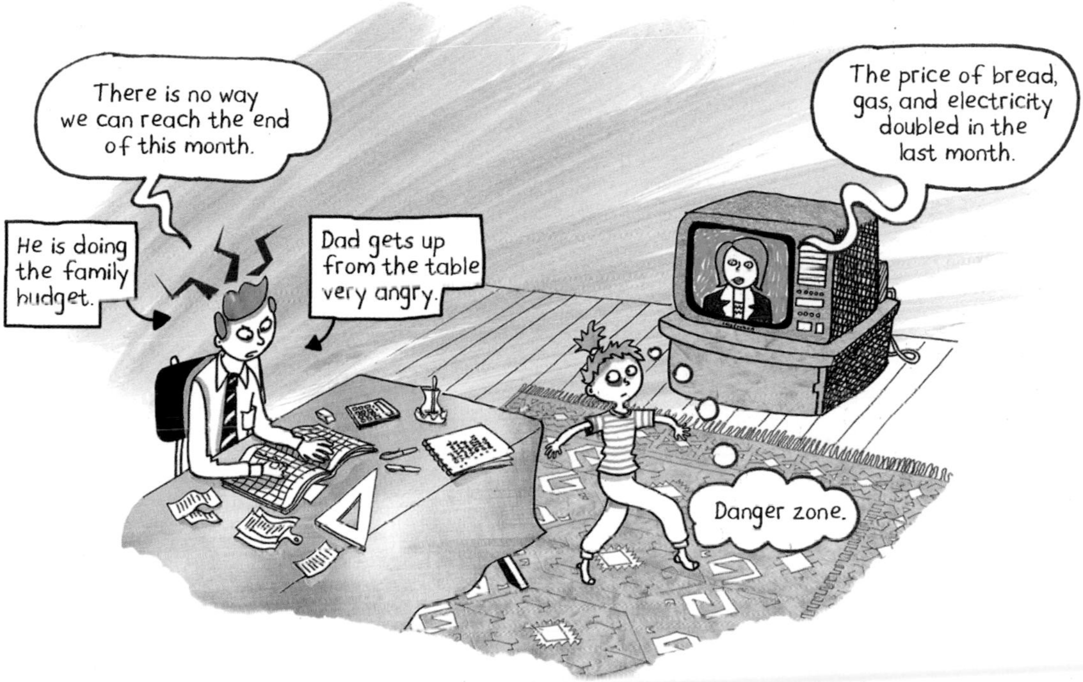

There is no way we can reach the end of this month.
He is doing the family budget.
Dad gets up from the table very angry.
The price of bread, gas, and electricity doubled in the last month.
Danger zone.

Our friend Engin's dad began exporting textiles. Overnight they were rich.

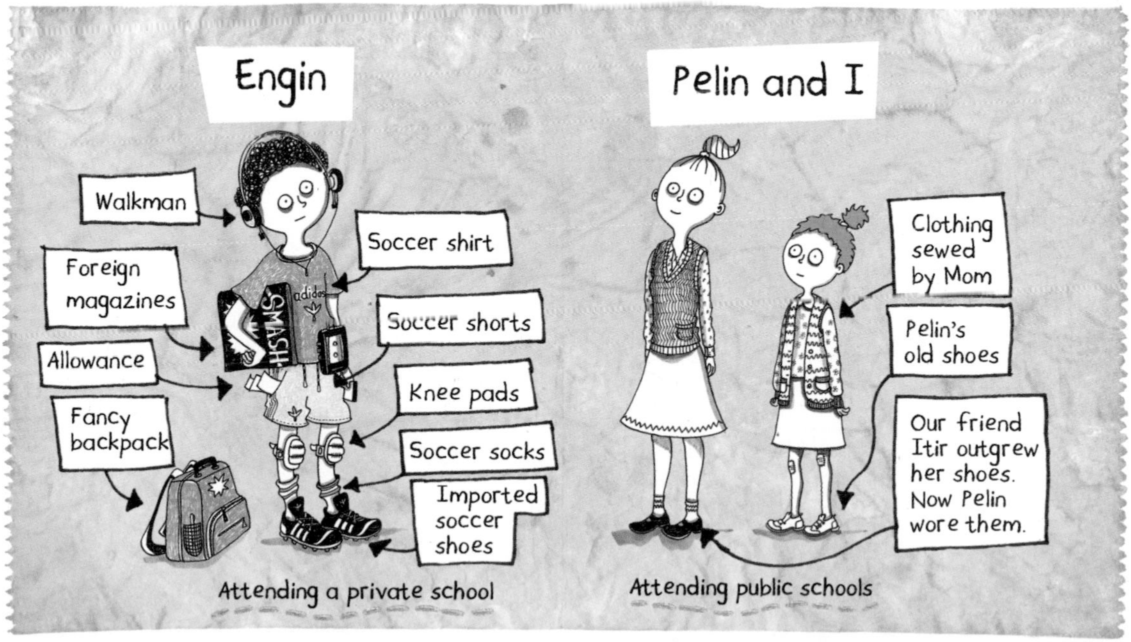

Engin
Pelin and I
Walkman
Foreign magazines
Allowance
Fancy backpack
Soccer shirt
Soccer shorts
Knee pads
Soccer socks
Imported soccer shoes
SMASH
adidas
Clothing sewed by Mom
Pelin's old shoes
Our friend Itir outgrew her shoes. Now Pelin wore them.
Attending a private school
Attending public schools

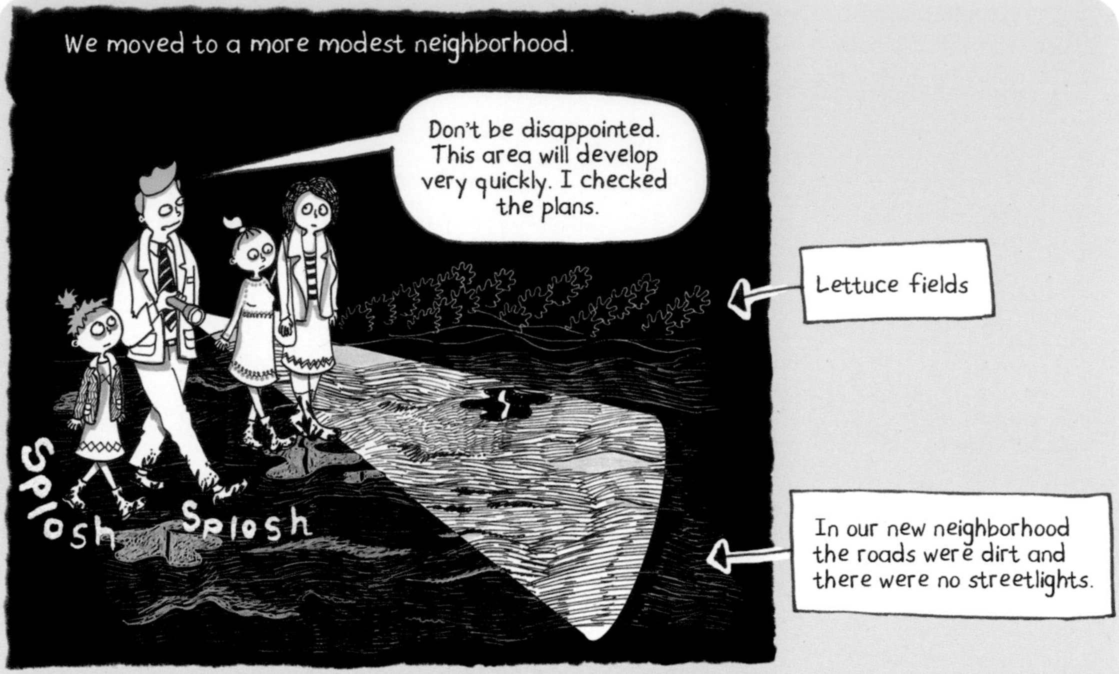
We moved to a more modest neighborhood.
Don't be disappointed. This area will develop very quickly. I checked the plans.
Lettuce fields
Splosh
Splosh
In our new neighborhood the roads were dirt and there were no streetlights.

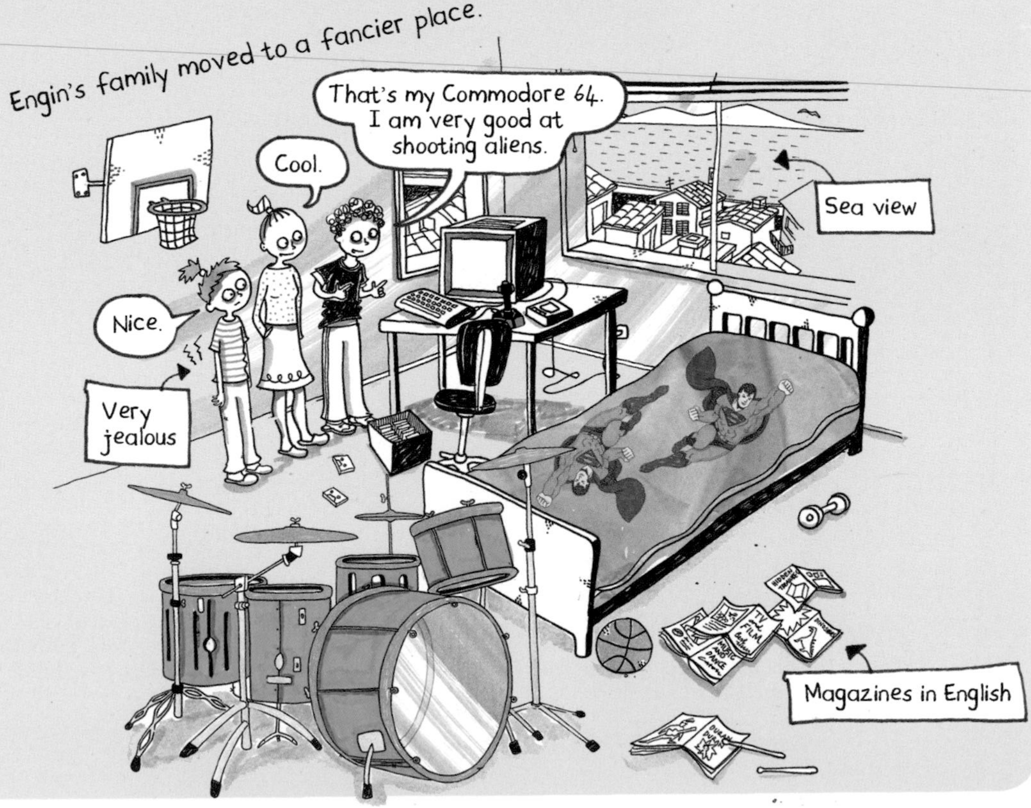
Engin's family moved to a fancier place.
That's my Commodore 64. I am very good at shooting aliens.
Cool.
Nice.
Very jealous
Sea view
Magazines in English

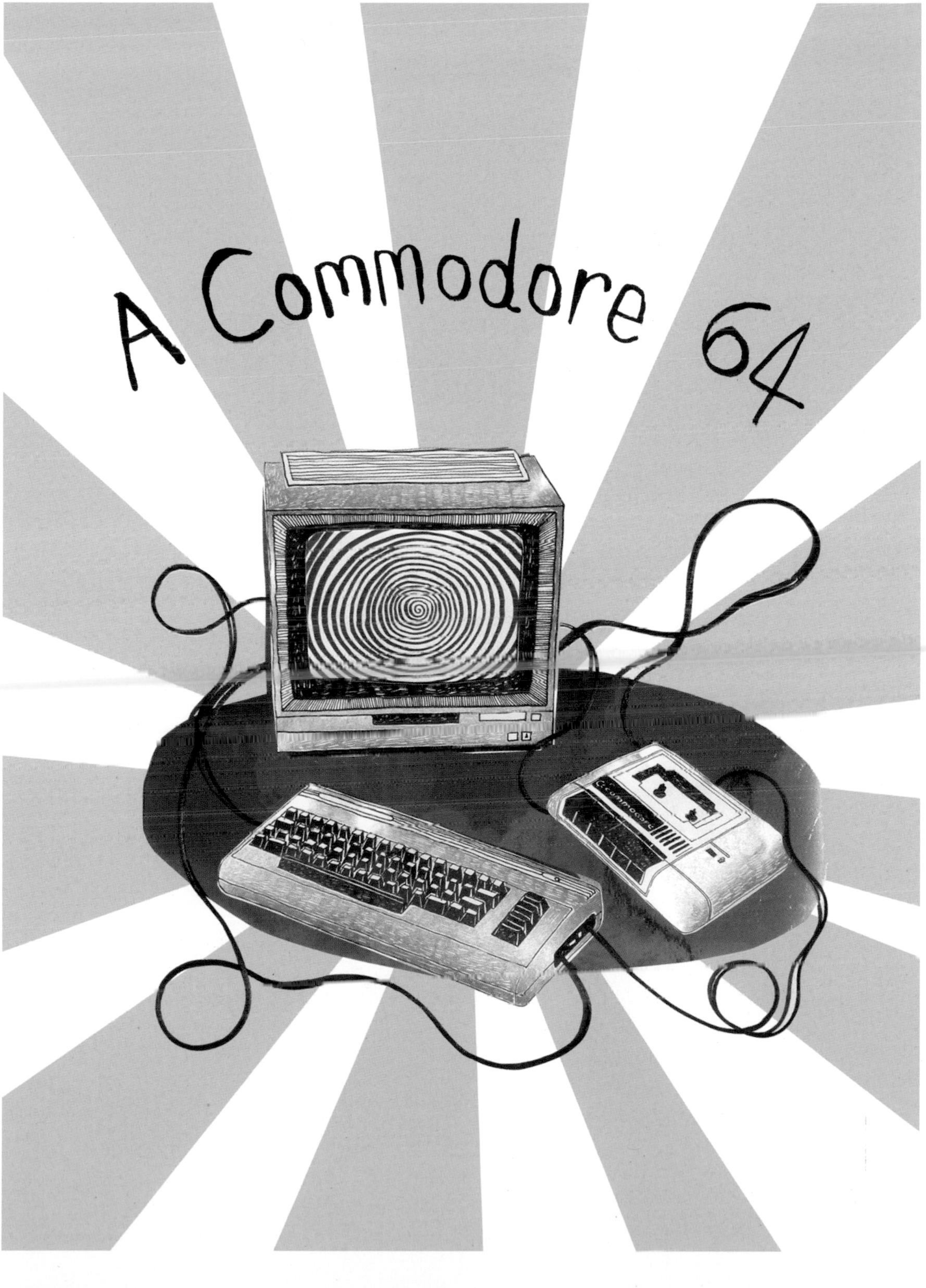
A Commodore 64
Commodore

At home:

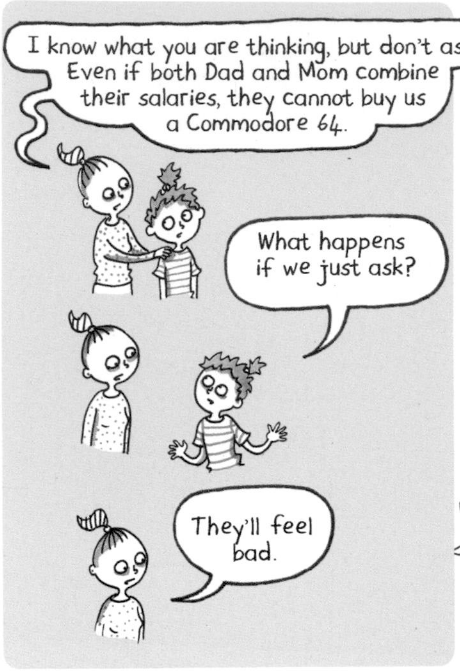
I know what you are thinking, but don't ask. Even if both Dad and Mom combine their salaries, they cannot buy us a Commodore 64.
What happens if we just ask?
They'll feel bad.

We used to spend each summer at the beach.

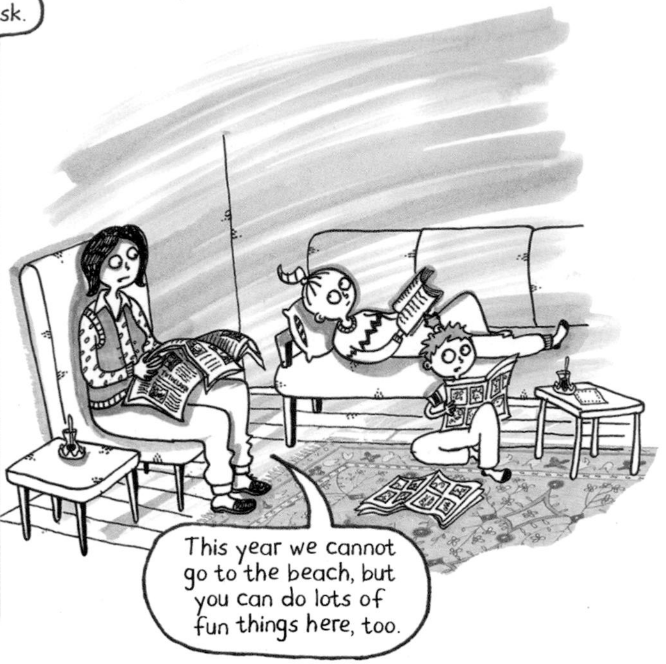
This year we cannot go to the beach, but you can do lots of fun things here, too.

Unexpectedly, Mom was right. I discovered Captain Cousteau that summer.

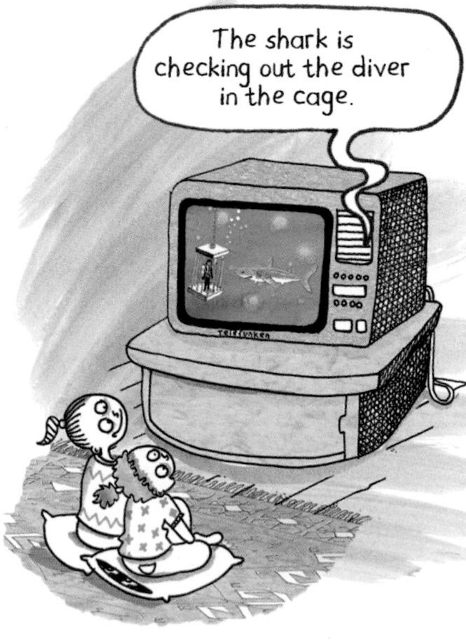
The shark is checking out the diver in the cage.

I wanted to learn to scuba dive, wander in different seas, discover sea creatures, and be just like him. I made a drawing of Captain Cousteau and myself.

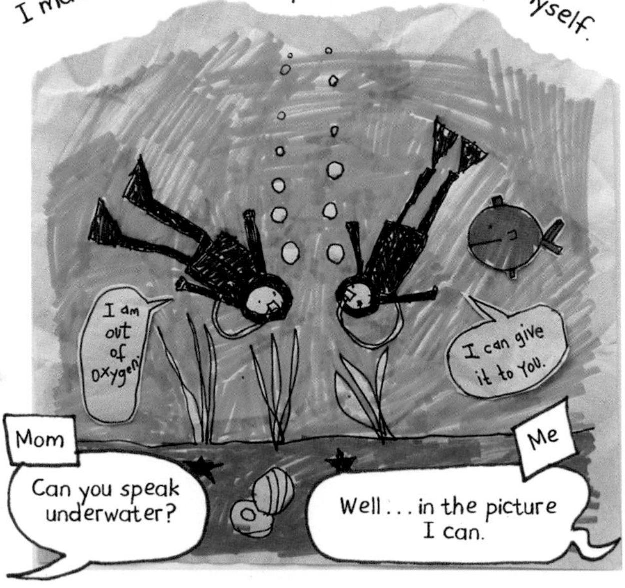
I am out of oxygen.
I can give it to you.
Mom
Me
Can you speak underwater?
Well . . . in the picture I can.

Turkish magazines were printed on low-quality paper and they didn't have many images. Foreign magazines had lots of images printed on glossy paper and they were super expensive.

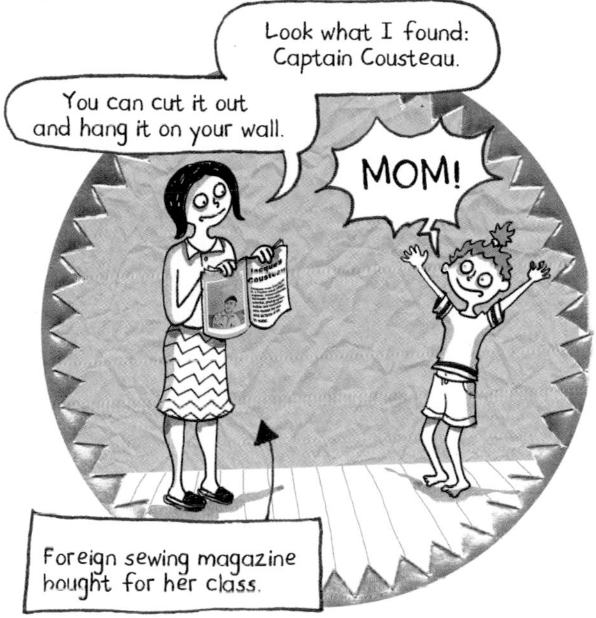
Look what I found: Captain Cousteau.
You can cut it out and hang it on your wall.
MOM!
Foreign sewing magazine bought for her class.

My friends had posters on their walls.

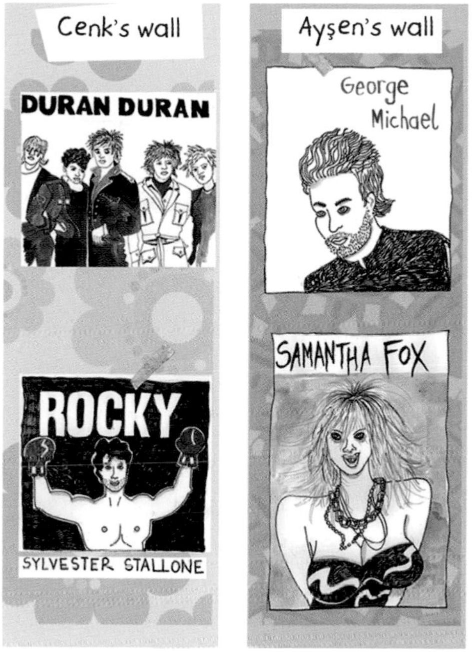
Cenk's wall
DURAN DURAN
ROCKY
SYLVESTER STALLONE
Ayşen's wall
George Michael
SAMANTHA FOX

I hung my favorite star's poster, too.

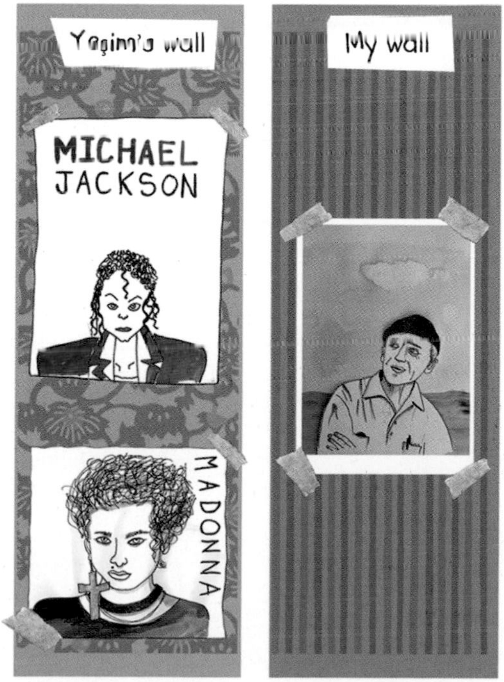
Yağım's wall
MICHAEL JACKSON
MADONNA
My wall

Following pop stars and wearing imported stuff was "in." Apparently, with my Captain Cousteau poster and my lack of knowledge, I was behind.

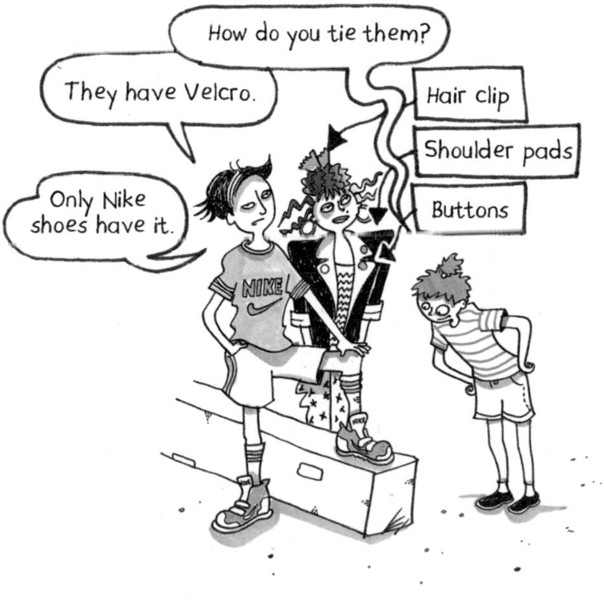
How do you tie them?
They have Velcro.
Only Nike shoes have it.
Hair clip
Shoulder pads
Buttons
NIKE

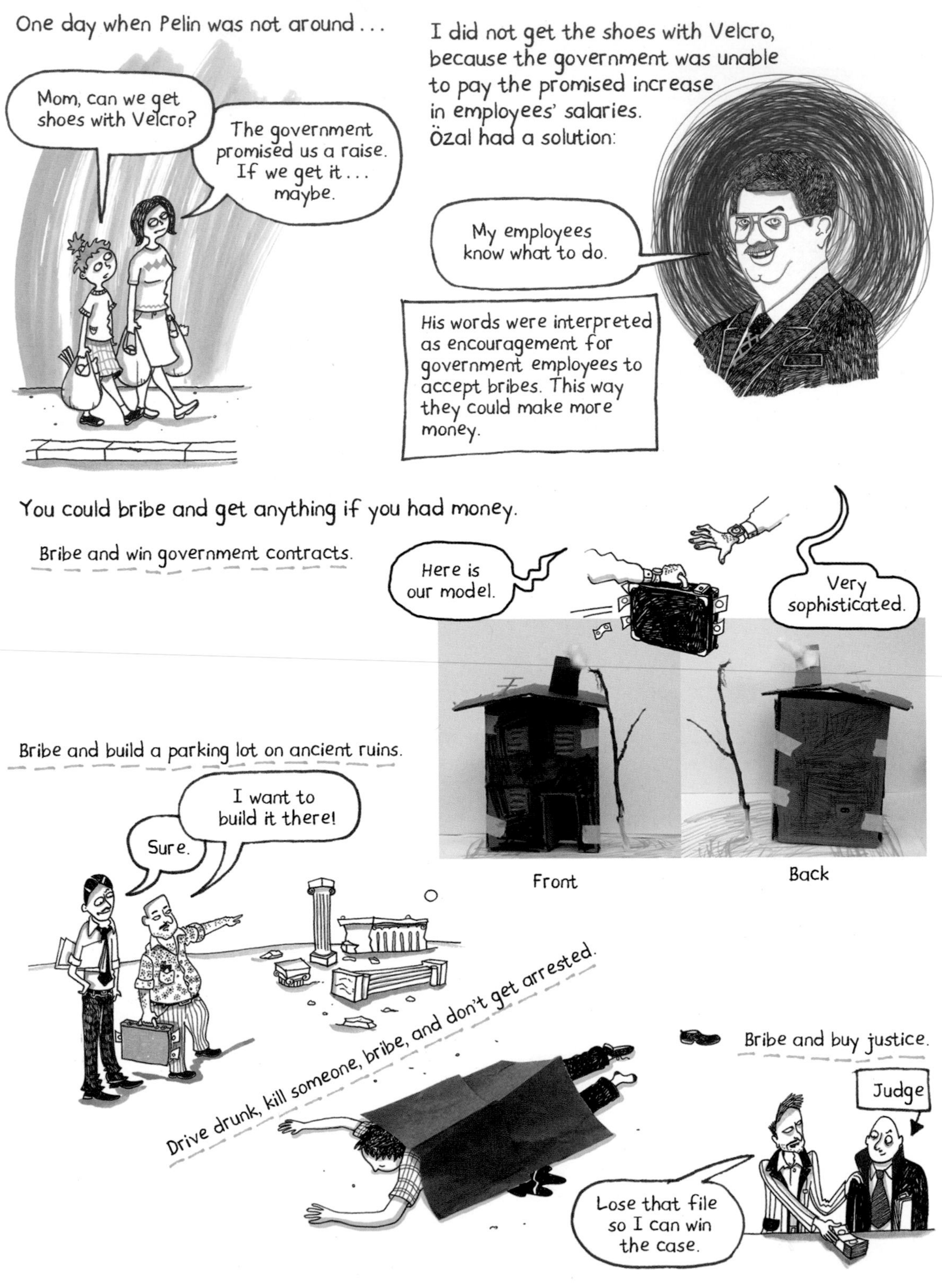
One day when Pelin was not around . . .
Mom, can we get shoes with Velcro?
The government promised us a raise. If we get it . . . maybe.
I did not get the shoes with Velcro, because the government was unable to pay the promised increase in employees' salaries. Özal had a solution:
My employees know what to do.
His words were interpreted as encouragement for government employees to accept bribes. This way they could make more money.
You could bribe and get anything if you had money.
Bribe and win government contracts.
Here is our model.
Very sophisticated.
Front
Back
Bribe and build a parking lot on ancient ruins.
I want to build it there!
Sure.
Drive drunk, kill someone, bribe, and don't get arrested.
Bribe and buy justice.
Judge
Lose that file so I can win the case.

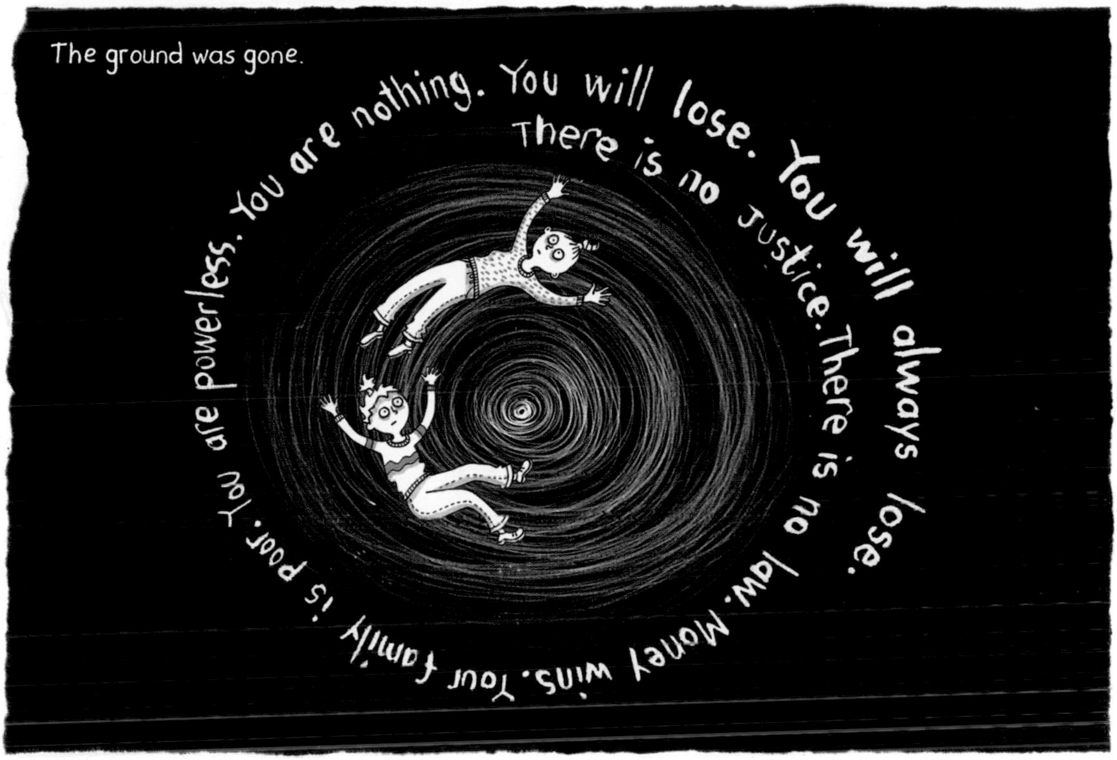
The ground was gone.
You are powerless. You are nothing. You will lose. You will always lose.
There is no justice. There is no law. Money wins. Your family is poor.

In my dad's mind the only way for my sister and me to have a secure future was to study engineering or medicine at a prestigious university, get a good job, make lots of money, and be powerful.

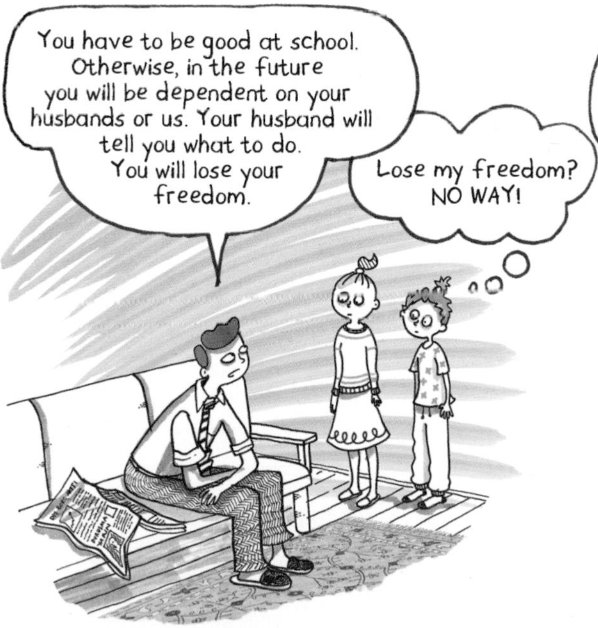
You have to be good at school. Otherwise, in the future you will be dependent on your husbands or us. Your husband will tell you what to do. You will lose your freedom.
Lose my freedom? NO WAY!

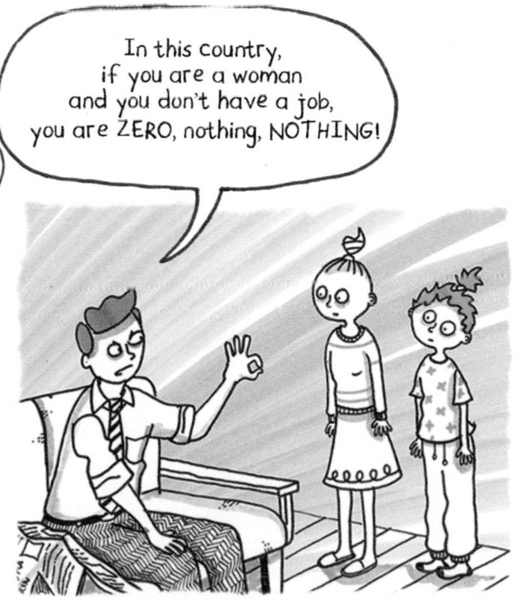
In this country, if you are a woman and you don't have a job, you are ZERO, nothing, NOTHING!

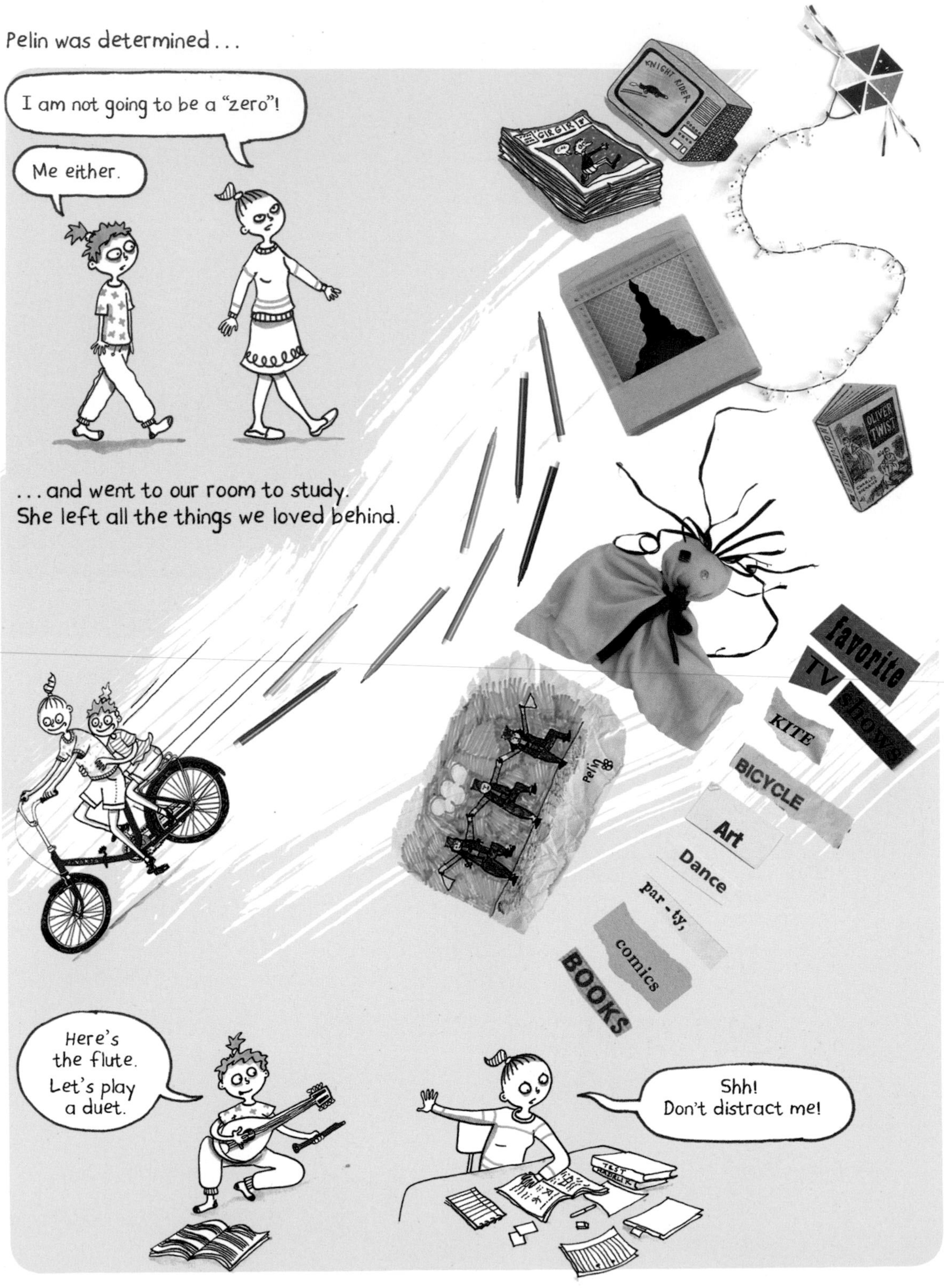
Pelin was determined . . .
I am not going to be a "zero"!
Me either.
KNIGHT RIDER
GIRGIR
OLIVER TWIST
. . . and went to our room to study.
She left all the things we loved behind.
favorite
TV
shows
KITE
BICYCLE
Art
Dance
par - ty,
comics
BOOKS
Pelin
Here's the flute. Let's play a duet.
Shh! Don't distract me!
TEST

Chapter 9

Approval

Our parents were not rich, so Pelin and I could only go to public schools.

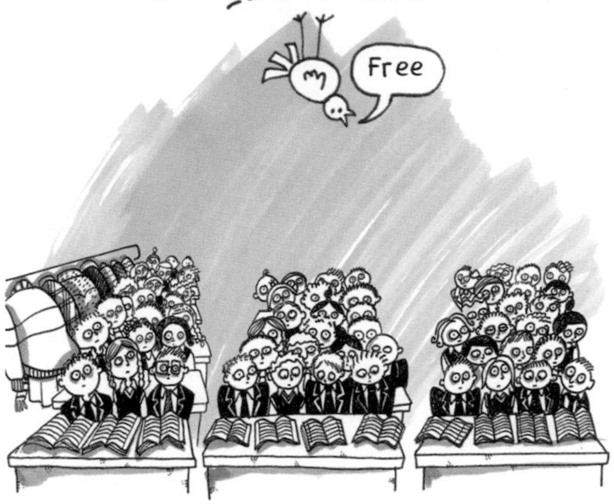
Free

There were sixty-three people in my secondary school class. It was good that there were so many of us, because there was no heating and the middle seats were very warm, except we could not move.

There were prestigious public schools and ordinary public schools.

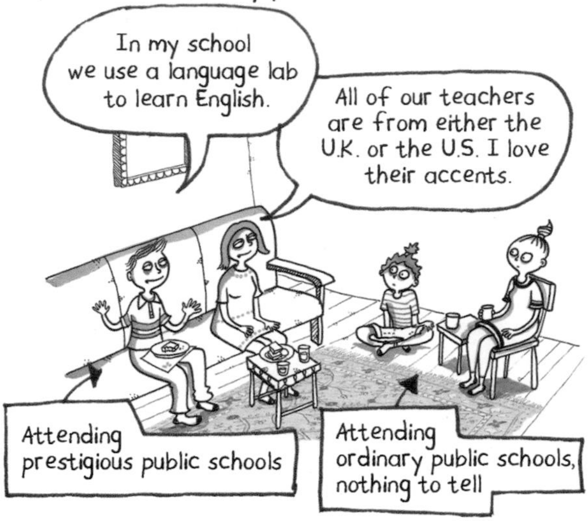
In my school we use a language lab to learn English.
All of our teachers are from either the U.K. or the U.S. I love their accents.
Attending prestigious public schools
Attending ordinary public schools, nothing to tell

In order to be admitted to a prestigious university, we had to follow a certain path.

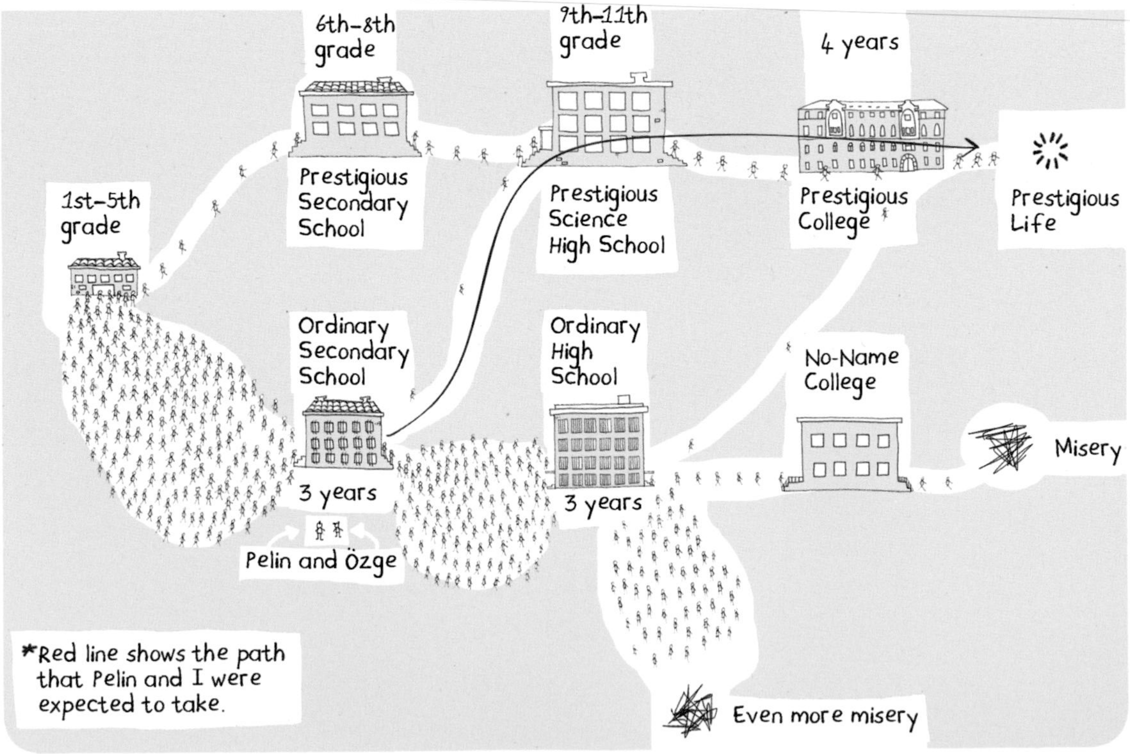
1st–5th grade
6th–8th grade
Prestigious Secondary School
9th–11th grade
Prestigious Science High School
4 years
Prestigious College
Prestigious Life
Ordinary Secondary School
3 years
Pelin and Özge
Ordinary High School
3 years
No-Name College
Misery
Even more misery
*Red line shows the path that Pelin and I were expected to take.

A lot of kids competed for places at the prestigious secondary schools, science high schools, and universities by scoring high on nationwide exams offered once a year.

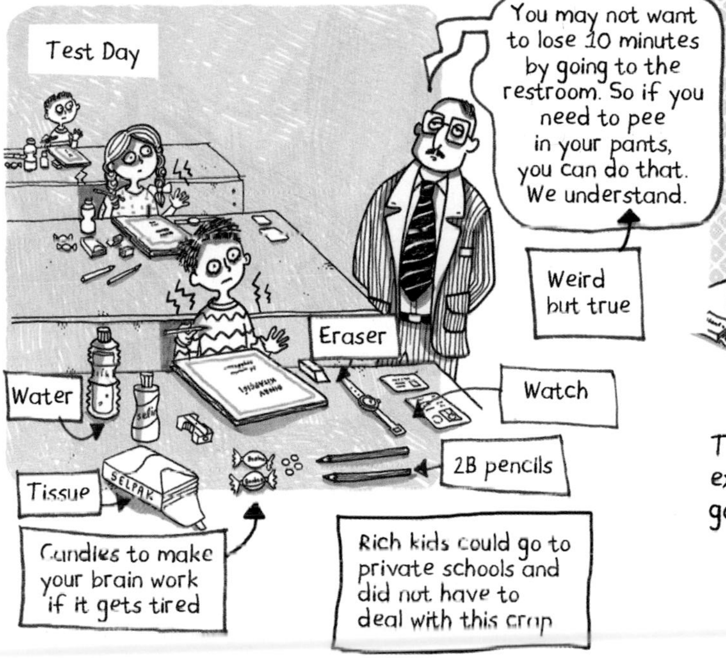
Test Day
You may not want to lose 10 minutes by going to the restroom. So if you need to pee in your pants, you can do that. We understand.
Weird but true
Eraser
Water
Watch
2B pencils
Tissue
SELPAK
Candies to make your brain work if it gets tired
Rich kids could go to private schools and did not have to deal with this crap

Accidents could happen. My friend Onur woke up sick on the morning of the secondary school exam.

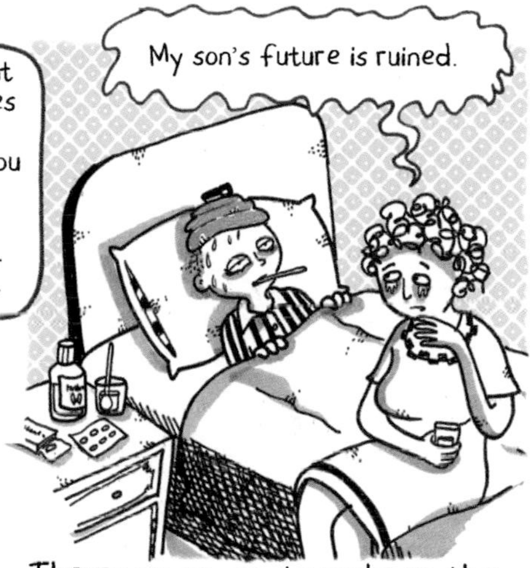
My son's future is ruined.

There was no way to make up the exam. So he had no choice but to go to an ordinary secondary school.

It was almost impossible to get into a prestigious school without attending a weekend school to study for the exams. This meant going to school seven days a week.

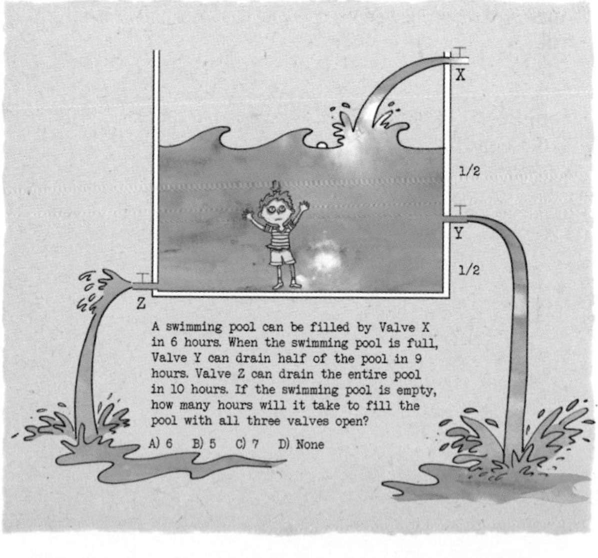
X
Y
Z
1/2
1/2
A swimming pool can be filled by Valve X in 6 hours. When the swimming pool is full, Valve Y can drain half of the pool in 9 hours. Valve Z can drain the entire pool in 10 hours. If the swimming pool is empty, how many hours will it take to fill the pool with all three valves open?
A) 6 B) 5 C) 7 D) None

Unfortunately, all weekend schools were private and that meant a huge burden on the family budget.

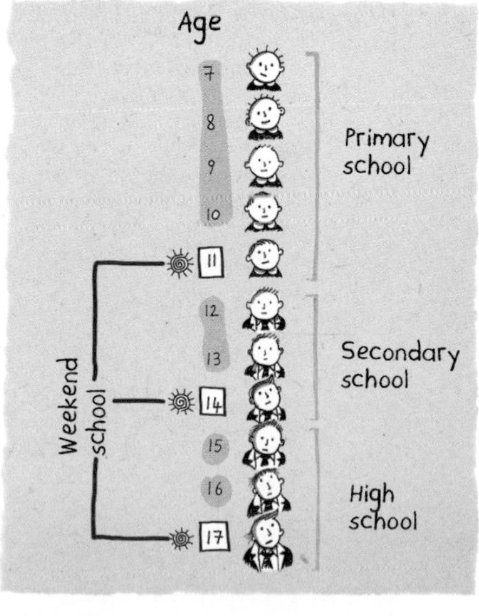
Age
7
8
9
10
11
12
13
14
15
16
17
Primary school
Secondary school
High school
Weekend school

Weekend schools were like factories. Students learned how to score well on multiple-choice exams.

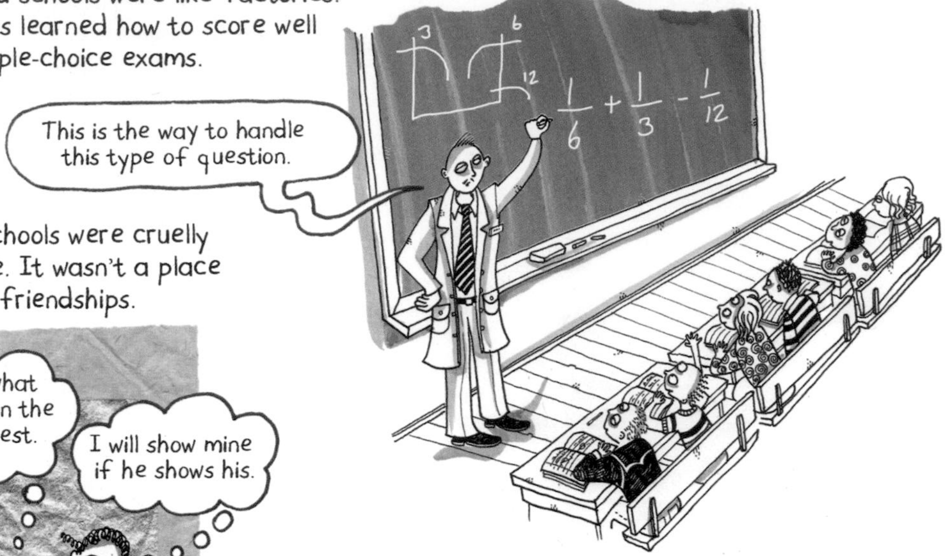
This is the way to handle this type of question.
1/6 + 1/3 - 1/12

Weekend schools were cruelly competitive. It wasn't a place to develop friendships.

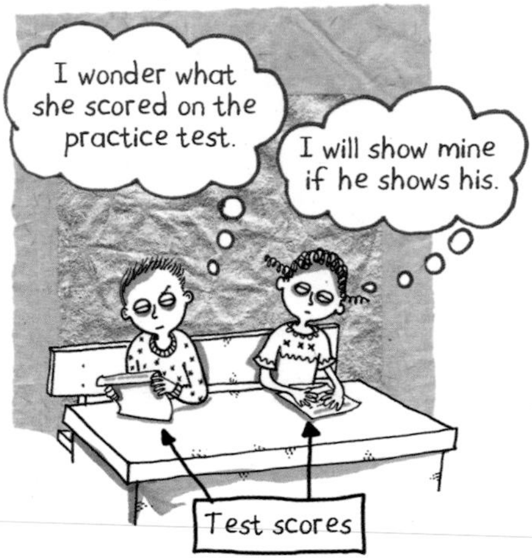
I wonder what she scored on the practice test.
I will show mine if he shows his.
Test scores

This was a strange game.

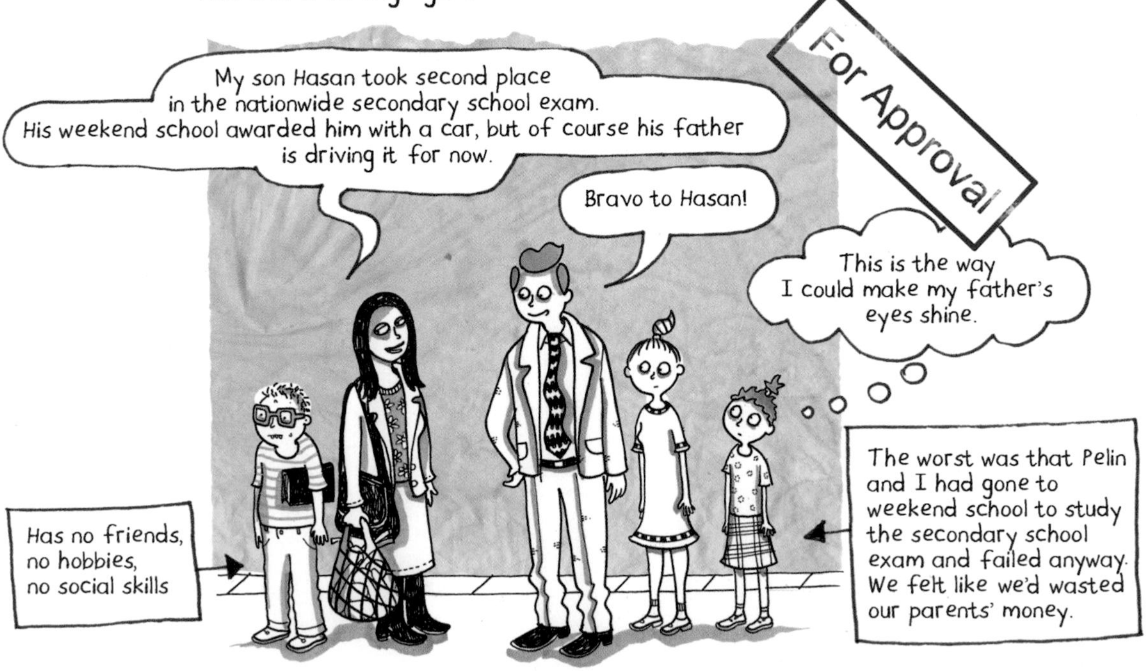
My son Hasan took second place in the nationwide secondary school exam. His weekend school awarded him with a car, but of course his father is driving it for now.
Bravo to Hasan!
For Approval
This is the way I could make my father's eyes shine.
Has no friends, no hobbies, no social skills
The worst was that Pelin and I had gone to weekend school to study the secondary school exam and failed anyway. We felt like we'd wasted our parents' money.

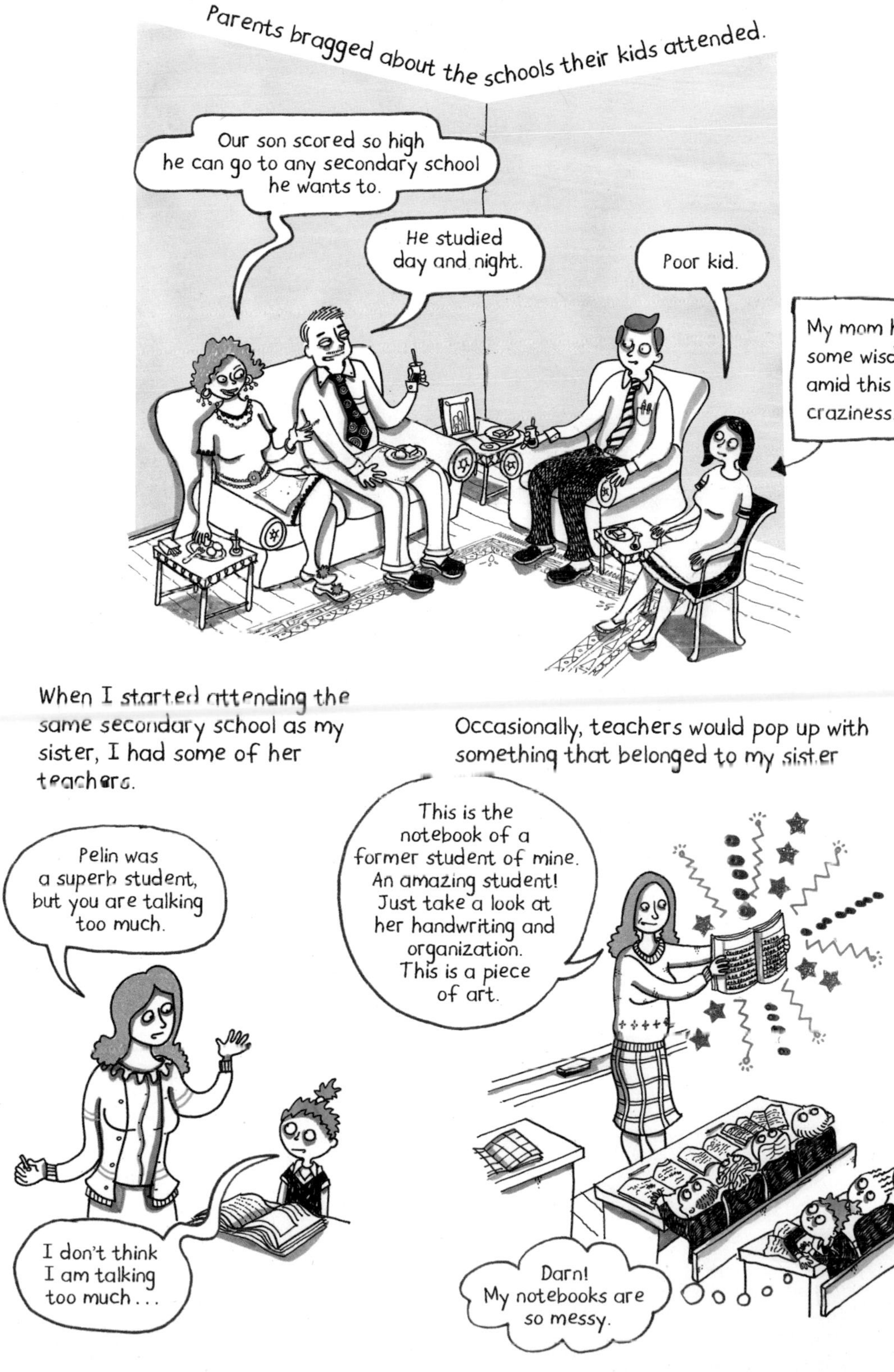

Parents bragged about the schools their kids attended.
Our son scored so high he can go to any secondary school he wants to.
He studied day and night.
Poor kid.
My mom had some wisdom amid this craziness.
When I started attending the same secondary school as my sister, I had some of her teachers.
Pelin was a superb student, but you are talking too much.
I don't think I am talking too much...
Occasionally, teachers would pop up with something that belonged to my sister
This is the notebook of a former student of mine. An amazing student! Just take a look at her handwriting and organization. This is a piece of art.
Darn! My notebooks are so messy.

Pelin was going to high school next year, and my father was worried about how to pay for the weekend school to help her prepare for the exam. But Pelin solved the problem herself.

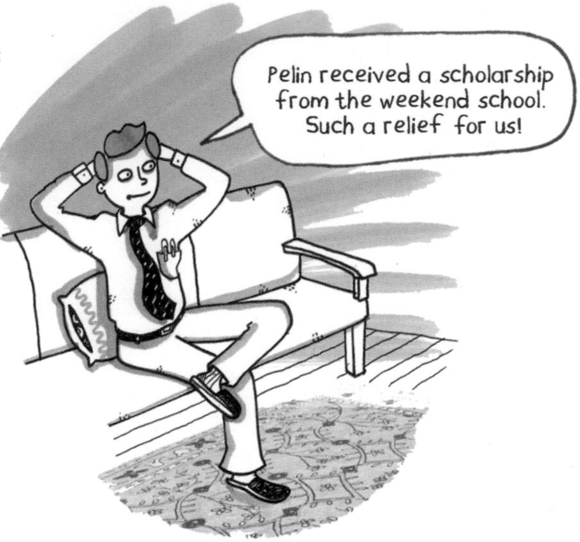
Pelin received a scholarship from the weekend school. Such a relief for us!

We had a corner for Pelin's trophies.

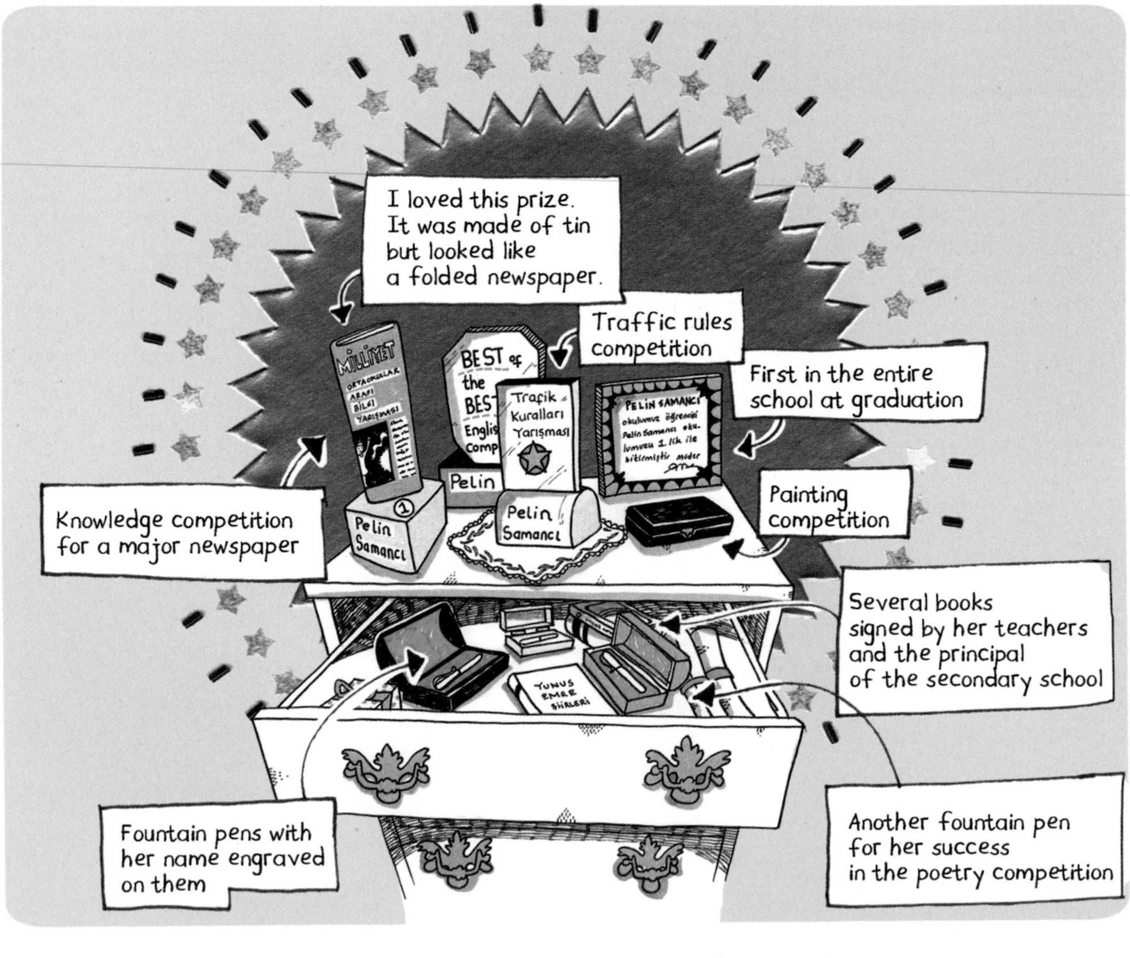
I loved this prize. It was made of tin but looked like a folded newspaper.
Traffic rules competition
First in the entire school at graduation
Knowledge competition for a major newspaper
Painting competition
Several books signed by her teachers and the principal of the secondary school
Fountain pens with her name engraved on them
Another fountain pen for her success in the poetry competition
MİLLİYET
BEST of the BEST
Trafik Kuralları Yarışması
Pelin
Pelin Samancı
Pelin Samancı
PELİN SAMANCI
YUNUS EMRE ŞİİRLERİ

I adored Pelin and yearned for the approval that she received.

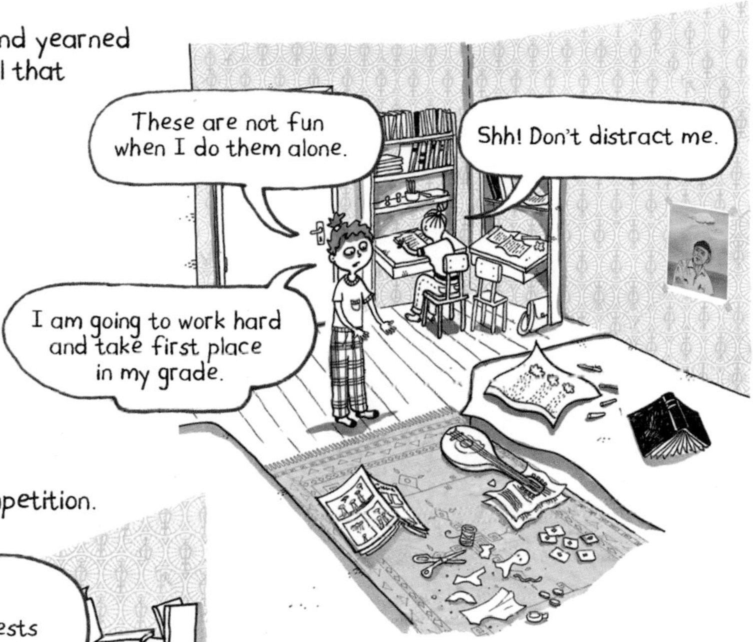
These are not fun when I do them alone.
Shh! Don't distract me.
I am going to work hard and take first place in my grade.

I became a part of the competition.

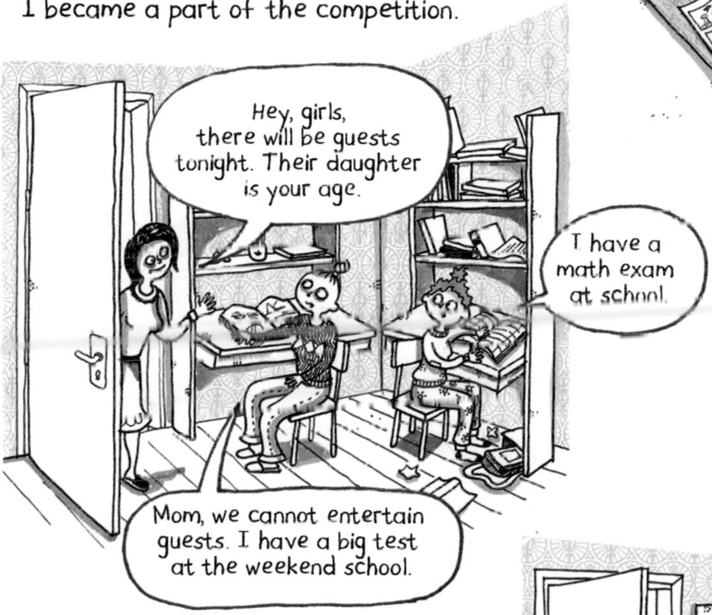
Hey, girls, there will be guests tonight. Their daughter is your age.
I have a math exam at school.
Mom, we cannot entertain guests. I have a big test at the weekend school.

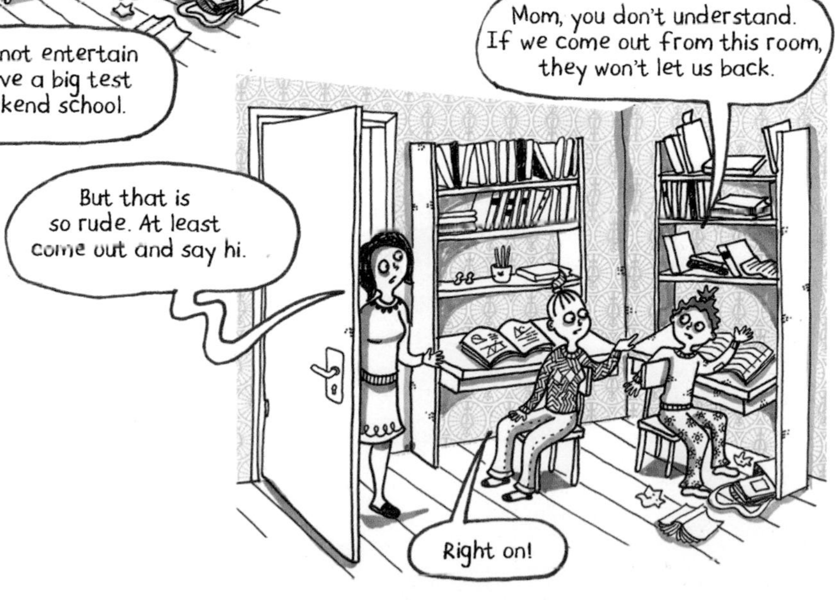
But that is so rude. At least come out and say hi.
Mom, you don't understand. If we come out from this room, they won't let us back.
Right on!

Mom was worried about us.

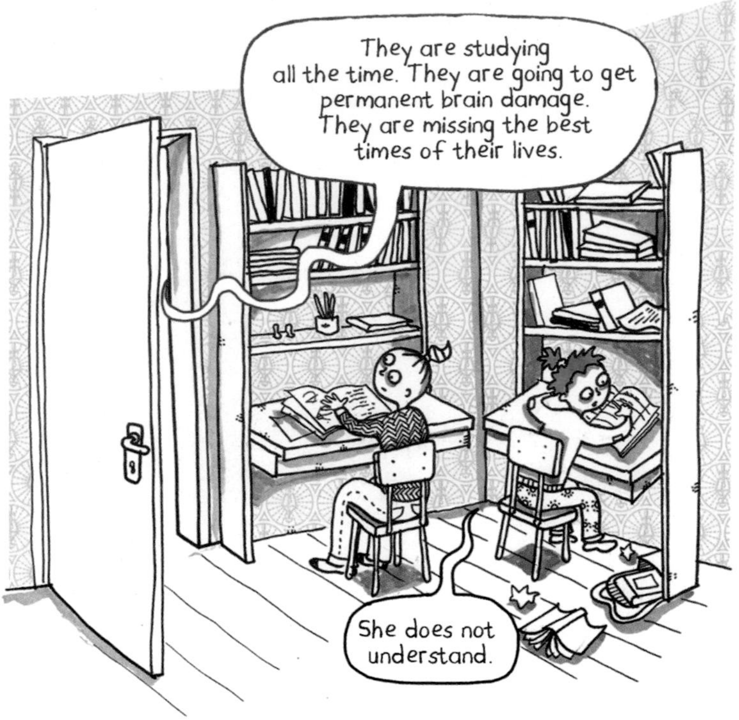
They are studying all the time. They are going to get permanent brain damage. They are missing the best times of their lives.
She does not understand.

Dad was proud . . .

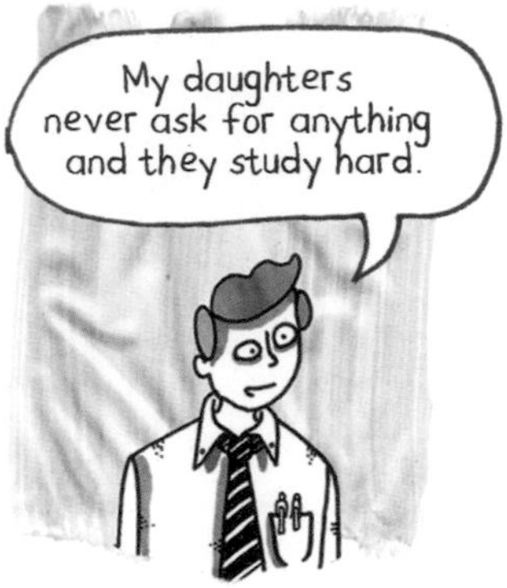
My daughters never ask for anything and they study hard.

Uncle Nihat was not . . .

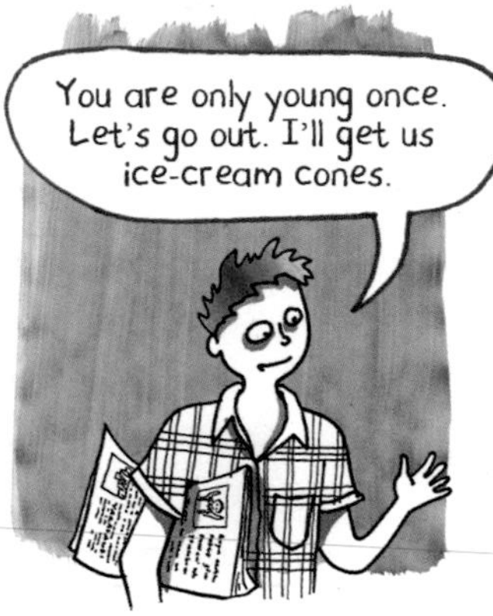
You are only young once. Let's go out. I'll get us ice-cream cones.

Pelin was not only a good student but also a good poet, painter, and performer.

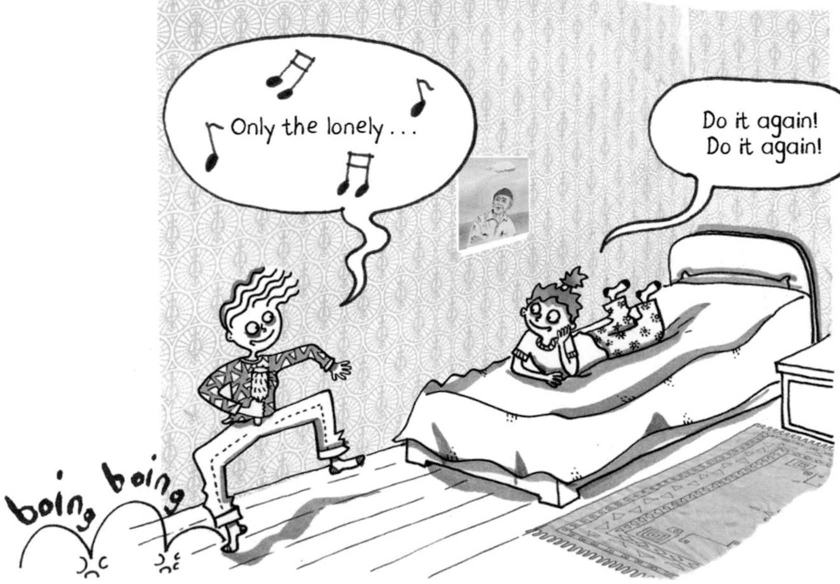
Only the lonely . . .
Do it again! Do it again!
boing boing

But that year she did not have time to perform. I did not have time to watch her.

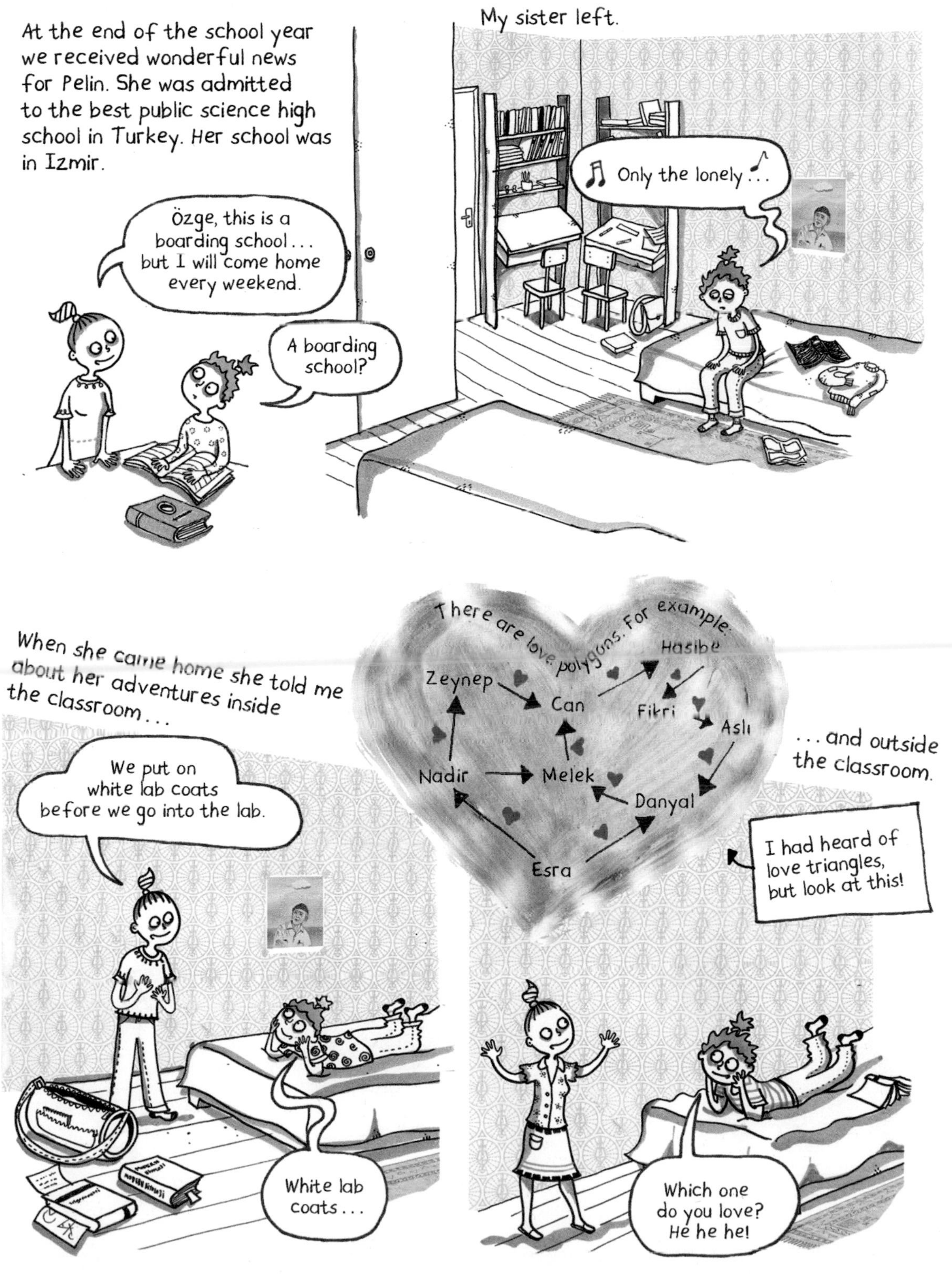
At the end of the school year we received wonderful news for Pelin. She was admitted to the best public science high school in Turkey. Her school was in Izmir.
Özge, this is a boarding school . . . but I will come home every weekend.
A boarding school?
My sister left.
Only the lonely . . .
When she came home she told me about her adventures inside the classroom . . .
We put on white lab coats before we go into the lab.
White lab coats . . .
There are love polygons. For example:
Zeynep
Can
Hasibe
Fikri
Aslı
Nadir
Melek
Danyal
Esra
. . . and outside the classroom.
I had heard of love triangles, but look at this!
Which one do you love? He he he!

Then one weekend . . .

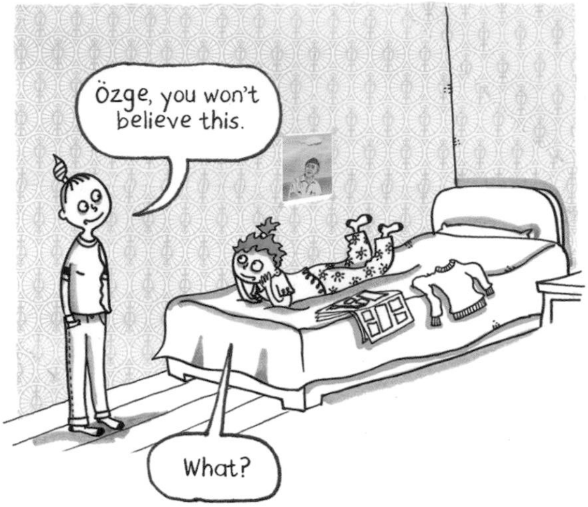
Özge, you won't believe this.
What?

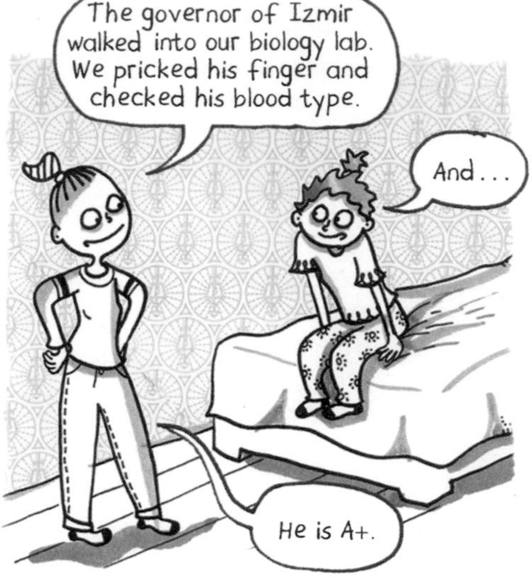
The governor of Izmir walked into our biology lab. We pricked his finger and checked his blood type.
And . . .
He is A+.

I wanted to go to her science high school and check the blood type of the governor . . .

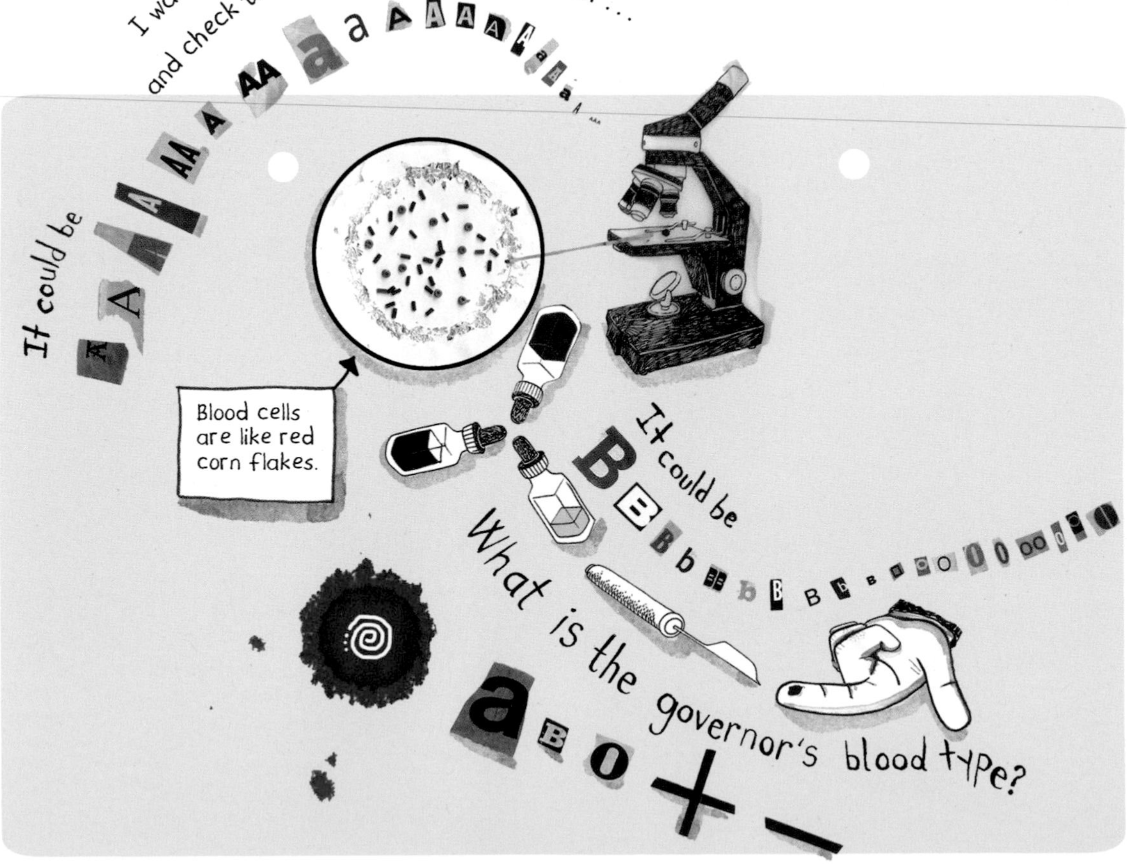
It could be
Blood cells are like red corn flakes.
It could be
What is the governor's blood type?

. . . and I wanted Dad's approval.

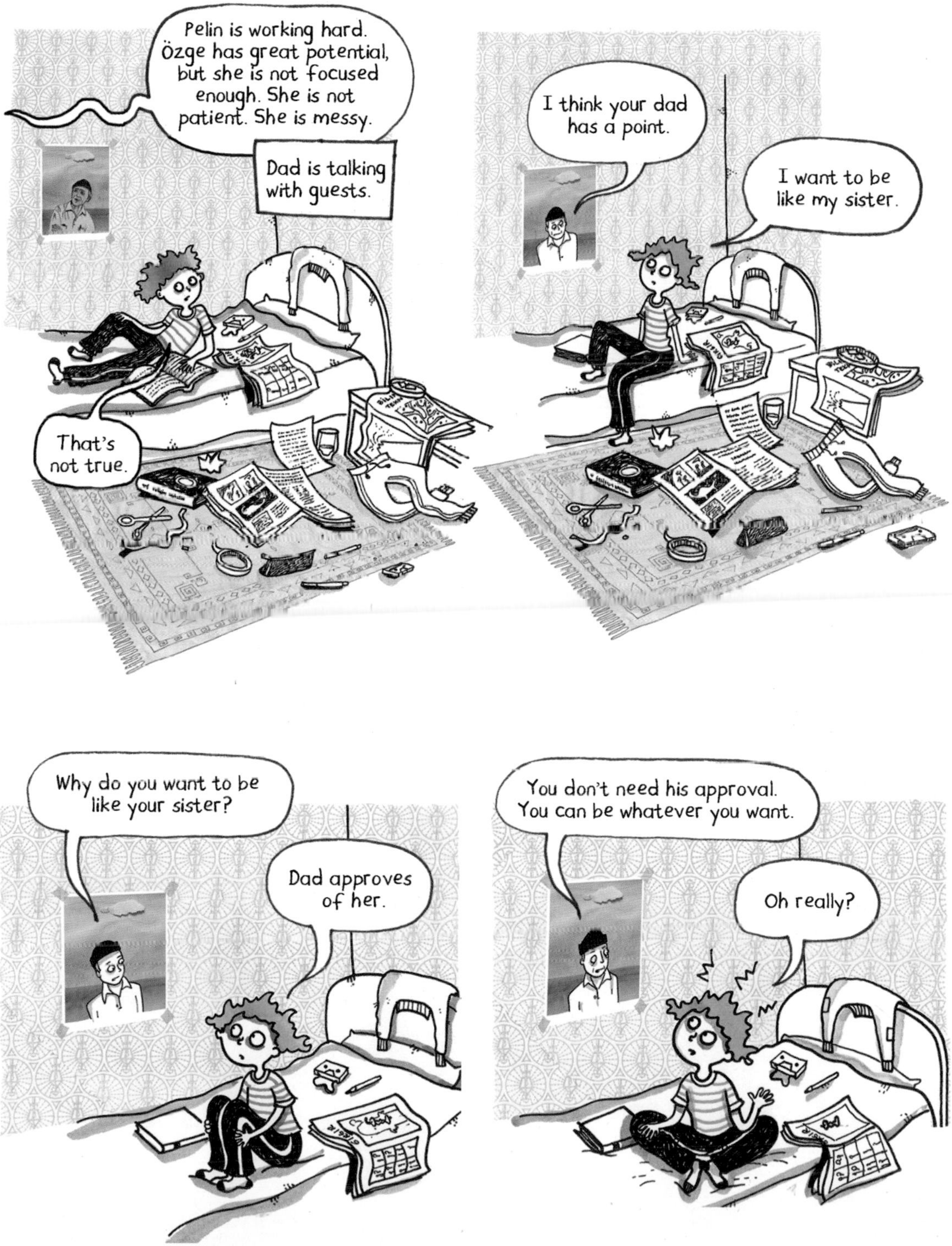
Pelin is working hard. Özge has great potential, but she is not focused enough. She is not patient. She is messy.
Dad is talking with guests.
That's not true.
I think your dad has a point.
I want to be like my sister.
Why do you want to be like your sister?
Dad approves of her.
You don't need his approval. You can be whatever you want.
Oh really?

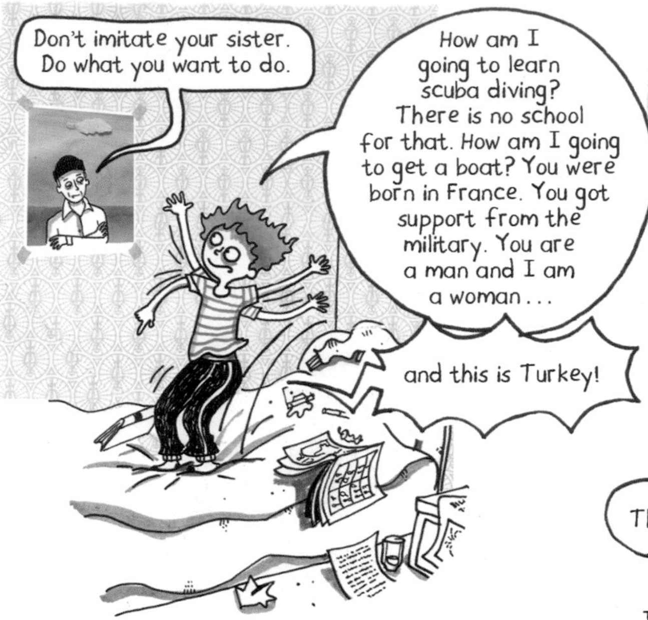
Don't imitate your sister. Do what you want to do.
How am I going to learn scuba diving? There is no school for that. How am I going to get a boat? You were born in France. You got support from the military. You are a man and I am a woman . . .
and this is Turkey!

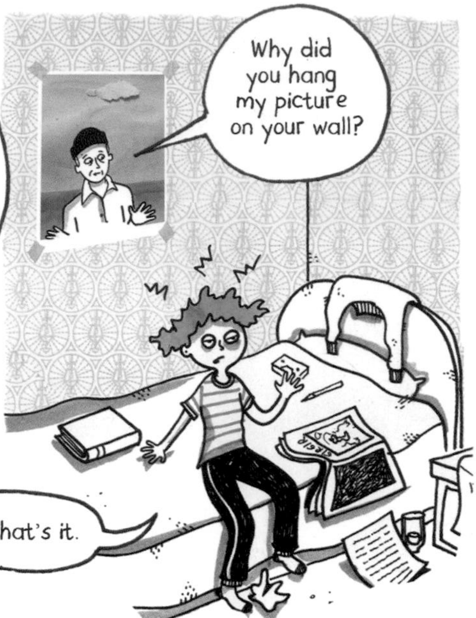
Why did you hang my picture on your wall?
That's it.

I got up . . .

. . . and silenced Jacques Cousteau's voice.

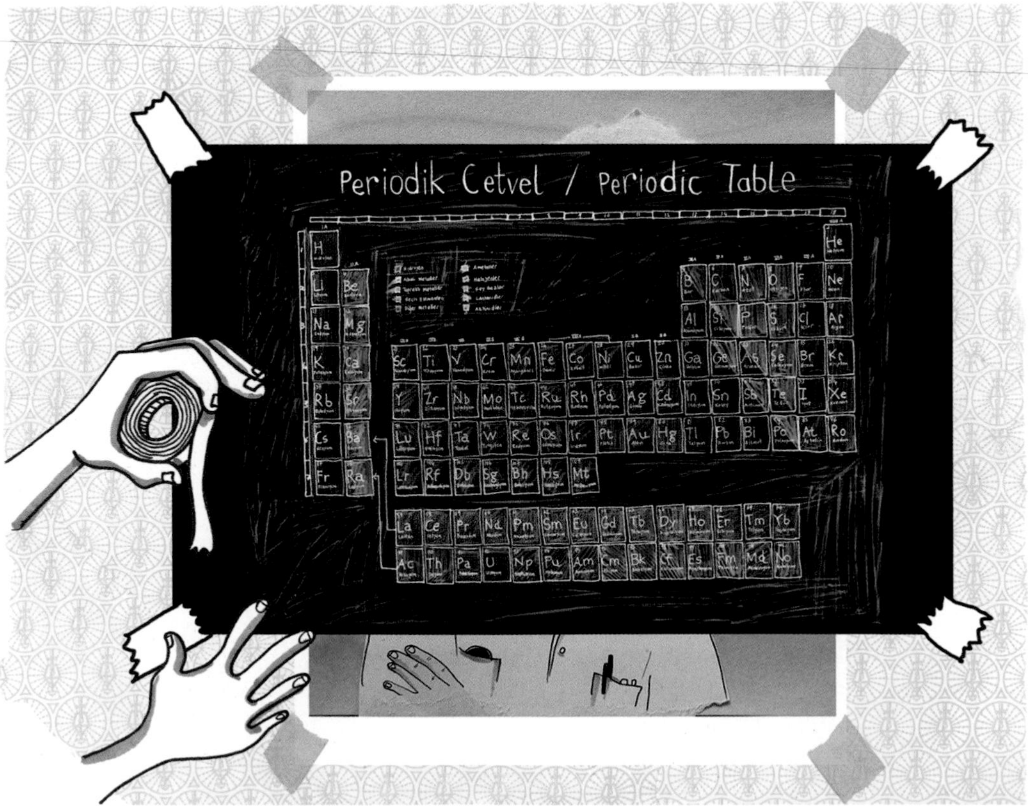
Periodik Cetvel / Periodic Table

Chapter 10

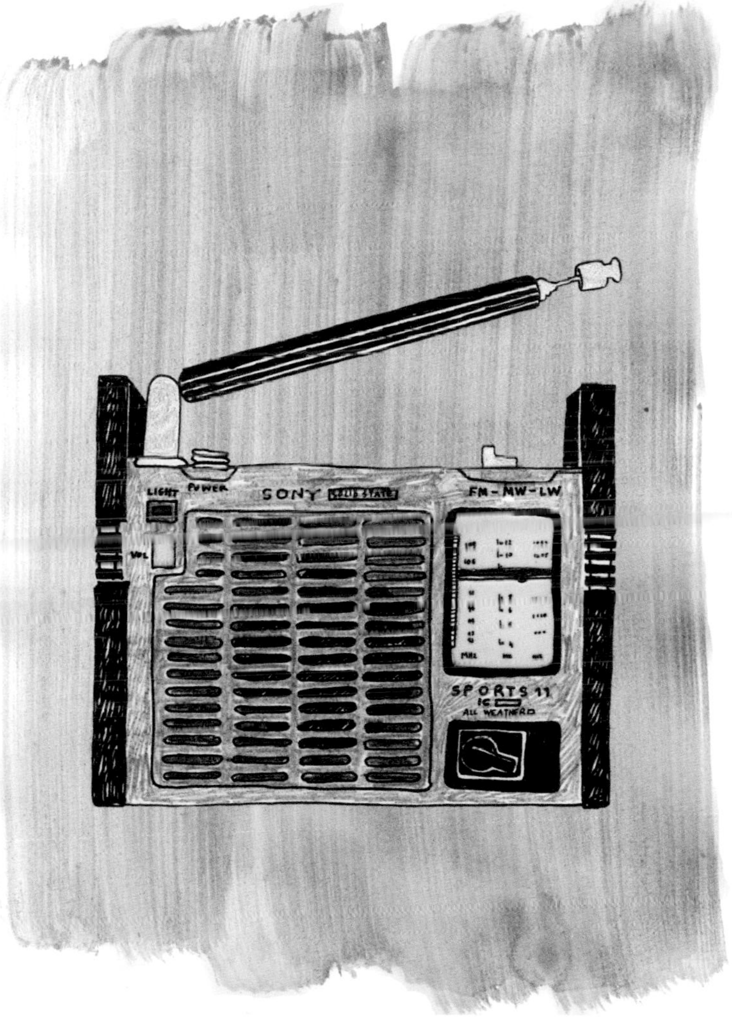

LIGHT
POWER
SONY
SOLID STATE
FM-MW-LW
VOL
SPORTS 11
IC
ALL WEATHERED

Broken Radio

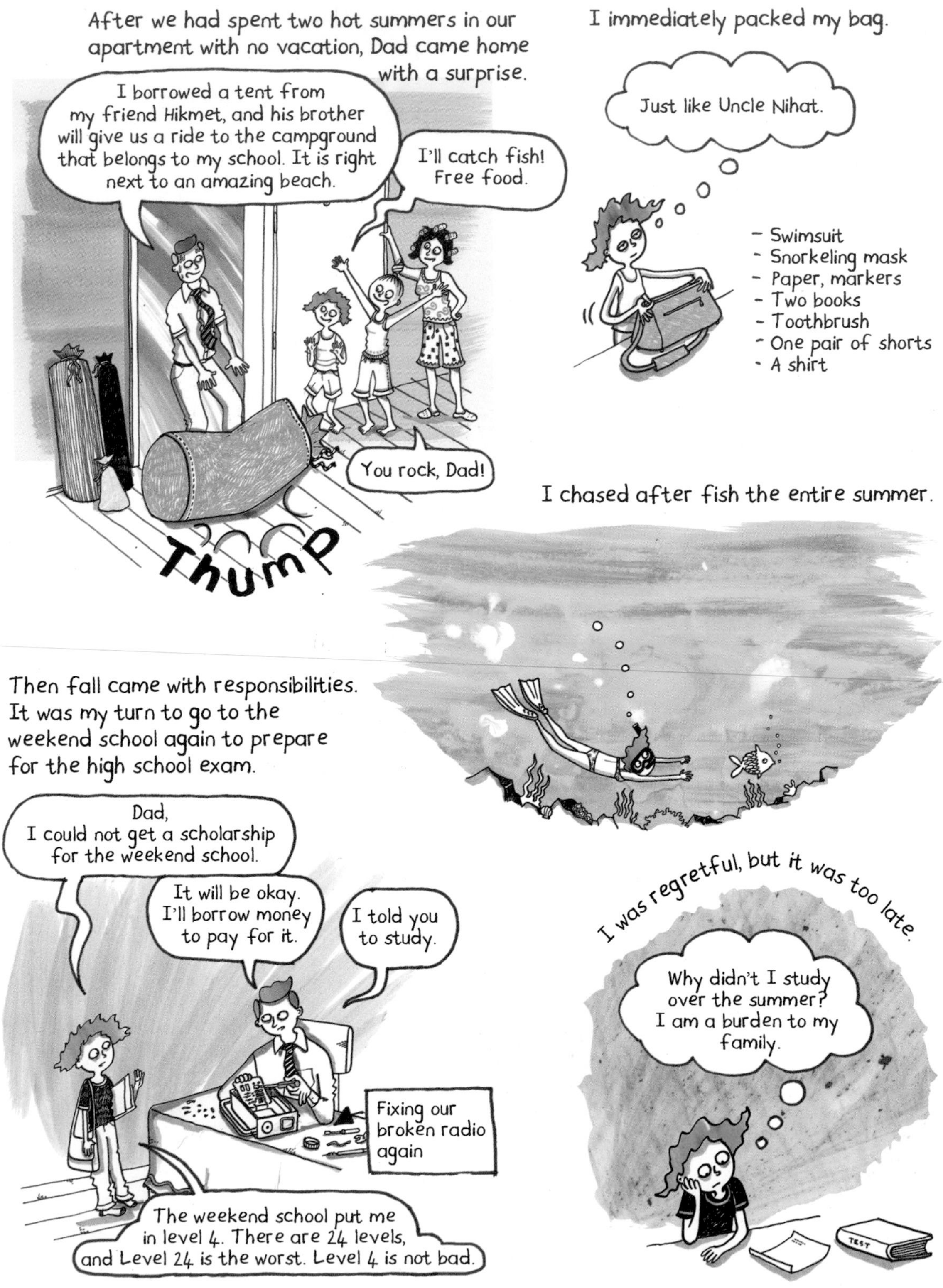

After we had spent two hot summers in our apartment with no vacation, Dad came home with a surprise.
I borrowed a tent from my friend Hikmet, and his brother will give us a ride to the campground that belongs to my school. It is right next to an amazing beach.
I'll catch fish! Free food.
You rock, Dad!
Thump
I immediately packed my bag.
Just like Uncle Nihat.
- Swimsuit
- Snorkeling mask
- Paper, markers
- Two books
- Toothbrush
- One pair of shorts
- A shirt
I chased after fish the entire summer.
Then fall came with responsibilities. It was my turn to go to the weekend school again to prepare for the high school exam.
Dad, I could not get a scholarship for the weekend school.
It will be okay. I'll borrow money to pay for it.
I told you to study.
Fixing our broken radio again
The weekend school put me in level 4. There are 24 levels, and Level 24 is the worst. Level 4 is not bad.
I was regretful, but it was too late.
Why didn't I study over the summer? I am a burden to my family.
TEST

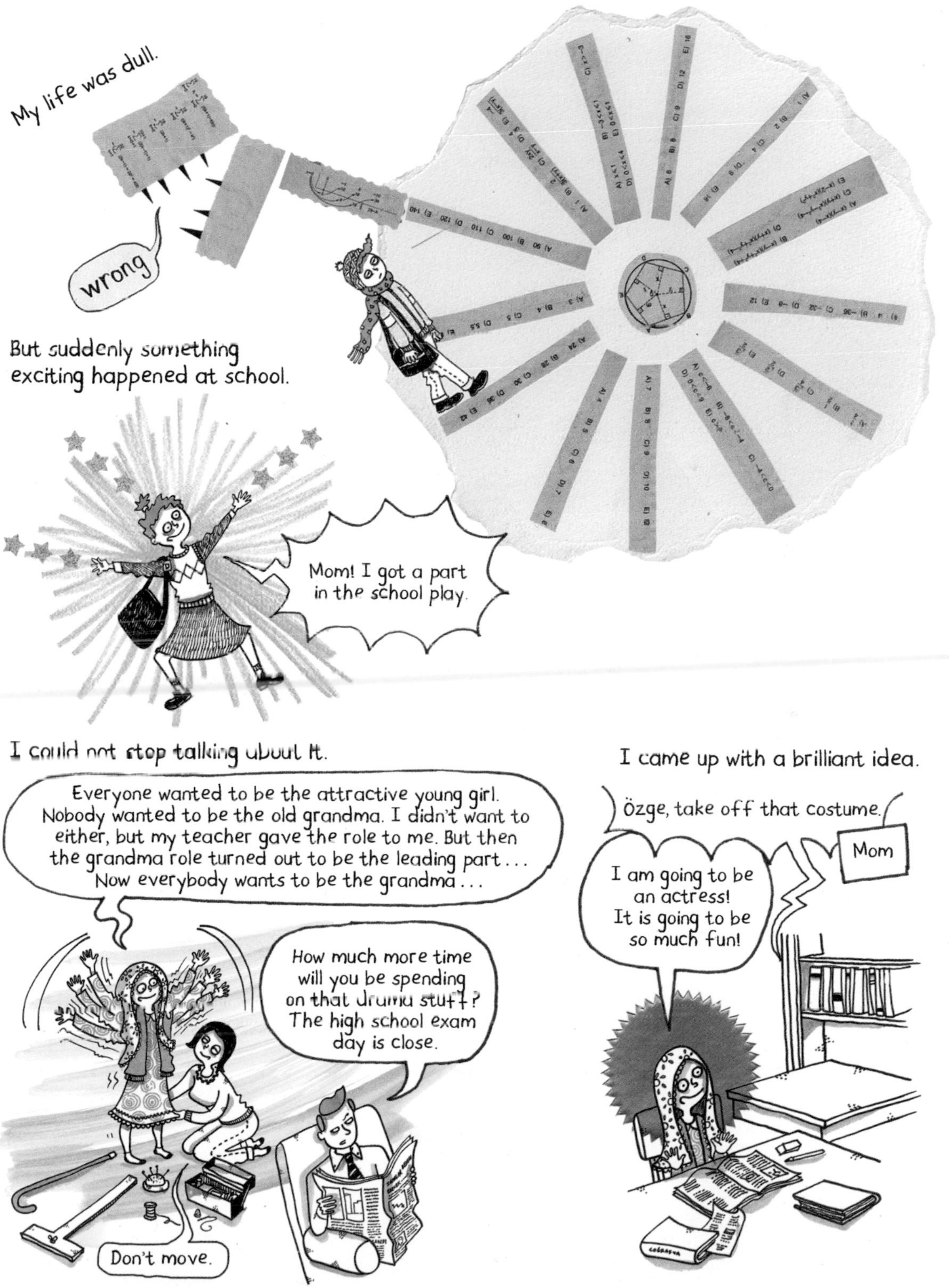

My life was dull.
wrong
But suddenly something exciting happened at school.
Mom! I got a part in the school play.
I could not stop talking about it.
Everyone wanted to be the attractive young girl. Nobody wanted to be the old grandma. I didn't want to either, but my teacher gave the role to me. But then the grandma role turned out to be the leading part . . . Now everybody wants to be the grandma . . .
How much more time will you be spending on that drama stuff? The high school exam day is close.
Don't move.
I came up with a brilliant idea.
Özge, take off that costume.
Mom
I am going to be an actress! It is going to be so much fun!

I immediately started telling everyone about my brilliant idea.

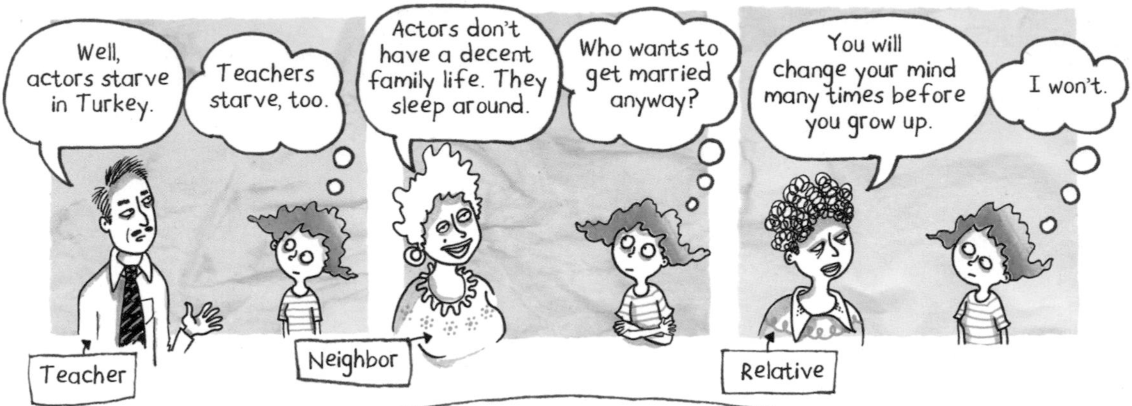
Well, actors starve in Turkey.
Teachers starve, too.
Actors don't have a decent family life. They sleep around.
Who wants to get married anyway?
You will change your mind many times before you grow up.
I won't.
Teacher
Neighbor
Relative

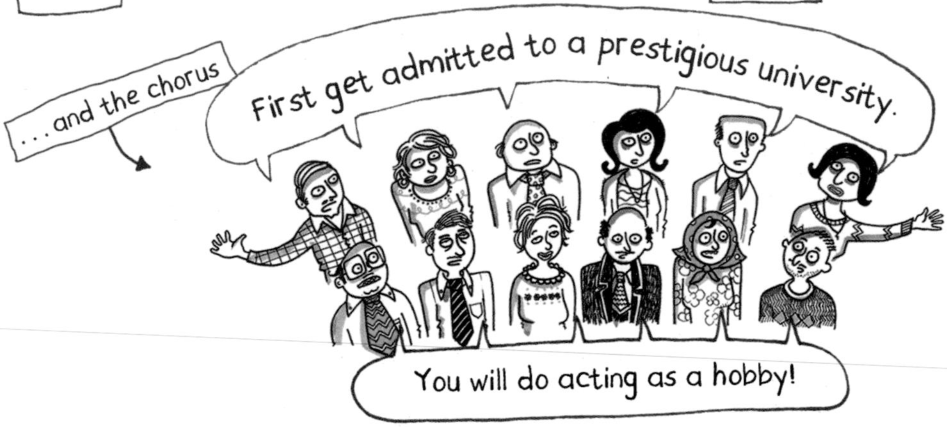
. . . and the chorus
First get admitted to a prestigious university.
You will do acting as a hobby!

After hearing the chorus I went back to studying.

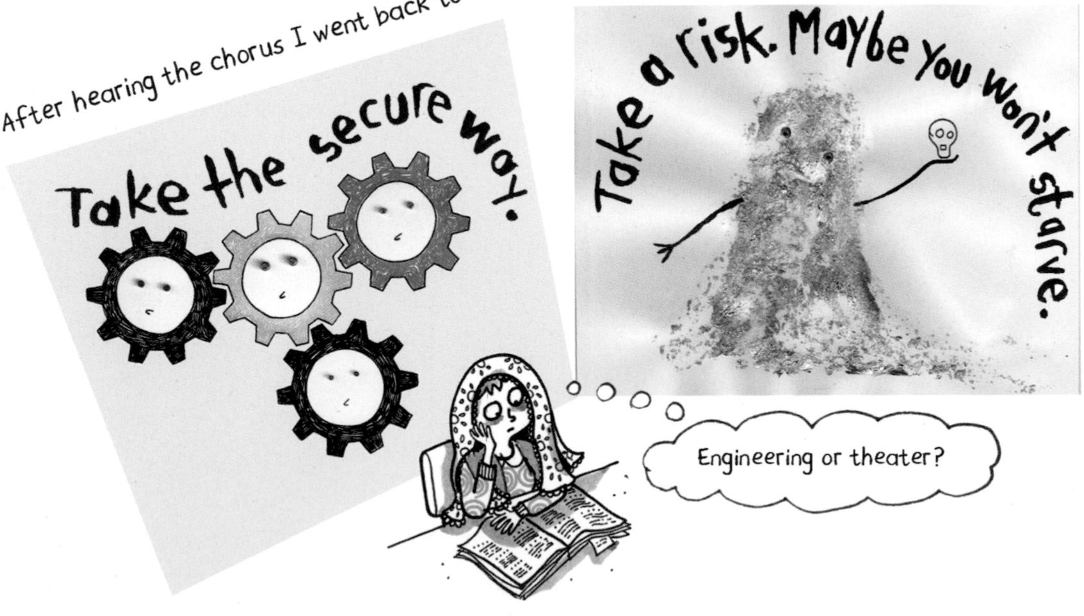
Take the secure way.
Take a risk. Maybe you won't starve.
Engineering or theater?

Our school play was a success, but my high school exam result was not.

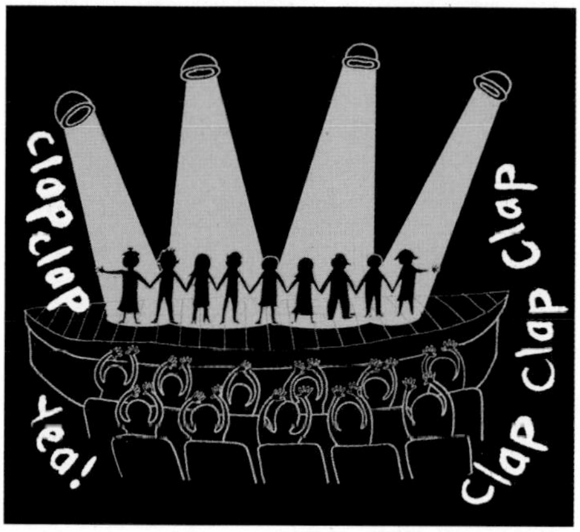

Clapclap
Yea!
Clap Clap Clap

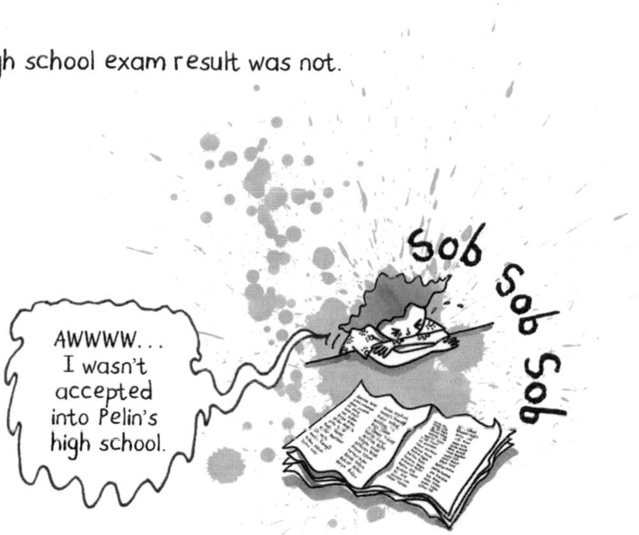

AWWWW... I wasn't accepted into Pelin's high school.
Sob Sob Sob

I was admitted to a less prestigious public school, Istanbul Atatürk Science High School.

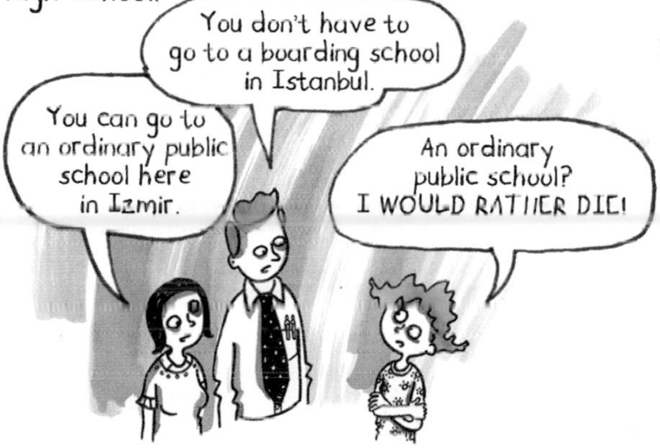

You can go to an ordinary public school here in Izmir.
You don't have to go to a boarding school in Istanbul.
An ordinary public school? I WOULD RATHER DIE!

I was 14. My wish to live in Istanbul had come true, but I was not happy.

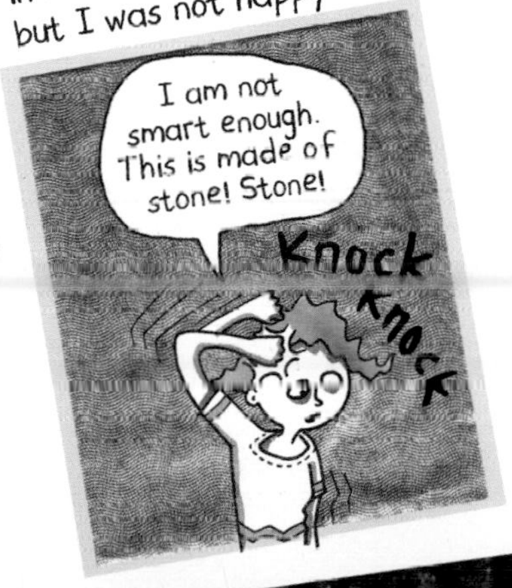

I am not smart enough. This is made of stone! Stone!
Knock Knock

Mom took me to Istanbul on an overnight bus.

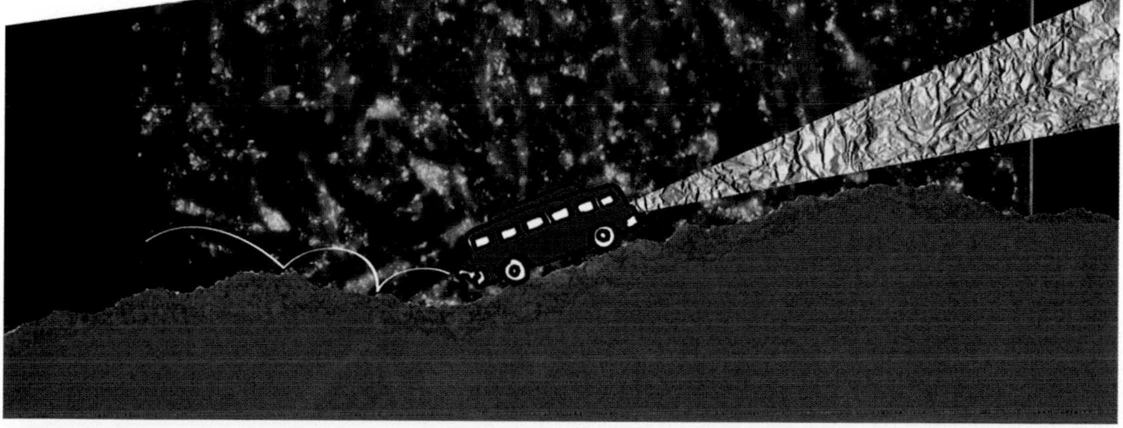

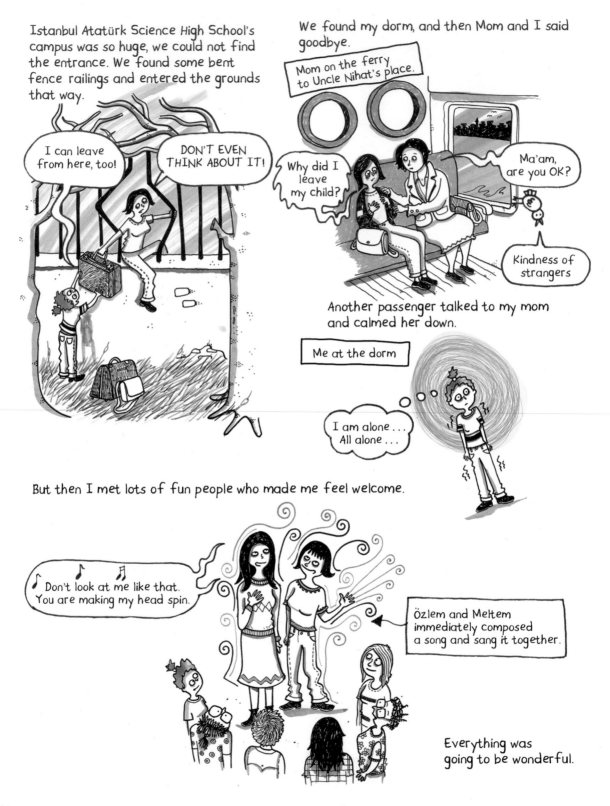

Istanbul Atatürk Science High School's campus was so huge, we could not find the entrance. We found some bent fence railings and entered the grounds that way.

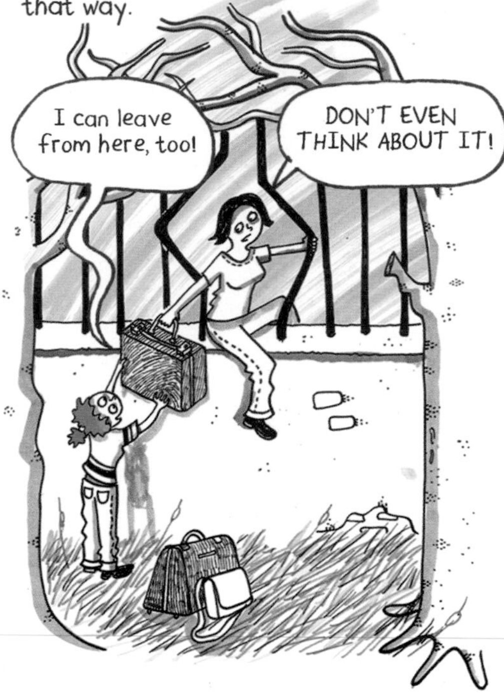
I can leave from here, too!
DON'T EVEN THINK ABOUT IT!

We found my dorm, and then Mom and I said goodbye.

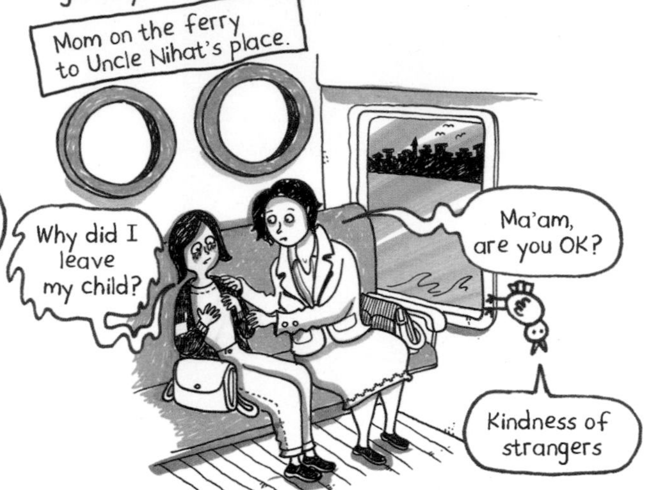
Mom on the ferry to Uncle Nihat's place.
Why did I leave my child?
Ma'am, are you OK?
Kindness of strangers

Another passenger talked to my mom and calmed her down.

Me at the dorm

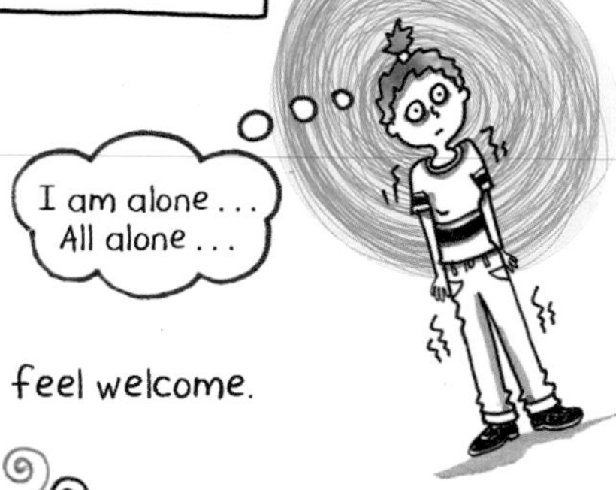
I am alone . . .
All alone . . .

But then I met lots of fun people who made me feel welcome.

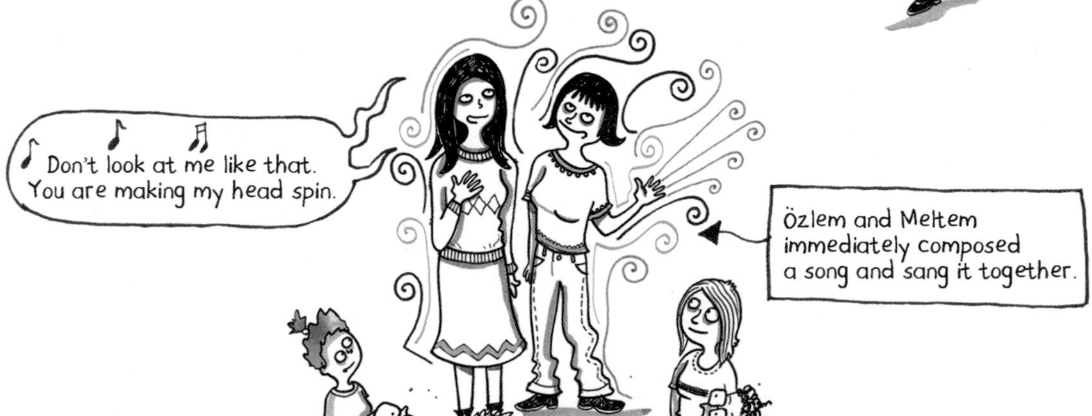
Don't look at me like that.
You are making my head spin.
Özlem and Meltem immediately composed a song and sang it together.

Everything was going to be wonderful.

But we all had to face reality in the morning. The teachers on duty had a cruel method of waking us up.

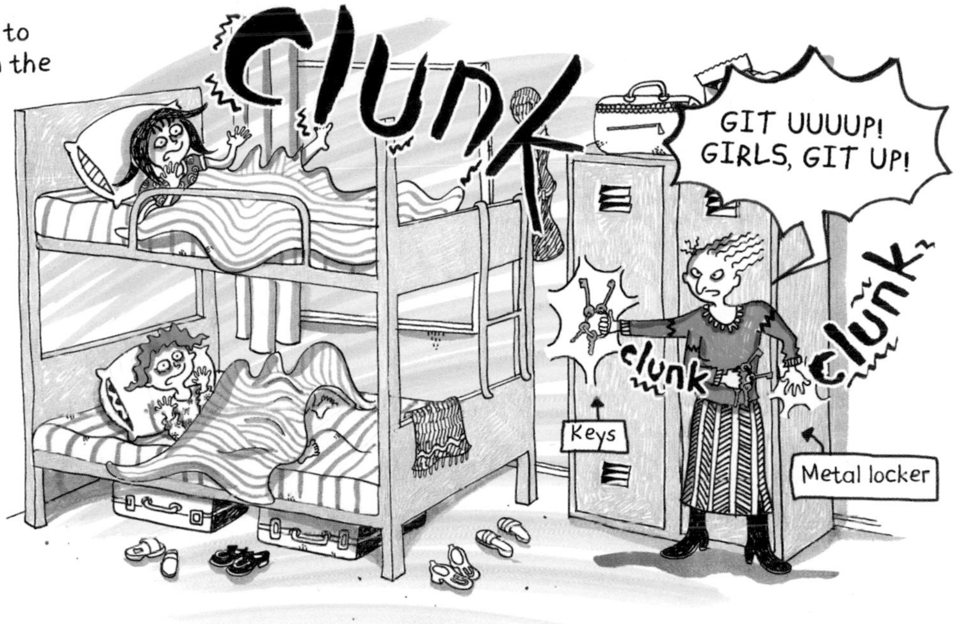
CLUNK
GIT UUUUP! GIRLS, GIT UP!
clunk
clunk
Keys
Metal locker

Breakfast was scary.

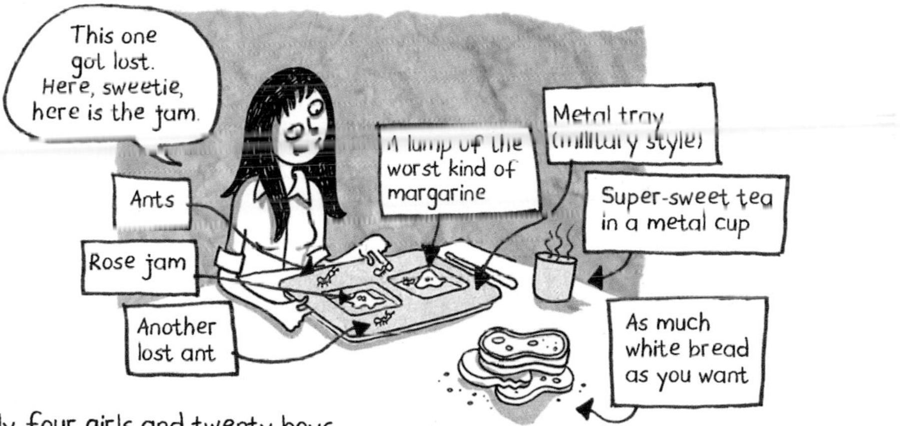
This one got lost. Here, sweetie, here is the jam.
Ants
Rose jam
Another lost ant
A lump of the worst kind of margarine
Metal tray (military style)
Super-sweet tea in a metal cup
As much white bread as you want

In our class there were only four girls and twenty boys.

Many of the boys in the school came from conservative families who were practicing Muslims.

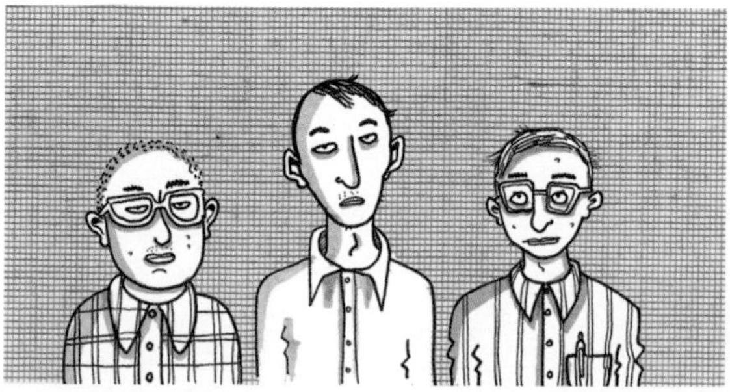

Many of the girls came from liberal families who were nonpracticing Muslims.

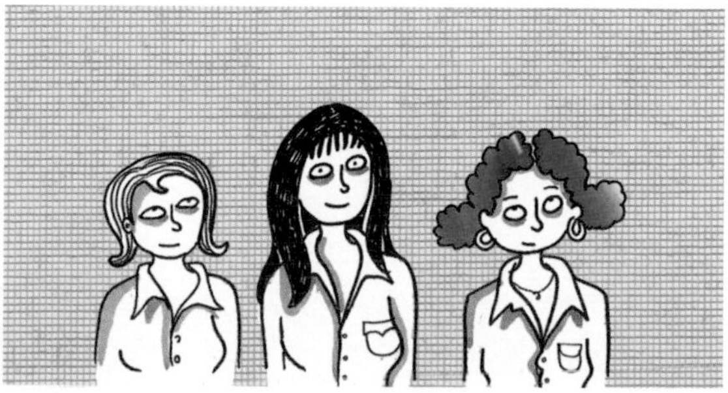

There were a few girls in the school who came from conservative families, but most conservative families were not inclined to send their daughters to a boarding school.

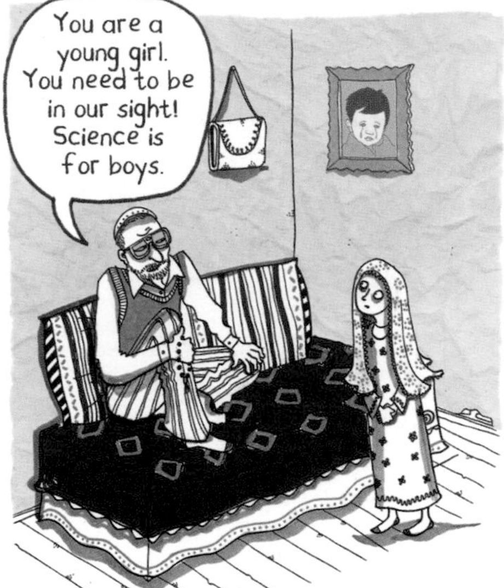
You are a young girl. You need to be in our sight! Science is for boys.

Most of the boys were intimidated by girls, so they simply ignored us.

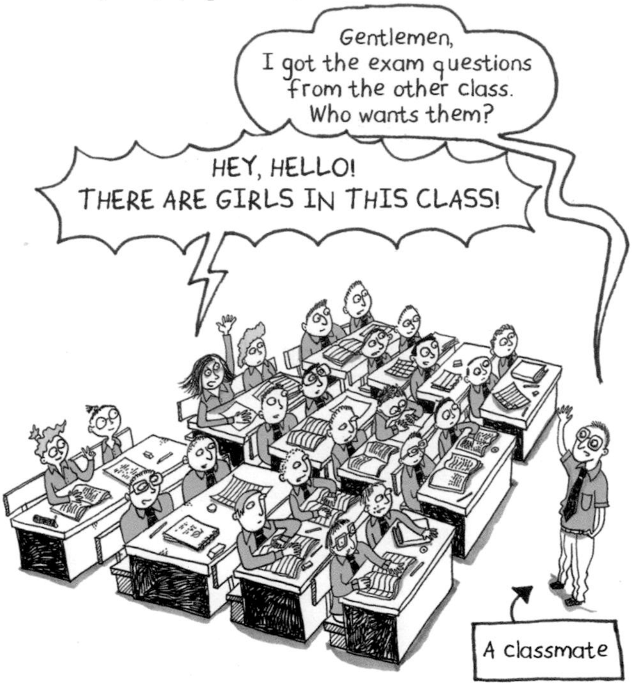
Gentlemen, I got the exam questions from the other class. Who wants them?
HEY, HELLO! THERE ARE GIRLS IN THIS CLASS!
A classmate

In the eyes of some of our male classmates we were promiscuous and valueless.

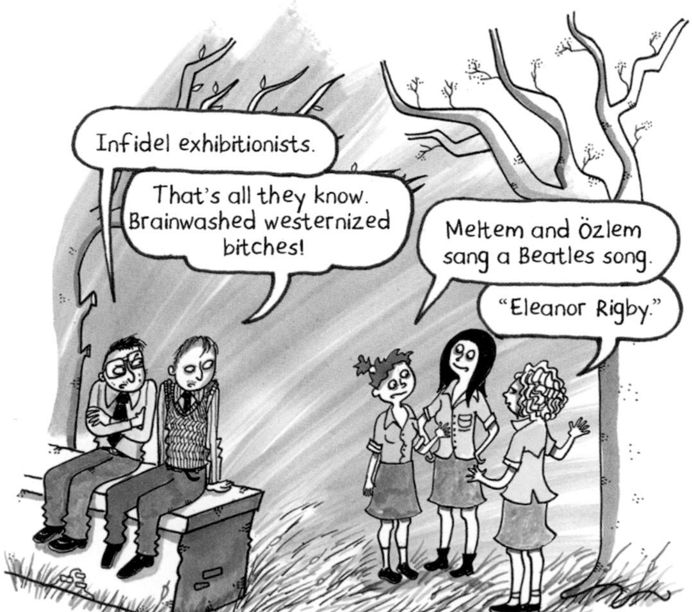
Infidel exhibitionists.
That's all they know. Brainwashed westernized bitches!
Meltem and Özlem sang a Beatles song.
"Eleanor Rigby."

In our eyes they were wearing blinders and were extremely dull.

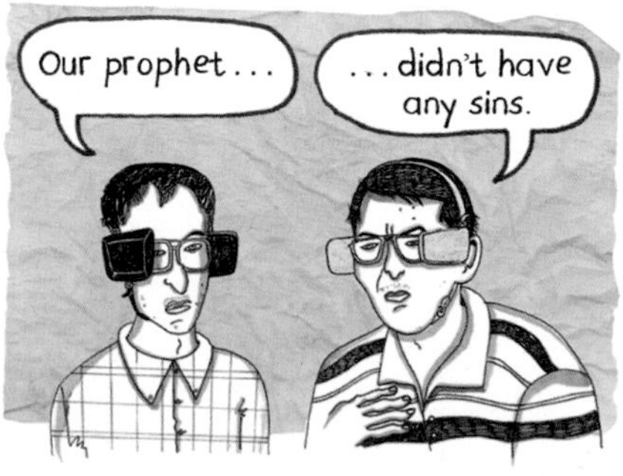
Our prophet . . .
. . . didn't have any sins.

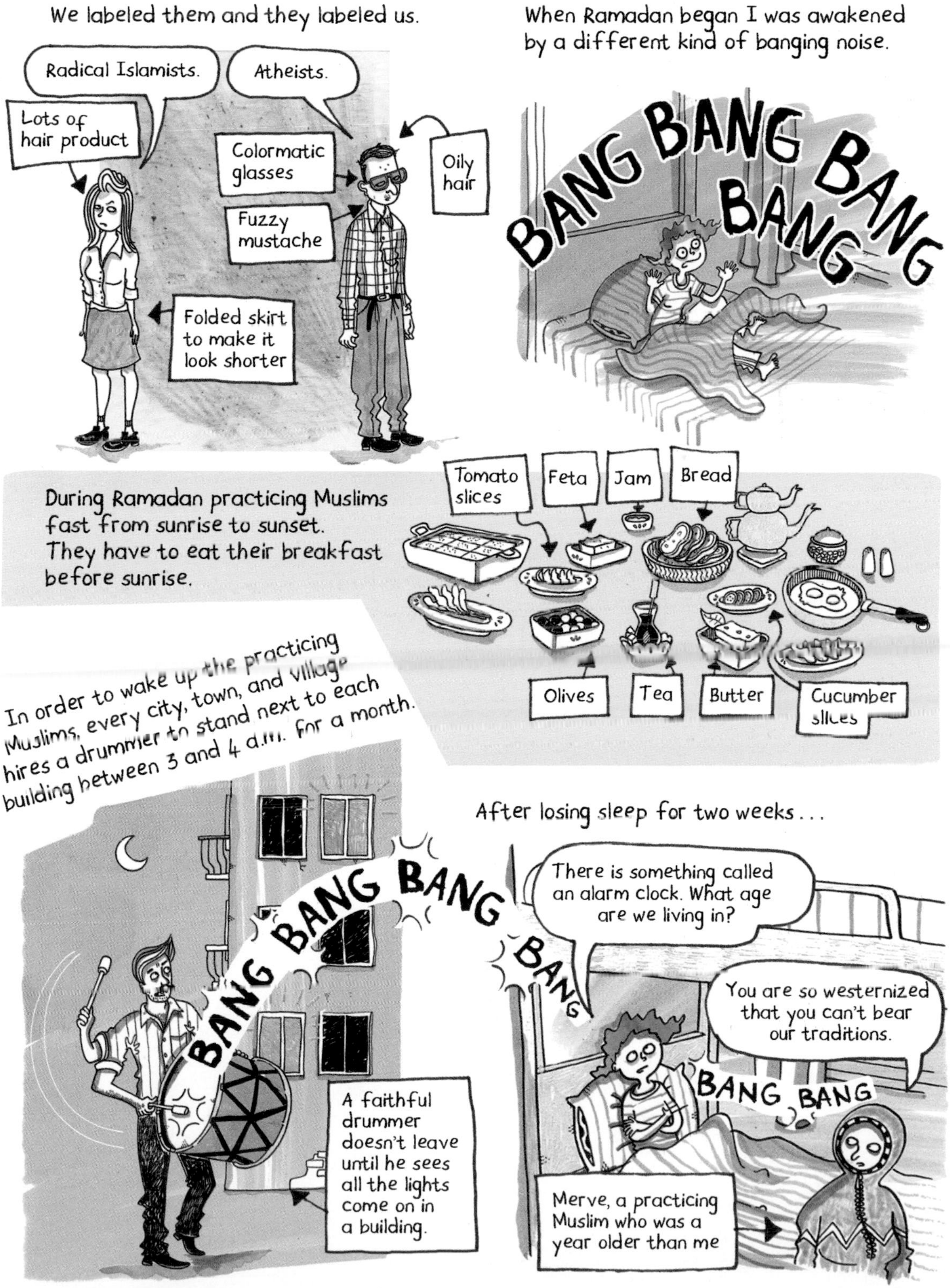

We labeled them and they labeled us.
Radical Islamists.
Atheists.
Lots of hair product
Colormatic glasses
Oily hair
Fuzzy mustache
Folded skirt to make it look shorter
When Ramadan began I was awakened by a different kind of banging noise.
BANG BANG BANG BANG BANG BANG
During Ramadan practicing Muslims fast from sunrise to sunset. They have to eat their breakfast before sunrise.
Tomato slices
Feta
Jam
Bread
Olives
Tea
Butter
Cucumber slices
In order to wake up the practicing Muslims, every city, town, and village hires a drummer to stand next to each building between 3 and 4 a.m. for a month.
BANG BANG BANG BANG
A faithful drummer doesn't leave until he sees all the lights come on in a building.
After losing sleep for two weeks . . .
There is something called an alarm clock. What age are we living in?
You are so westernized that you can't bear our traditions.
BANG BANG
Merve, a practicing Muslim who was a year older than me

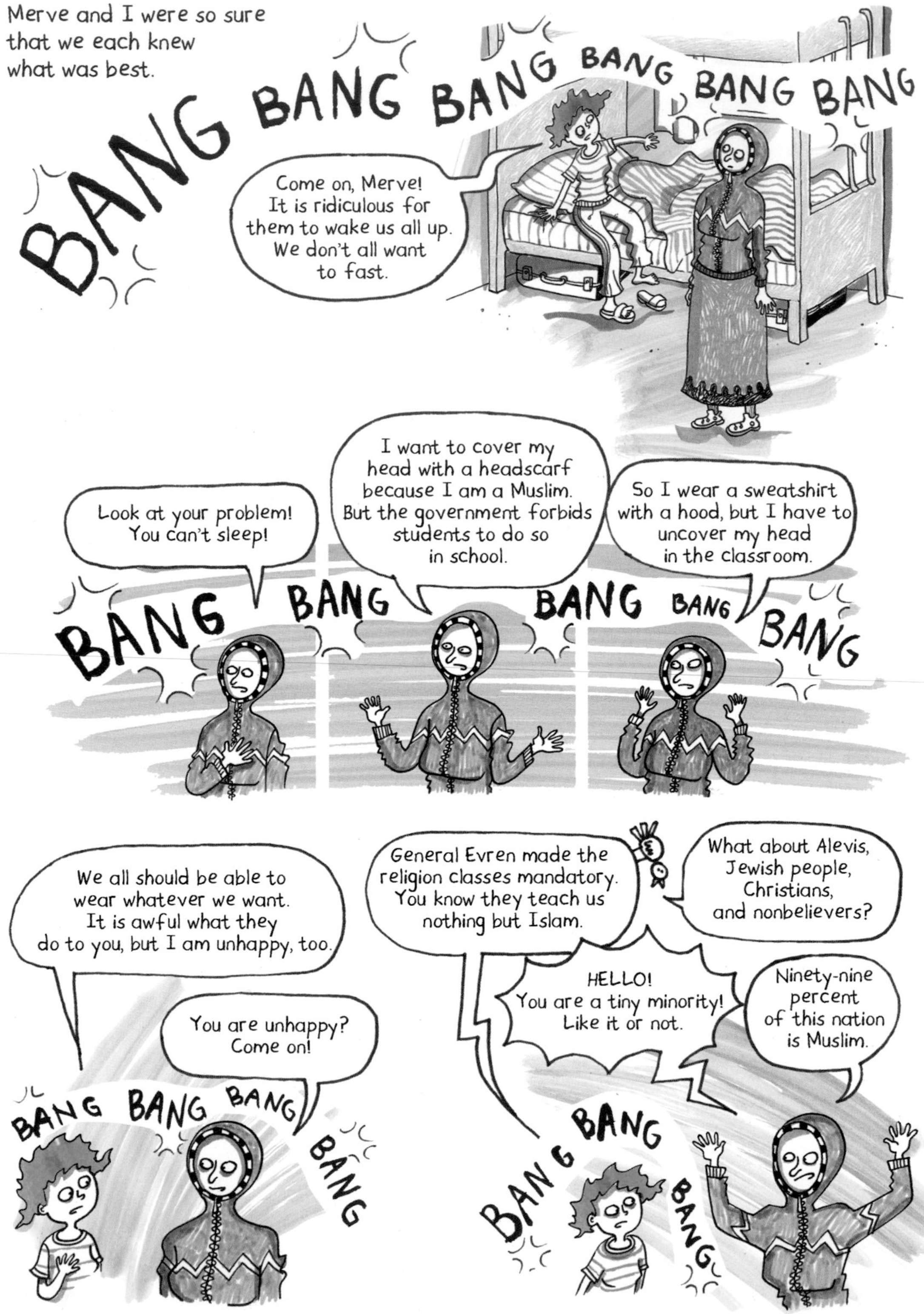
Merve and I were so sure that we each knew what was best.
BANG BANG BANG BANG BANG BANG
Come on, Merve! It is ridiculous for them to wake us all up. We don't all want to fast.
Look at your problem! You can't sleep!
BANG
I want to cover my head with a headscarf because I am a Muslim. But the government forbids students to do so in school.
BANG
So I wear a sweatshirt with a hood, but I have to uncover my head in the classroom.
BANG BANG BANG
We all should be able to wear whatever we want. It is awful what they do to you, but I am unhappy, too.
You are unhappy? Come on!
BANG BANG BANG BANG
General Evren made the religion classes mandatory. You know they teach us nothing but Islam.
What about Alevis, Jewish people, Christians, and nonbelievers?
HELLO! You are a tiny minority! Like it or not.
Ninety-nine percent of this nation is Muslim.
BANG BANG BANG

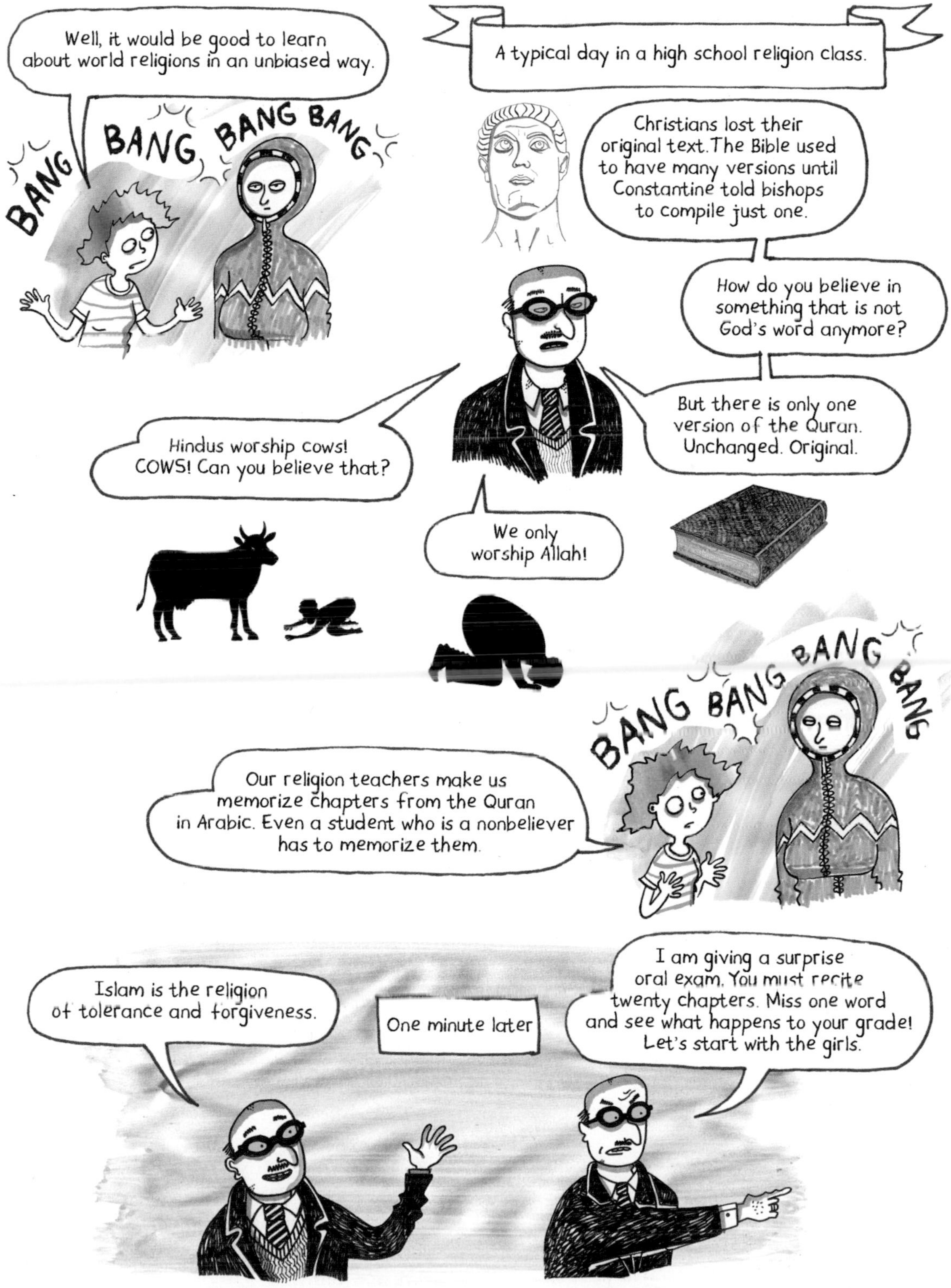
Well, it would be good to learn about world religions in an unbiased way.
BANG BANG, BANG BANG
A typical day in a high school religion class.
Christians lost their original text. The Bible used to have many versions until Constantine told bishops to compile just one.
How do you believe in something that is not God's word anymore?
But there is only one version of the Quran. Unchanged. Original.
Hindus worship cows! COWS! Can you believe that?
We only worship Allah!
BANG BANG BANG BANG
Our religion teachers make us memorize chapters from the Quran in Arabic. Even a student who is a nonbeliever has to memorize them.
Islam is the religion of tolerance and forgiveness.
One minute later
I am giving a surprise oral exam. You must recite twenty chapters. Miss one word and see what happens to your grade! Let's start with the girls.

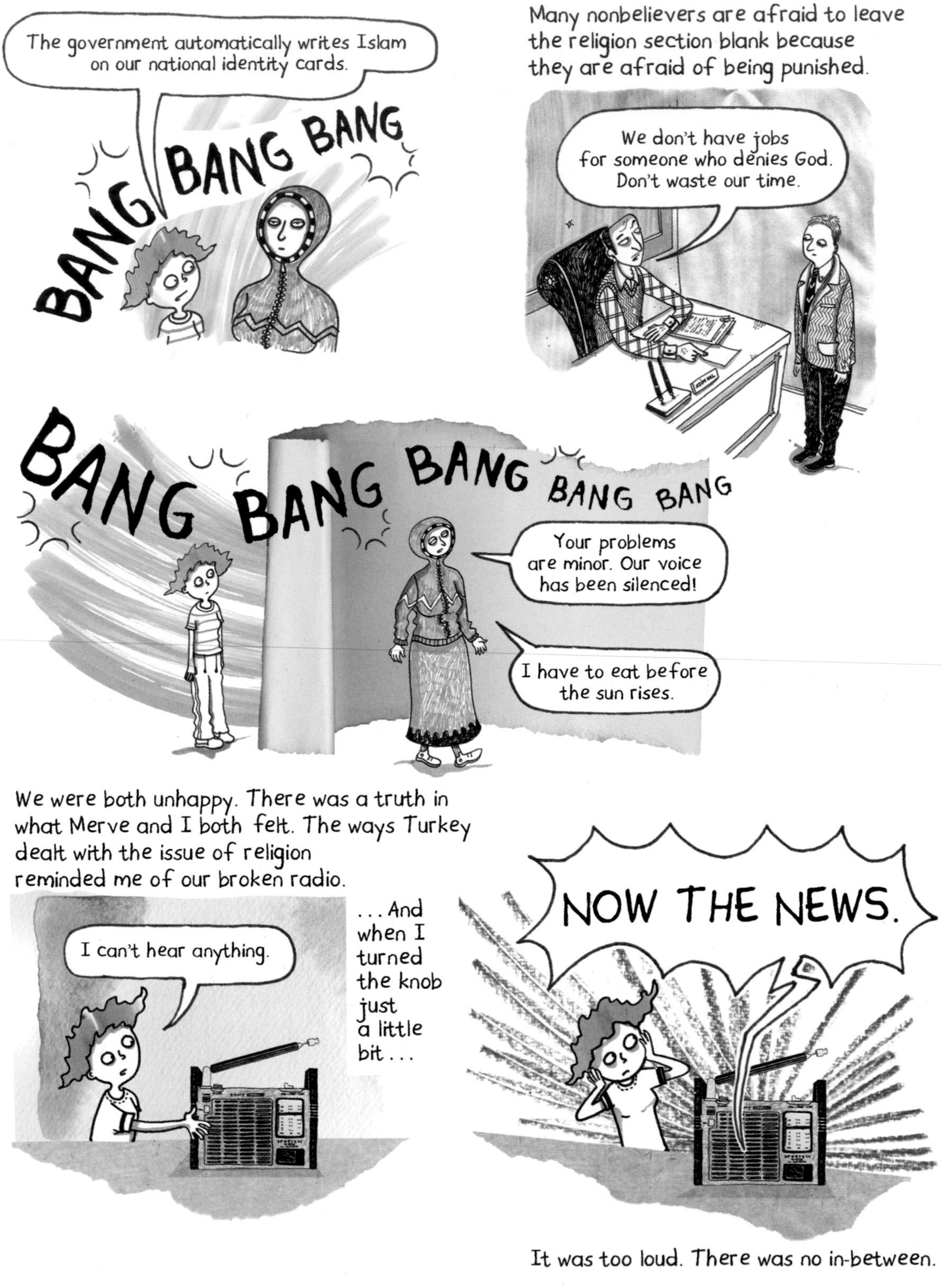
The government automatically writes Islam on our national identity cards.
BANG BANG BANG
Many nonbelievers are afraid to leave the religion section blank because they are afraid of being punished.
We don't have jobs for someone who denies God. Don't waste our time.
BANG BANG BANG BANG BANG
Your problems are minor. Our voice has been silenced!
I have to eat before the sun rises.
We were both unhappy. There was a truth in what Merve and I both felt. The ways Turkey dealt with the issue of religion reminded me of our broken radio.
I can't hear anything.
. . . And when I turned the knob just a little bit . . .
NOW THE NEWS.
It was too loud. There was no in-between.

Chapter 11

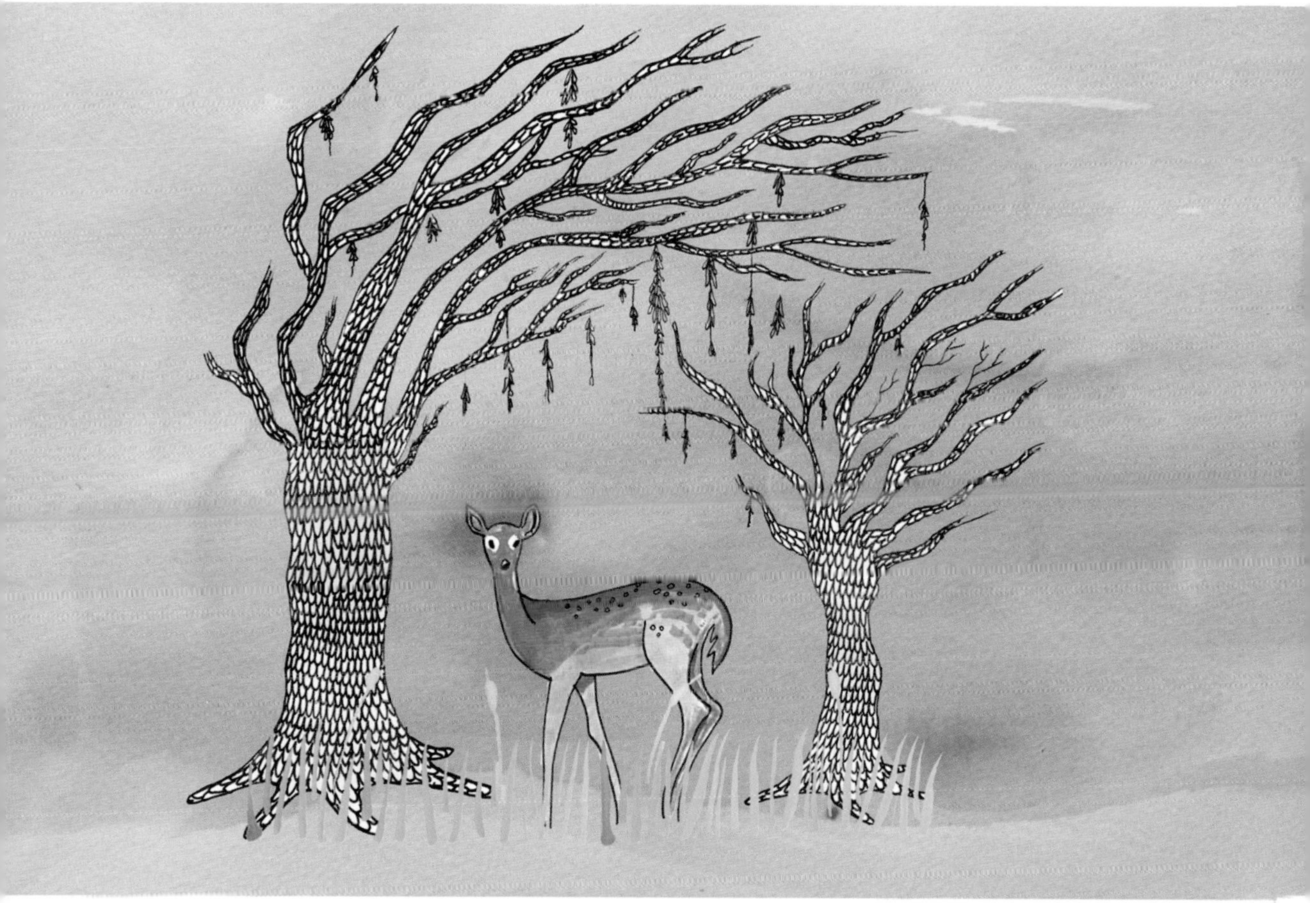

Hunting Ground

The most ironic thing in our high school was the principal.

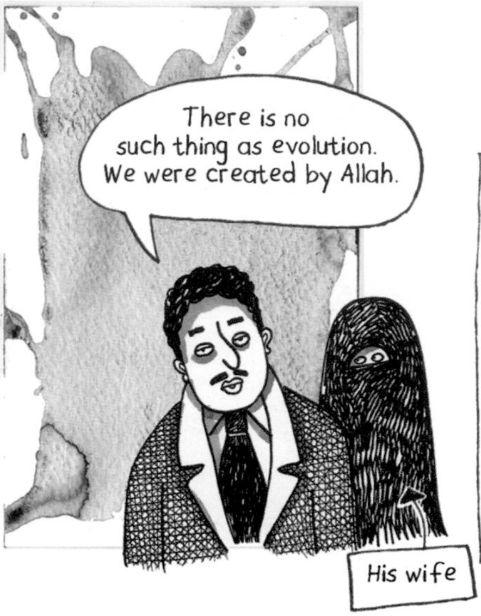
There is no such thing as evolution. We were created by Allah.
His wife

The polarization of the student body was a product of the principal's and some of the teachers' efforts.

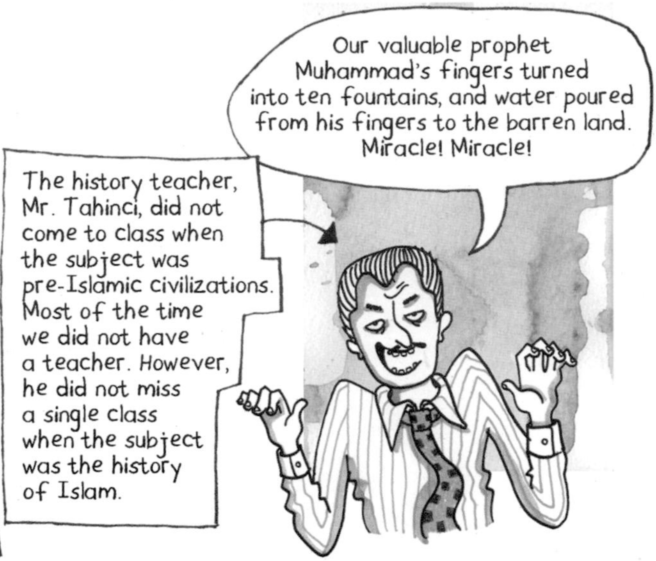
The history teacher, Mr. Tahinci, did not come to class when the subject was pre-Islamic civilizations. Most of the time we did not have a teacher. However, he did not miss a single class when the subject was the history of Islam.
Our valuable prophet Muhammad's fingers turned into ten fountains, and water poured from his fingers to the barren land. Miracle! Miracle!

The Turkish literature teacher, Mr. Çetin, was a rich businessman who owned a factory. He did not need that little teacher's salary. He used his teaching position to organize religious students.

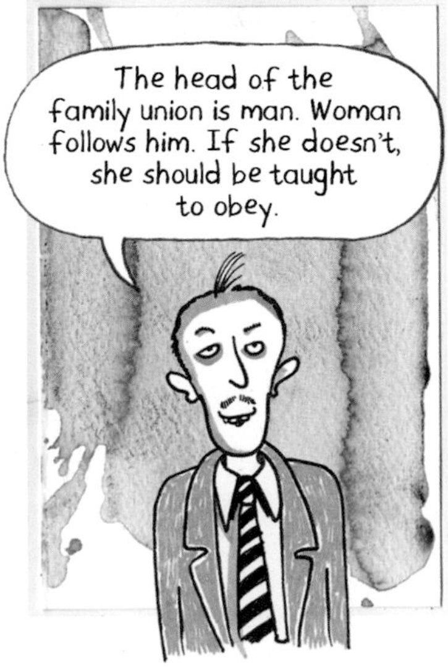
The head of the family union is man. Woman follows him. If she doesn't, she should be taught to obey.

The religion and ethics teacher, Mr. Mahluki, had a bunch of theories, mostly about women's blood circulation.

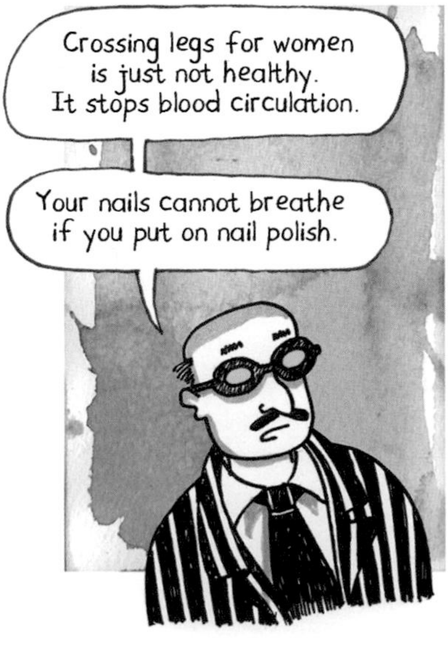
Crossing legs for women is just not healthy. It stops blood circulation.
Your nails cannot breathe if you put on nail polish.

The principal and these teachers assigned an older student from the conservative and religious side to help us during study hours.

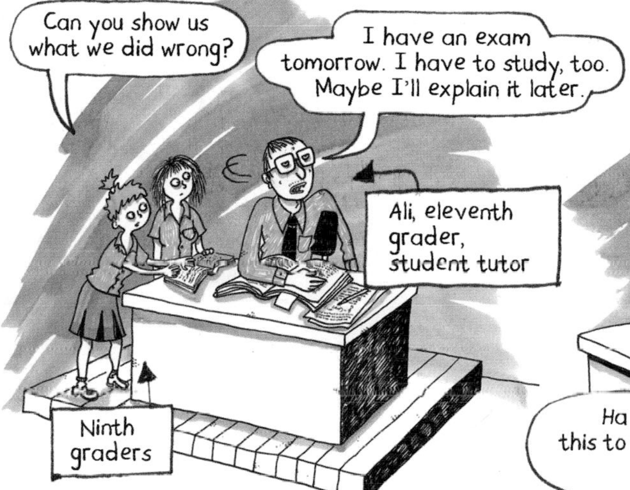
Can you show us what we did wrong?
I have an exam tomorrow. I have to study, too. Maybe I'll explain it later.
Ali, eleventh grader, student tutor
Ninth graders

Ali did not look at our faces while talking to us girls. He liked talking to and helping religious boys.

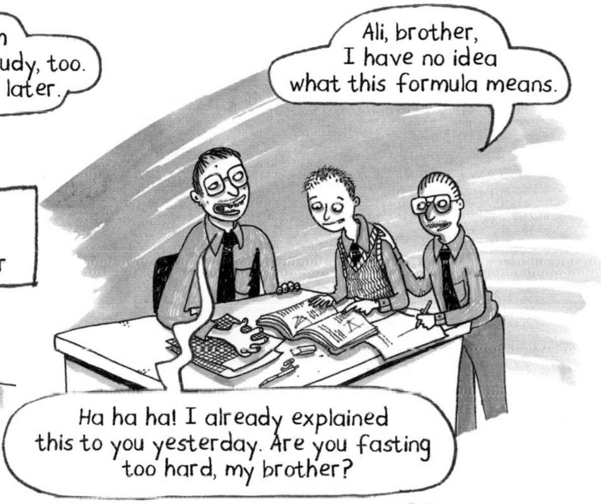
Ali, brother, I have no idea what this formula means.
Ha ha ha! I already explained this to you yesterday. Are you fasting too hard, my brother?

These teachers invited Muslim boys from low-income families to special places called lighthouses.

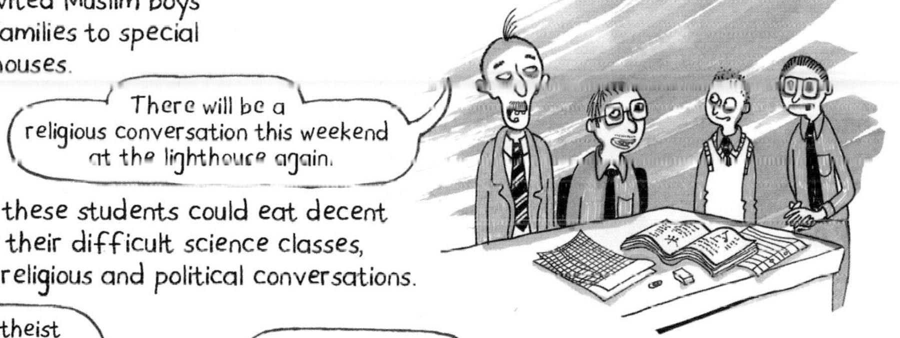
There will be a religious conversation this weekend at the lighthouse again.

In the lighthouses these students could eat decent food, get help for their difficult science classes, and participate in religious and political conversations.

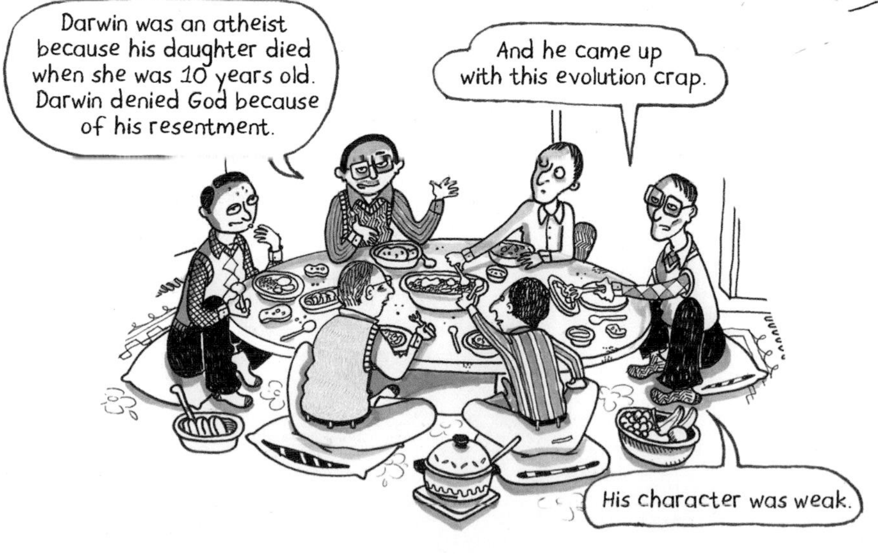
Darwin was an atheist because his daughter died when she was 10 years old. Darwin denied God because of his resentment.
And he came up with this evolution crap.
His character was weak.

These houses were funded by Gülen Foundation, a private organization whose aim was to move Turkey toward conservative and Islamic values.

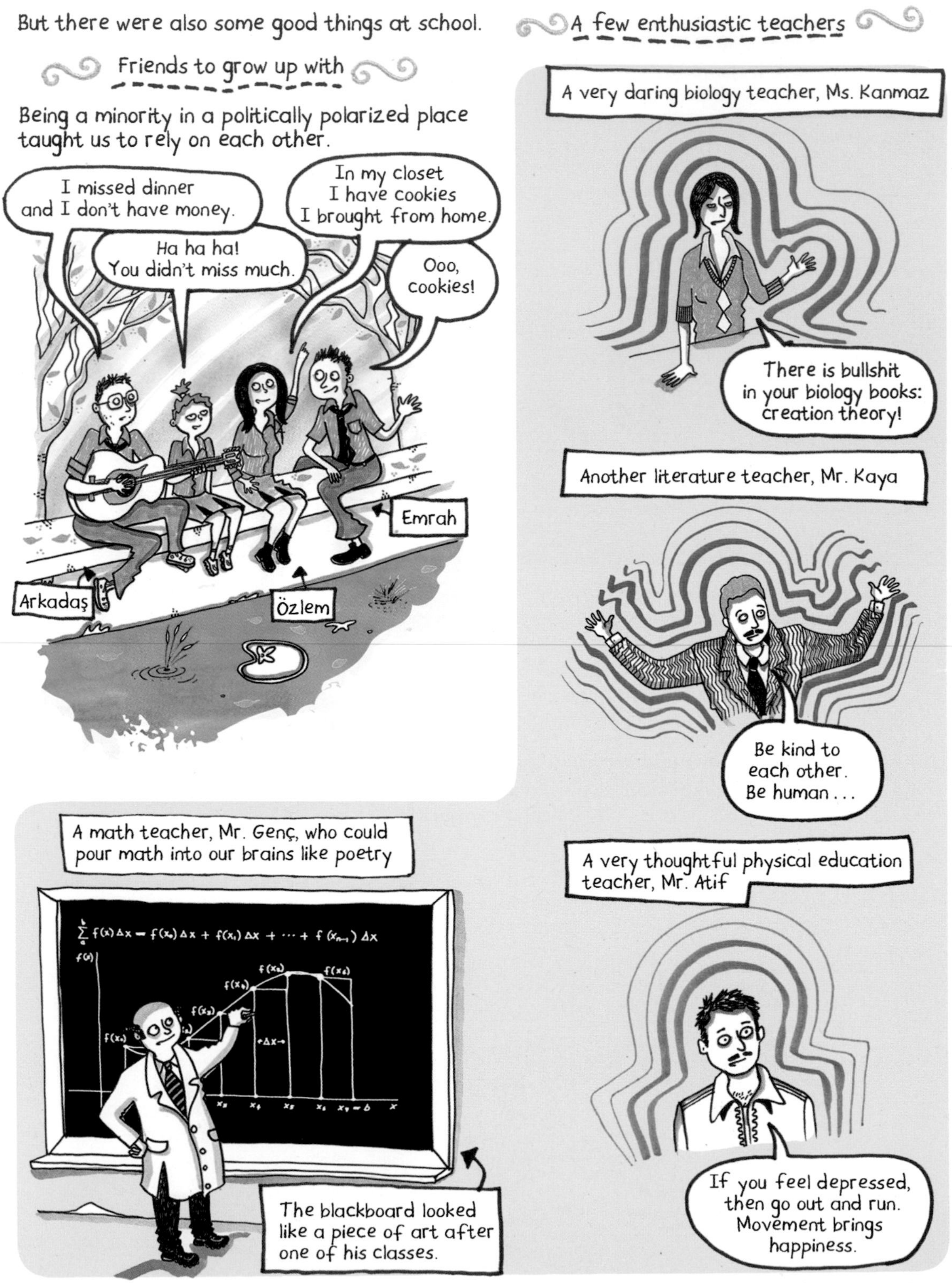
But there were also some good things at school.
Friends to grow up with
Being a minority in a politically polarized place taught us to rely on each other.
I missed dinner and I don't have money.
Ha ha ha! You didn't miss much.
In my closet I have cookies I brought from home.
Ooo, cookies!
Arkadaş
Özlem
Emrah
A few enthusiastic teachers
A very daring biology teacher, Ms. Kanmaz
There is bullshit in your biology books: creation theory!
Another literature teacher, Mr. Kaya
Be kind to each other. Be human . . .
A math teacher, Mr. Genç, who could pour math into our brains like poetry
$\sum_a^b f(x)\Delta x = f(x_0)\Delta x + f(x_1)\Delta x + \cdots + f(x_{n-1})\Delta x$
The blackboard looked like a piece of art after one of his classes.
A very thoughtful physical education teacher, Mr. Atif
If you feel depressed, then go out and run. Movement brings happiness.

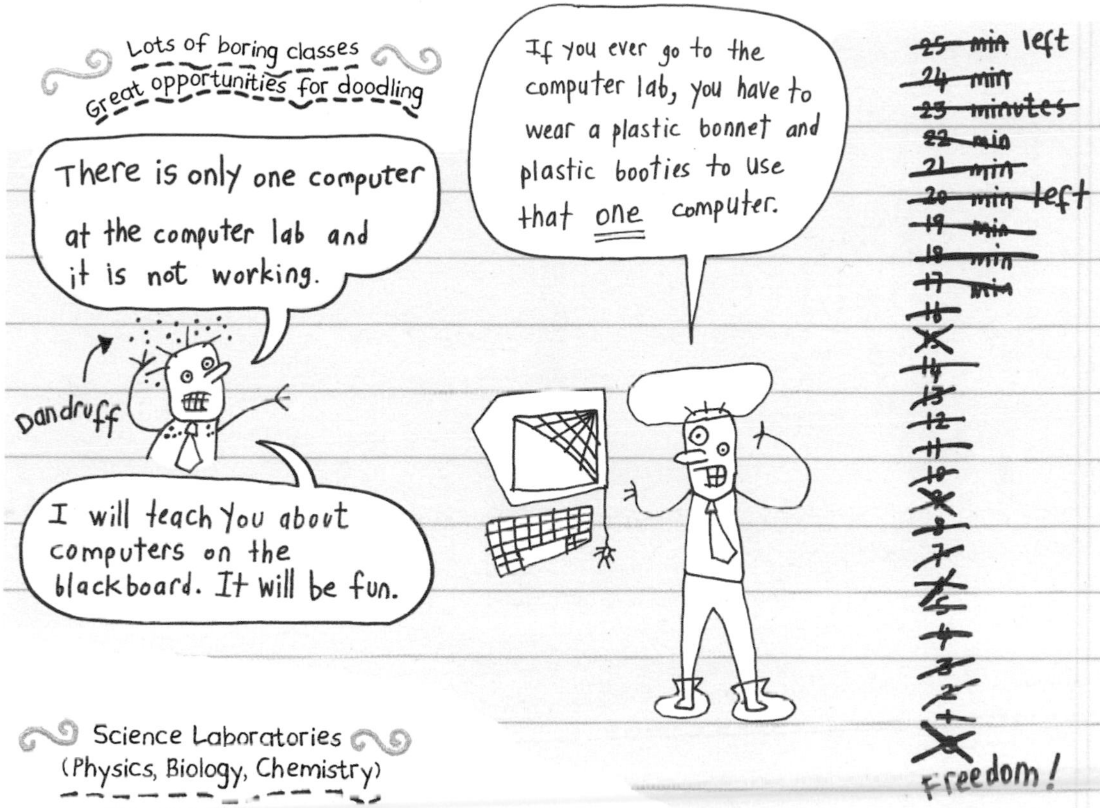
Lots of boring classes
Great opportunities for doodling
There is only one computer at the computer lab and it is not working.
Dandruff
I will teach you about computers on the blackboard. It will be fun.
If you ever go to the computer lab, you have to wear a plastic bonnet and plastic booties to use that one computer.
25 min left
24 min
23 minutes
22 min
21 min
20 min left
19 min
18 min
17 min
16
14
13
12
11
10
8
7
5
4
3
2
1
Freedom!

Science Laboratories
(Physics, Biology, Chemistry)

In an ordinary public school
we would have only seen
a microscope in our dreams.

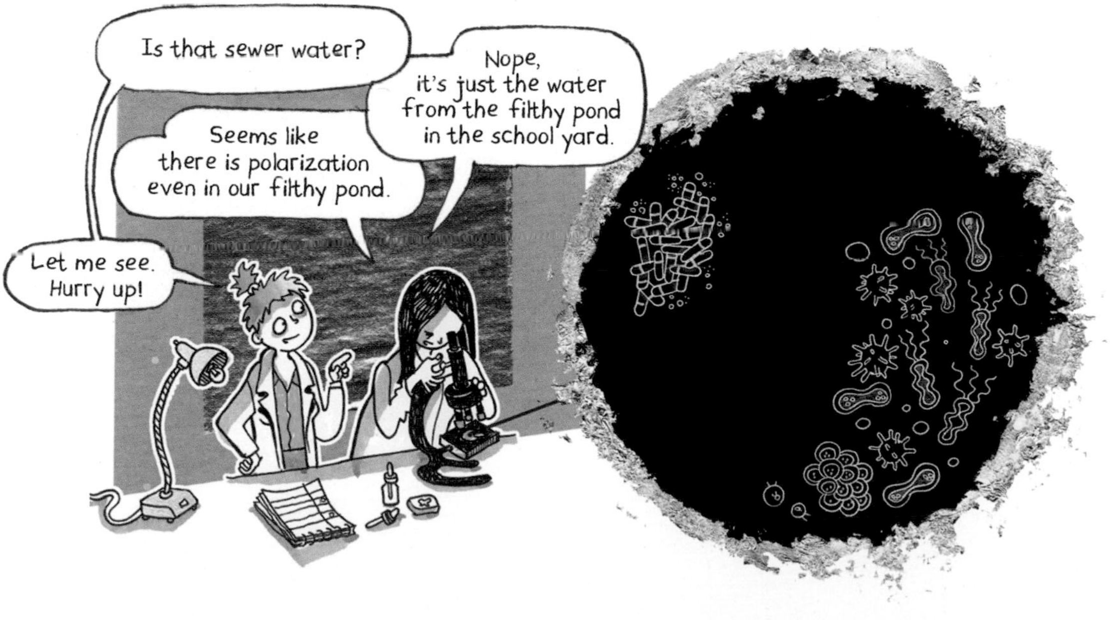
Is that sewer water?
Nope, it's just the water from the filthy pond in the school yard.
Seems like there is polarization even in our filthy pond.
Let me see. Hurry up!

Adventures

We would sneak out over the wall, but we could not reenter the school until morning since they locked the doors at night.

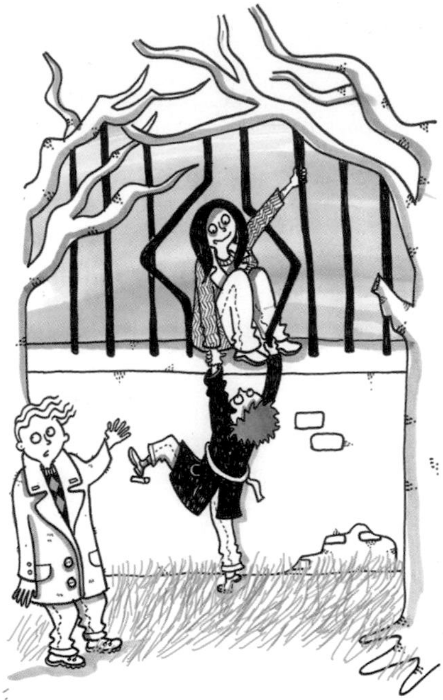

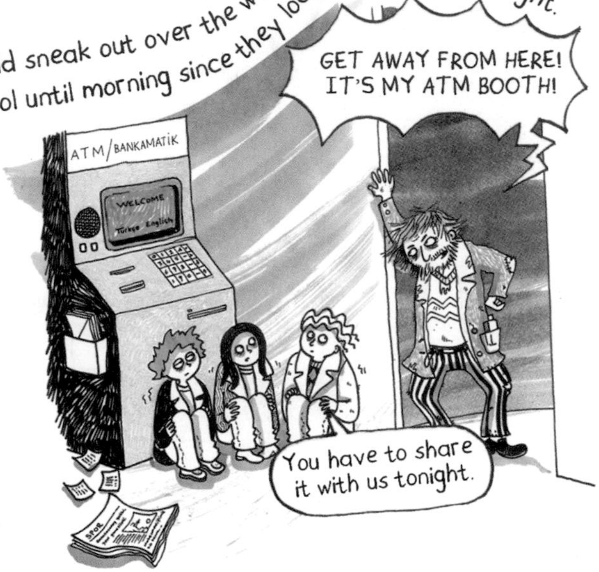
GET AWAY FROM HERE! IT'S MY ATM BOOTH!
ATM/BANKAMATİK
WELCOME
You have to share it with us tonight.

And the beautiful school yard

In the time of the Ottoman Empire some of the sultans loved hunting. Our school was established on land that once was the hunting ground of Sultan Murat IV of the Ottoman Empire.

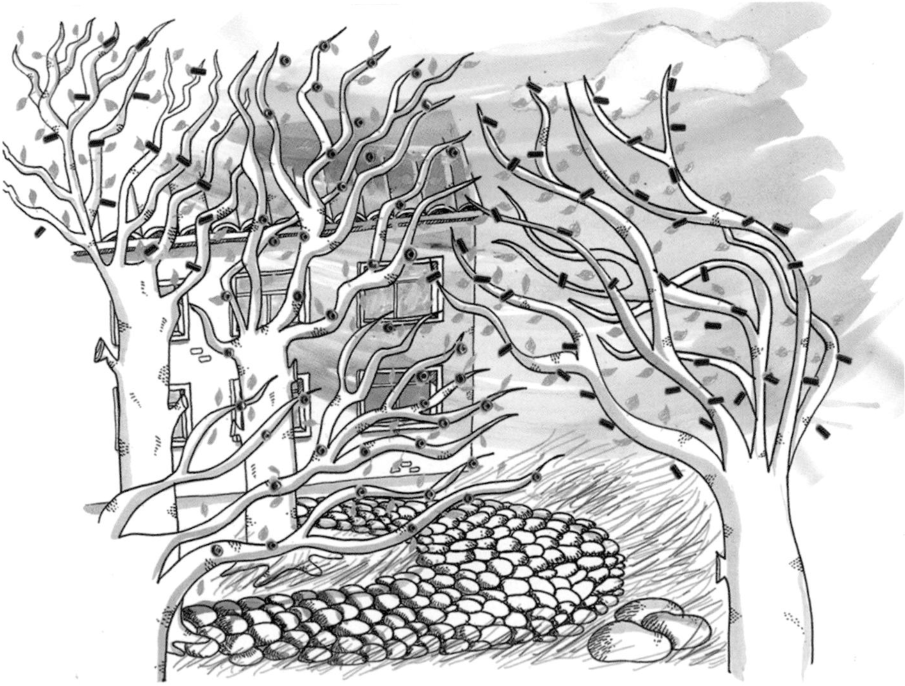

In our school there was not too much to do other than study.

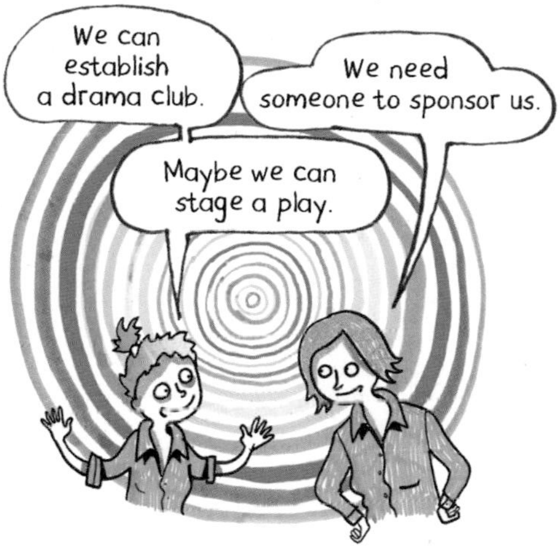
We can establish a drama club.
We need someone to sponsor us.
Maybe we can stage a play.

We thought that one of our favorite teachers, Mr. Kaya, could help us.

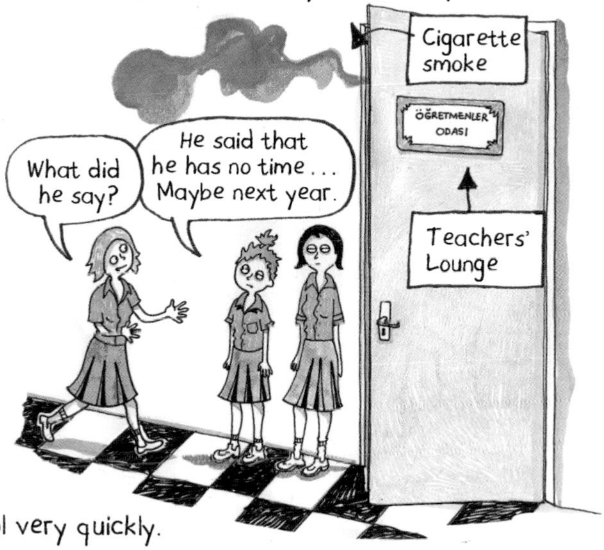
Cigarette smoke
ÖĞRETMENLER ODASI
Teachers' Lounge
What did he say?
He said that he has no time . . . Maybe next year.

The word spread through our little school very quickly.

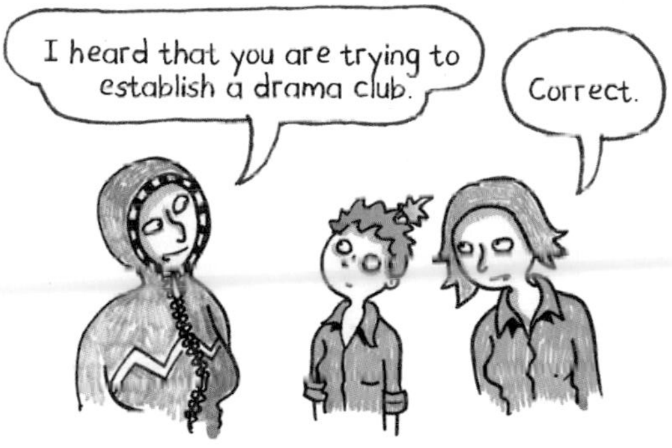
I heard that you are trying to establish a drama club.
Correct.

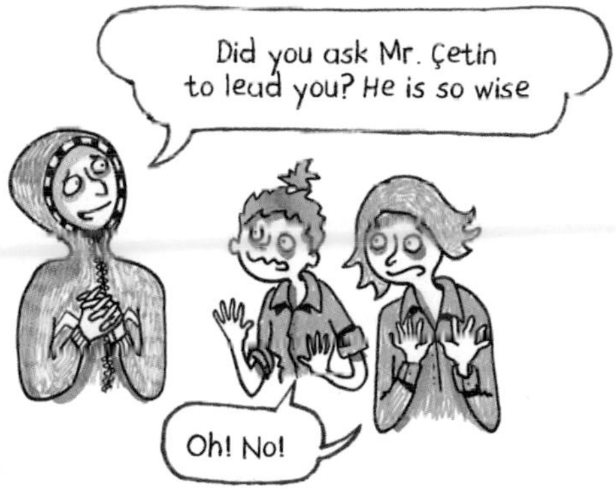
Did you ask Mr. Çetin to lead you? He is so wise
Oh! No!

Within a couple days Mr. Çetin established a drama club.

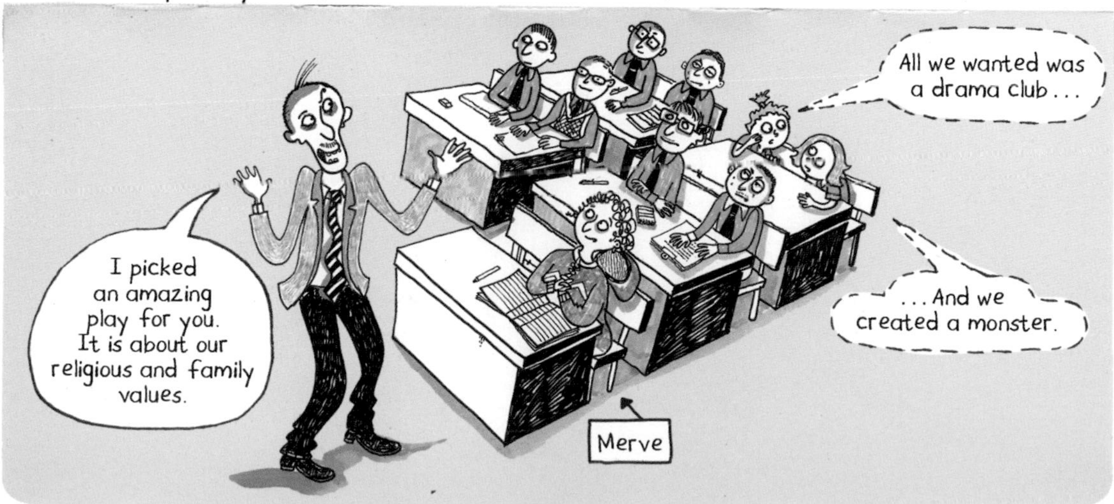
All we wanted was a drama club . . .
I picked an amazing play for you. It is about our religious and family values.
. . . And we created a monster.
Merve

We read the "amazing" play that Mr. Çetin picked for us.

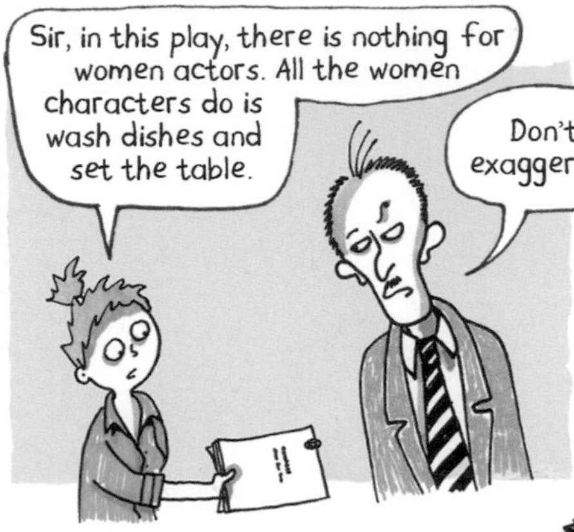
Sir, in this play, there is nothing for women actors. All the women characters do is wash dishes and set the table.
Don't exaggerate.

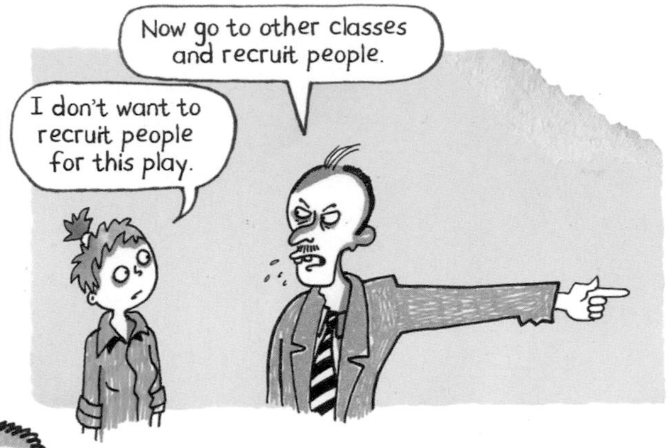
Now go to other classes and recruit people.
I don't want to recruit people for this play.

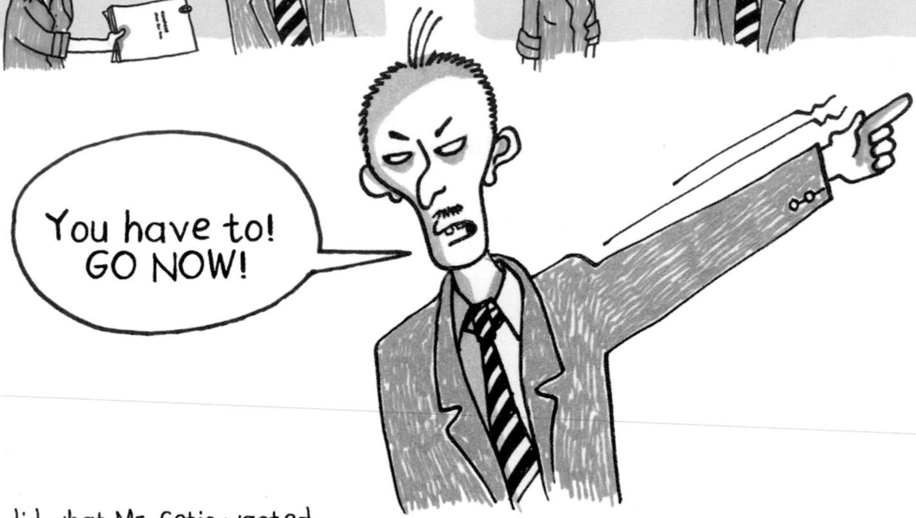
You have to! GO NOW!

I did what Mr. Çetin wanted but in my own way.

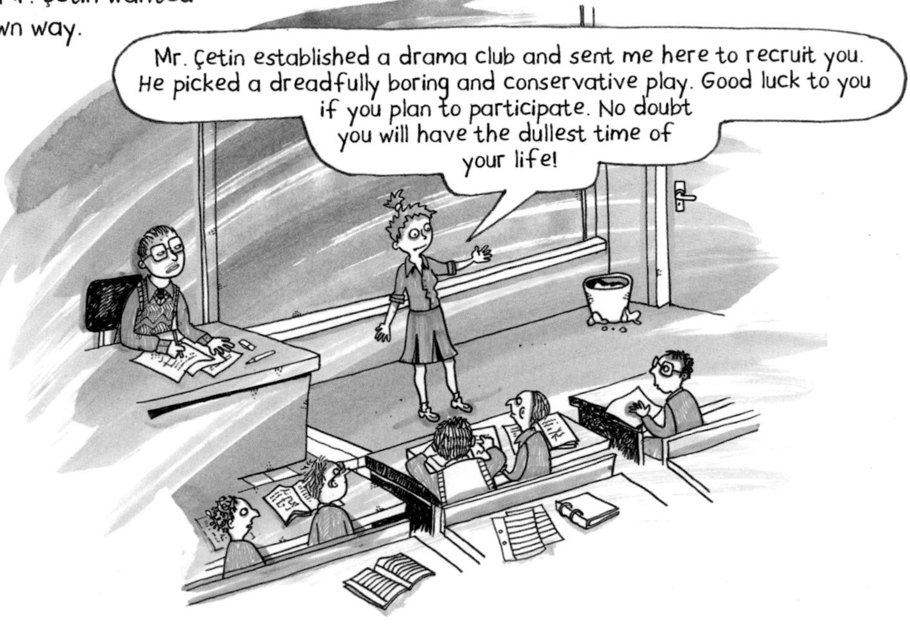
Mr. Çetin established a drama club and sent me here to recruit you. He picked a dreadfully boring and conservative play. Good luck to you if you plan to participate. No doubt you will have the dullest time of your life!

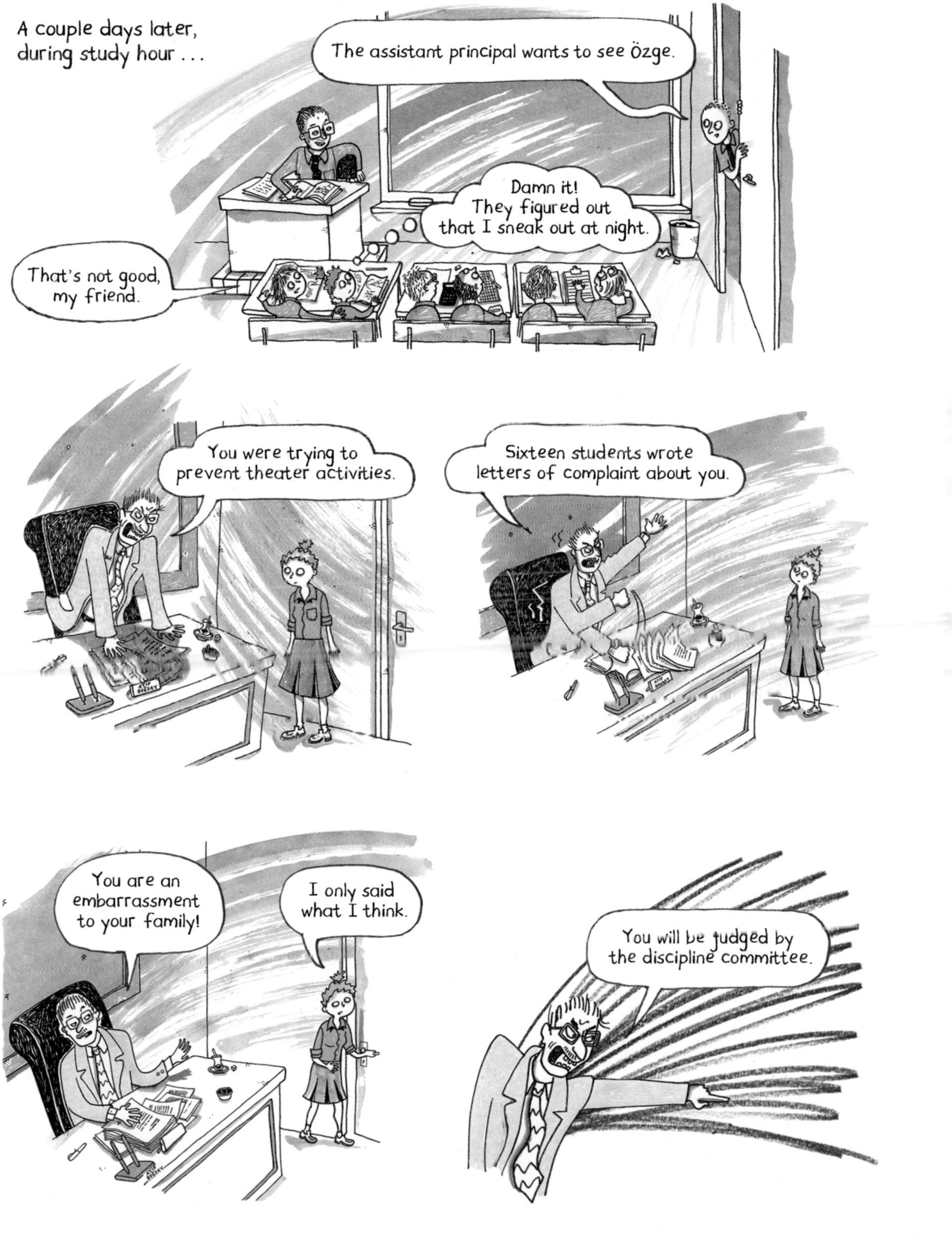

A couple days later, during study hour . . .
The assistant principal wants to see Özge.
Damn it! They figured out that I sneak out at night.
That's not good, my friend.
You were trying to prevent theater activities.
Sixteen students wrote letters of complaint about you.
You are an embarrassment to your family!
I only said what I think.
You will be judged by the discipline committee.

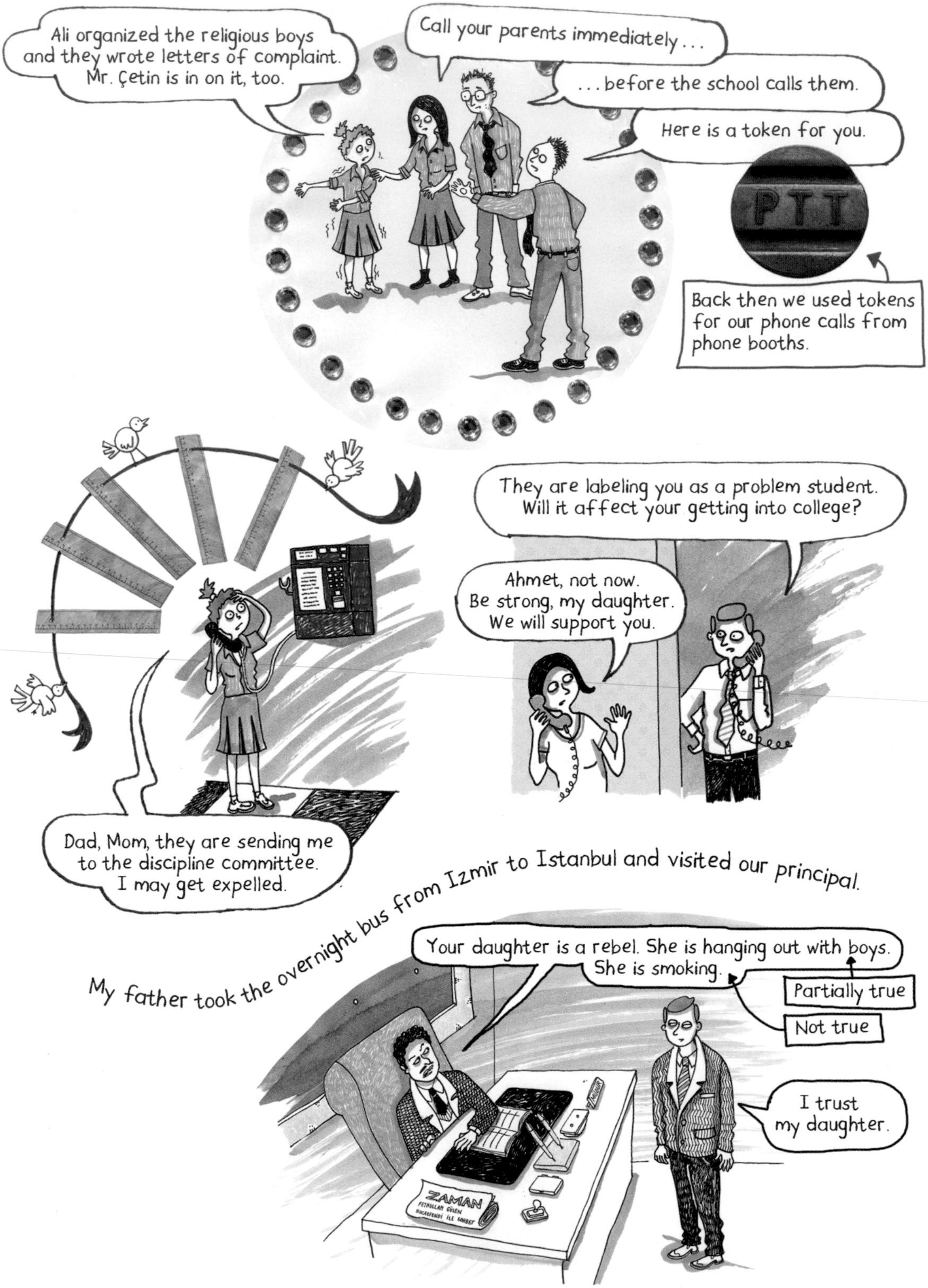

Ali organized the religious boys and they wrote letters of complaint. Mr. Çetin is in on it, too.
Call your parents immediately . . .
. . . before the school calls them.
Here is a token for you.
PTT
Back then we used tokens for our phone calls from phone booths.
They are labeling you as a problem student. Will it affect your getting into college?
Ahmet, not now. Be strong, my daughter. We will support you.
Dad, Mom, they are sending me to the discipline committee. I may get expelled.
My father took the overnight bus from Izmir to Istanbul and visited our principal.
Your daughter is a rebel. She is hanging out with boys. She is smoking.
Partially true
Not true
I trust my daughter.
ZAMAN

I took a long walk with my dad in the school's garden.

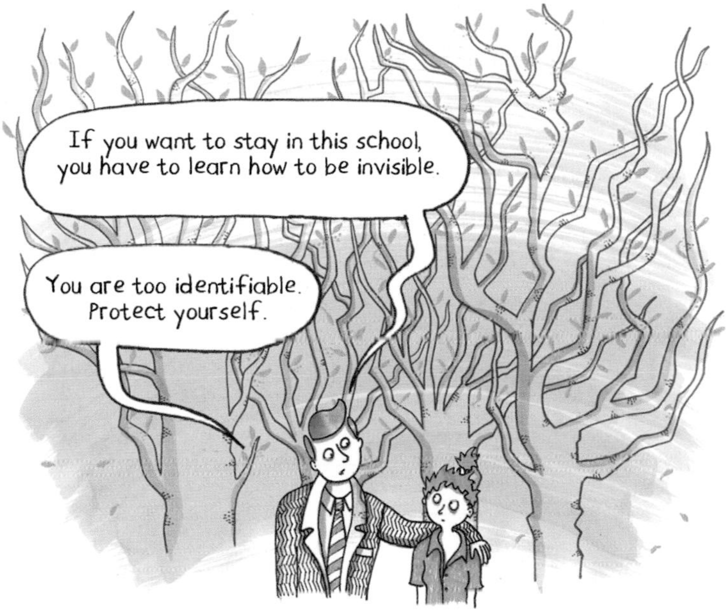
If you want to stay in this school, you have to learn how to be invisible.
You are too identifiable. Protect yourself.

My father went home, and I was left with the spirits of the animals who were hunted in that garden.

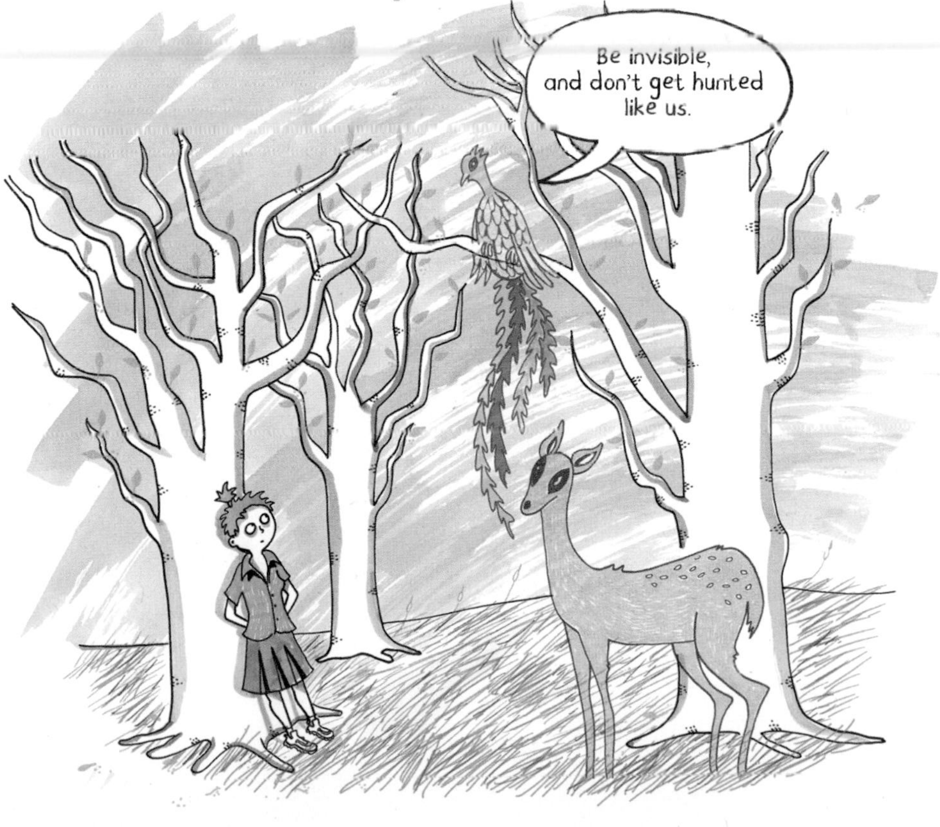
Be invisible, and don't get hunted like us.

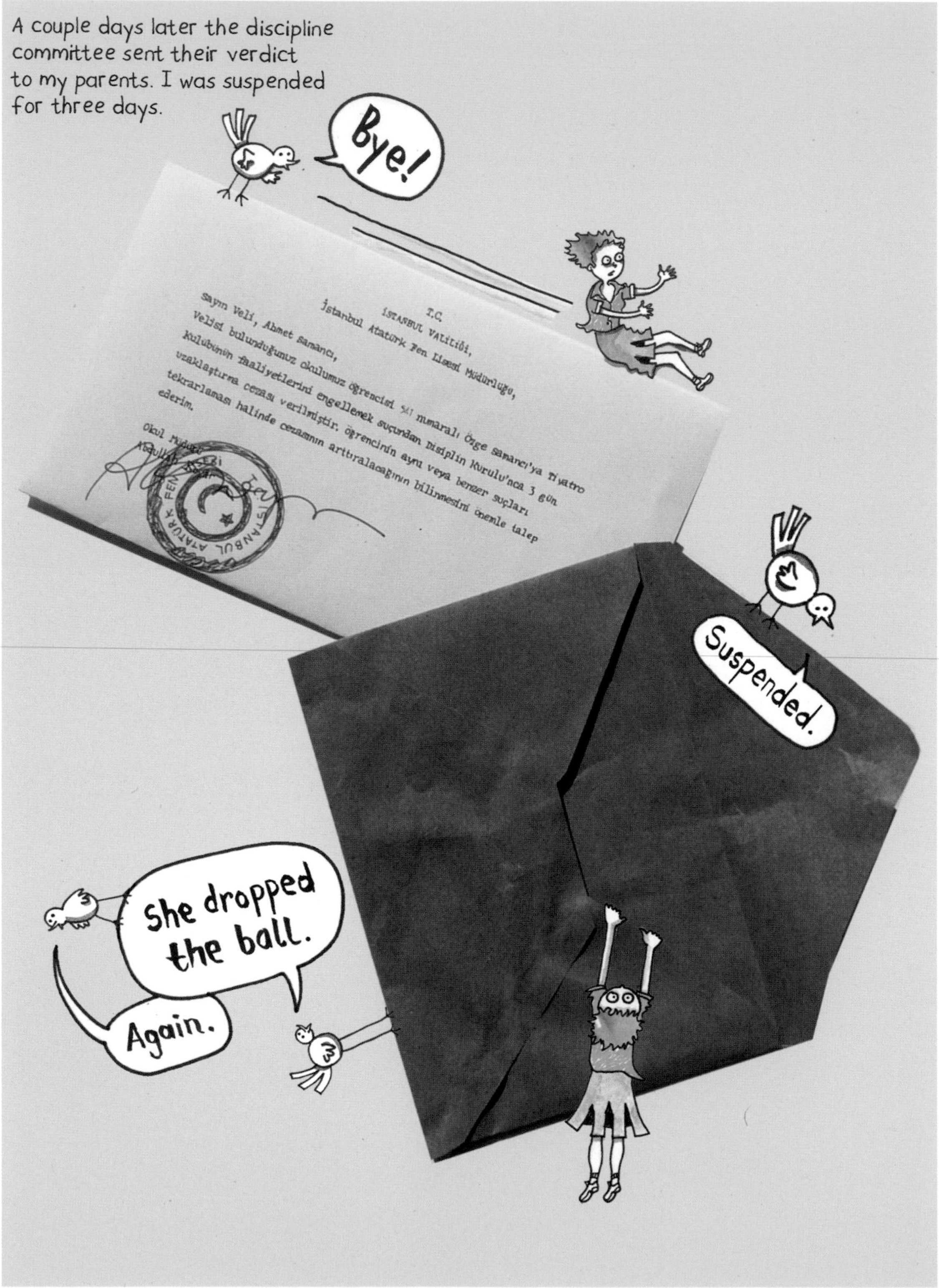
A couple days later the discipline committee sent their verdict to my parents. I was suspended for three days.
Bye!
T.C.
İSTANBUL VALİLİĞİ,
İstanbul Atatürk Fen Lisesi Müdürlüğü,
Sayın Veli, Ahmet Samancı,
Velisi bulunduğunuz okulumuz öğrencisi numaralı Özge Samancı'ya Tiyatro
Kulubünün faaliyetlerini engellemek suçundan Disiplin Kurulu'nca 3 gün
uzaklaştırma cezası verilmiştir. öğrencinin aynı veya benzer suçları
tekrarlaması halinde cezasının arttıralacağının bilinmesini önemle talep
ederim.
Okul Müdürü
Suspended.
She dropped the ball.
Again.

After my eventful year in high school I returned home for the summer.
My family had good news to share. Pelin had been accepted to a prestigious college, Bosphorus University in Istanbul. We were going to be in the same city.

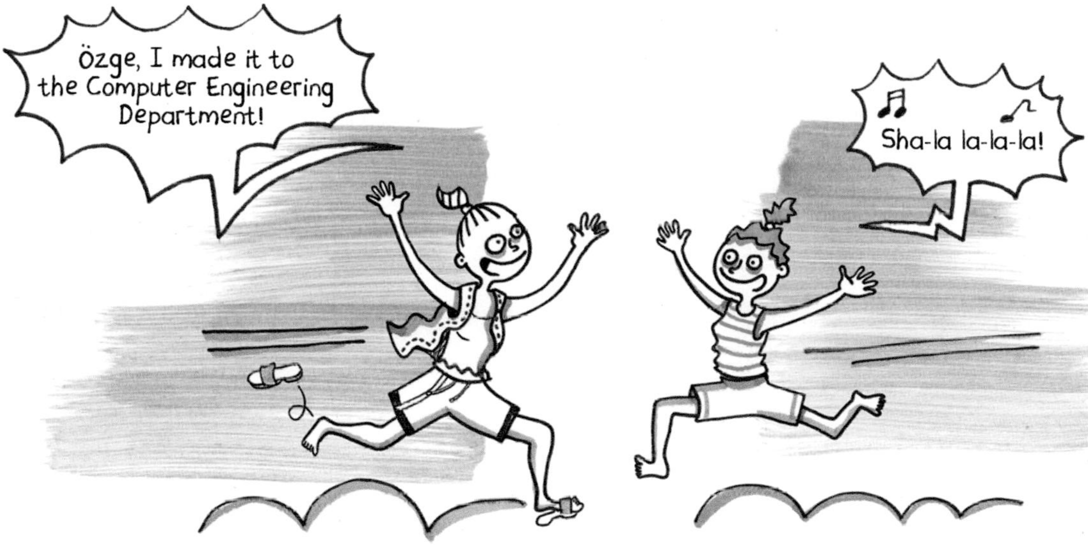
Özge, I made it to the Computer Engineering Department!
Sha-la la-la-la!

We never had a computer. Pelin was not interested in computers . . . but whatever . . . it was very prestigious

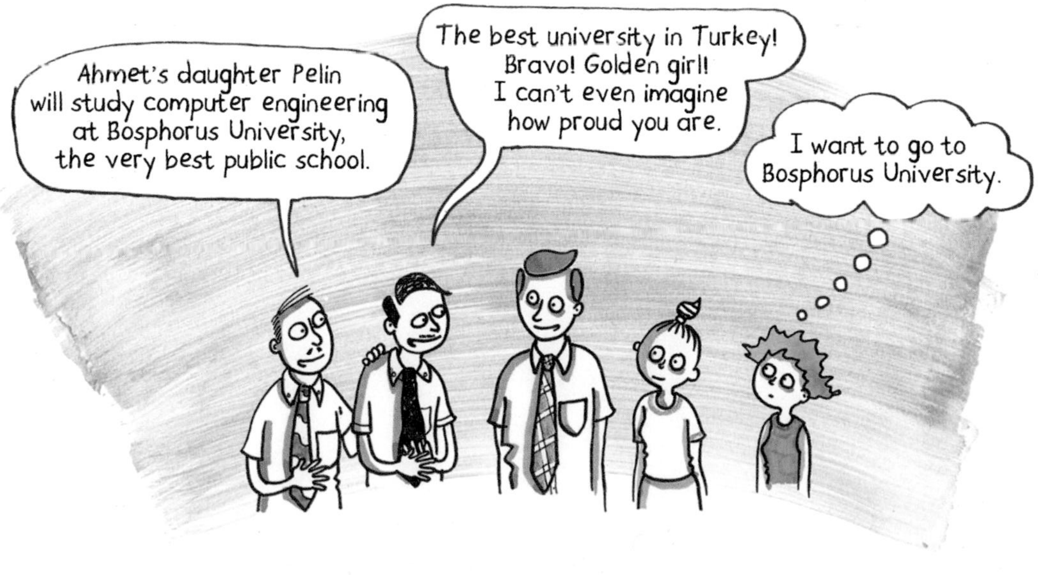
Ahmet's daughter Pelin will study computer engineering at Bosphorus University, the very best public school.
The best university in Turkey! Bravo! Golden girl! I can't even imagine how proud you are.
I want to go to Bosphorus University.

Once school started again, I kept getting in trouble. Administrators sent rebel students to the discipline committee for minor infractions.

I received three more disciplinary punishments in the second year of high school.

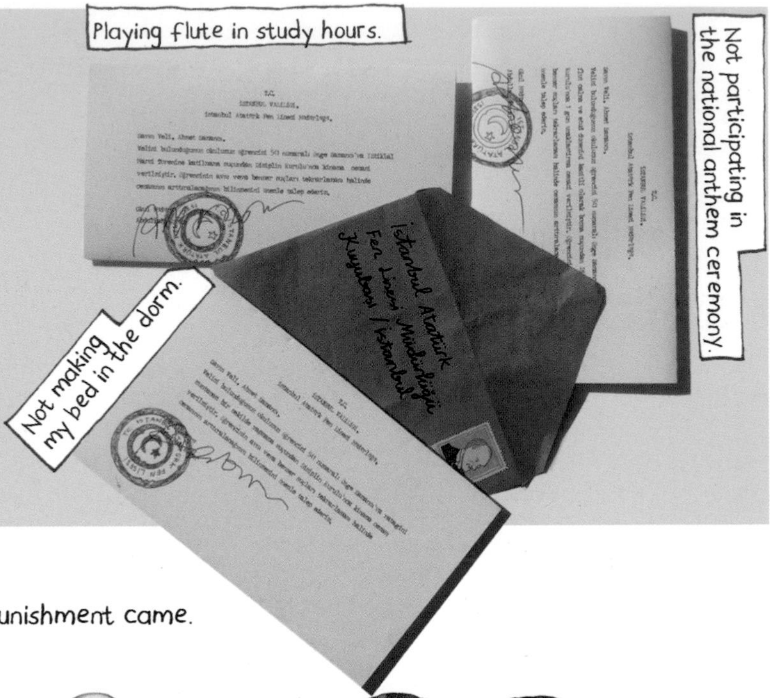
Playing flute in study hours.
Not participating in the national anthem ceremony.
Not making my bed in the dorm.
İstanbul Atatürk Fen Lisesi Müdürlüğü Kuyubaşı / İstanbul

Then my fourth disciplinary punishment came.

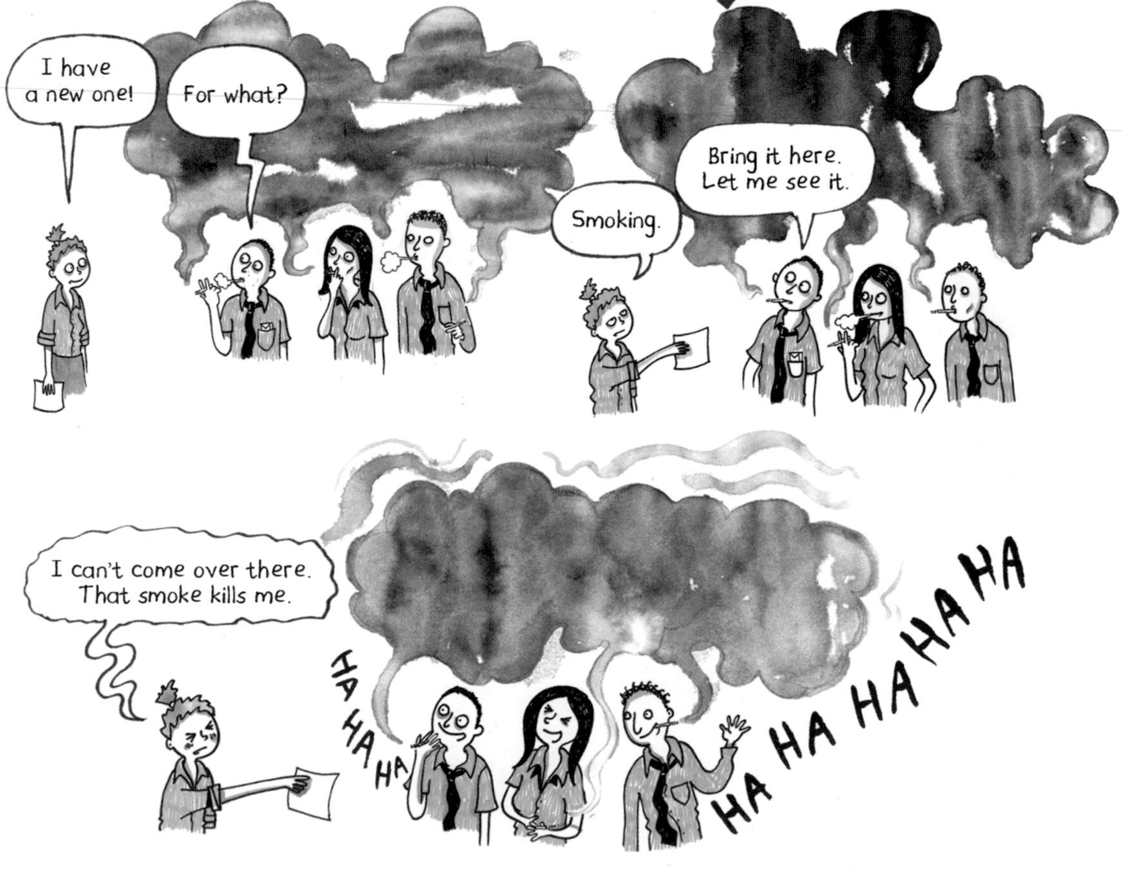
I have a new one!
For what?
Smoking.
Bring it here. Let me see it.
I can't come over there. That smoke kills me.
HA HA HA
HA HA HA HA HA HA

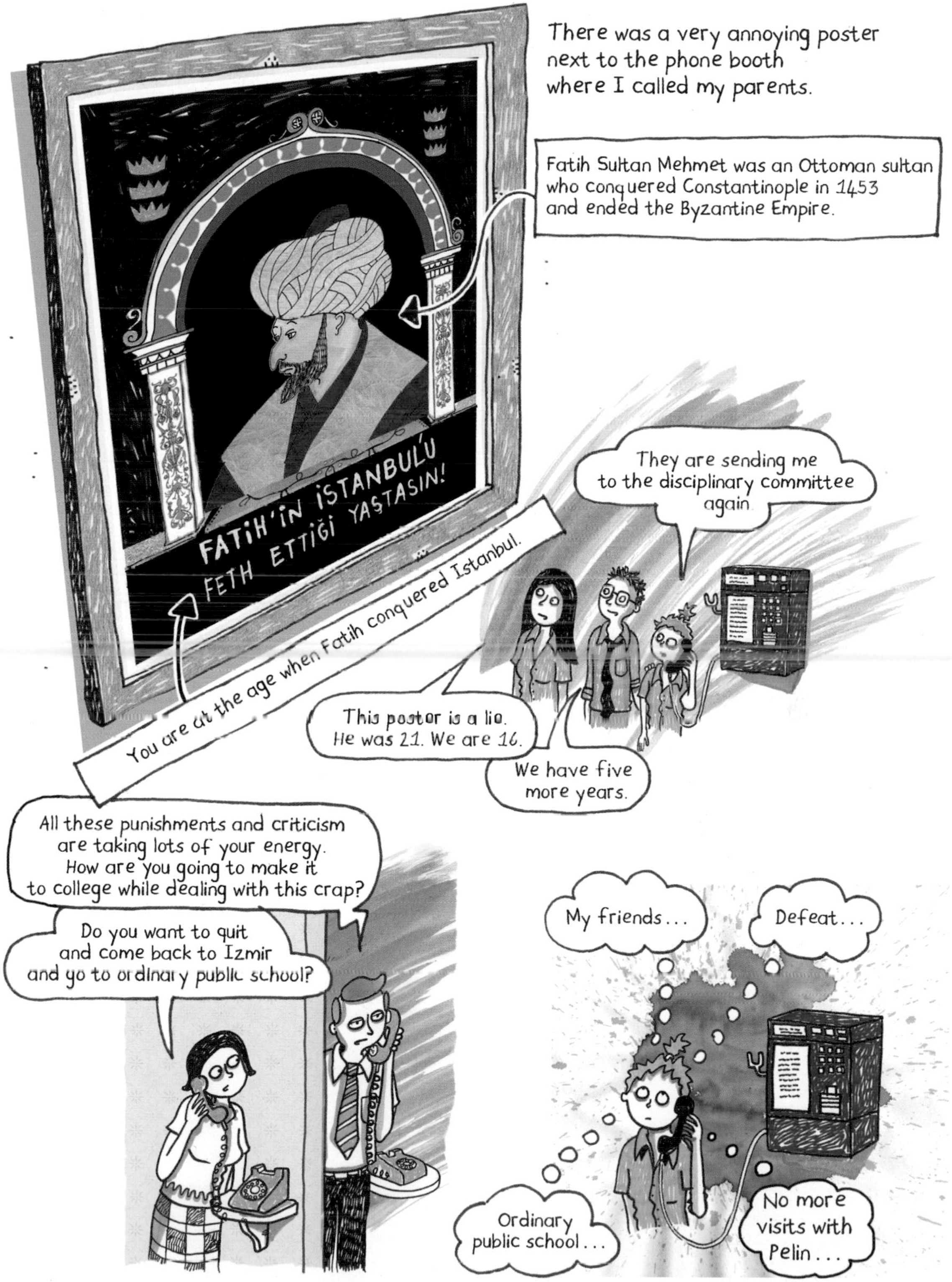
There was a very annoying poster next to the phone booth where I called my parents.
Fatih Sultan Mehmet was an Ottoman sultan who conquered Constantinople in 1453 and ended the Byzantine Empire.
FATİH'İN İSTANBUL'U FETH ETTİĞİ YAŞTASIN!
You are at the age when Fatih conquered Istanbul.
They are sending me to the disciplinary committee again.
This poster is a lie. He was 21. We are 16.
We have five more years.
All these punishments and criticism are taking lots of your energy. How are you going to make it to college while dealing with this crap?
Do you want to quit and come back to Izmir and go to ordinary public school?
My friends...
Defeat...
Ordinary public school...
No more visits with Pelin...

Does quitting mean accepting defeat?

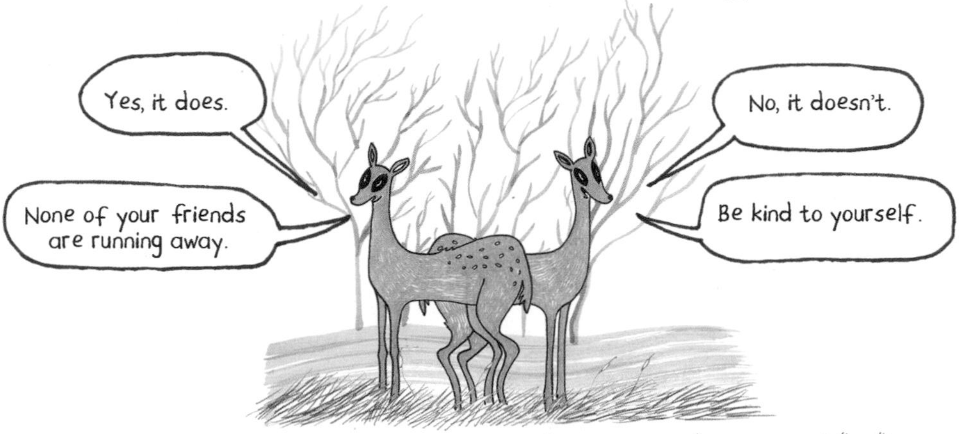
Yes, it does.
None of your friends are running away.
No, it doesn't.
Be kind to yourself.

I decided to leave the hunting ground.

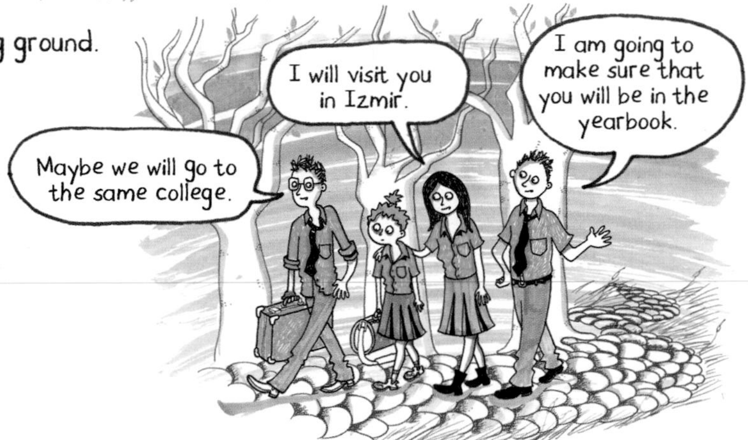
Maybe we will go to the same college.
I will visit you in Izmir.
I am going to make sure that you will be in the yearbook.

I looked back one more time before I left.

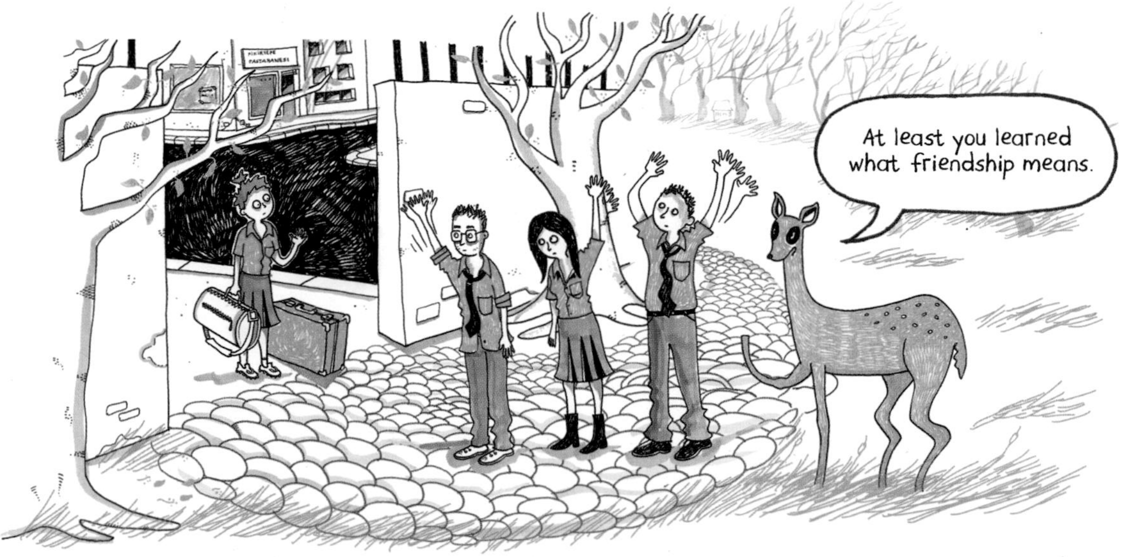
At least you learned what friendship means.

Chapter 12

Potato

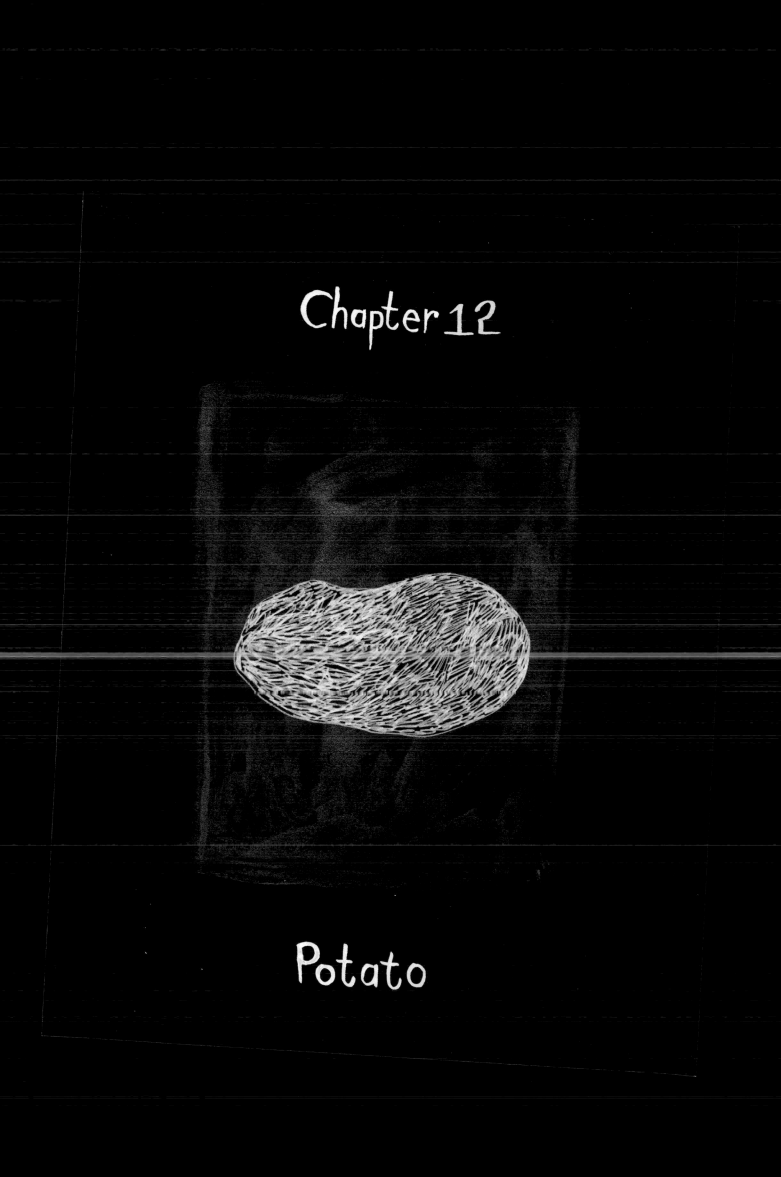

I had spent my whole life in schools, but I had never seen something this beautiful.

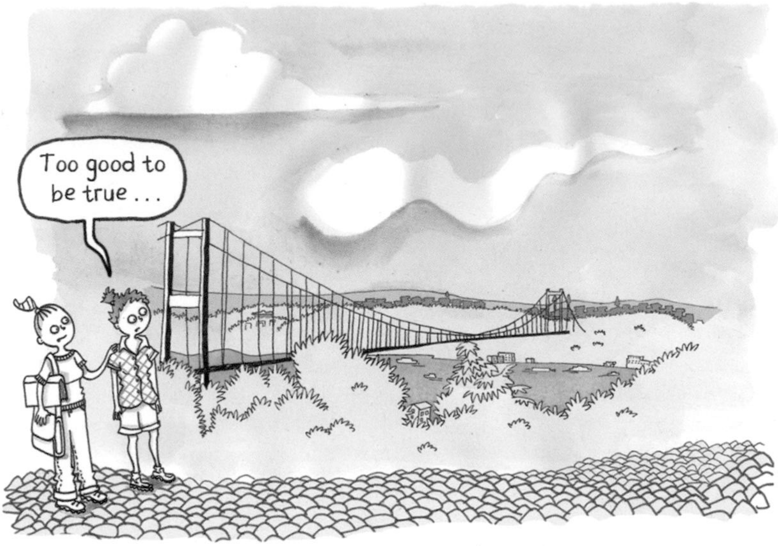
Too good to be true . . .

While I was completing my last year at an ordinary high school in Izmir, I went to Istanbul to visit my sister at Bosphorus University. She had always visited me. I had never seen the university before.

Students were lying on the grass . . .

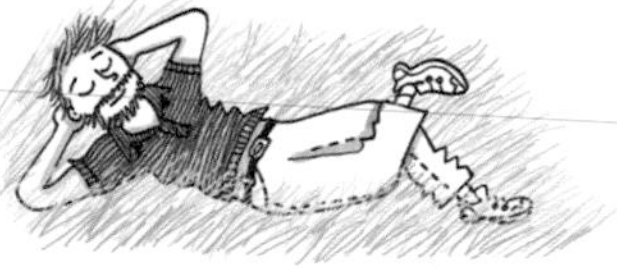

making out . . .

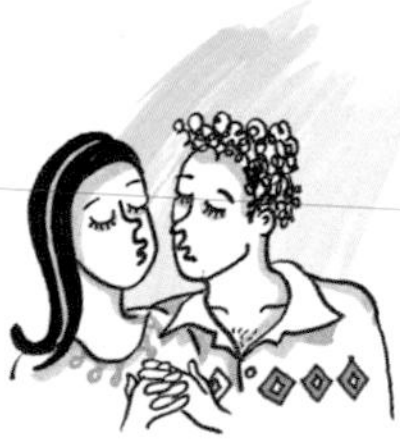

playing music . . .

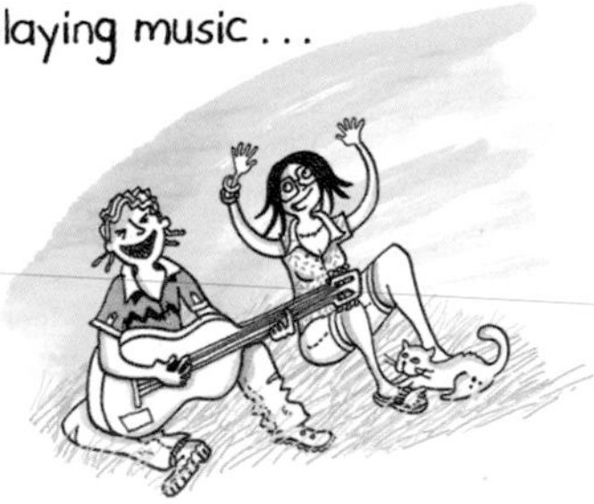

This school had an outdoor swimming pool. There were no public swimming pools in Izmir or Istanbul.

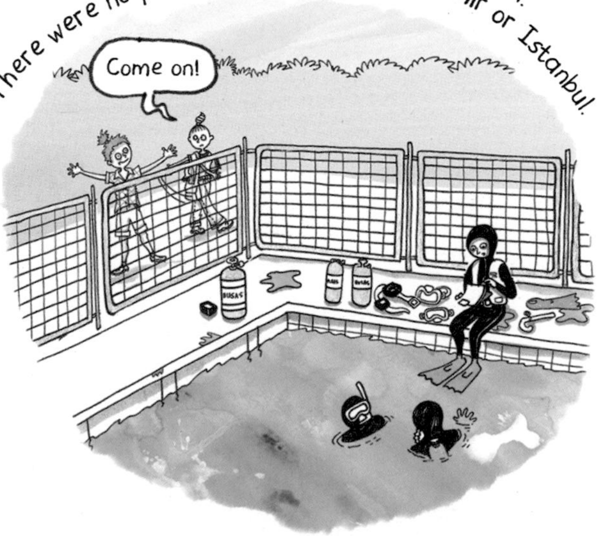
Come on!

I heard a voice in my head.

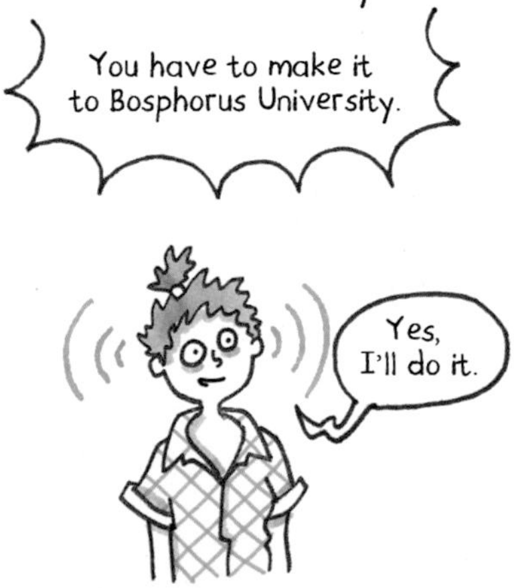
You have to make it to Bosphorus University.
Yes, I'll do it.

I wished I could study civil or mechanical engineering at Bosphorus University. That would surely please me, my dad, my teachers, and everybody.

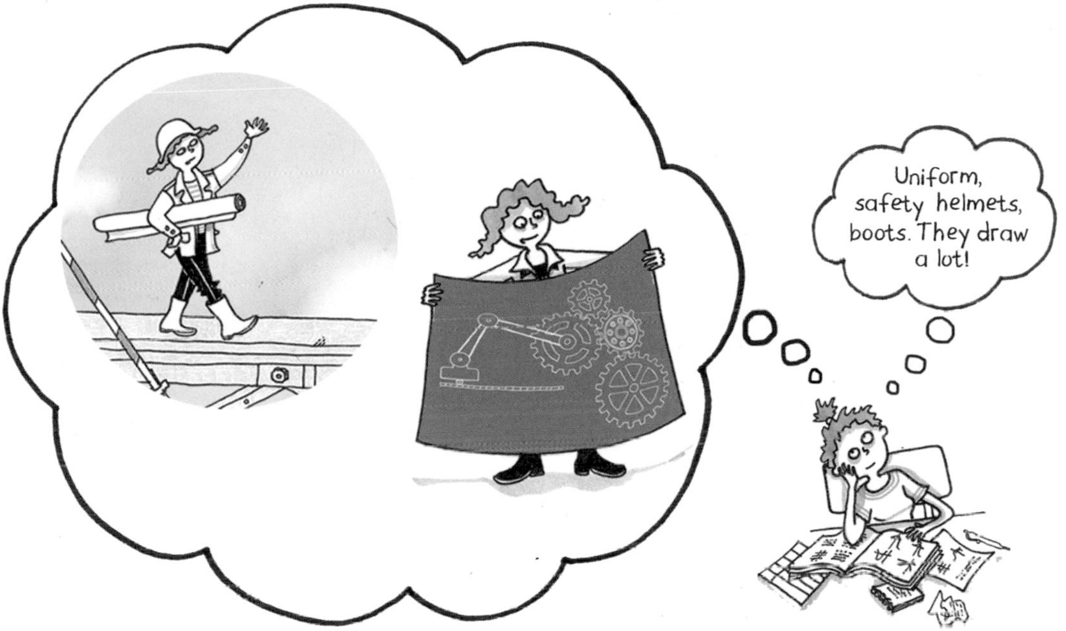

Uniform, safety helmets, boots. They draw a lot!

But Bosphorus University engineering departments admitted top students, and my practice test results at the weekend school were not that good. I decided I was willing to study any major at Bosphorus University.

Before we took the college entrance examination we filled out a college and major preference form. On the basis of our score in the exam, we were admitted to a school and assigned a major.

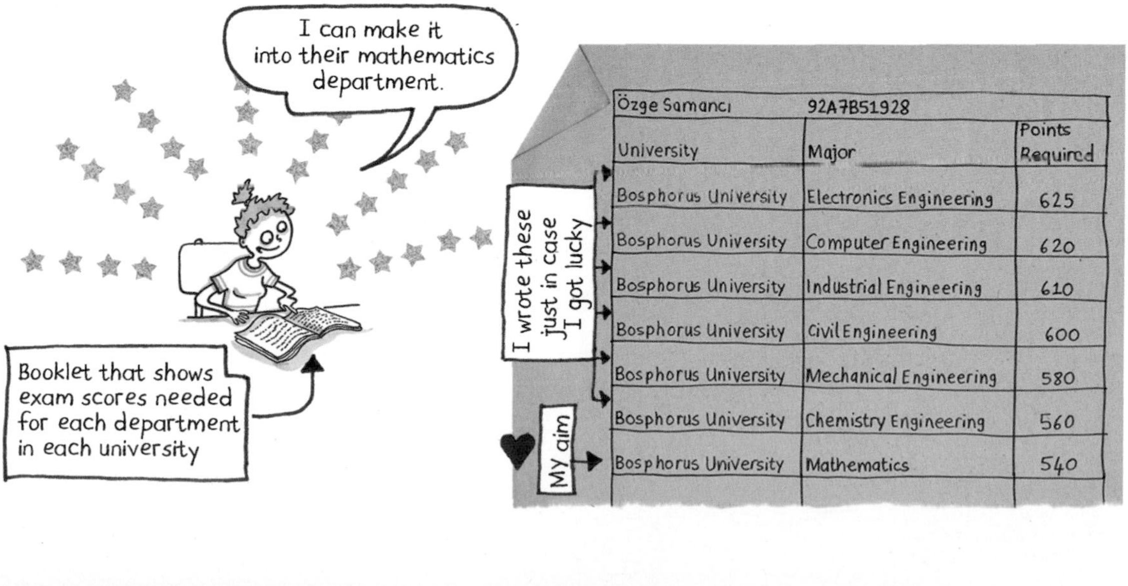

I can make it into their mathematics department.
Booklet that shows exam scores needed for each department in each university
I wrote these just in case I got lucky
My aim

Özge Samancı	92A7B51928	
University	Major	Points Required
Bosphorus University	Electronics Engineering	625
Bosphorus University	Computer Engineering	620
Bosphorus University	Industrial Engineering	610
Bosphorus University	Civil Engineering	600
Bosphorus University	Mechanical Engineering	580
Bosphorus University	Chemistry Engineering	560
Bosphorus University	Mathematics	540

While I was filling out my form, my father and I argued.

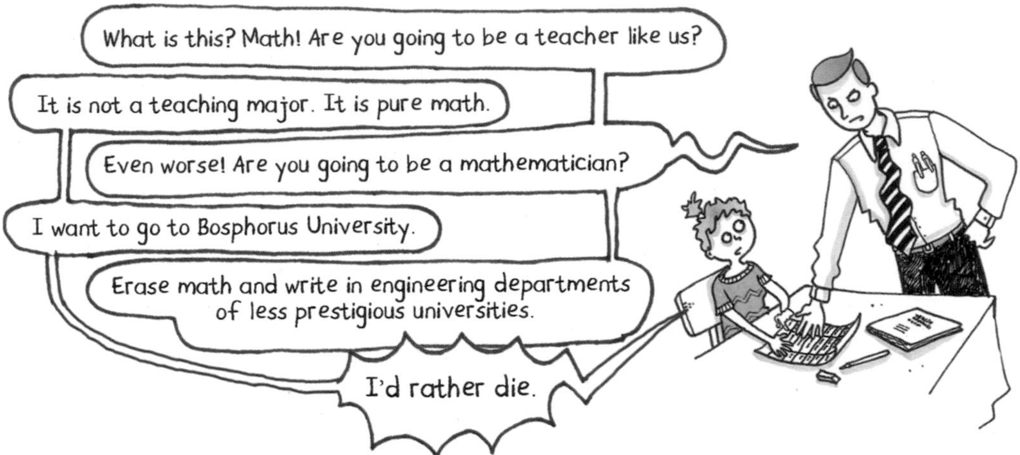
What is this? Math! Are you going to be a teacher like us?
It is not a teaching major. It is pure math.
Even worse! Are you going to be a mathematician?
I want to go to Bosphorus University.
Erase math and write in engineering departments of less prestigious universities.
I'd rather die.

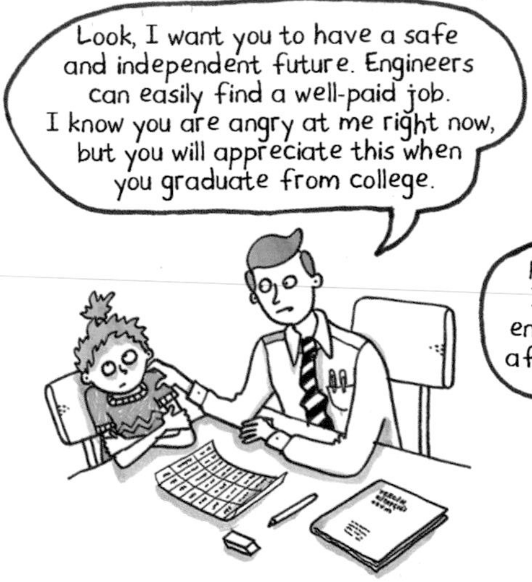
Look, I want you to have a safe and independent future. Engineers can easily find a well-paid job. I know you are angry at me right now, but you will appreciate this when you graduate from college.

My mom got involved.

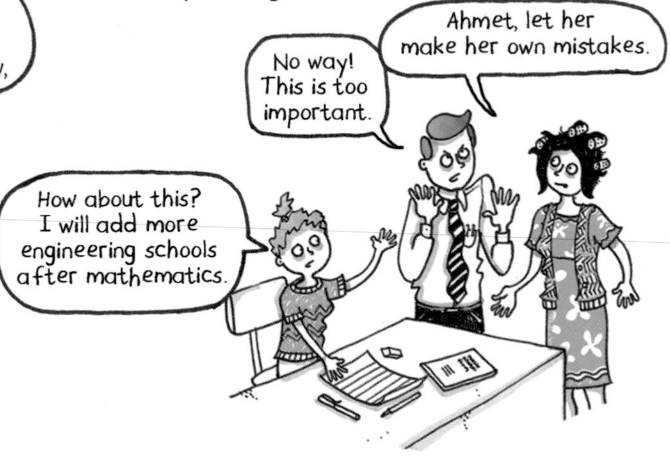
Ahmet, let her make her own mistakes.
No way! This is too important.
How about this? I will add more engineering schools after mathematics.

During the three-hour-long exam my father waited outside.

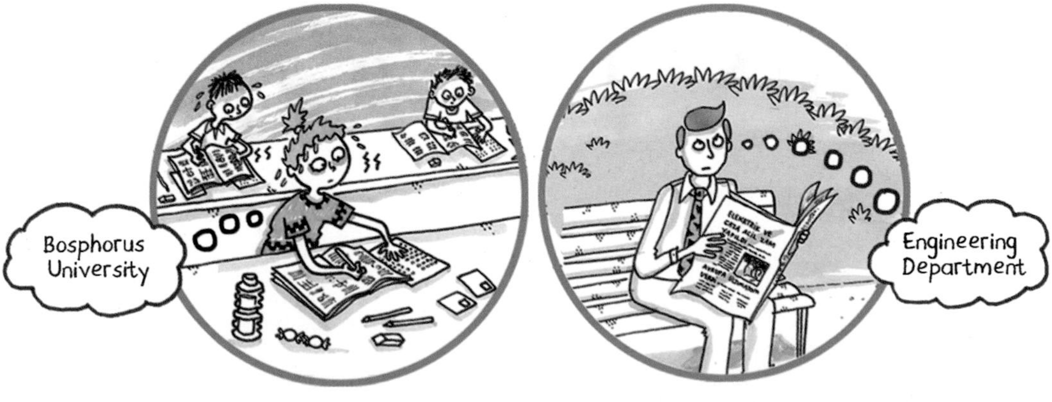
Bosphorus University
Engineering Department

A month later they announced the results. I made it into the less prestigious math department of my sister's school.

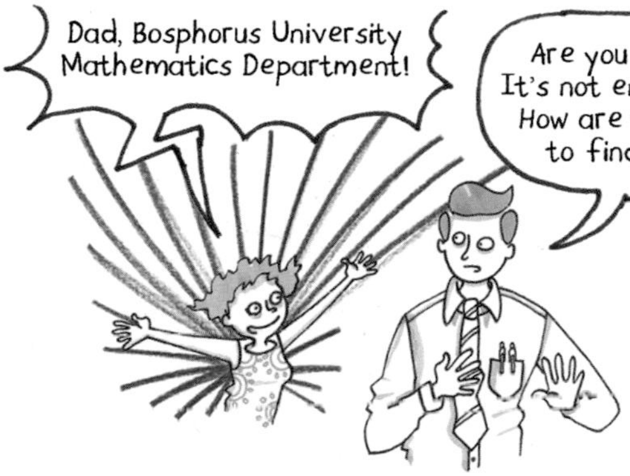
Dad, Bosphorus University Mathematics Department!
Are you serious? It's not engineering? How are you going to find a job?

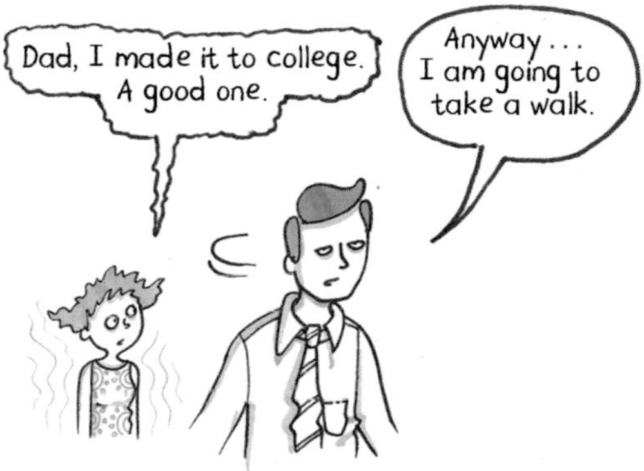
Dad, I made it to college. A good one.
Anyway . . . I am going to take a walk.

I wasn't particularly good at mathematics, but who cares! I made it to Bosphorus University. I was reunited with my sister and two of my close friends from Atatürk Science High School.

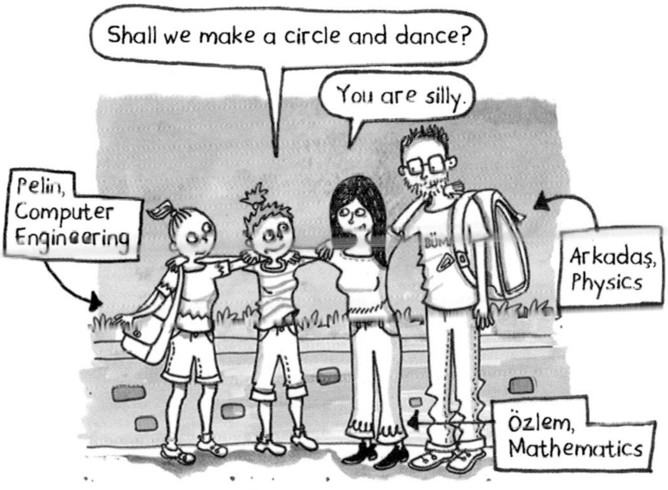
Shall we make a circle and dance?
You are silly.
Pelin, Computer Engineering
Arkadaş, Physics
Özlem, Mathematics

Could life be better than this?

One morning I was waiting for Özlem to go to our class together.

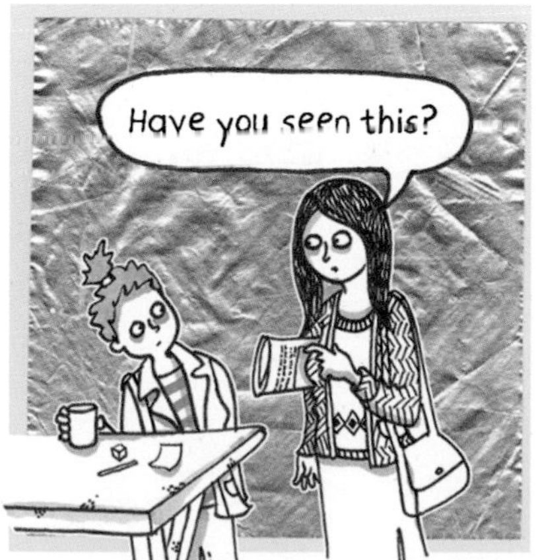
Have you seen this?

According to the newspaper, Mr. Atif, our physical education teacher from high school, was a terrorist.

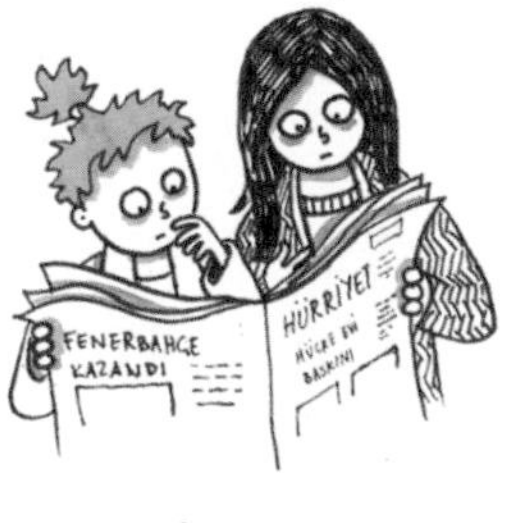
FENERBAHCE KAZANDI
HÜRRIYET

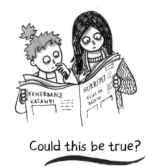

Could this be true?

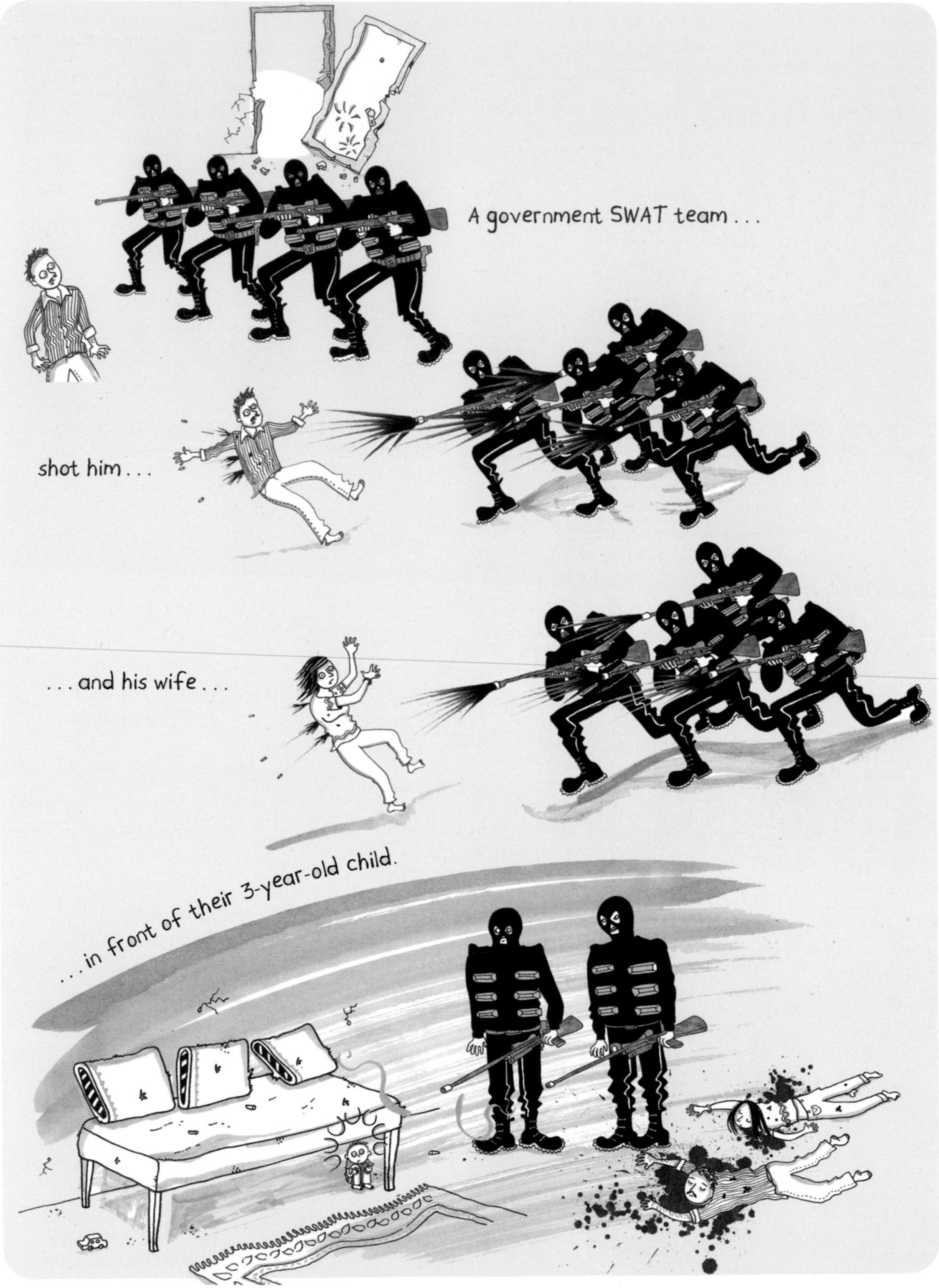
A government SWAT team . . .
shot him . . .
. . . and his wife . . .
. . . in front of their 3-year-old child.

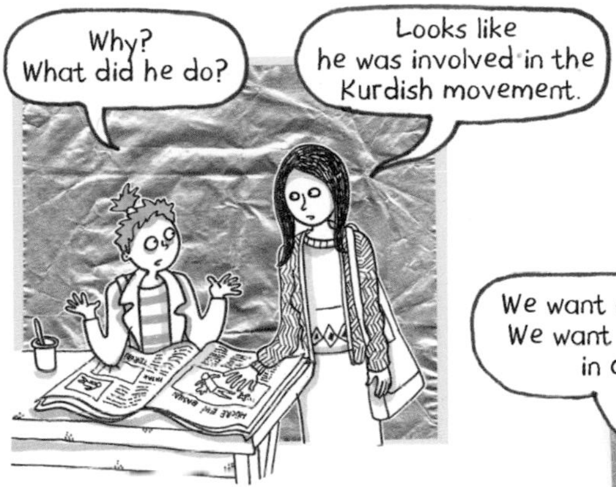
Why?
What did he do?
Looks like
he was involved in the
Kurdish movement.

Ever since the Turkish War of Independence there had been a conflict between the Kurds and the Turks. Now there was a violent war raging between them in eastern Turkey. Thousands of people were dying. Kurds demanded their rights and expressed various opinions about what those rights should be.

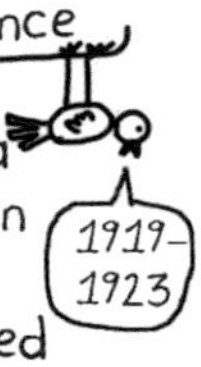
1919–
1923

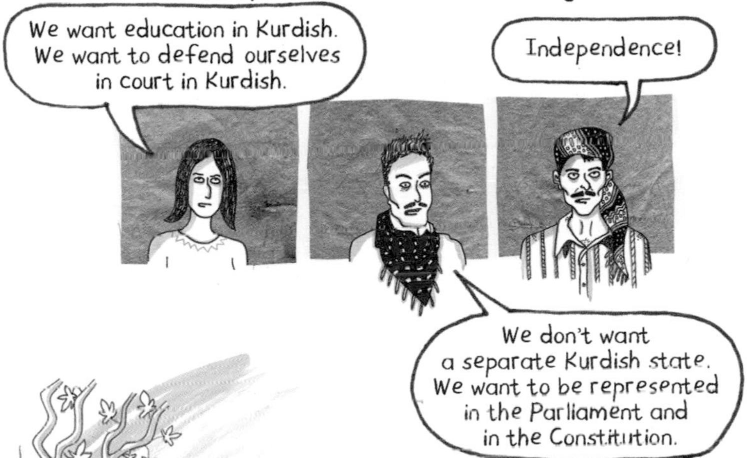
We want education in Kurdish.
We want to defend ourselves
in court in Kurdish.
Independence!
We don't want
a separate Kurdish state.
We want to be represented
in the Parliament and
in the Constitution.

Our teacher was executed with no trial. We silently walked to our class.

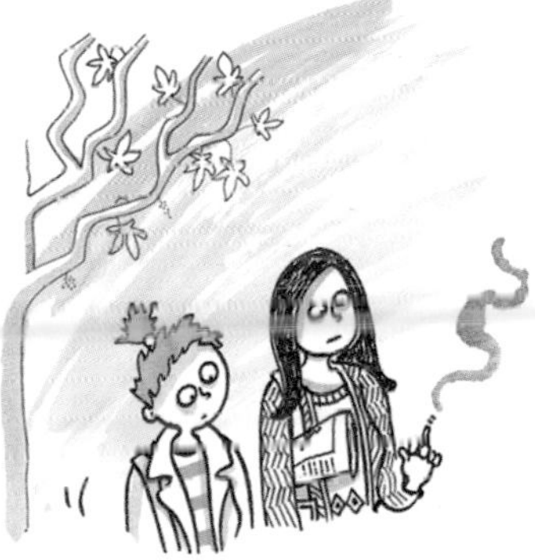

Education in Kurdish was not a possibility, but education in English was highly in demand. Bosphorus University modeled itself on the American education system, and all courses were taught in English. Sometimes being there felt absurd. Everybody's native language was Turkish, but we all spoke English.

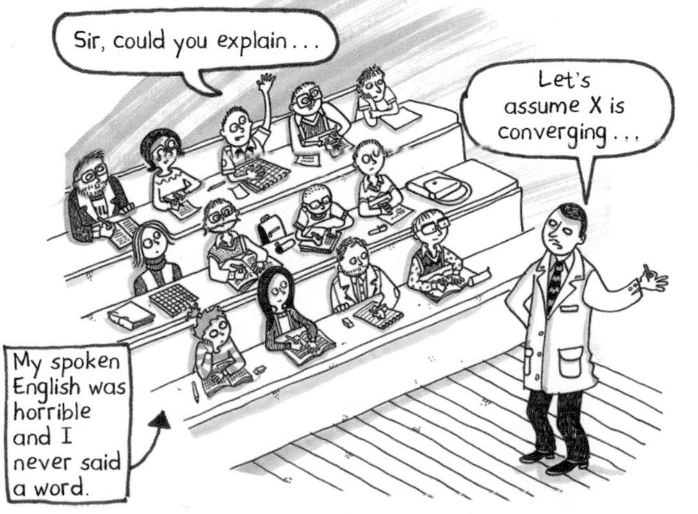
Sir, could you explain . . .
Let's
assume X is
converging . . .
My spoken
English was
horrible
and I
never said
a word.

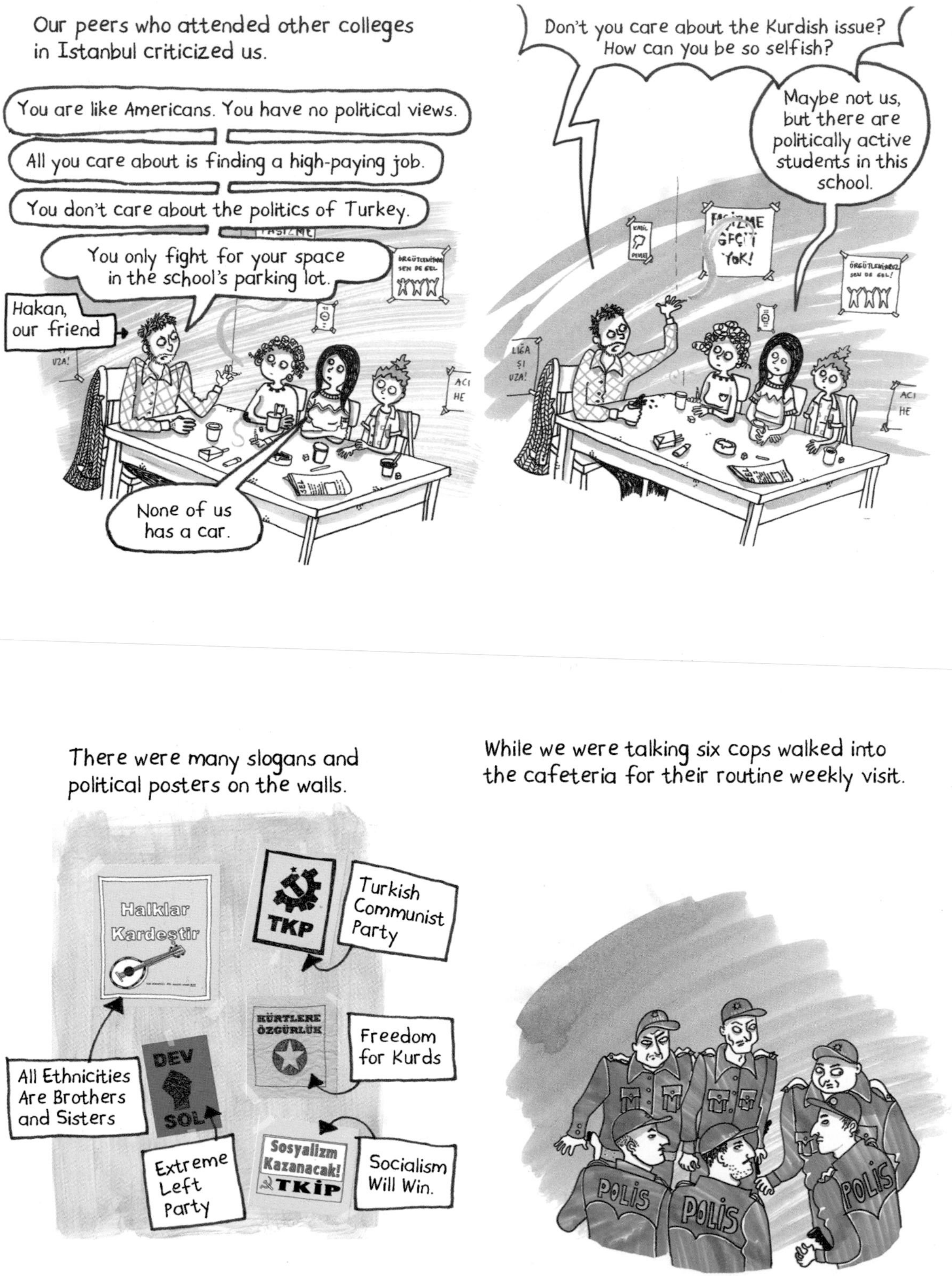
Our peers who attended other colleges in Istanbul criticized us.
You are like Americans. You have no political views.
All you care about is finding a high-paying job.
You don't care about the politics of Turkey.
You only fight for your space in the school's parking lot.
Hakan, our friend
None of us has a car.
Don't you care about the Kurdish issue? How can you be so selfish?
Maybe not us, but there are politically active students in this school.
FAŞİZME GEÇİT YOK!
There were many slogans and political posters on the walls.
Halklar Kardestir
TKP
Turkish Communist Party
KÜRTLERE ÖZGÜRLÜK
Freedom for Kurds
All Ethnicities Are Brothers and Sisters
DEV SOL
Extreme Left Party
Sosyalizm Kazanacak!
TKİP
Socialism Will Win.
While we were talking six cops walked into the cafeteria for their routine weekly visit.
POLİS
POLİS
POLİS

They were checking the posters and ripping down anything about either communism or Kurds.

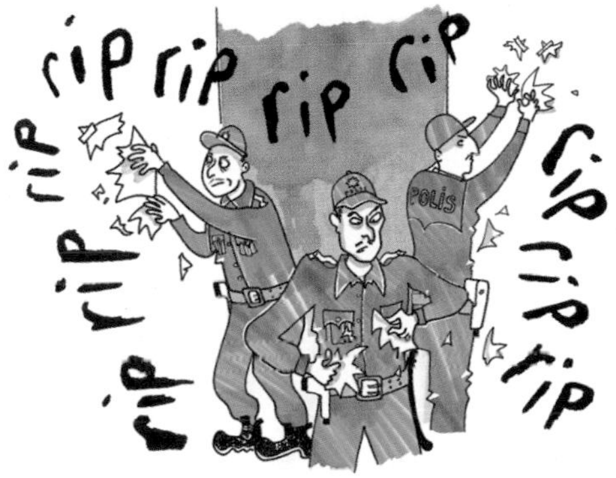
rip rip rip rip
rip rip rip rip rip rip
POLIS

A policeman hesitated at one poster.

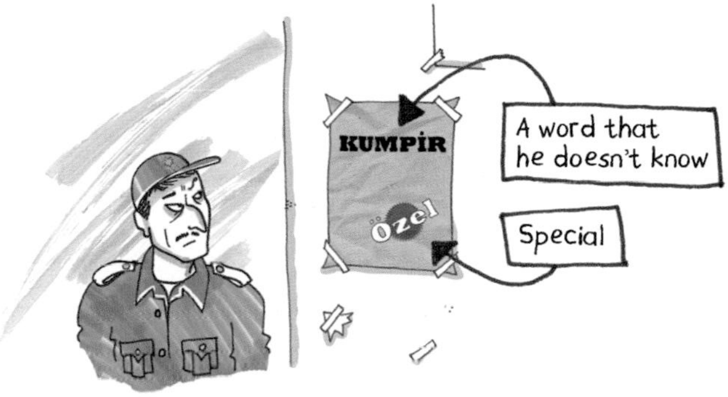
KUMPİR
Özel
A word that he doesn't know
Special

Then he tore it apart.

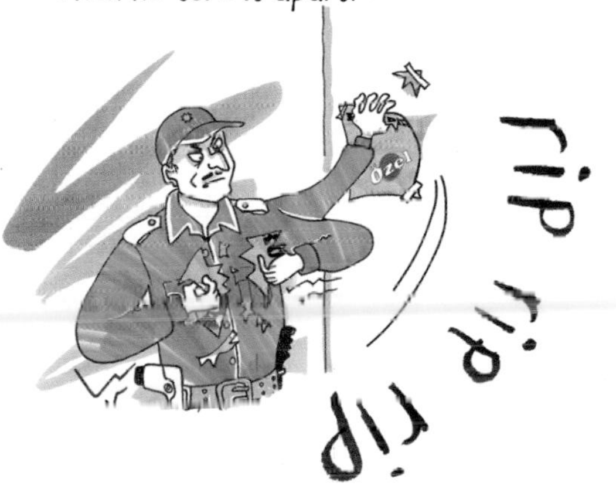
Özel
rip rip rip

We could not help it—we started laughing.

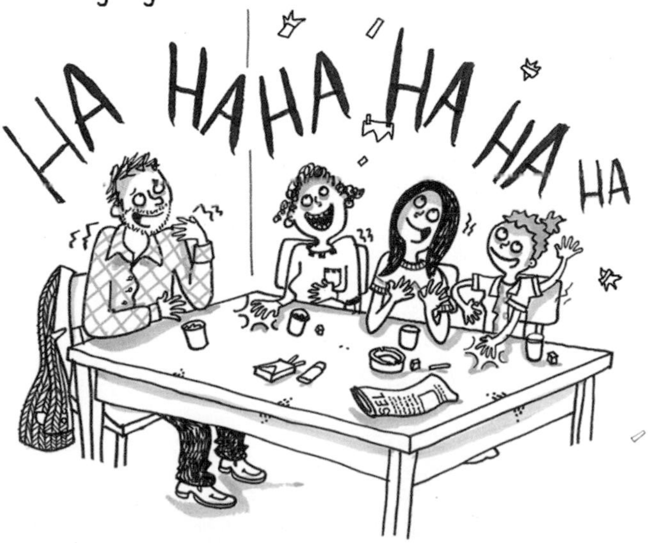
HA HAHA HA HA HA

Of course, that was not the smartest thing to do.

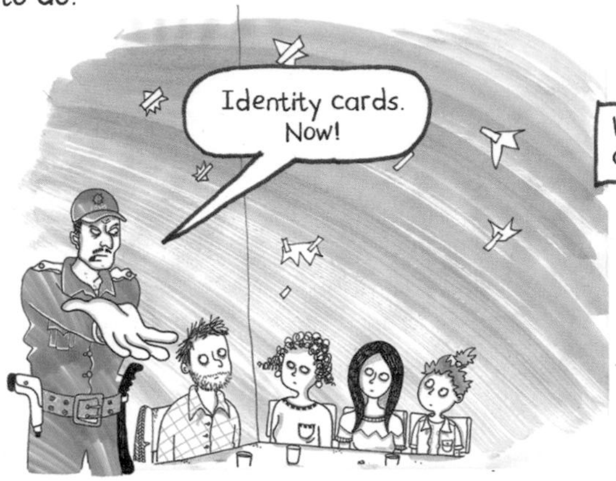
Identity cards. Now!

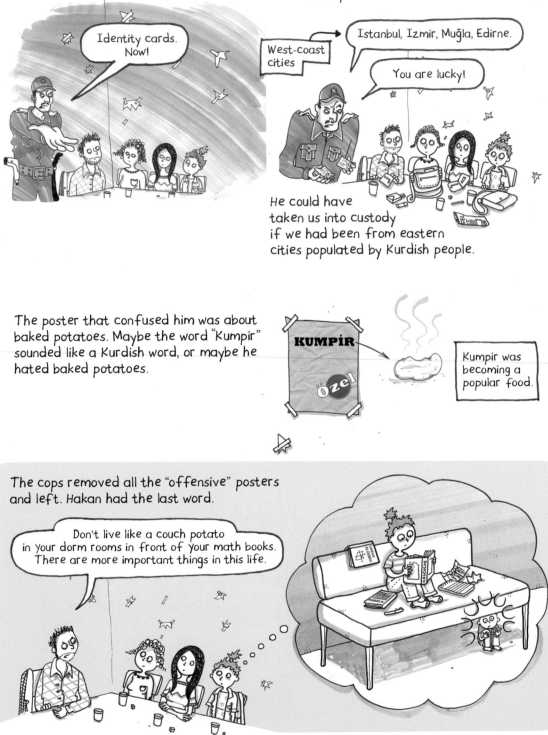

He checked our identities and looked at our birthplaces.

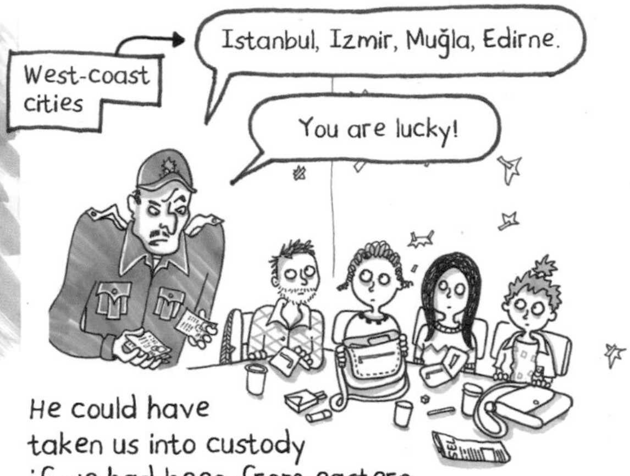
West-coast cities
Istanbul, Izmir, Muğla, Edirne.
You are lucky!

He could have taken us into custody if we had been from eastern cities populated by Kurdish people.

The poster that confused him was about baked potatoes. Maybe the word "Kumpir" sounded like a Kurdish word, or maybe he hated baked potatoes.

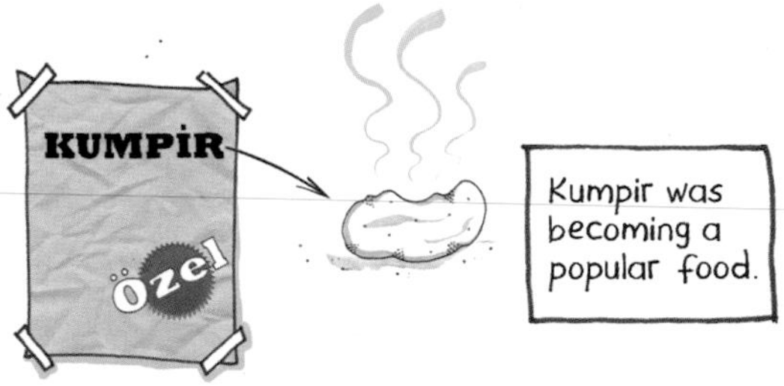
KUMPİR
Özel
Kumpir was becoming a popular food.

The cops removed all the "offensive" posters and left. Hakan had the last word.

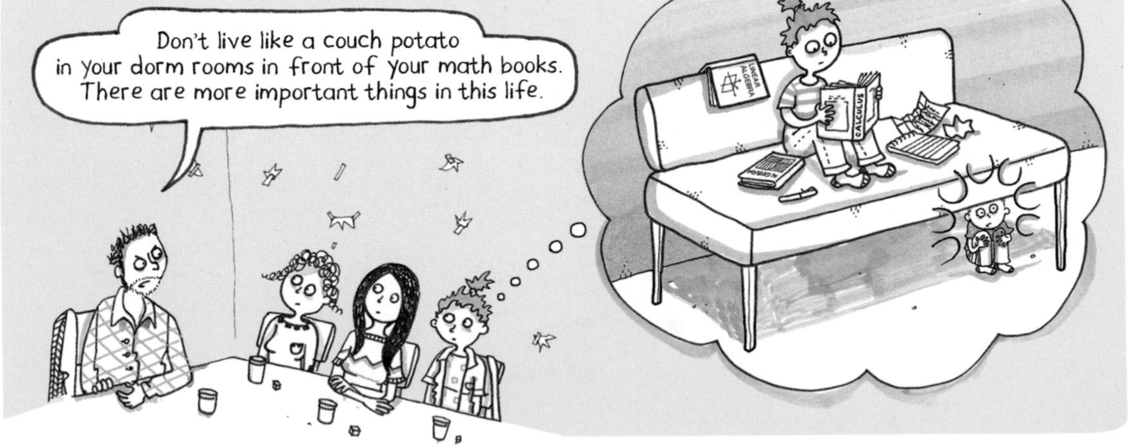
Don't live like a couch potato in your dorm rooms in front of your math books. There are more important things in this life.
LINEAR ALGEBRA
CALCULUS

Chapter 13

Sun Behind the Clouds

One day, I walked into the school cafeteria and saw that my roommate Ceyda was wearing heavy eye makeup. I was not going to miss this opportunity.

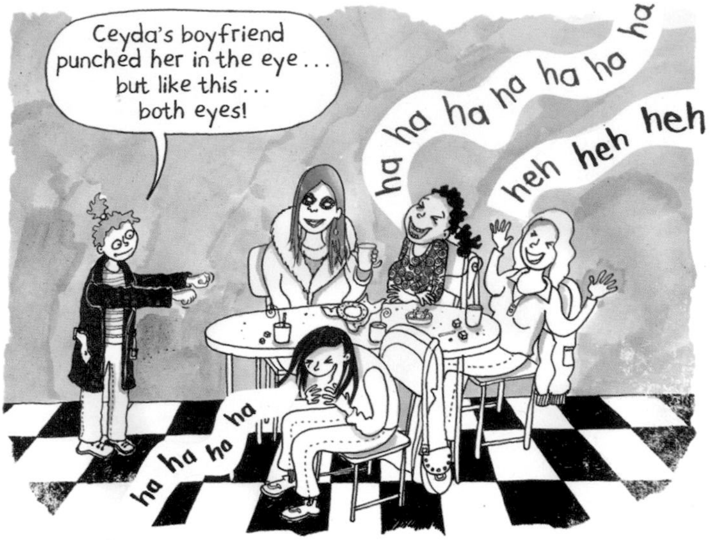
Ceyda's boyfriend punched her in the eye . . . but like this . . . both eyes!
ha ha ha ha ha ha ha
heh heh heh
ha ha ha ha

The next day, Uncle Nihat came to visit me and we took a minibus to his house late at night. As usual, the greedy driver packed the minibus with an impossible number of passengers. There was no space to move, and it was hard to breathe.

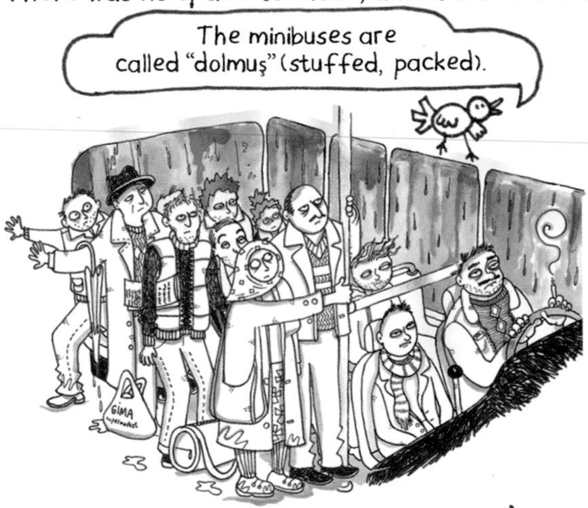
The minibuses are called "dolmuş" (stuffed, packed).
GİMA

A mile ahead there was a traffic cop. All the standing passengers crouched to protect the driver from getting a ticket for carrying standing passengers. The cops could not see them in the windows.

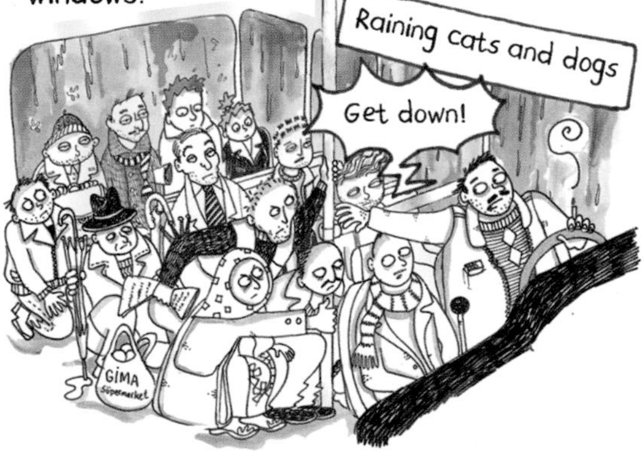
Raining cats and dogs
Get down!
GİMA Süpermarket

After we made it safely past the cops, the driver picked up a couple more passengers from the road, and the standing passengers rebelled.

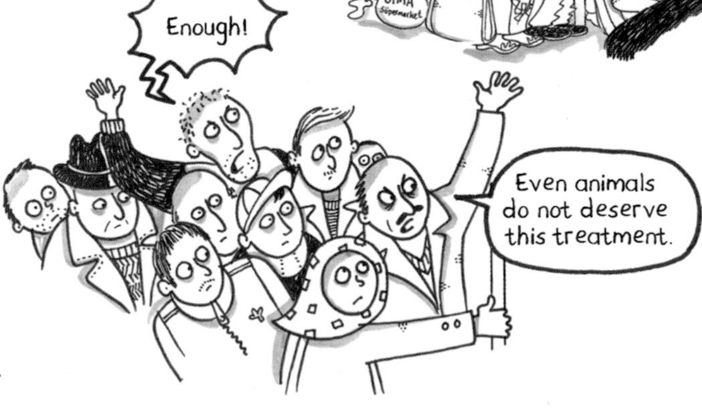
Enough!
Even animals do not deserve this treatment.

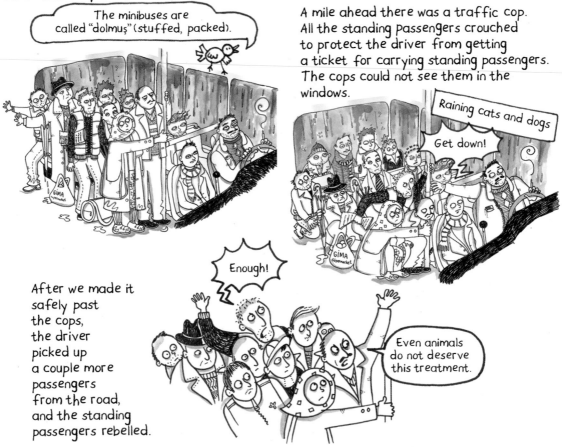

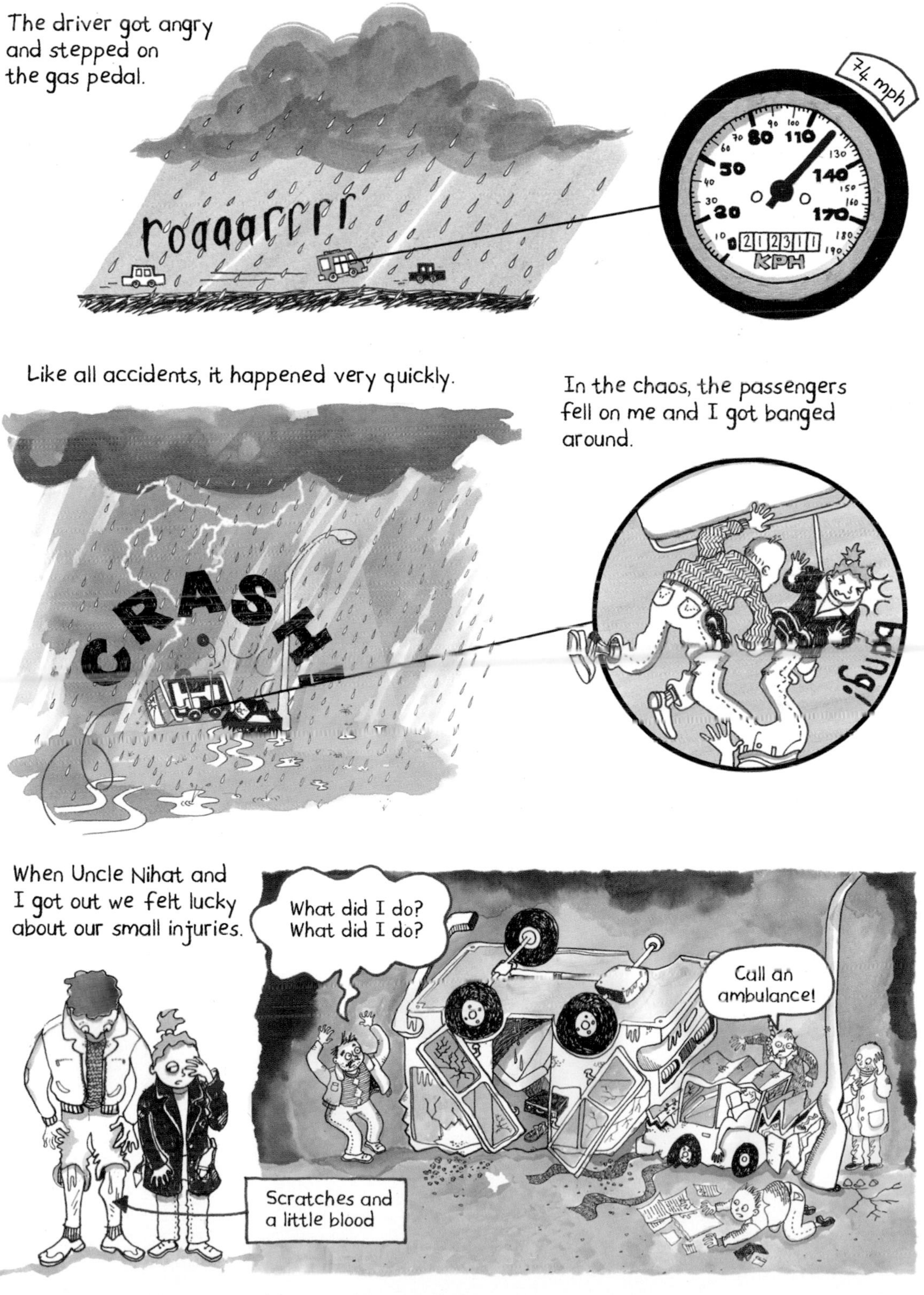
The driver got angry and stepped on the gas pedal.
roaaarrrr
74 mph
KPH
Like all accidents, it happened very quickly.
CRASH
In the chaos, the passengers fell on me and I got banged around.
bang!
When Uncle Nihat and I got out we felt lucky about our small injuries.
What did I do? What did I do?
Call an ambulance!
Scratches and a little blood

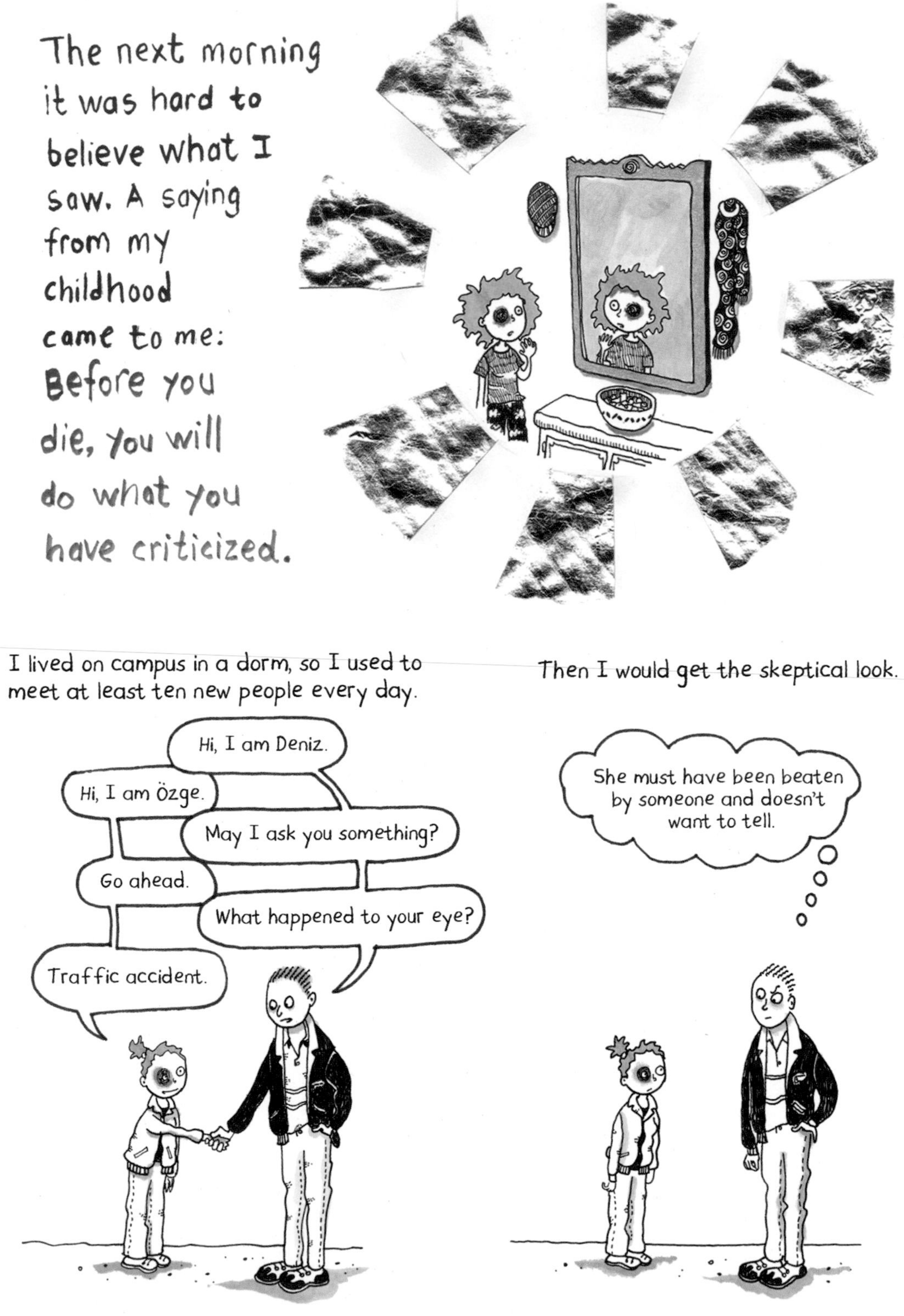

The next morning it was hard to believe what I saw. A saying from my childhood came to me: Before you die, you will do what you have criticized.
I lived on campus in a dorm, so I used to meet at least ten new people every day.
Hi, I am Deniz.
Hi, I am Özge.
May I ask you something?
Go ahead.
What happened to your eye?
Traffic accident.
Then I would get the skeptical look.
She must have been beaten by someone and doesn't want to tell.

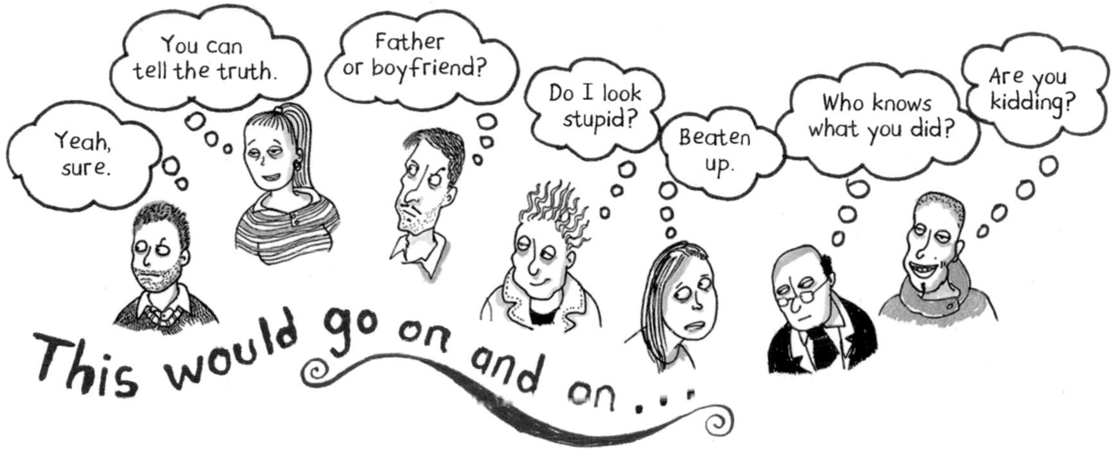
Yeah, sure.
You can tell the truth.
Father or boyfriend?
Do I look stupid?
Beaten up.
Who knows what you did?
Are you kidding?
This would go on and on . . .

After a while I got tired of it and started telling people what they wanted to hear.

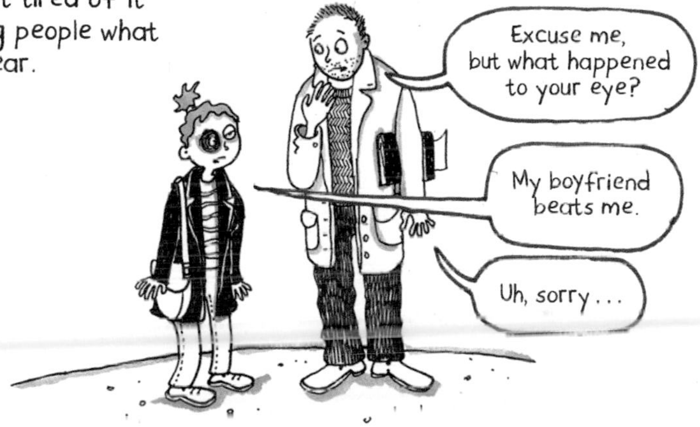
Excuse me, but what happened to your eye?
My boyfriend beats me.
Uh, sorry . . .

My spirits were low. A couple days later I got bad news. I received my grades. My GPA was equal to my short height. Out of a possible 4.0 my GPA was 1.58. I failed all my math classes.

Student Number : 9261526
Last Name : SAMANCI
First Name : ÖZGE

1993/1994-1 1.Sm

AE 111	ADVANCED ENGLISH I	3	BB
MATH131	CALCULUS I	4	F
MATH161	INTRO. TO FUNDAMENTALS MATHEMATICS I	3	F
PE 101	STEP	1	AA
PHIL131	LOGIC I	3	CB
PHYS101	PHYSICS I	4	CC

Sem. ->Cr.Att: 18+ 0 Cr.Comp.: 11+ 0 Hr.Pts.:28,5 SPA:1,58
Aft.Sem->Cr.Att: 18+ 0 Cr.Comp.: 11+ 0 Hr.Pts.:28,5 GPA:1,58

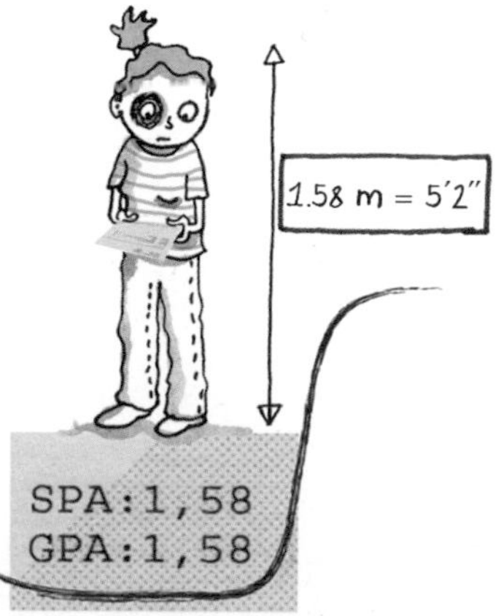
1.58 m = 5′2″
SPA:1,58
GPA:1,58

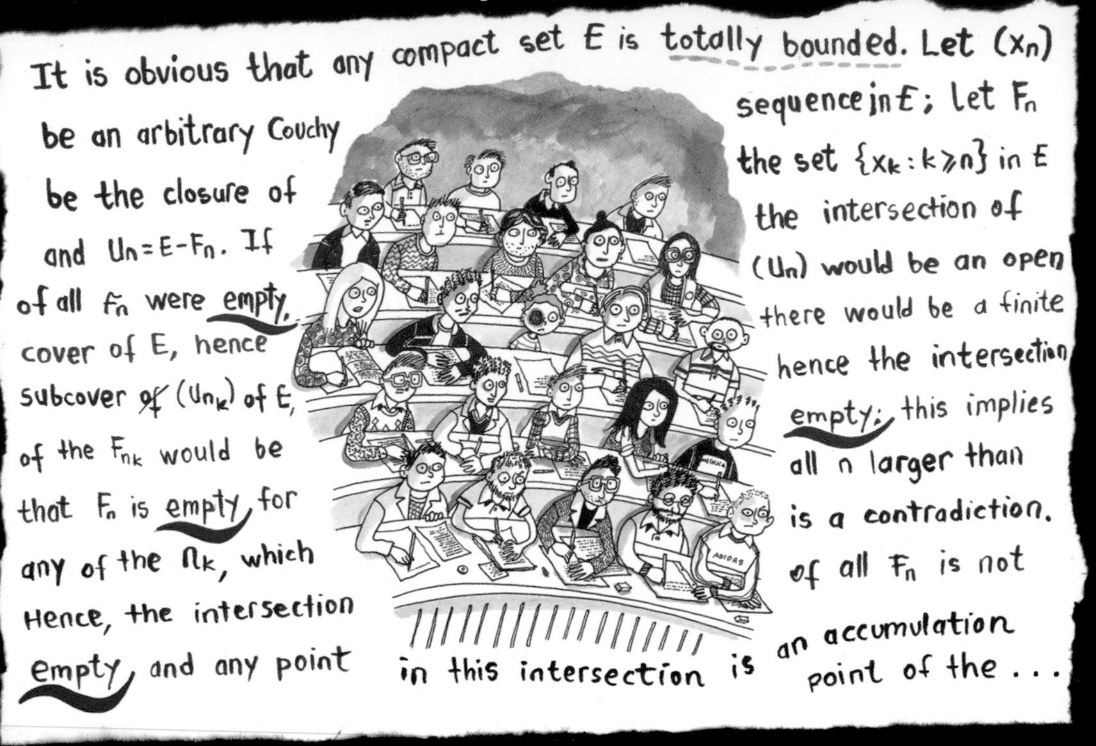

It is obvious that any compact set E is totally bounded. Let (x_n)

be an arbitrary Cauchy | sequence in E; let F_n
be the closure of | the set $\{x_k : k \geq n\}$ in E
and $U_n = E - F_n$. If | the intersection of
of all F_n were empty, | (U_n) would be an open
cover of E, hence | there would be a finite
subcover of (U_{n_k}) of E, | hence the intersection
of the F_{n_k} would be | empty; this implies
that F_n is empty, for | all n larger than
any of the n_k, which | is a contradiction.
Hence, the intersection | of all F_n is not
empty, and any point | in this intersection is | an accumulation point of the . . .

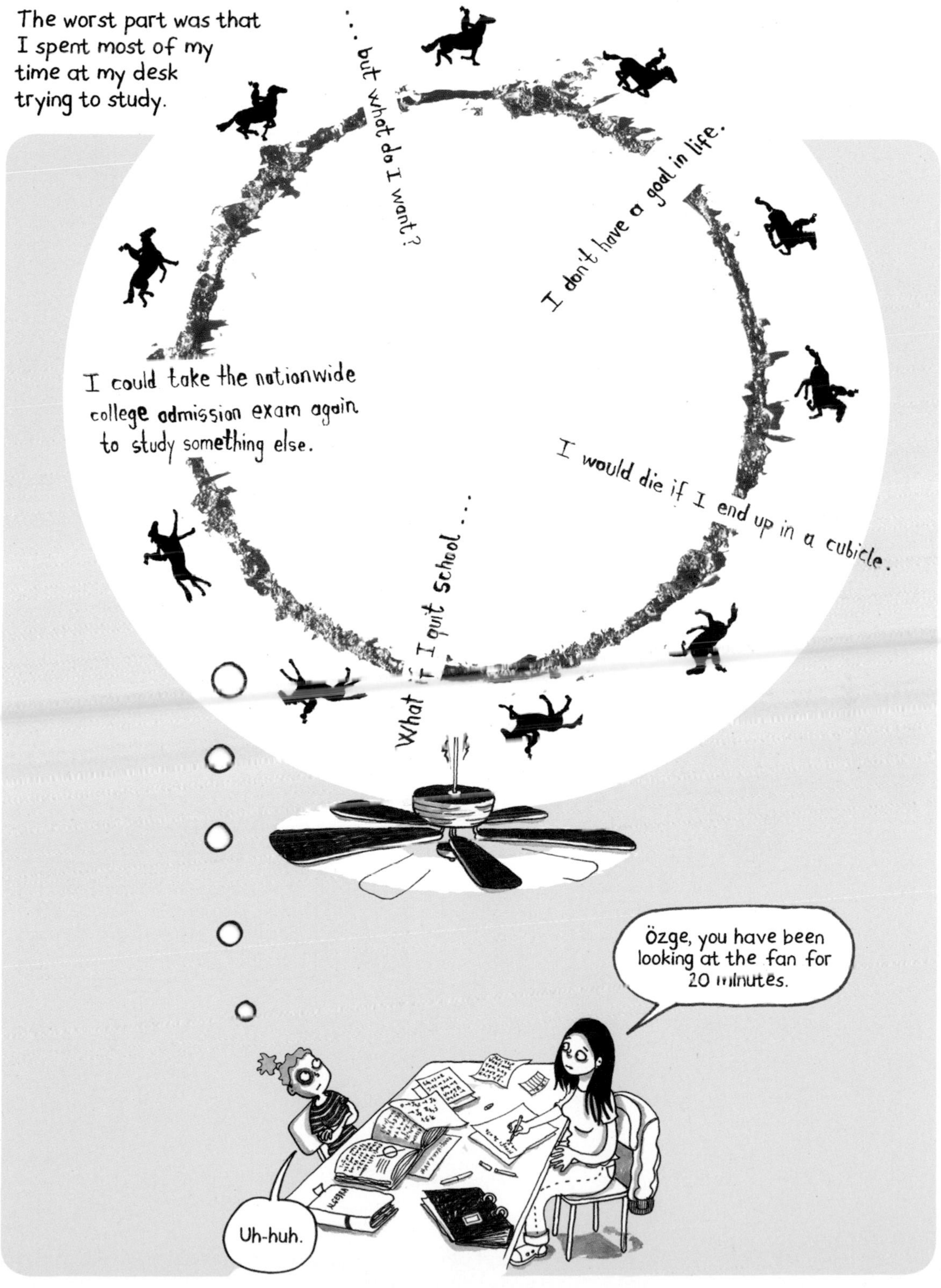
The worst part was that I spent most of my time at my desk trying to study.
. . . but what do I want?
I don't have a goal in life.
I would die if I end up in a cubicle.
What if I quit school . . .
I could take the nationwide college admission exam again to study something else.
Özge, you have been looking at the fan for 20 minutes.
Uh-huh.

Our parents made it clear to Pelin and me that we had one job—to be good full-time students. We wanted to do this to please our parents but also because they were still giving us a monthly allowance.

I am useless.

ATM

lütfen paranızı alınız.

Money sent by Mom and Dad, who were barely making it through the month on their teacher salaries.

I felt guilty if I did anything except try to study and look at the fan.

I shouldn't be here. I should be studying.

Nikahına benii çağır sevgilim istersen şahidin olurum senin ♪

More beer

Nuts

Back then it was legal to drink on campus.

The campus had one of the most pleasurable views of the Bosphorus Strait if you knew how to enjoy it . . .

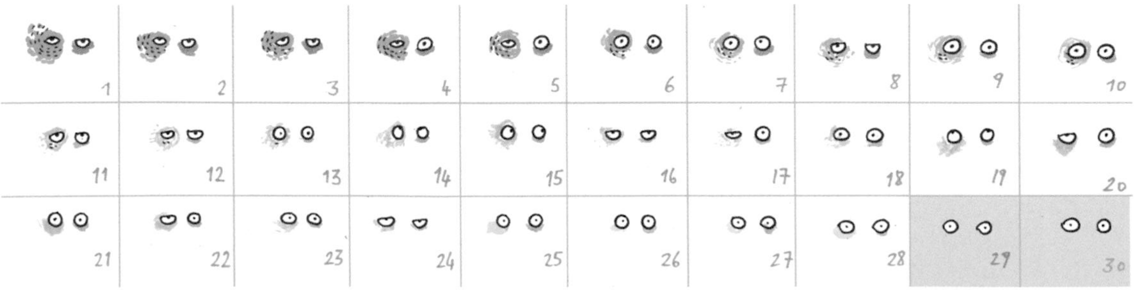

1	2	3	4	5	6	7	8	9	10
11	12	13	14	15	16	17	18	19	20
21	22	23	24	25	26	27	28	29	30

It had been two days since my purple eye had healed.

I was dragging my feet to my dreadful calculus class. There were two choices through campus: a shortcut or a long way.

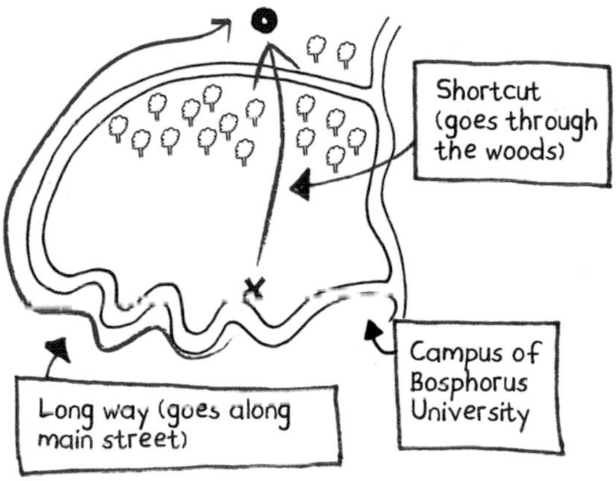
Shortcut (goes through the woods)
Campus of Bosphorus University
Long way (goes along main street)

I decided to take the shortcut.

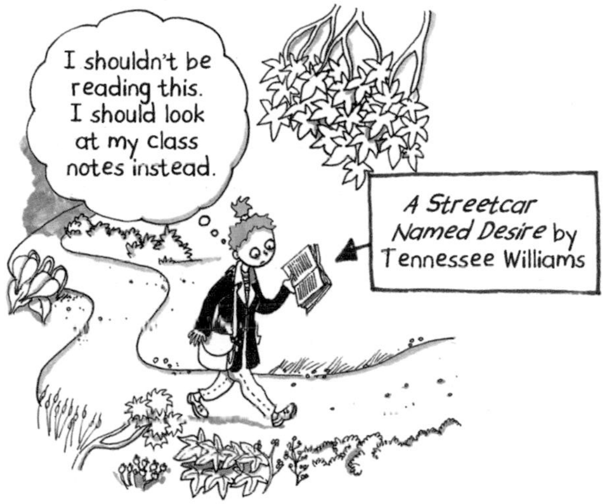
I shouldn't be reading this. I should look at my class notes instead.
A Streetcar Named Desire by Tennessee Williams

There was someone behind me.

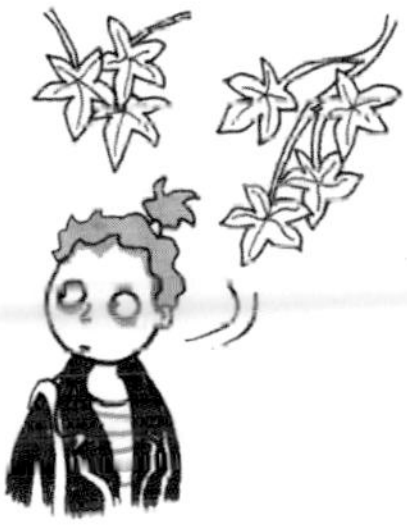

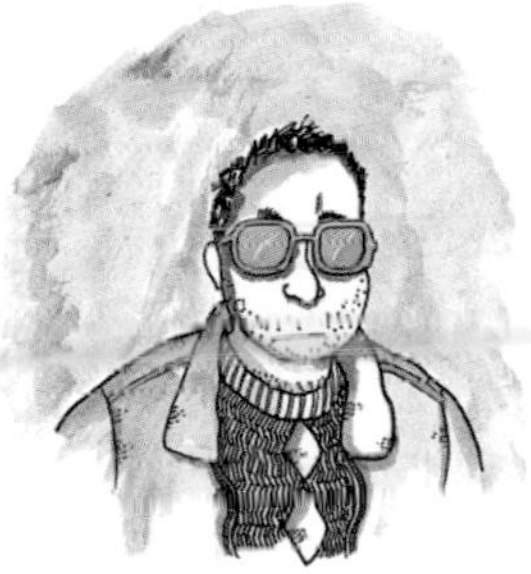

It was a guy who did not look like a student.

I sped up.

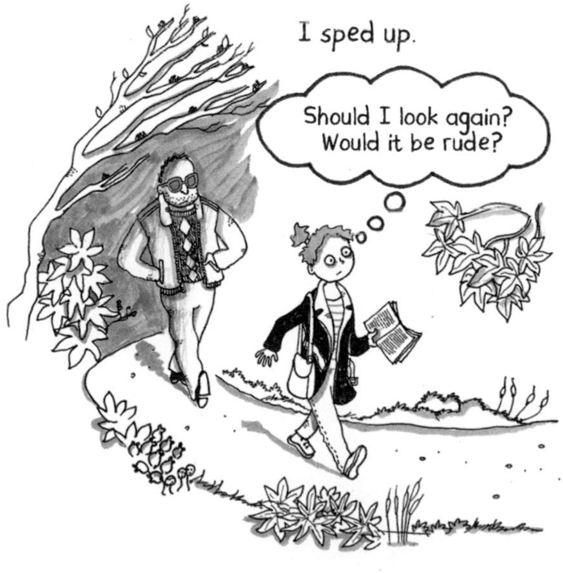
Should I look again? Would it be rude?

Suddenly I heard his voice.

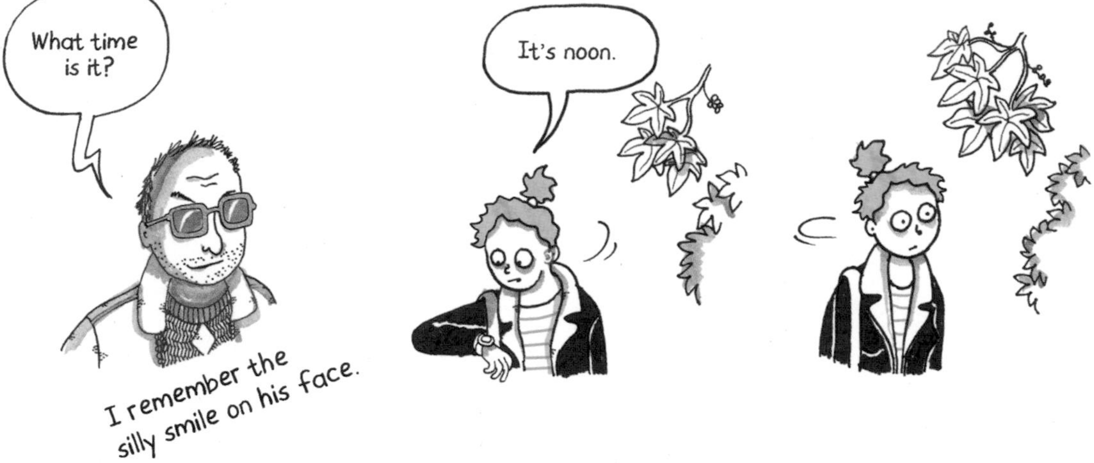
What time is it?
It's noon.
I remember the silly smile on his face.

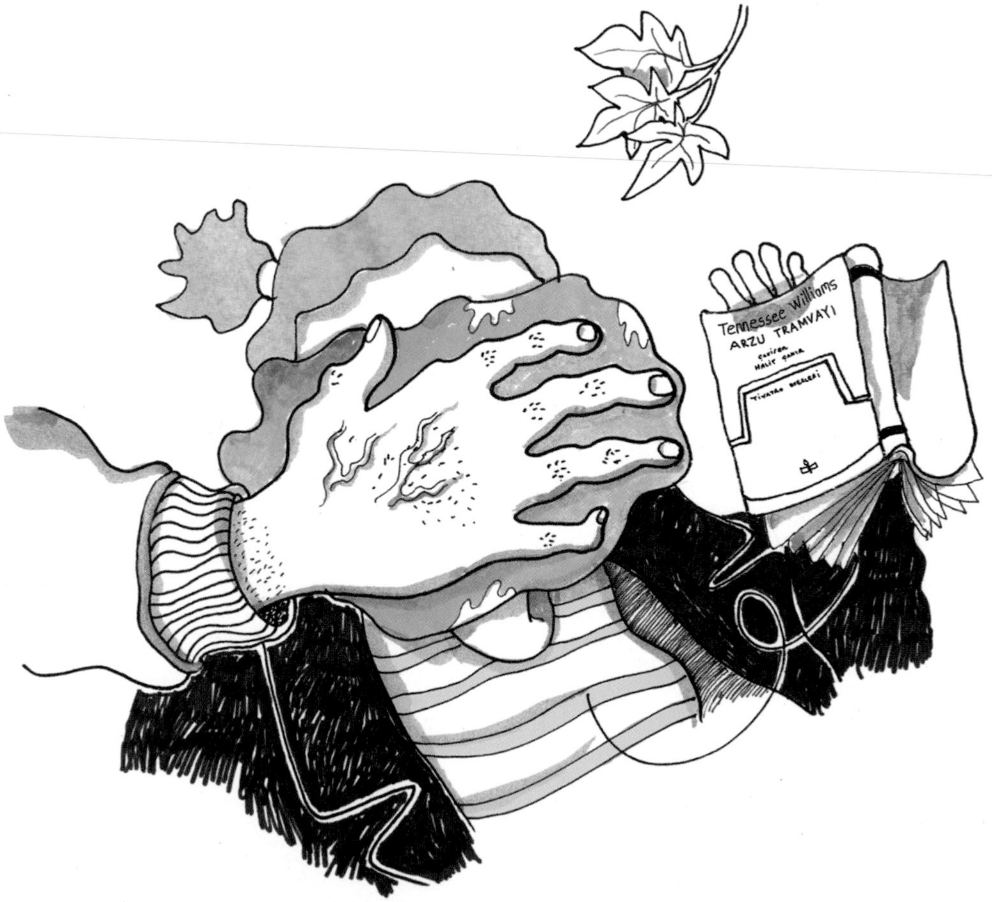
Tennessee Williams
ARZU TRAMVAYI

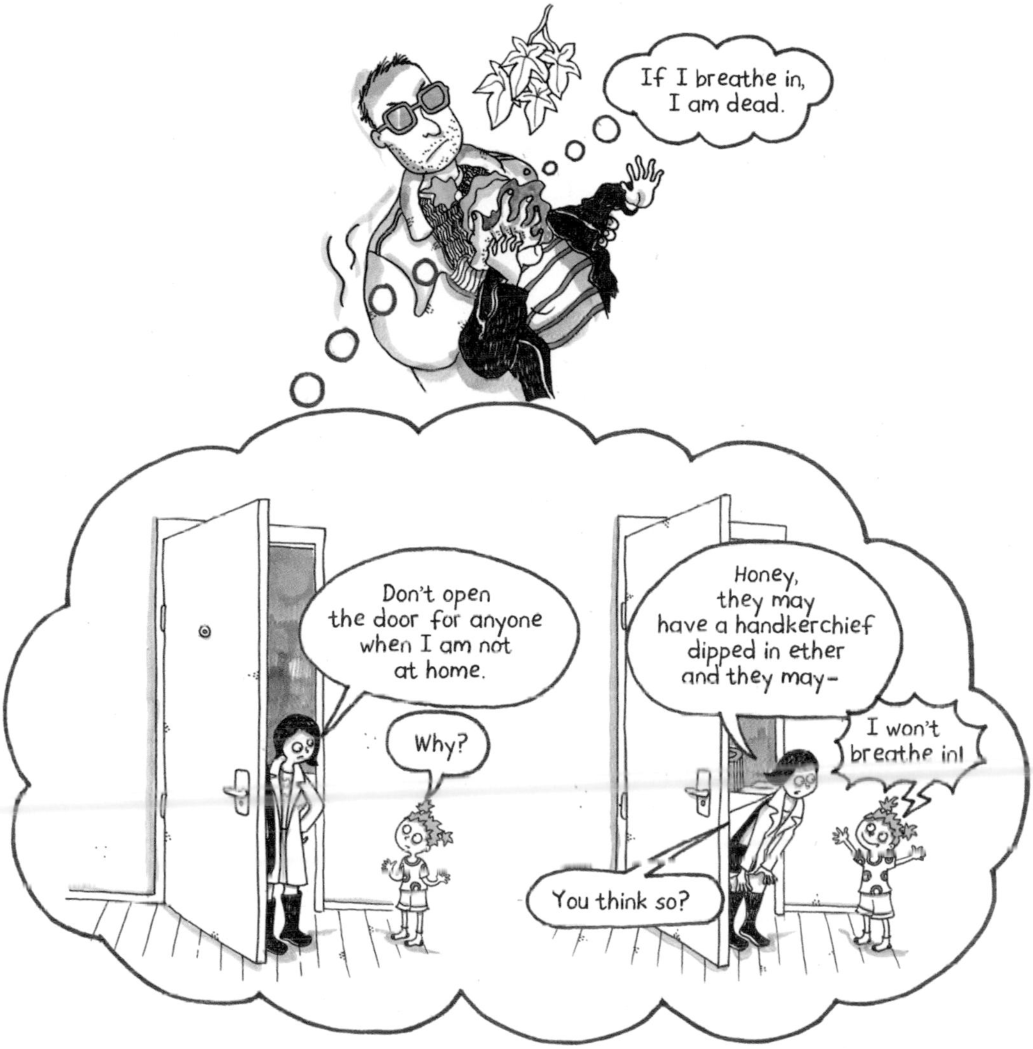
If I breathe in, I am dead.
Don't open the door for anyone when I am not at home.
Why?
Honey, they may have a handkerchief dipped in ether and they may-
I won't breathe in!
You think so?

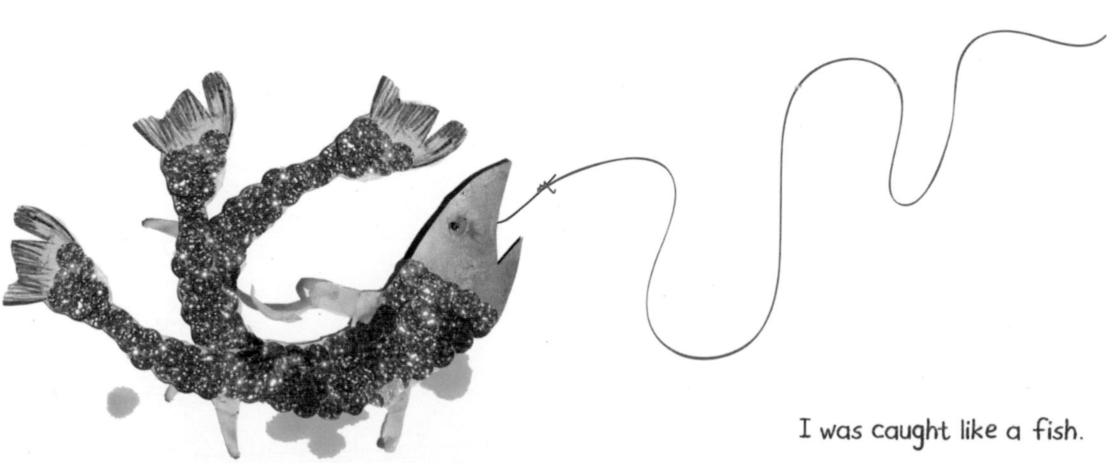

I was caught like a fish.

I held my breath as if I were underwater.
My brain was racing with thoughts.

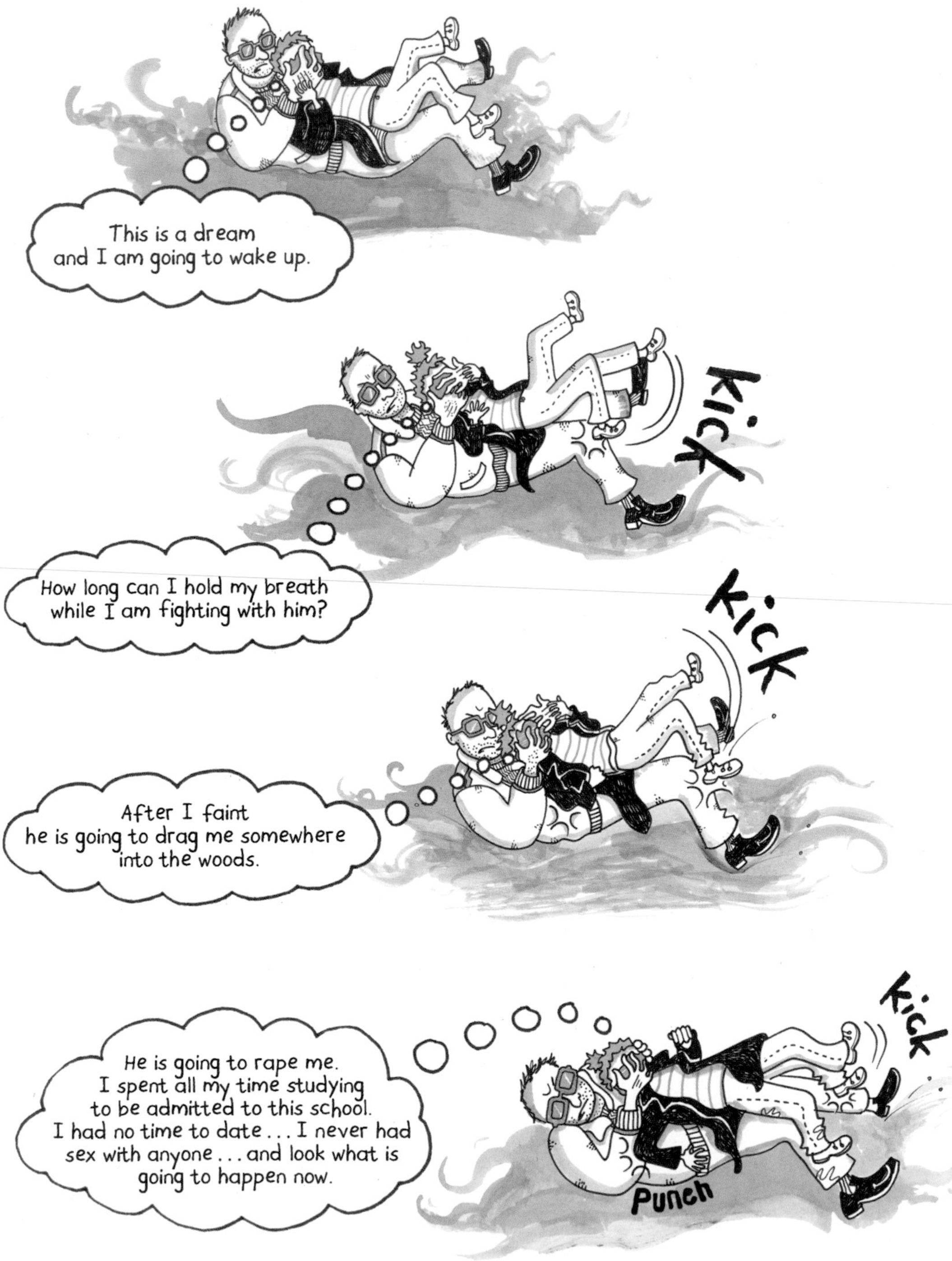
This is a dream and I am going to wake up.
KICK
How long can I hold my breath while I am fighting with him?
KICK
After I faint he is going to drag me somewhere into the woods.
KICK
He is going to rape me. I spent all my time studying to be admitted to this school. I had no time to date . . . I never had sex with anyone . . . and look what is going to happen now.
Punch

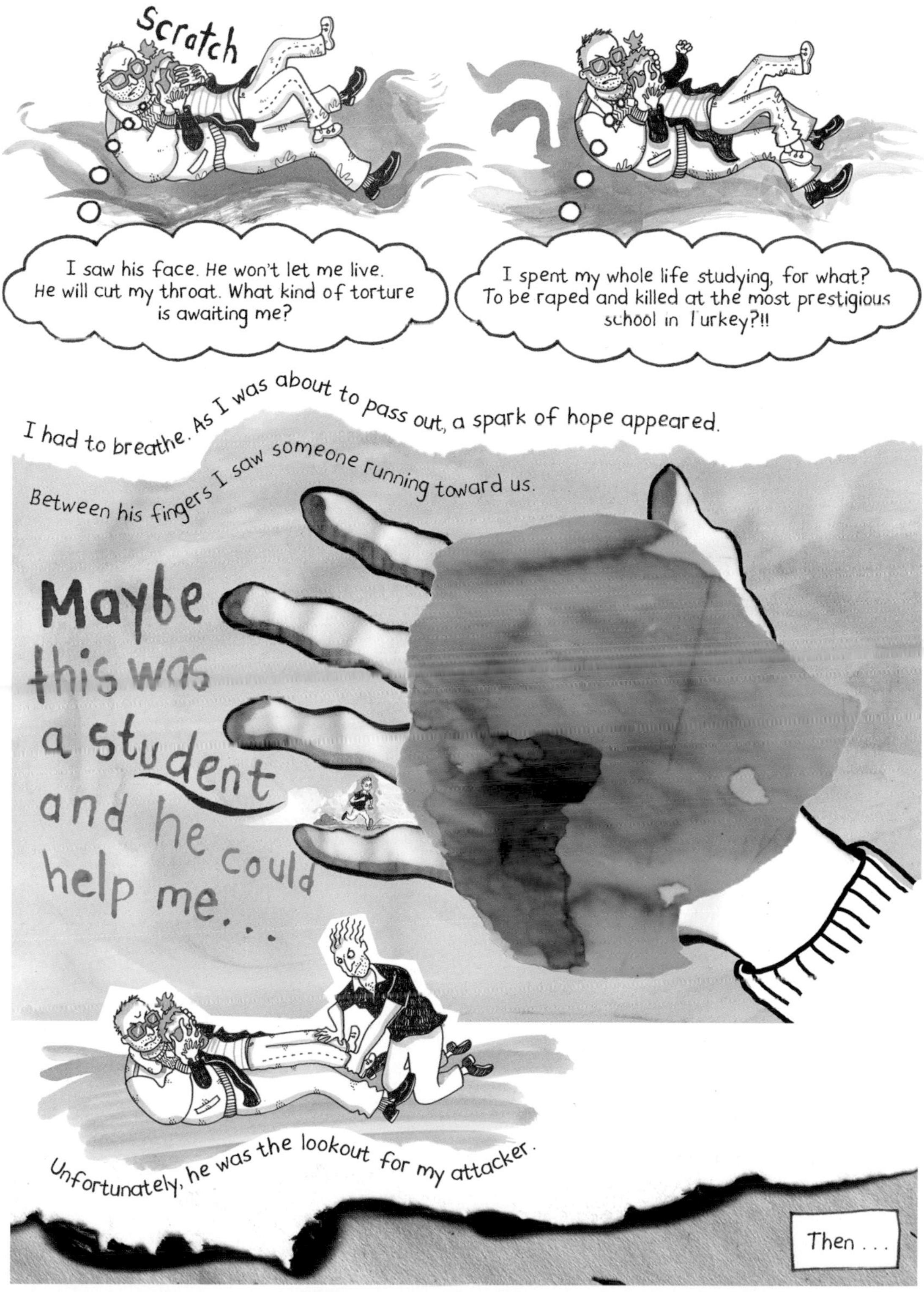
Scratch
I saw his face. He won't let me live. He will cut my throat. What kind of torture is awaiting me?
I spent my whole life studying, for what? To be raped and killed at the most prestigious school in Turkey?!!
I had to breathe. As I was about to pass out, a spark of hope appeared.
Between his fingers I saw someone running toward us.
Maybe this was a student and he could help me...
Unfortunately, he was the lookout for my attacker.
Then . . .

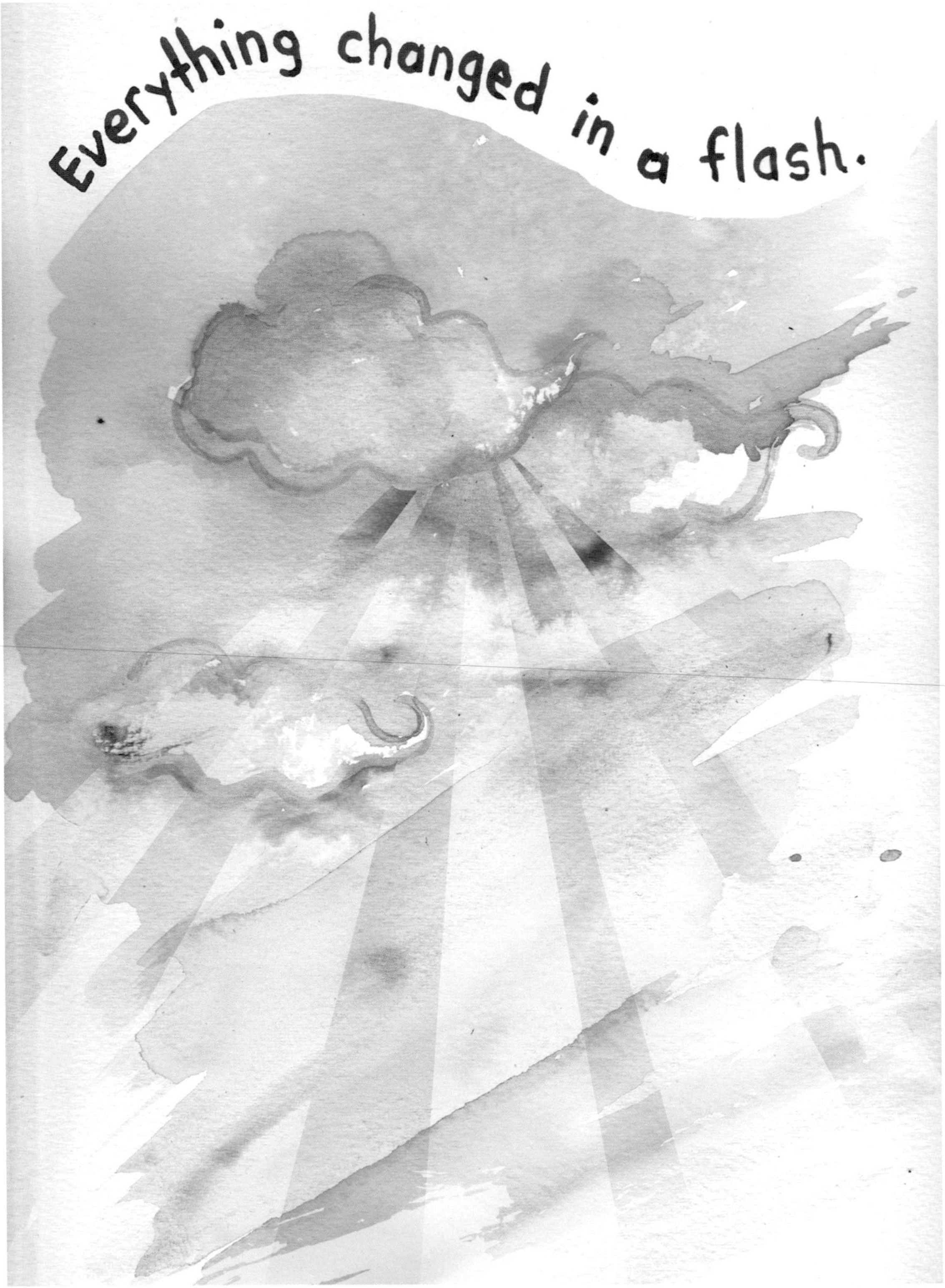
Everything changed in a flash.

The two attackers suddenly left me.

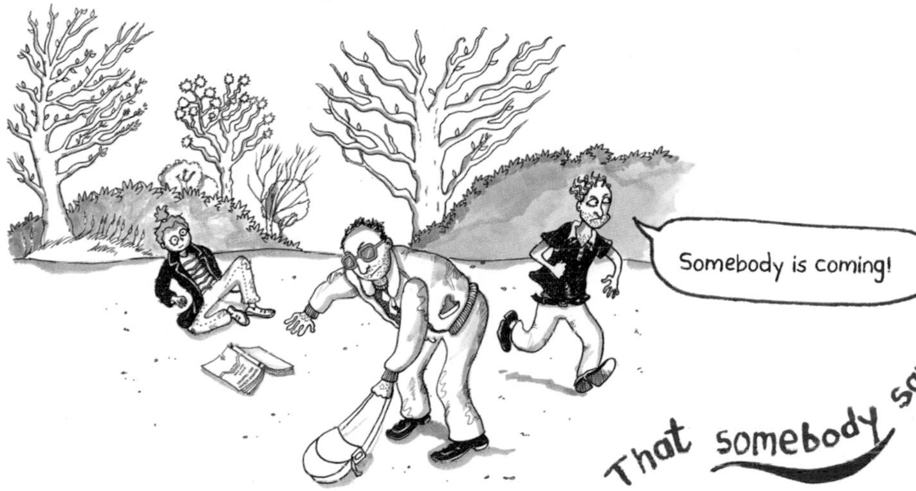

Somebody is coming!

That somebody saved my life.

I didn't faint and they only took my bag.

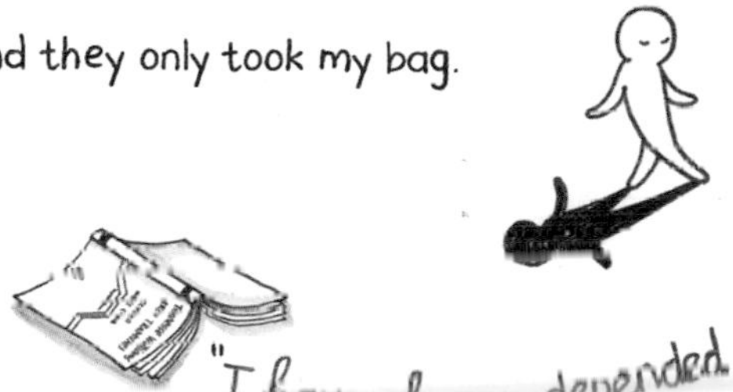

"I have always depended on the kindness of strangers."
T. Williams, A Streetcar Named Desire

After they left I started screaming.

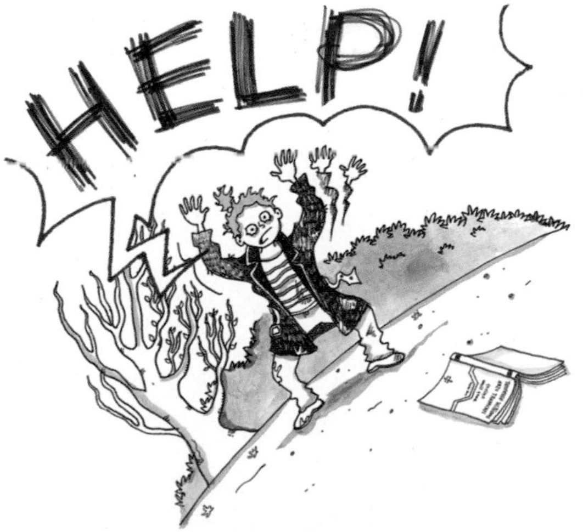

HELP!

Apparently there was also someone coming from the direction that they were going, and they started to run back toward me.

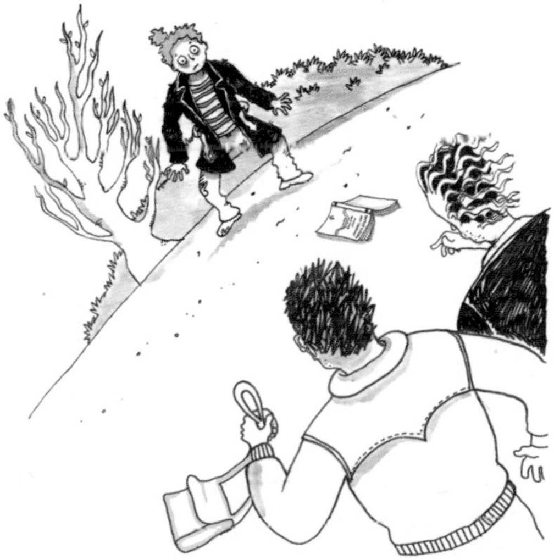

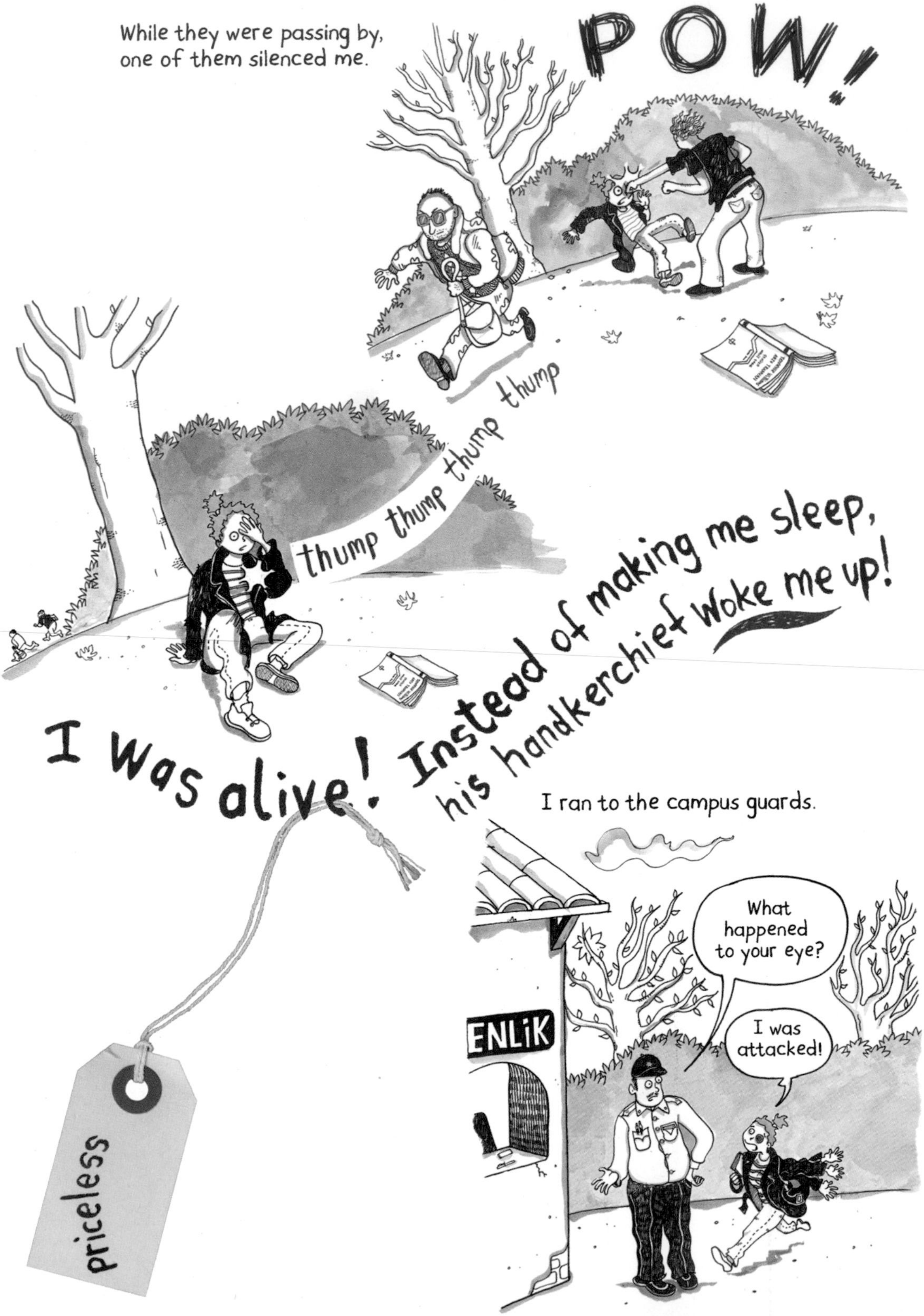
While they were passing by, one of them silenced me.
POW!
thump thump thump thump
I was alive! Instead of making me sleep, his handkerchief woke me up!
priceless
I ran to the campus guards.
ENLiK
What happened to your eye?
I was attacked!

Chapter 14

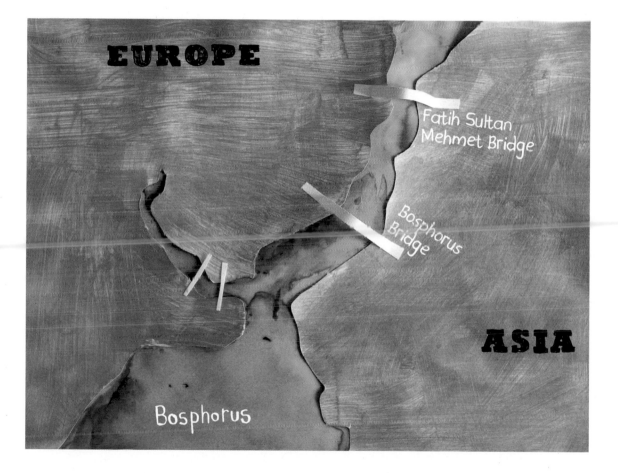

EUROPE

Fatih Sultan
Mehmet Bridge

Bosphorus
Bridge

ASIA

Bosphorus

In Between

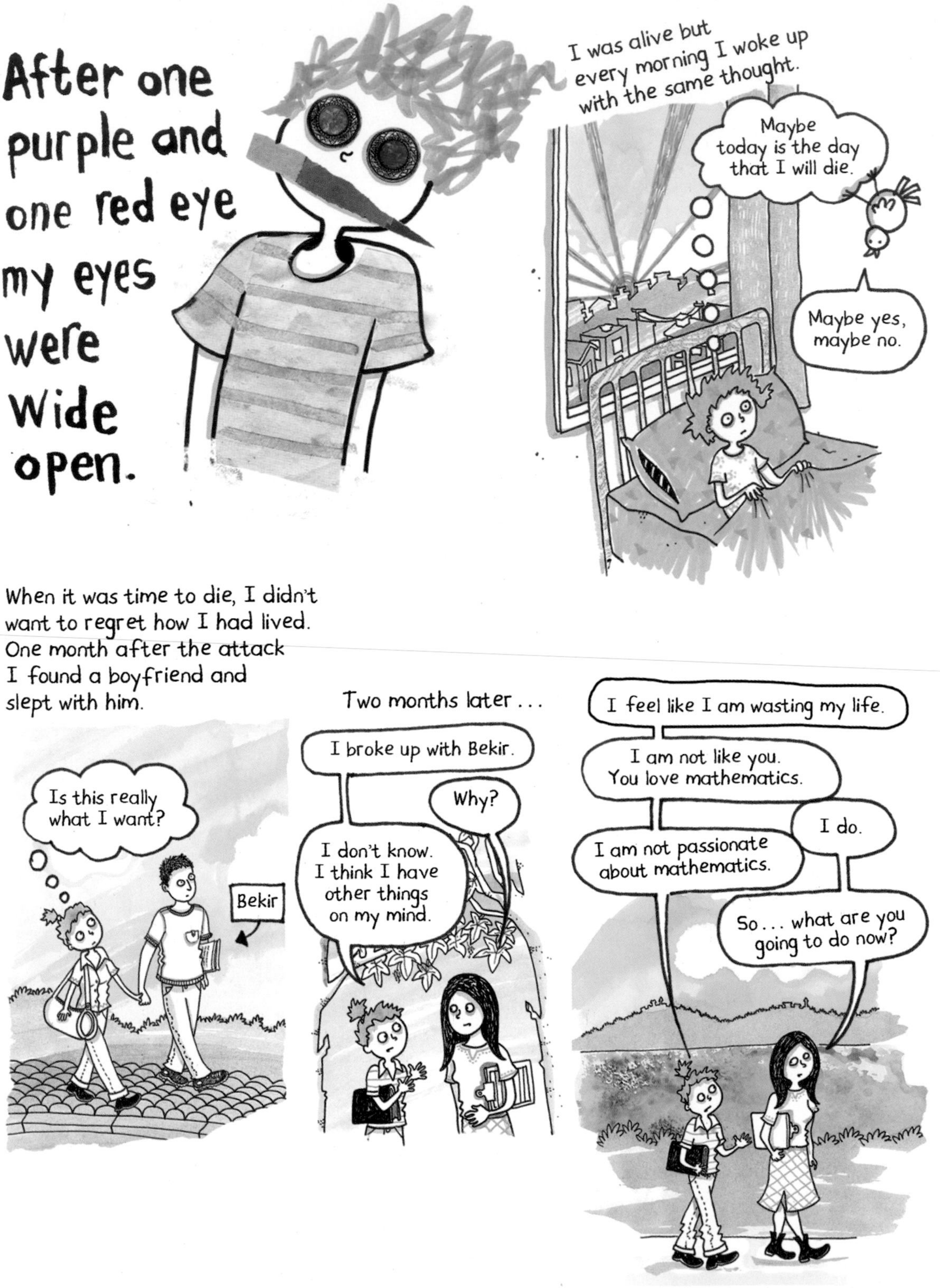
After one purple and one red eye my eyes were wide open.
I was alive but every morning I woke up with the same thought.
Maybe today is the day that I will die.
Maybe yes, maybe no.
When it was time to die, I didn't want to regret how I had lived. One month after the attack I found a boyfriend and slept with him.
Is this really what I want?
Bekir
Two months later . . .
I broke up with Bekir.
Why?
I don't know. I think I have other things on my mind.
I feel like I am wasting my life.
I am not like you. You love mathematics.
I do.
I am not passionate about mathematics.
So . . . what are you going to do now?

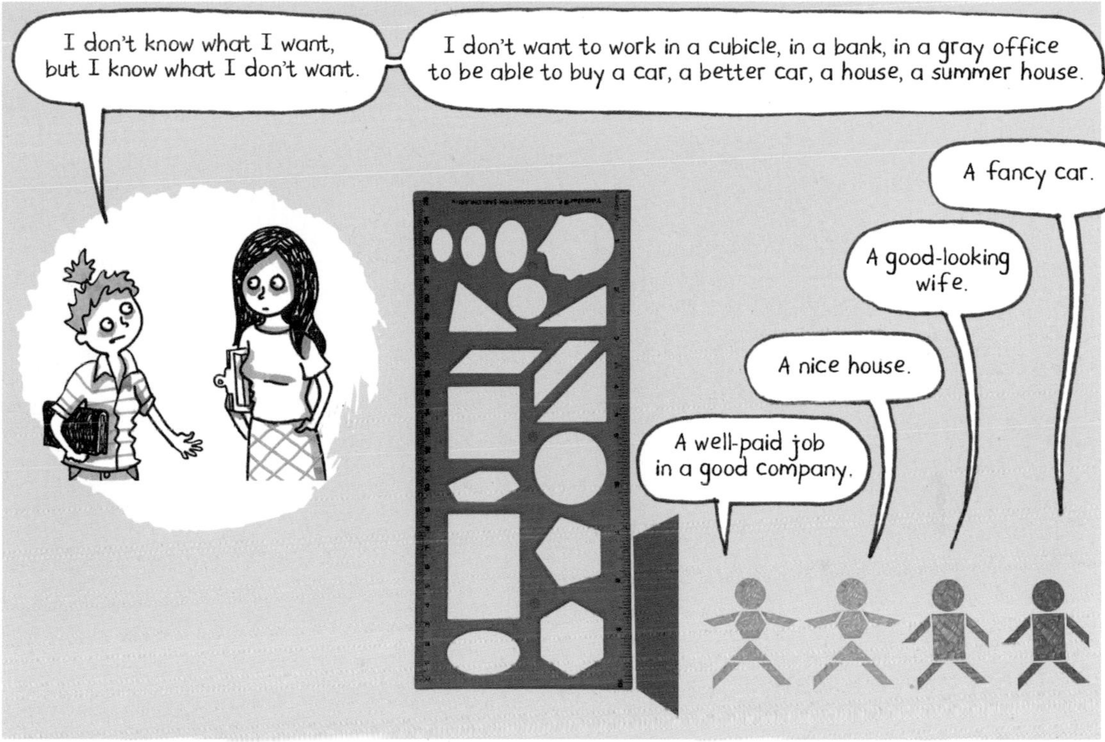
I don't know what I want, but I know what I don't want.
I don't want to work in a cubicle, in a bank, in a gray office to be able to buy a car, a better car, a house, a summer house.
A well-paid job in a good company.
A nice house.
A good-looking wife.
A fancy car.

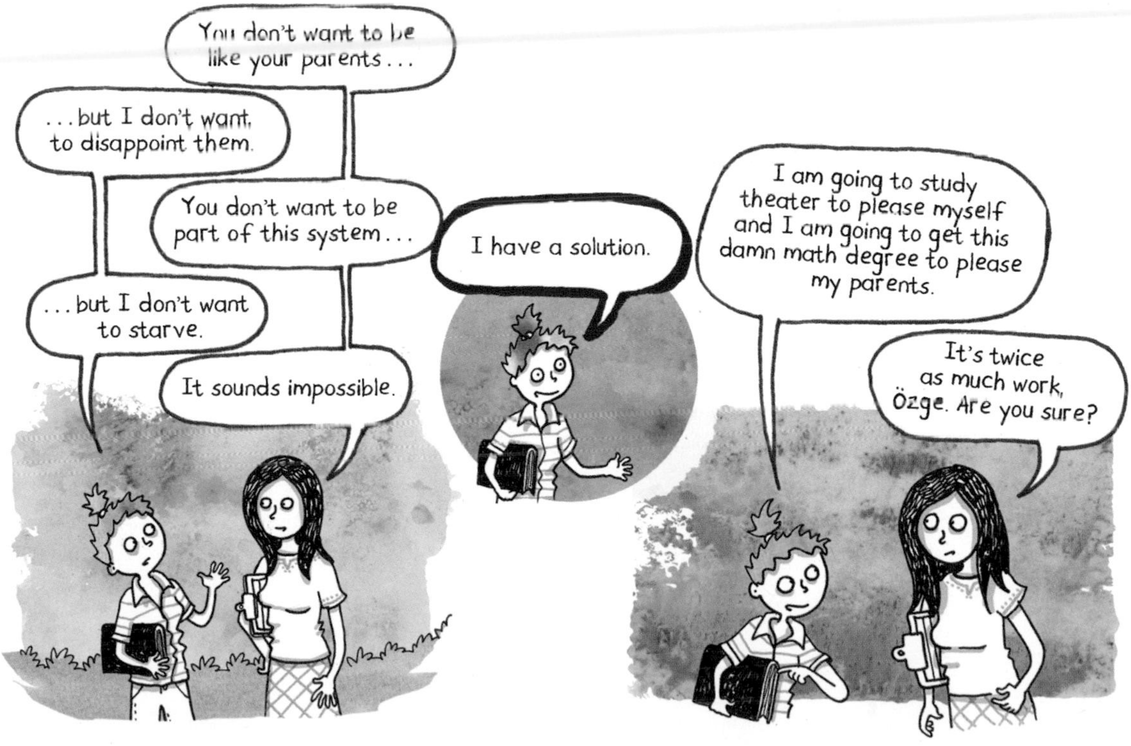
You don't want to be like your parents...
...but I don't want to disappoint them.
You don't want to be part of this system...
...but I don't want to starve.
It sounds impossible.
I have a solution.
I am going to study theater to please myself and I am going to get this damn math degree to please my parents.
It's twice as much work, Özge. Are you sure?

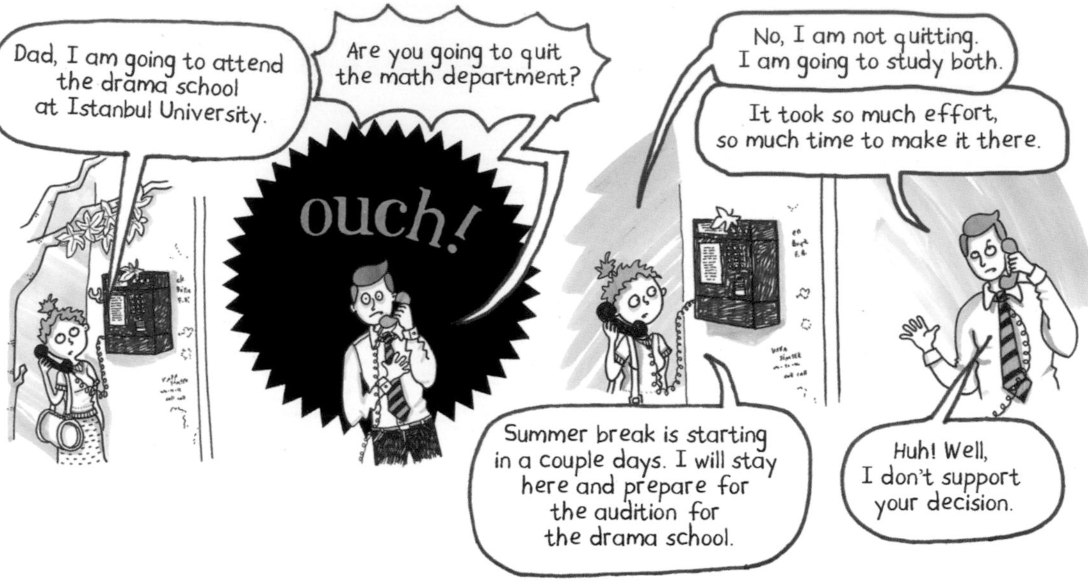
Dad, I am going to attend the drama school at Istanbul University.
Are you going to quit the math department?
ouch!
No, I am not quitting. I am going to study both.
It took so much effort, so much time to make it there.
Summer break is starting in a couple days. I will stay here and prepare for the audition for the drama school.
Huh! Well, I don't support your decision.

The next day or so . . .

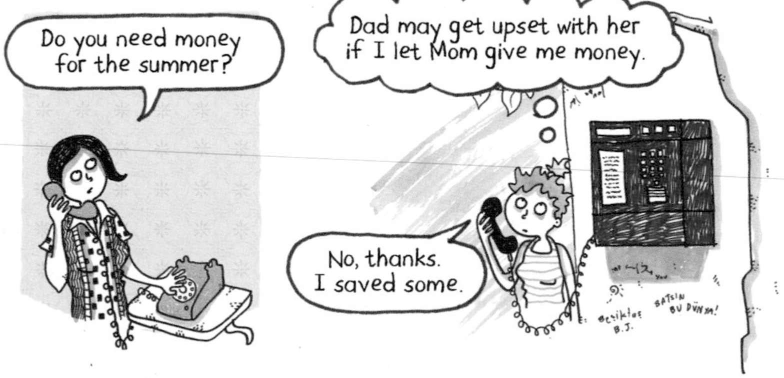
Do you need money for the summer?
Dad may get upset with her if I let Mom give me money.
No, thanks. I saved some.

I had no money to stay at school. My friends and my sister had already left for the break. I could not ask Uncle Nihat. He was unemployed.

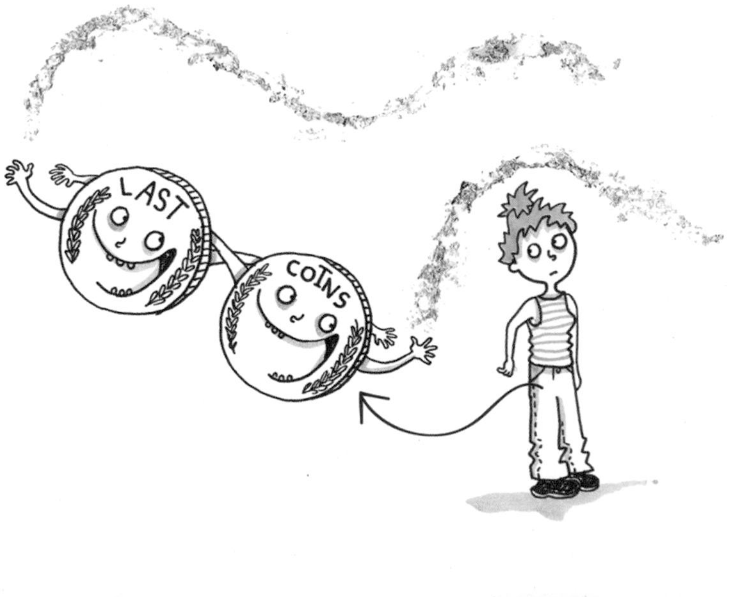
LAST
COINS

I minimalized my living costs.

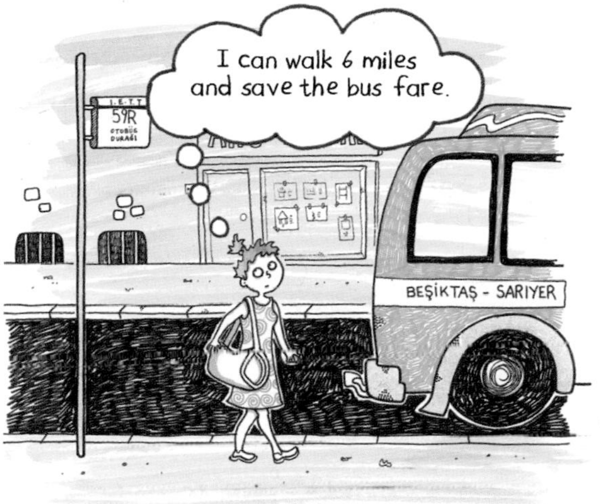
I can walk 6 miles and save the bus fare.
59R
BEŞİKTAŞ - SARIYER

My dorm was closing for break, but my sister's dorm stayed open for summer school students. Luckily, dorms in public schools were free and I could stay in her room while she was gone. While I was moving, I discovered a treasure.

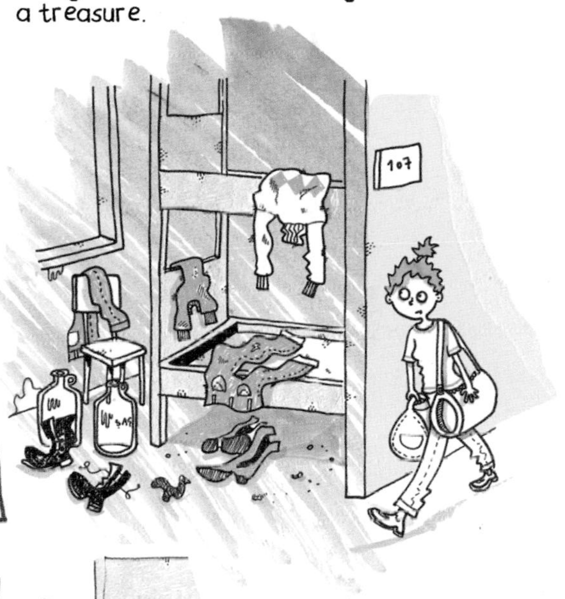
107
Students went back home and they abandoned things they didn't want: their old shoes, sweaters, refundable water bottles, etc.

I visited the empty rooms one by one and collected their leftovers.

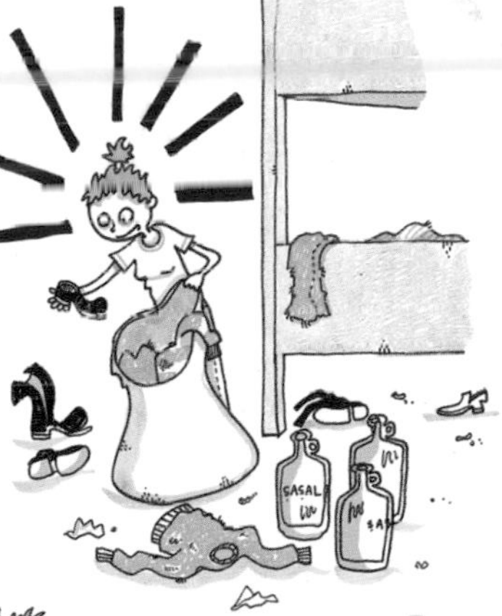

. . . and took them to the guy who sold old stuff just outside the campus gate.

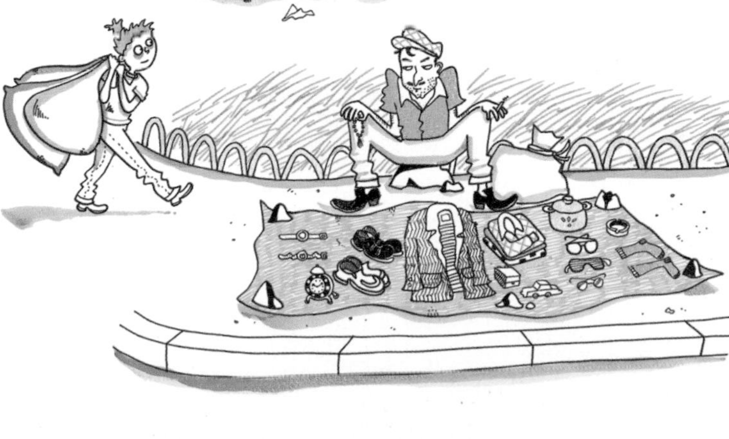

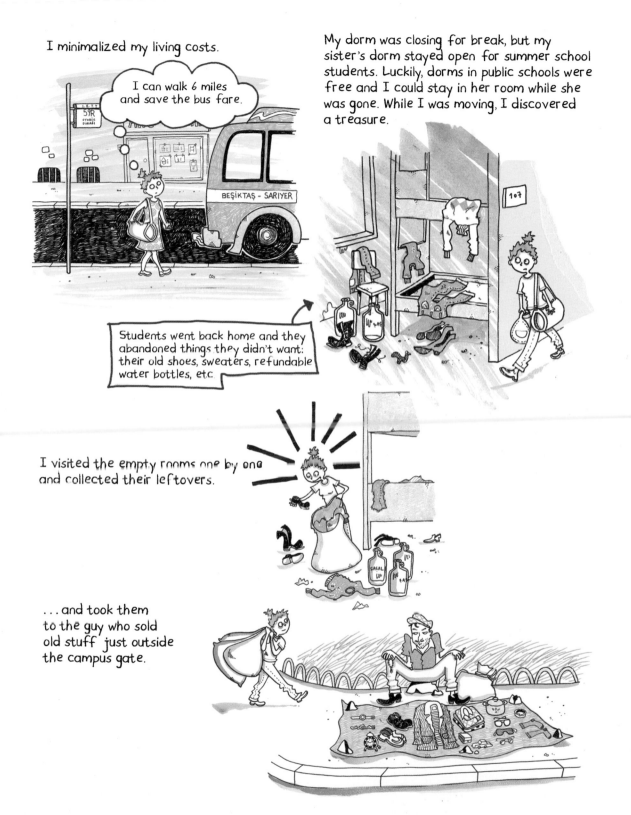

He gave me cash and whispered in my ear.

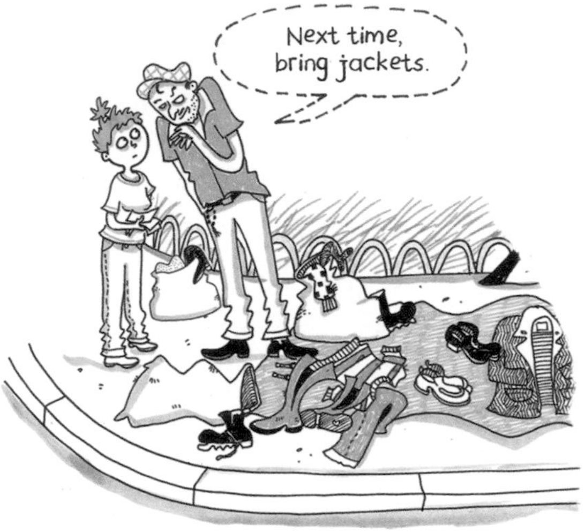

Next time, bring jackets.

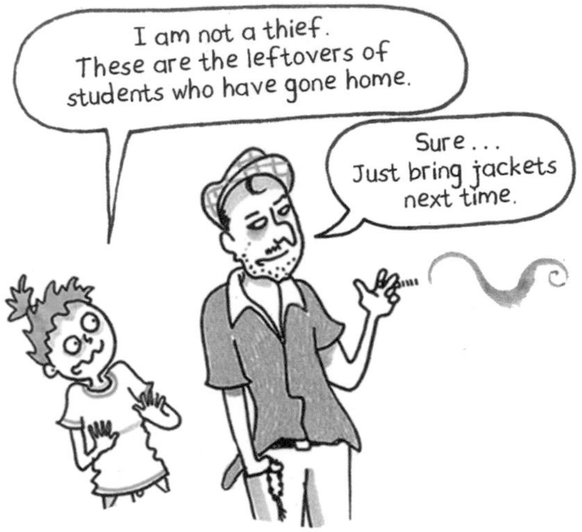

I am not a thief. These are the leftovers of students who have gone home.
Sure . . . Just bring jackets next time.

With the money I was able to stay in Istanbul and prepare for the audition for the drama school. Surprisingly, I passed it. During the first year in the drama school we were writing, directing, and acting out short stories. I loved writing and directing. My friends loved my ideas. I was truly happy.

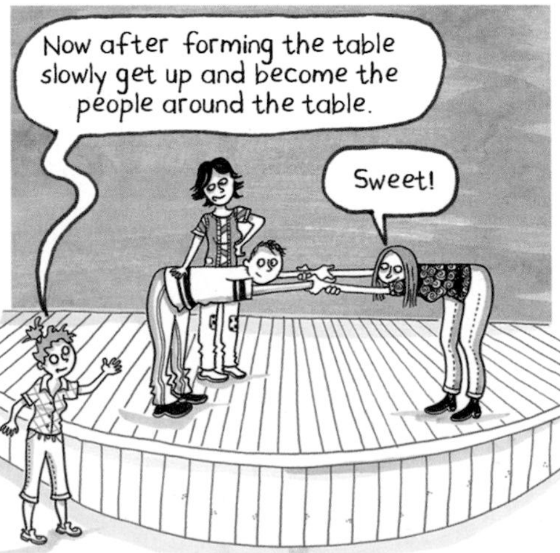

Now after forming the table slowly get up and become the people around the table.
Sweet!

But after the first year it was all acting. I was not an actor.

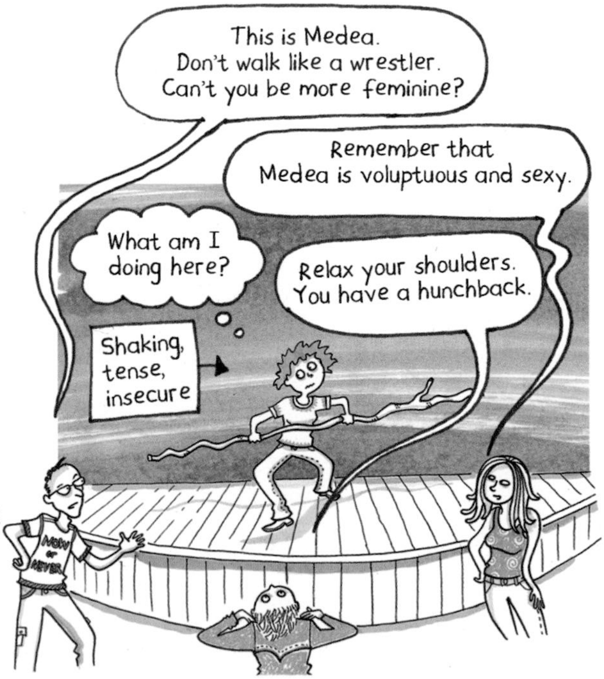

This is Medea. Don't walk like a wrestler. Can't you be more feminine?
Remember that Medea is voluptuous and sexy.
What am I doing here?
Relax your shoulders. You have a hunchback.
Shaking, tense, insecure

I was trying so hard to succeed in two different schools.
I was literally running from one continent to another to please both Dad and myself.

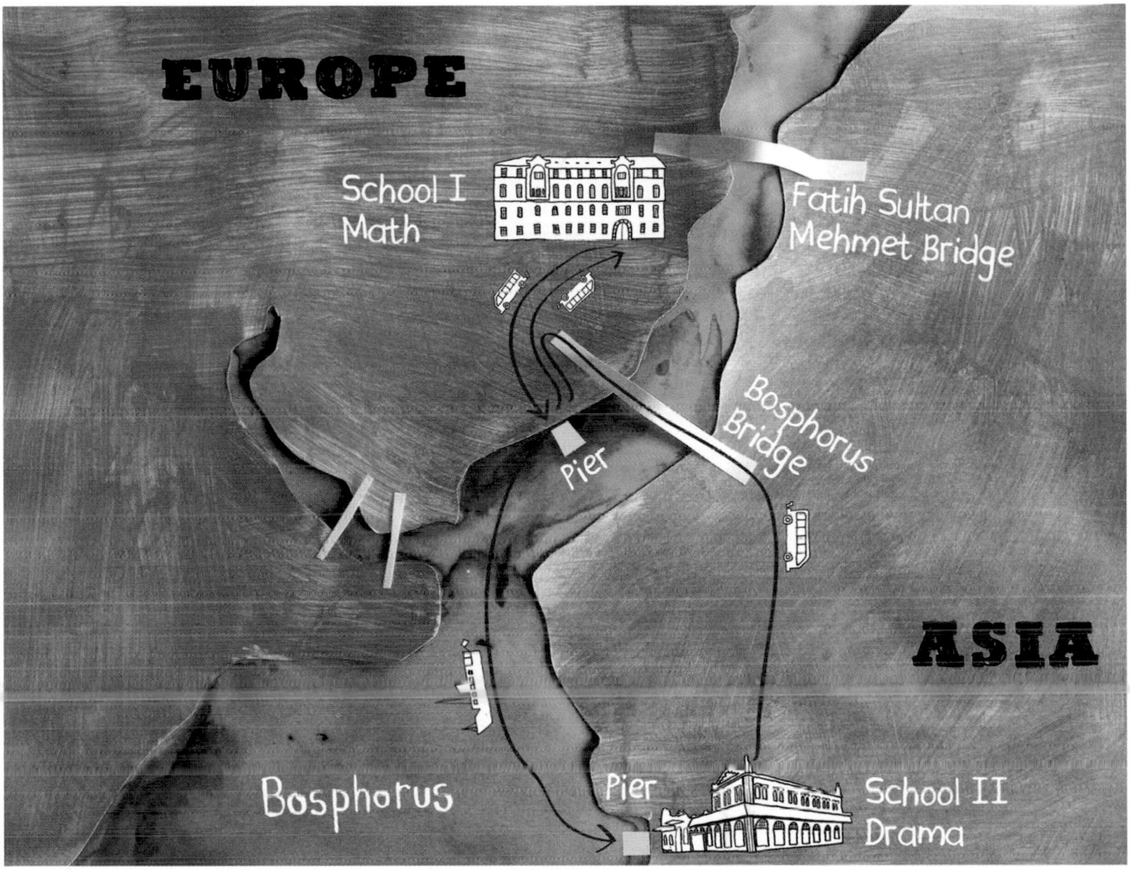
EUROPE
School I
Math
Fatih Sultan
Mehmet Bridge
Bosphorus
Bridge
Pier
ASIA
Bosphorus
Pier
School II
Drama

I hated receiving money from my parents. I began tutoring high school students at their homes. I had five students that I visited on a weekly basis.

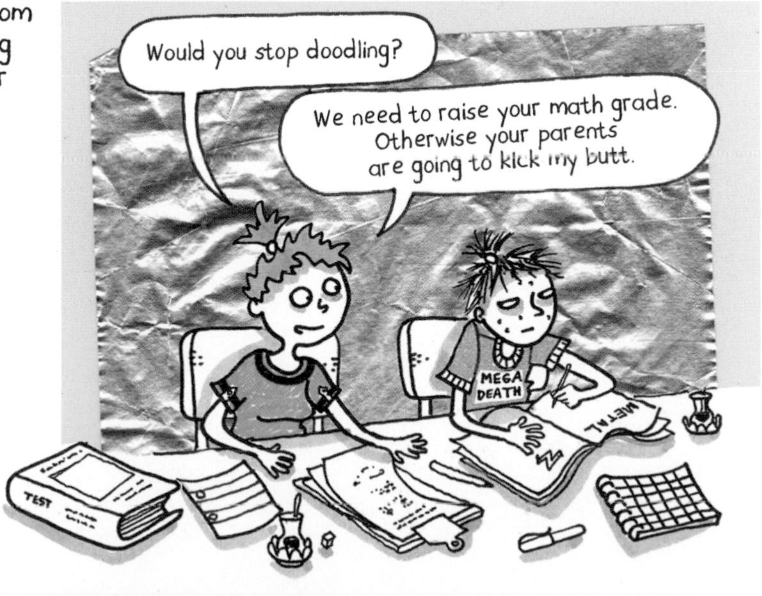
Would you stop doodling?
We need to raise your math grade. Otherwise your parents are going to kick my butt.
MEGA DEATH
METAL
TEST

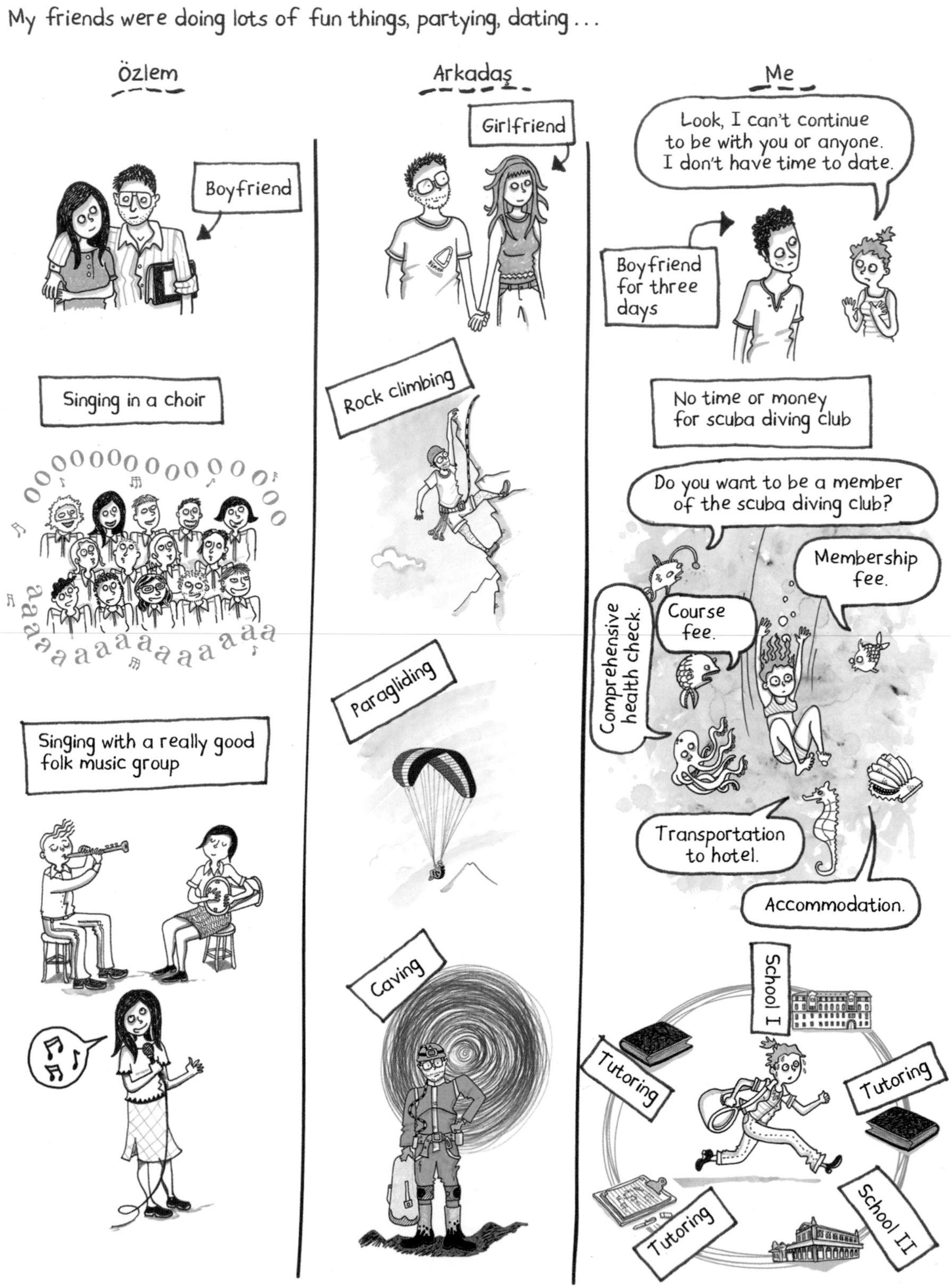

My friends were doing lots of fun things, partying, dating . . .
Özlem
Boyfriend
Singing in a choir
Singing with a really good folk music group
Arkadaş
Girlfriend
Rock climbing
Paragliding
Caving
Me
Look, I can't continue to be with you or anyone. I don't have time to date.
Boyfriend for three days
No time or money for scuba diving club
Do you want to be a member of the scuba diving club?
Membership fee.
Course fee.
Comprehensive health check.
Transportation to hotel.
Accommodation.
School I
Tutoring
Tutoring
Tutoring
School II

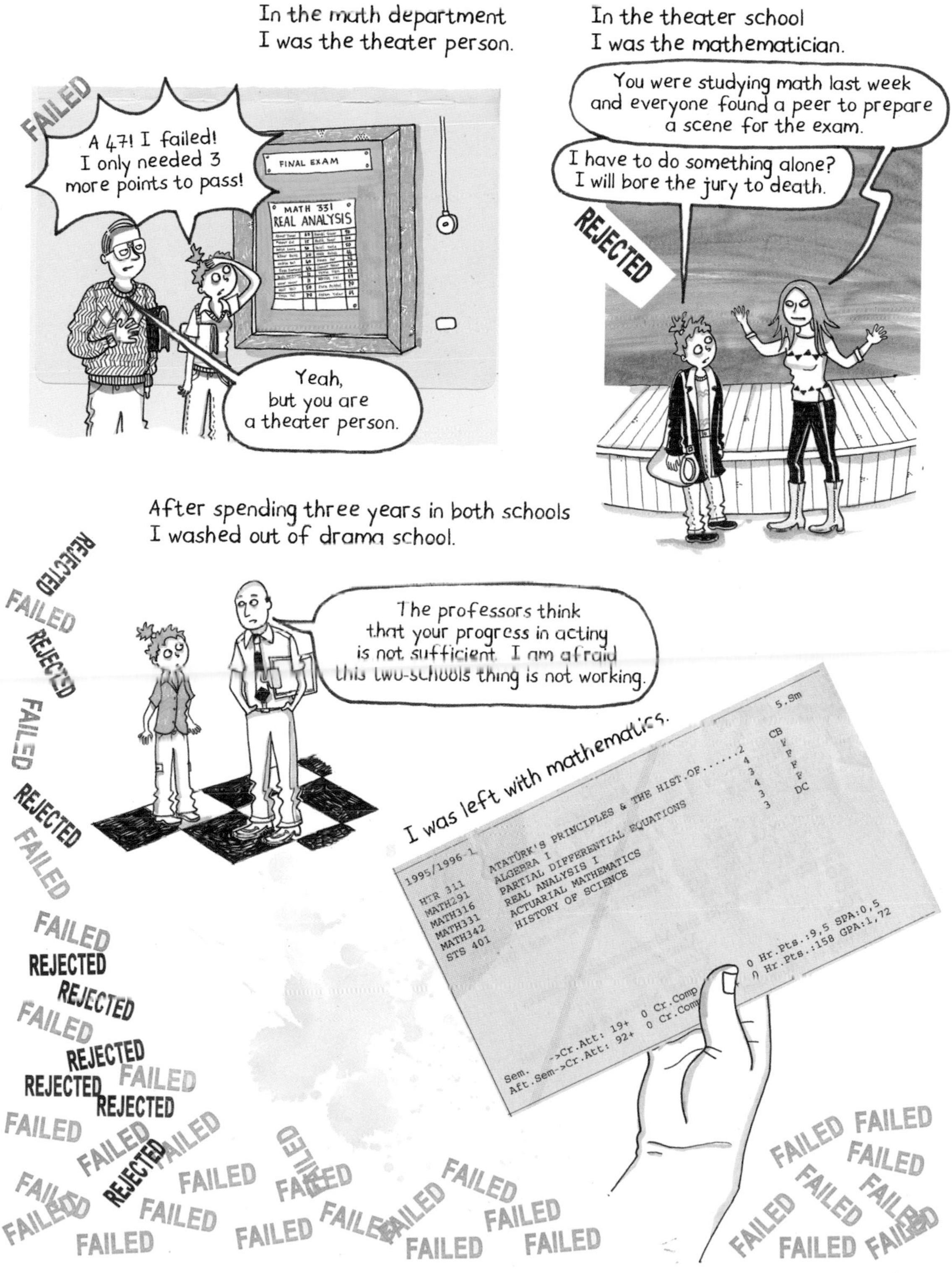
In the math department
I was the theater person.
FAILED
A 47! I failed! I only needed 3 more points to pass!
FINAL EXAM
MATH 331
REAL ANALYSIS
Yeah, but you are a theater person.
In the theater school
I was the mathematician.
You were studying math last week and everyone found a peer to prepare a scene for the exam.
I have to do something alone? I will bore the jury to death.
REJECTED
After spending three years in both schools
I washed out of drama school.
The professors think that your progress in acting is not sufficient. I am afraid this two-schools thing is not working.
I was left with mathematics.
1995/1996-1
5.Sm
HTR 311 ATATÜRK'S PRINCIPLES & THE HIST.OF......2 CB
MATH291 ALGEBRA I 4 F
MATH316 PARTIAL DIFFERENTIAL EQUATIONS 3 F
MATH331 REAL ANALYSIS I 4 F
MATH342 ACTUARIAL MATHEMATICS 3 F
STS 401 HISTORY OF SCIENCE 3 DC
Sem. ->Cr.Att: 19+ 0 Cr.Comp
Aft.Sem->Cr.Att: 92+ 0 Cr.Comp
0 Hr.Pts.:9,5 SPA:0,5
0 Hr.Pts.:158 GPA:1,72
REJECTED
FAILED
REJECTED
FAILED
REJECTED
FAILED
FAILED
REJECTED
REJECTED
FAILED
REJECTED
REJECTED FAILED
REJECTED
FAILED
FAILED
FAILED
FAILED
FAILED
FAILED
FAILED
FAILED
FAILED
FAILED FAILED
FAILED
FAILED
FAILED
FAILED
FAILED

My friends Arkadaş and Özlem graduated.

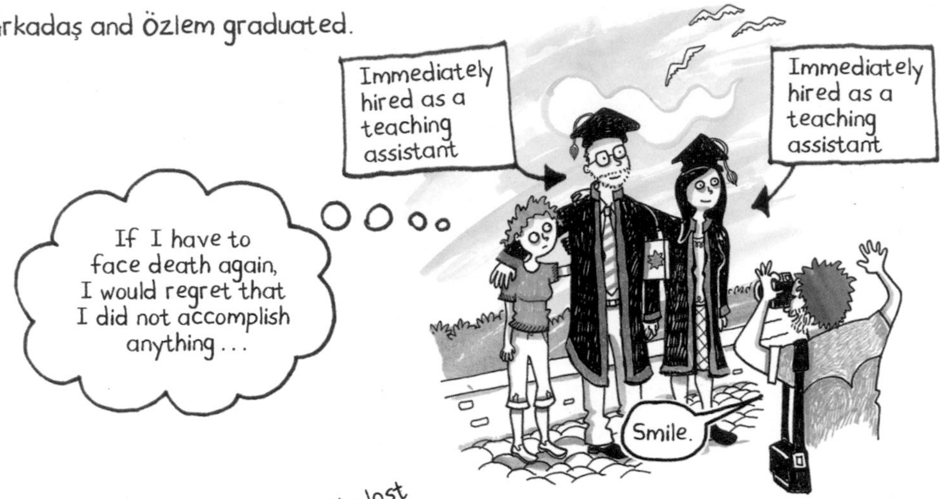
If I have to face death again, I would regret that I did not accomplish anything . . .
Immediately hired as a teaching assistant
Immediately hired as a teaching assistant
Smile.

In those three years I had gradually lost my self-esteem and finally hit a wall.

Either I could not sleep or I could not get up.

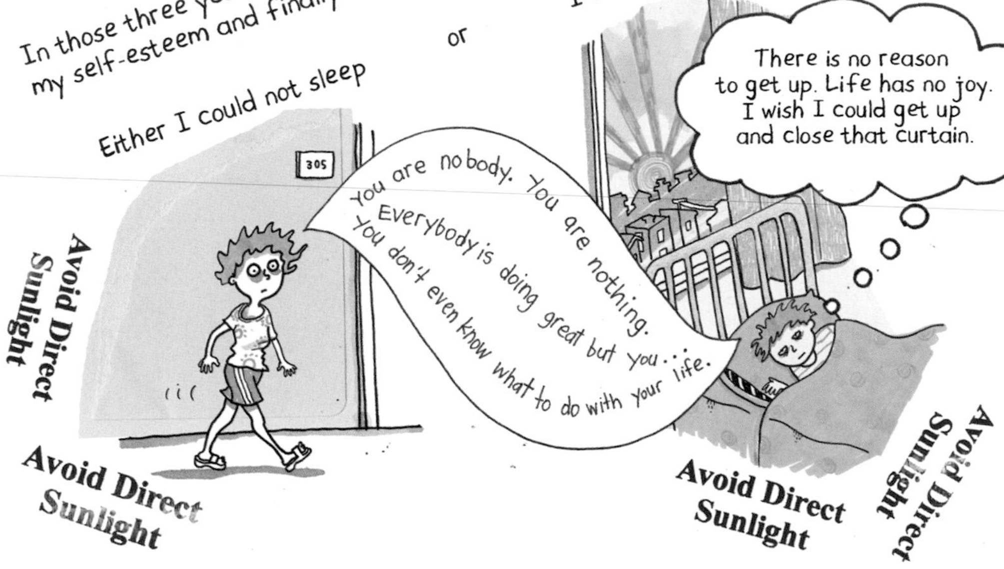
305
You are nobody. You are nothing.
Everybody is doing great but you . . .
You don't even know what to do with your life.
There is no reason to get up. Life has no joy. I wish I could get up and close that curtain.
Avoid Direct Sunlight
Avoid Direct Sunlight
Avoid Direct Sunlight
Avoid Direct Sunlight

When I was able to get up I imagined having a button on my arm. I wanted to switch it off and disappear.

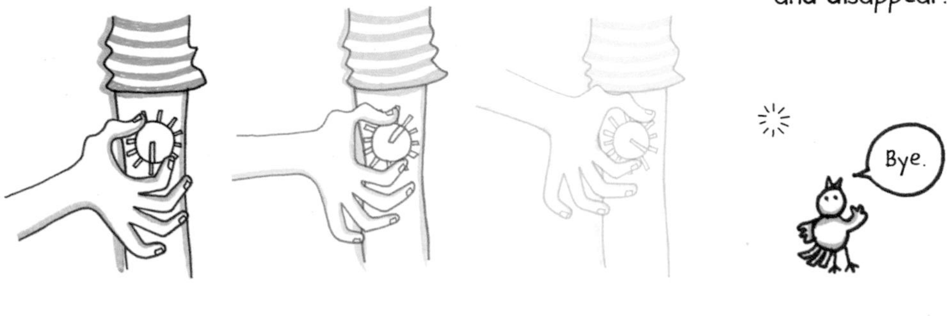
Bye.

Whenever I had energy I was edgy or angry . . .

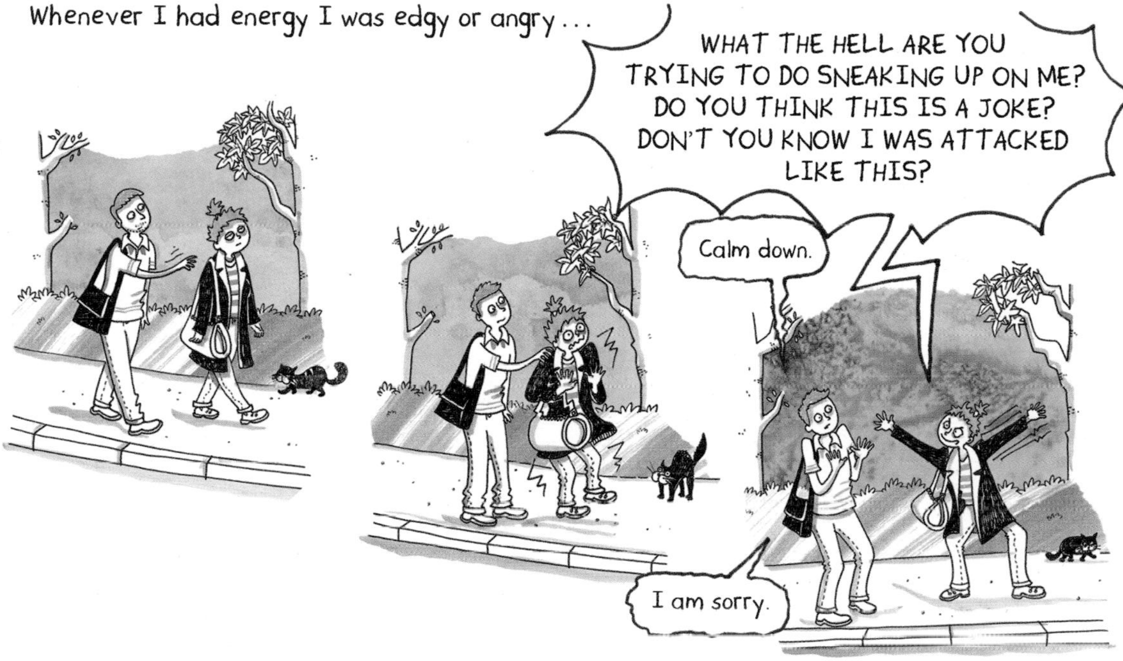
WHAT THE HELL ARE YOU TRYING TO DO SNEAKING UP ON ME? DO YOU THINK THIS IS A JOKE? DON'T YOU KNOW I WAS ATTACKED LIKE THIS?
Calm down.
I am sorry.

. . . or I stared at the TV and doodled.

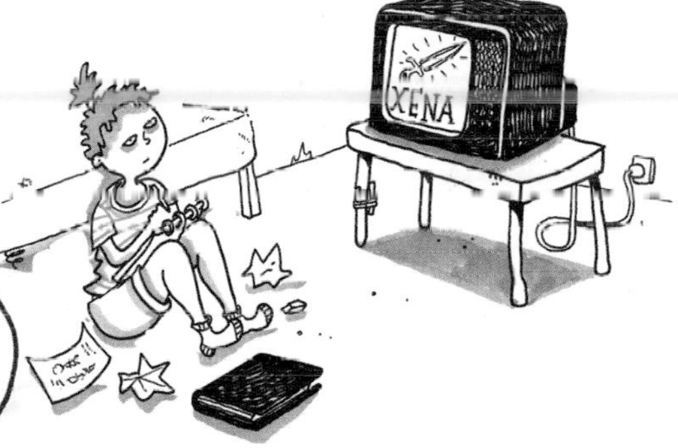
XENA

My poet-painter-performer sister was not happy either. I was not cut out to be a mathematician. She was not cut out to be a computer engineer.

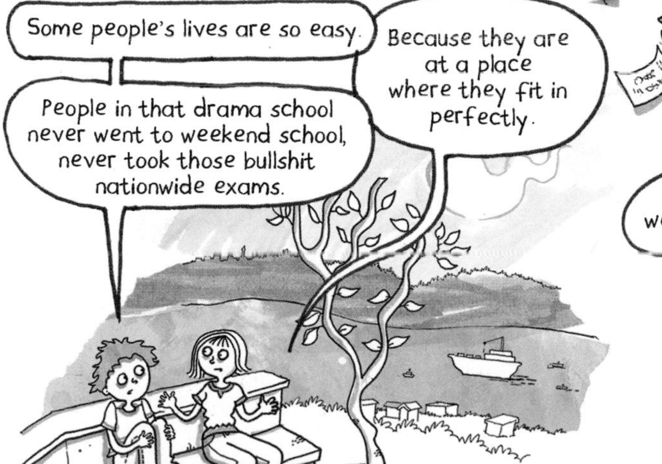
Some people's lives are so easy.
People in that drama school never went to weekend school, never took those bullshit nationwide exams.
Because they are at a place where they fit in perfectly.
After graduation she started working in a bank.

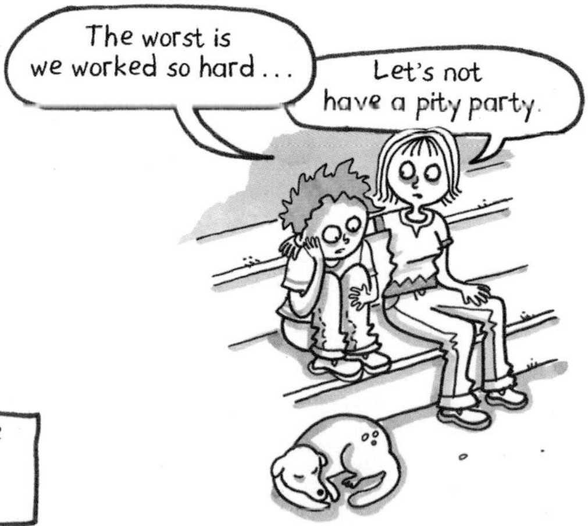
The worst is we worked so hard . . .
Let's not have a pity party.

Neither my sister nor my friends would let me off the hook.
My friends took action. Özlem tutored me two days a week.

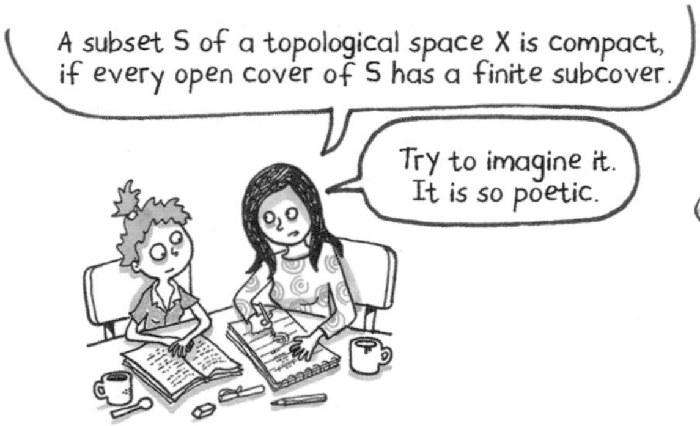
A subset S of a topological space X is compact, if every open cover of S has a finite subcover.
Try to imagine it. It is so poetic.

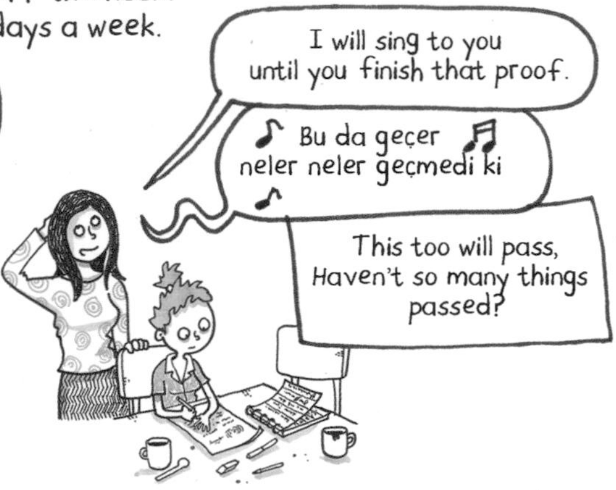
I will sing to you until you finish that proof.
Bu da geçer neler neler geçmedi ki
This too will pass, Haven't so many things passed?

Some weekends Arkadaş invited me to his parents' home and he tutored me.

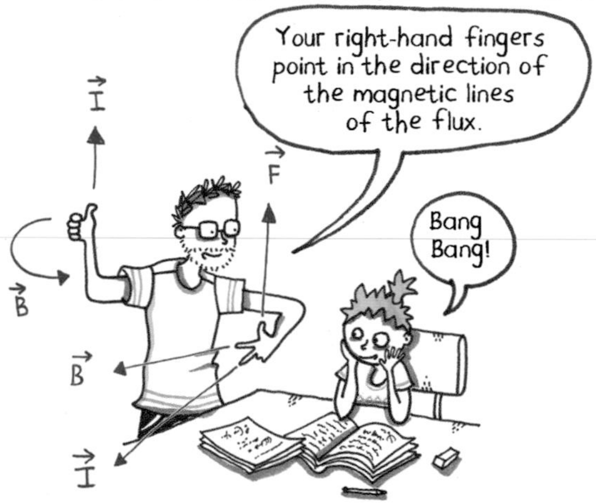
Your right-hand fingers point in the direction of the magnetic lines of the flux.
Bang Bang!

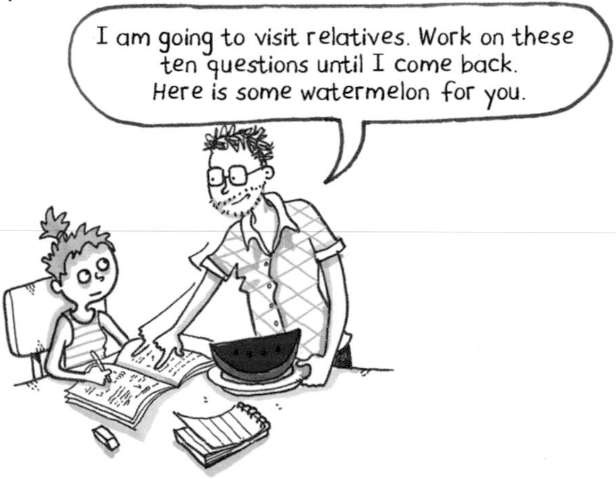
I am going to visit relatives. Work on these ten questions until I come back. Here is some watermelon for you.

Since I did not graduate on time
I was not allowed to stay in the dorm.
My sister and I rented a cheap
apartment with no heat in Istanbul.

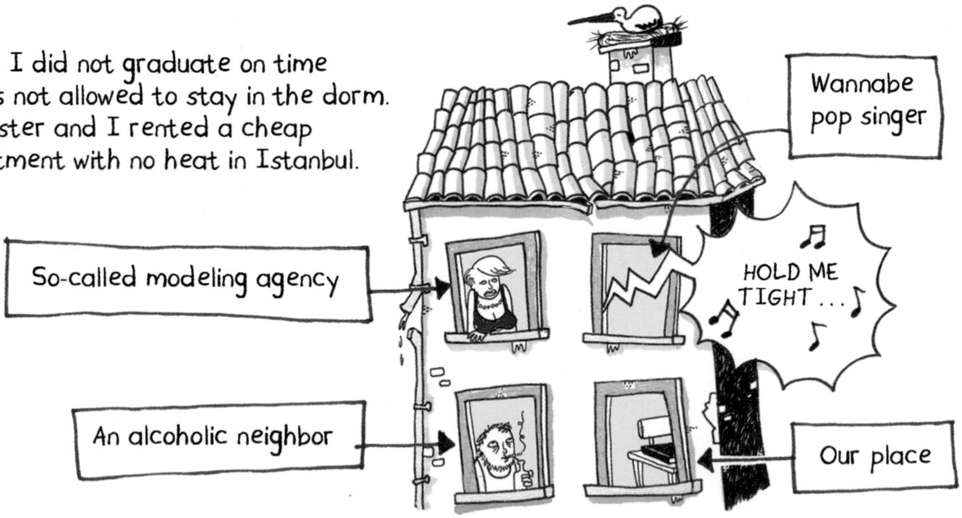
Wannabe pop singer
HOLD ME TIGHT . . .
So-called modeling agency
An alcoholic neighbor
Our place

My friend Nalan and I were taking the same courses and we studied together almost every day.

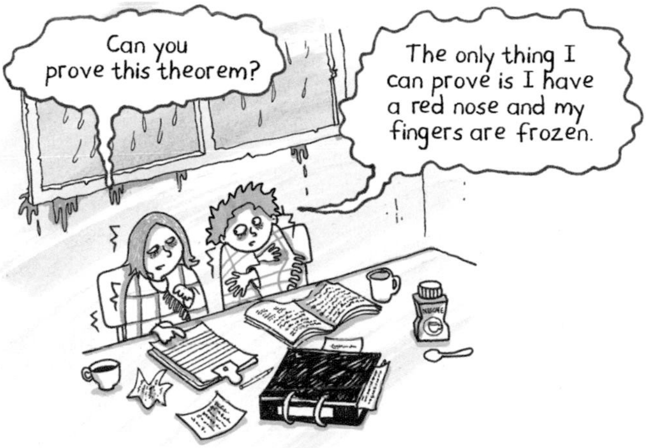
Can you prove this theorem?
The only thing I can prove is I have a red nose and my fingers are frozen.

Two years after my friends graduated I only needed one last elective course to graduate.

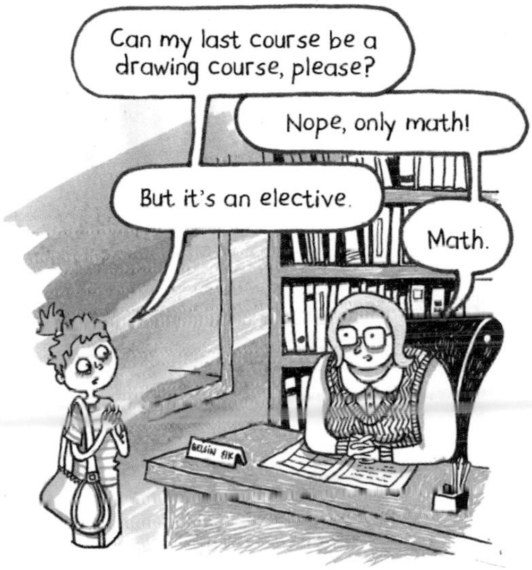
Can my last course be a drawing course, please?
Nope, only math!
But it's an elective.
Math.

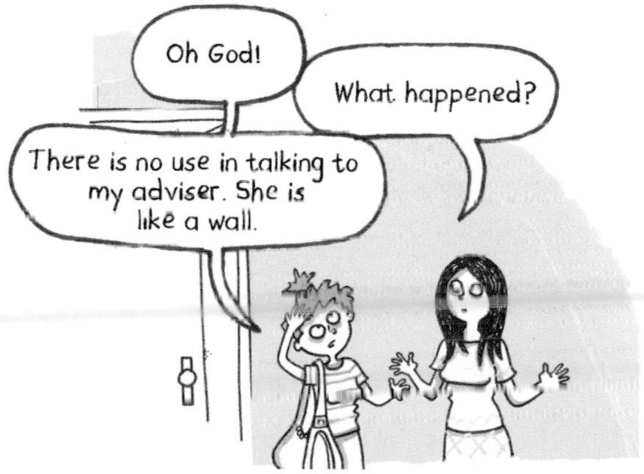
Oh God!
What happened?
There is no use in talking to my adviser. She is like a wall.

Özlem and I crashed on a bench.

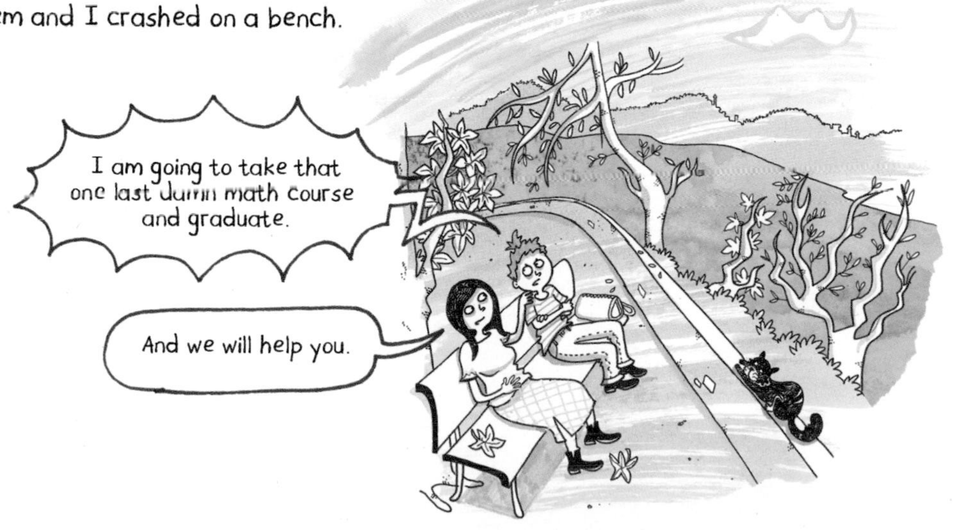
I am going to take that one last damn math course and graduate.
And we will help you.

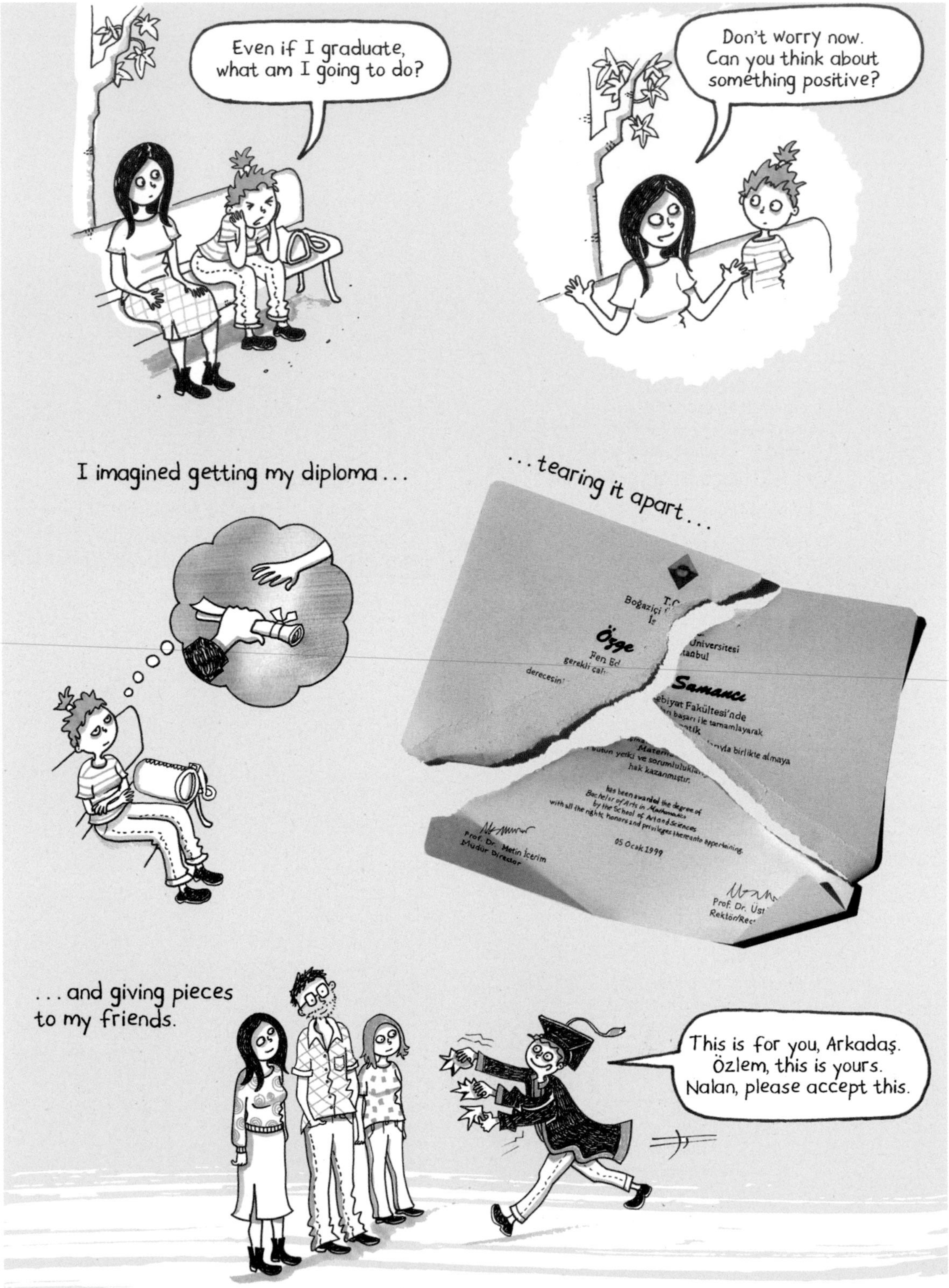
Even if I graduate, what am I going to do?
Don't worry now. Can you think about something positive?
I imagined getting my diploma . . .
. . . tearing it apart . . .
. . . and giving pieces to my friends.
This is for you, Arkadaş. Özlem, this is yours. Nalan, please accept this.

Chapter 15

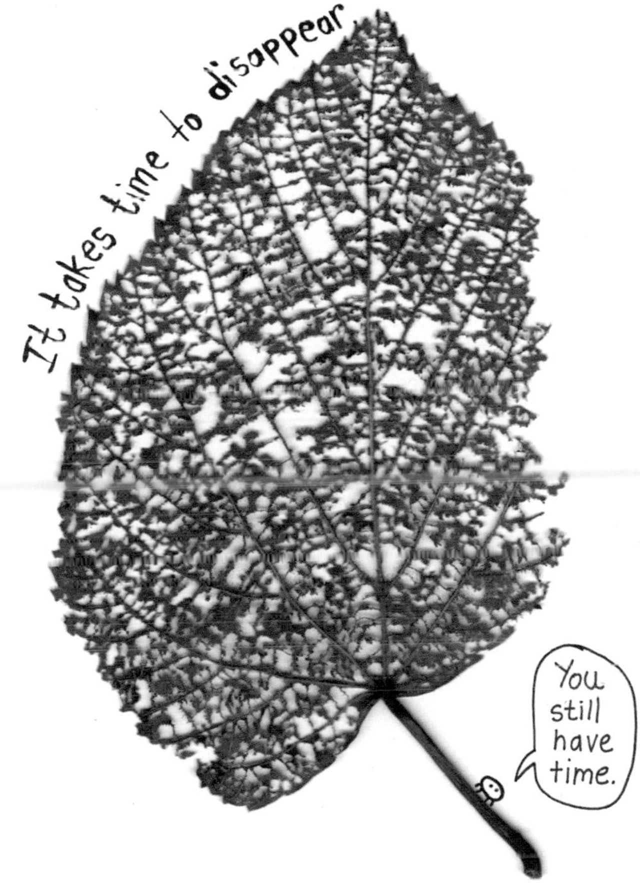
It takes time to disappear.
You still have time.

Beginning

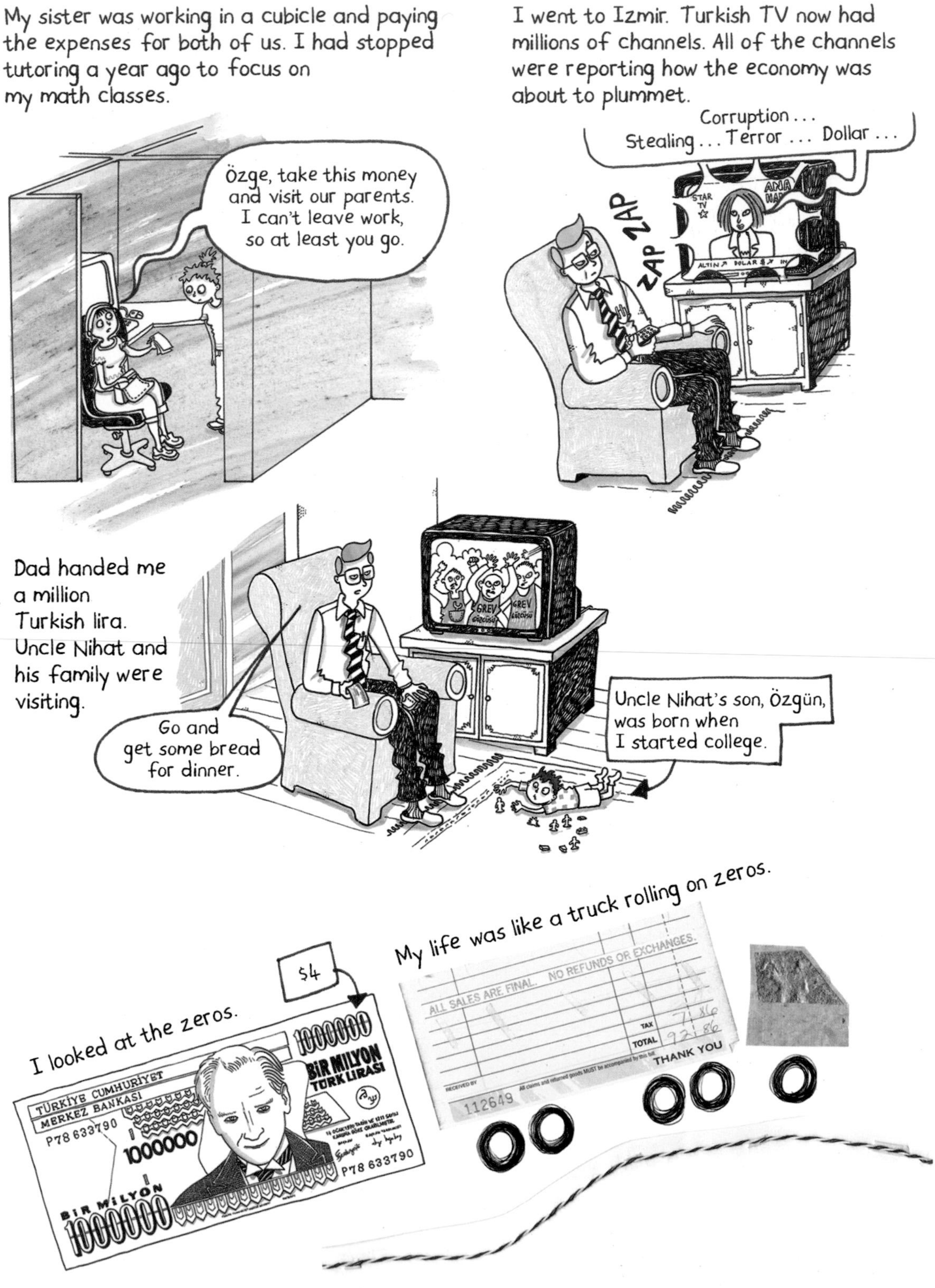
My sister was working in a cubicle and paying the expenses for both of us. I had stopped tutoring a year ago to focus on my math classes.
Özge, take this money and visit our parents. I can't leave work, so at least you go.
I went to Izmir. Turkish TV now had millions of channels. All of the channels were reporting how the economy was about to plummet.
Corruption . . . Stealing . . . Terror . . . Dollar . . .
STAR TV
ZAP ZAP ZAP
Dad handed me a million Turkish lira. Uncle Nihat and his family were visiting.
GREV
GREV
Go and get some bread for dinner.
Uncle Nihat's son, Özgün, was born when I started college.
I looked at the zeros.
$4
TÜRKİYE CUMHURİYET MERKEZ BANKASI
BİR MİLYON TÜRK LİRASI
1000000
P78 633790
My life was like a truck rolling on zeros.
ALL SALES ARE FINAL. NO REFUNDS OR EXCHANGES.
TAX 7.86
TOTAL 92.86
THANK YOU
112649

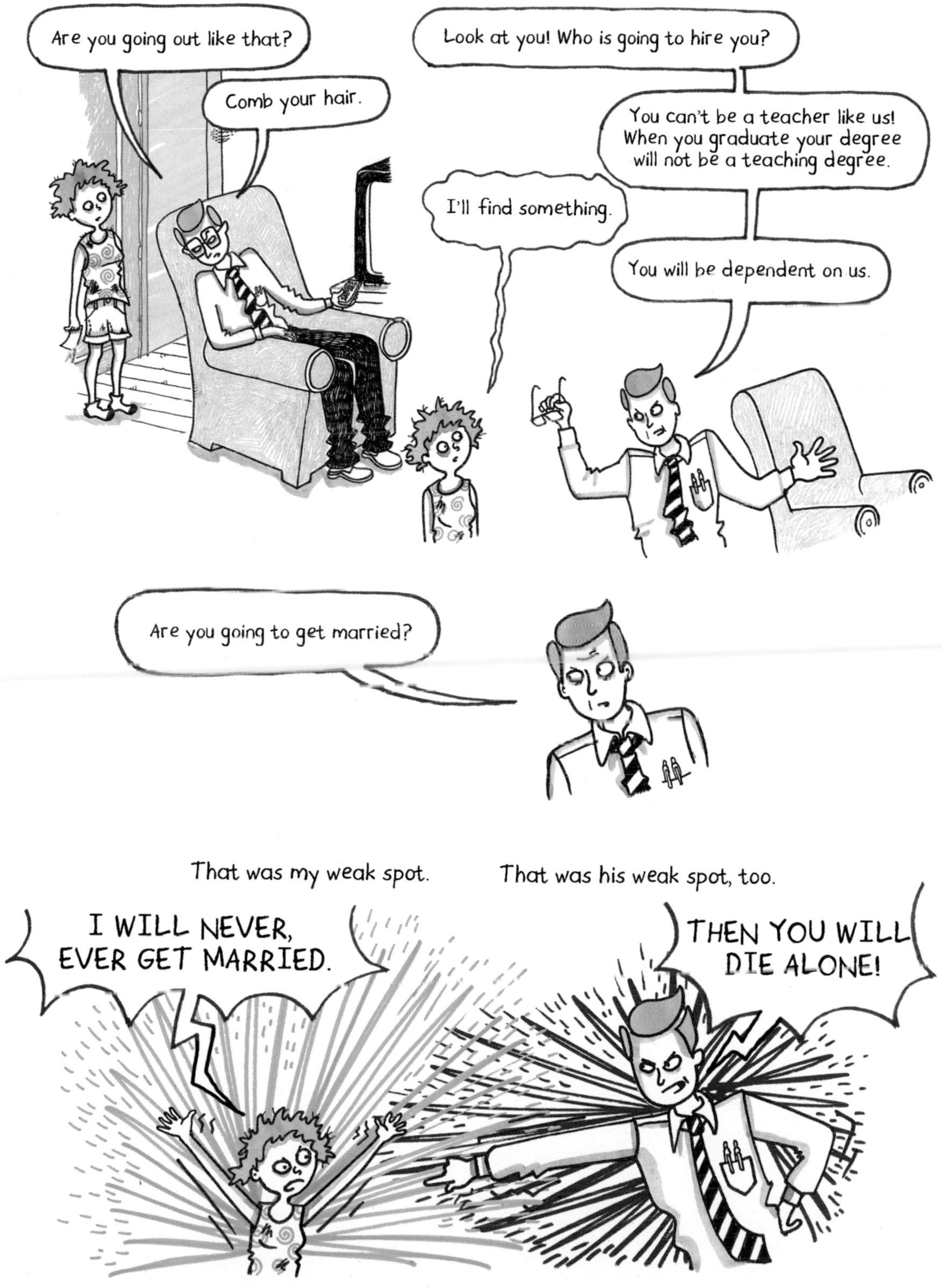
Are you going out like that?
Comb your hair.
Look at you! Who is going to hire you?
I'll find something.
You can't be a teacher like us! When you graduate your degree will not be a teaching degree.
You will be dependent on us.
Are you going to get married?
That was my weak spot.
That was his weak spot, too.
I WILL NEVER, EVER GET MARRIED.
THEN YOU WILL DIE ALONE!

I went to the grocery store and Mom came along.

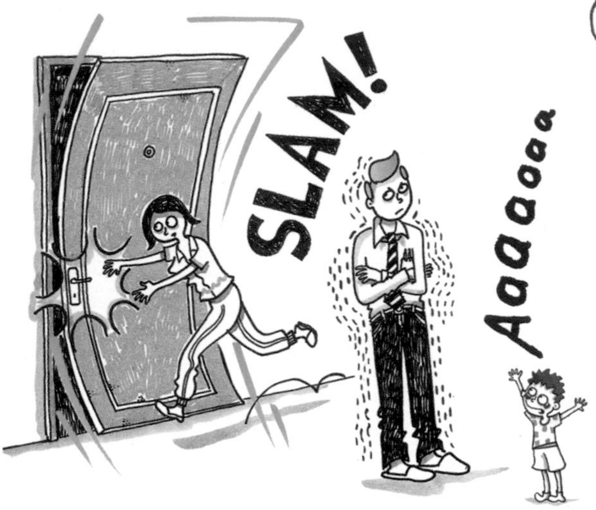
SLAM!
Aaaaaaa

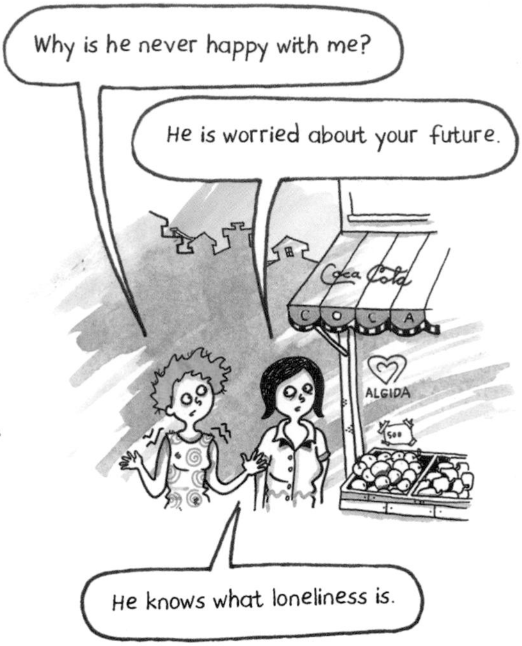
Why is he never happy with me?
He is worried about your future.
Coca Cola
COCA
ALGIDA
He knows what loneliness is.

After I came back from the store I hid in my old room. Mom was using it for sewing.

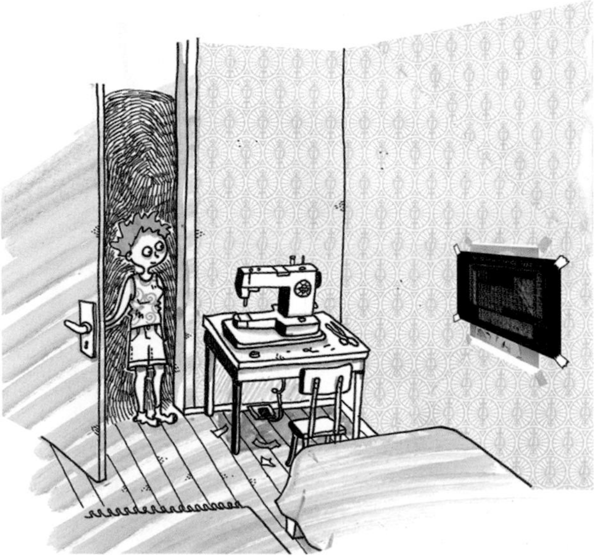

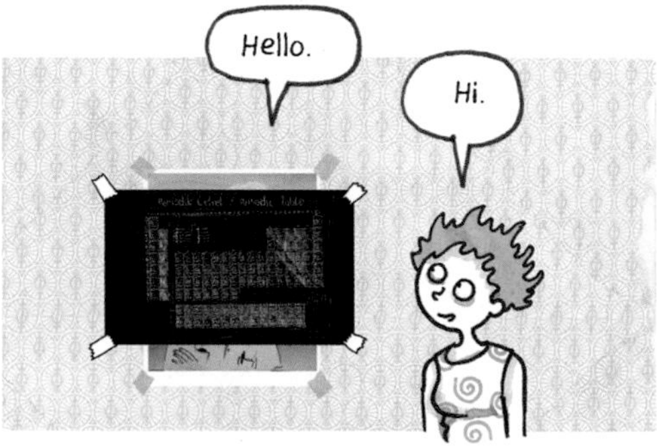
Hello.
Hi.

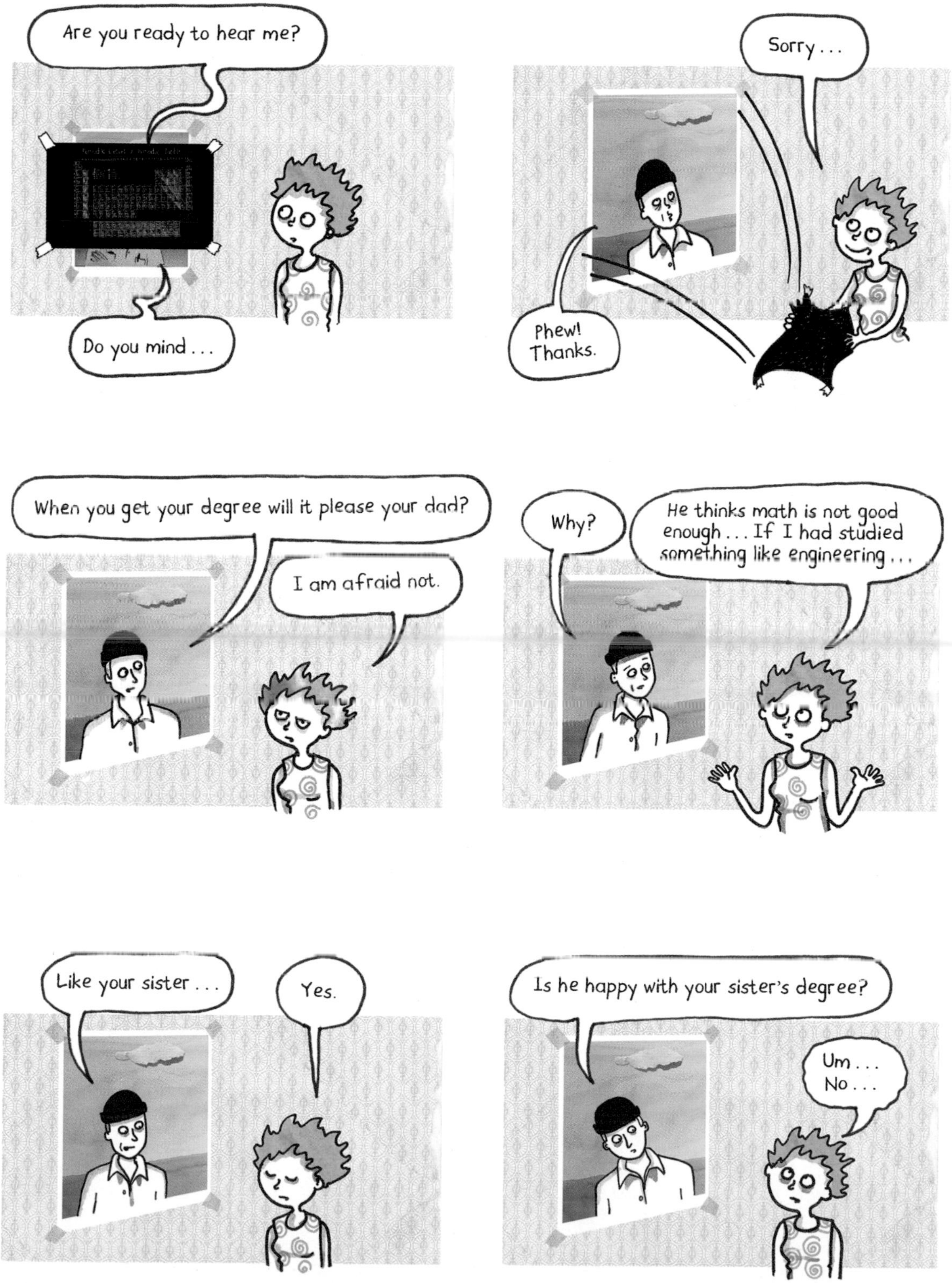
Are you ready to hear me?
Do you mind . . .
Sorry . . .
Phew! Thanks.
When you get your degree will it please your dad?
I am afraid not.
Why?
He thinks math is not good enough . . . If I had studied something like engineering . . .
Like your sister . . .
Yes.
Is he happy with your sister's degree?
Um . . . No . . .

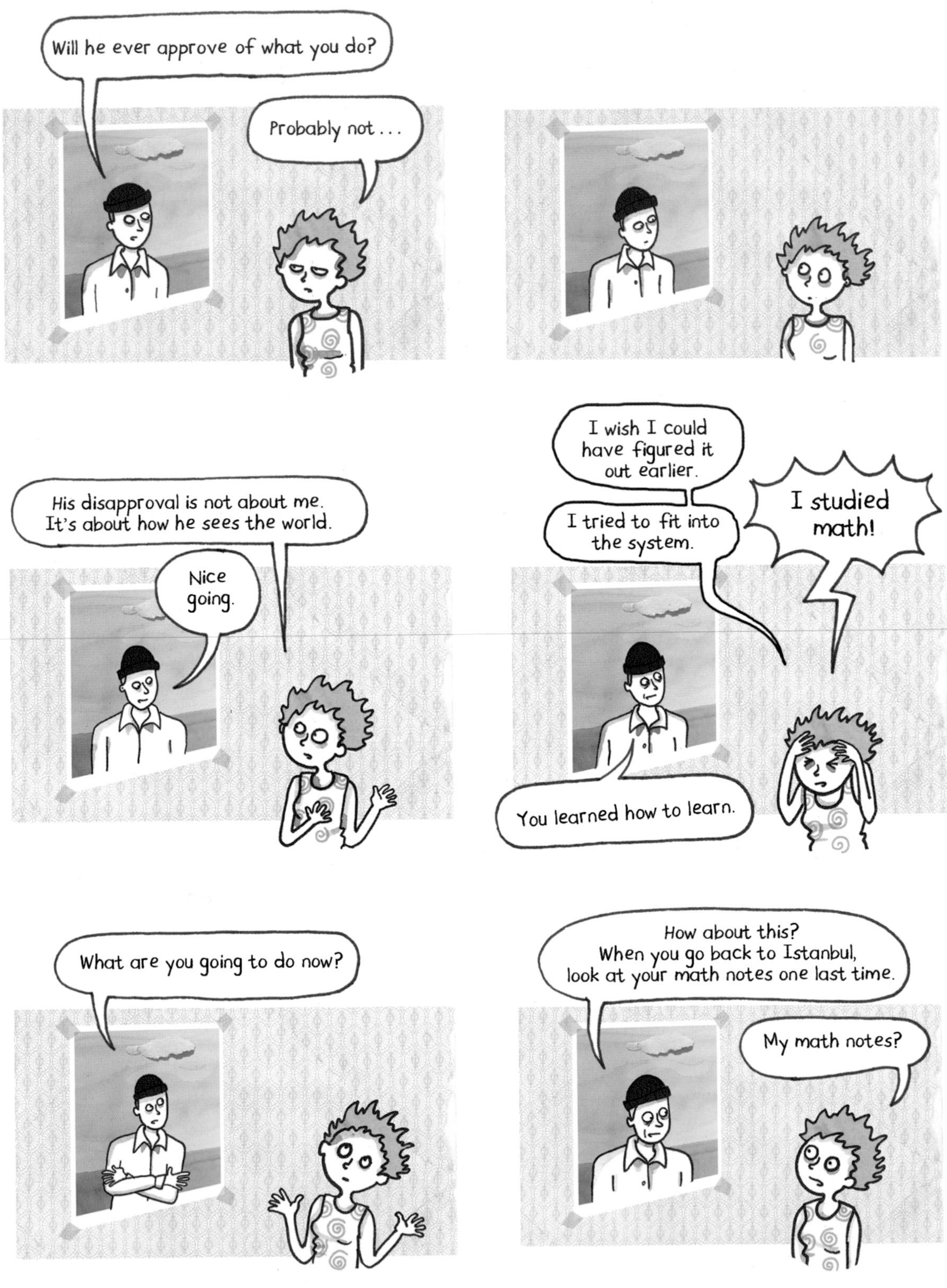
Will he ever approve of what you do?
Probably not . . .
His disapproval is not about me. It's about how he sees the world.
Nice going.
I wish I could have figured it out earlier.
I tried to fit into the system.
I studied math!
You learned how to learn.
What are you going to do now?
How about this? When you go back to Istanbul, look at your math notes one last time.
My math notes?

On the last day of my stay, Mom helped me make peace with my dad.

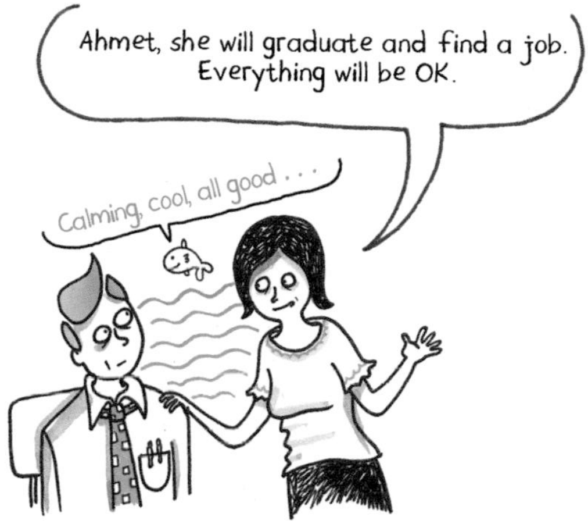
Ahmet, she will graduate and find a job. Everything will be OK.
Calming, cool, all good . . .

And they all said goodbye to me.

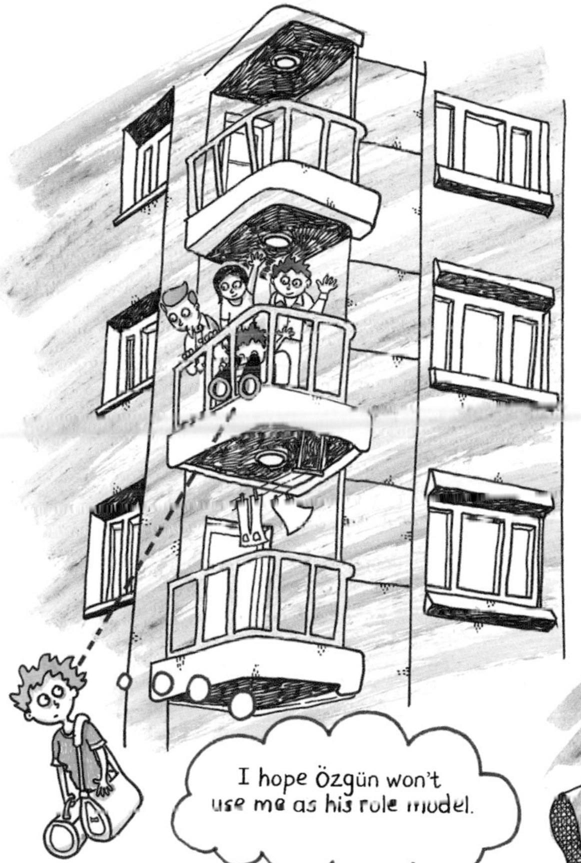
I hope Özgün won't use me as his role model.

On the bus, on my way back to Istanbul, I couldn't stop thinking.

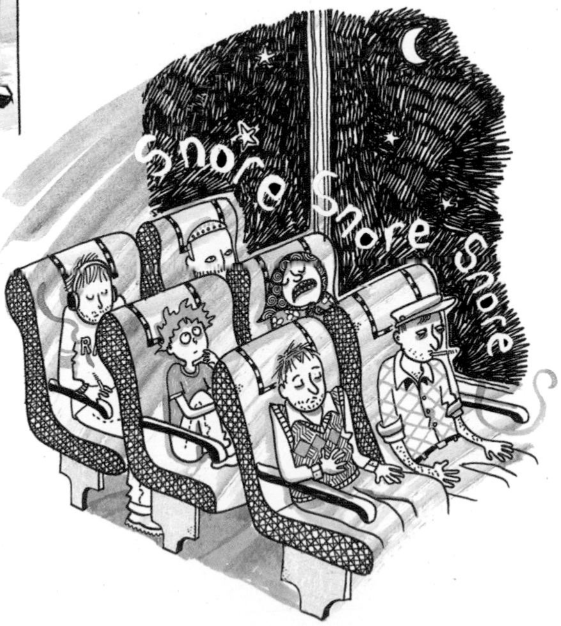
Snore Snore Snore Snore

A part of me was like my uncle . . .

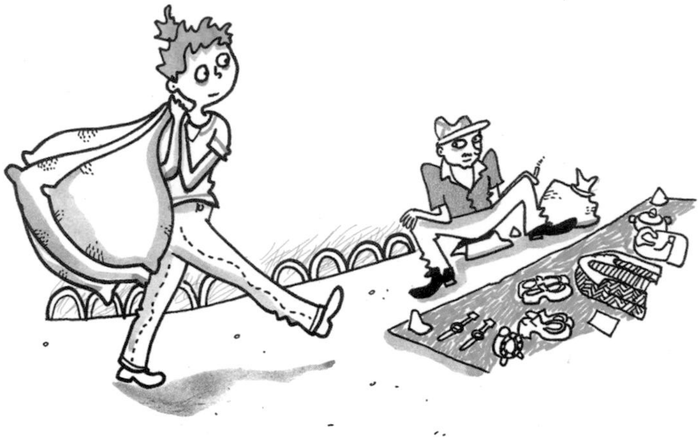

A part of me was like my dad . . .

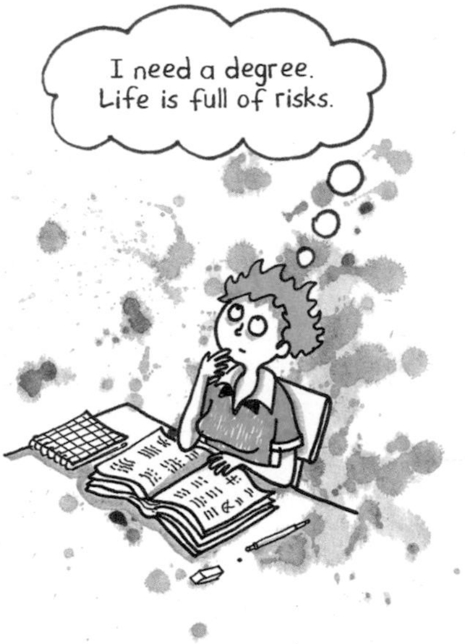
I need a degree.
Life is full of risks.

A part of me followed my sister . . .

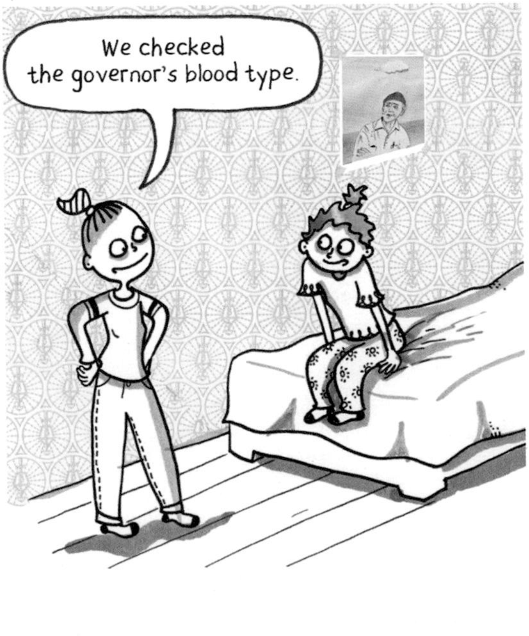
We checked the governor's blood type.

A part of me needed Mom's protection to deal with the world.

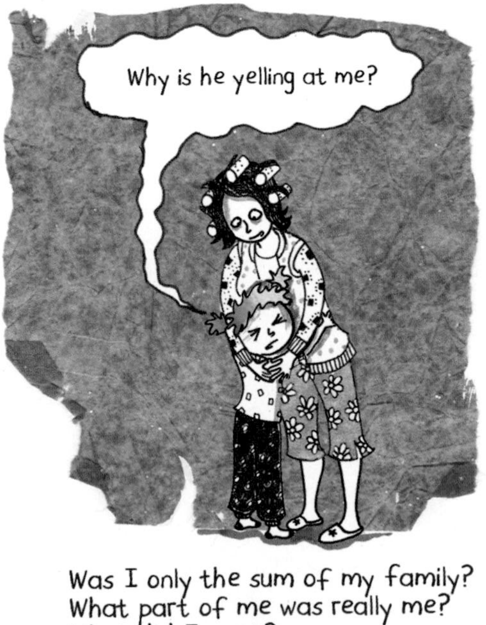
Why is he yelling at me?

Was I only the sum of my family?
What part of me was really me?
What did I want?

In the midst of the noise that I grew up with I could not hear my own voice.

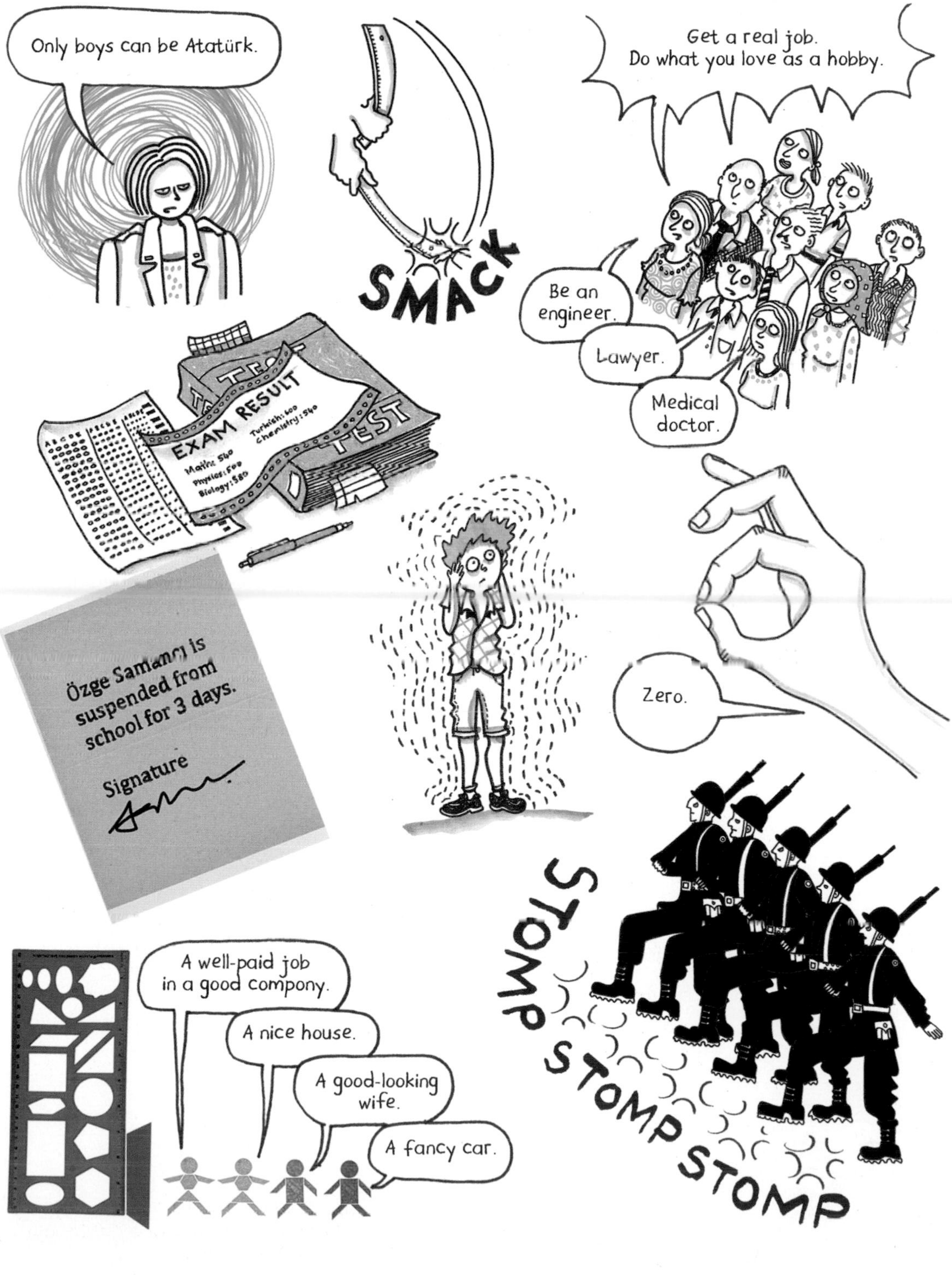

Only boys can be Atatürk.
SMACK
Get a real job.
Do what you love as a hobby.
Be an engineer.
Lawyer.
Medical doctor.
TEST
EXAM RESULT
Math: 540
Physics: 500
Biology: 580
Turkish: 600
Chemistry: 540
Özge Samanci is suspended from school for 3 days.
Signature
Zero.
STOMP STOMP STOMP STOMP
A well-paid job in a good compony.
A nice house.
A good-looking wife.
A fancy car.

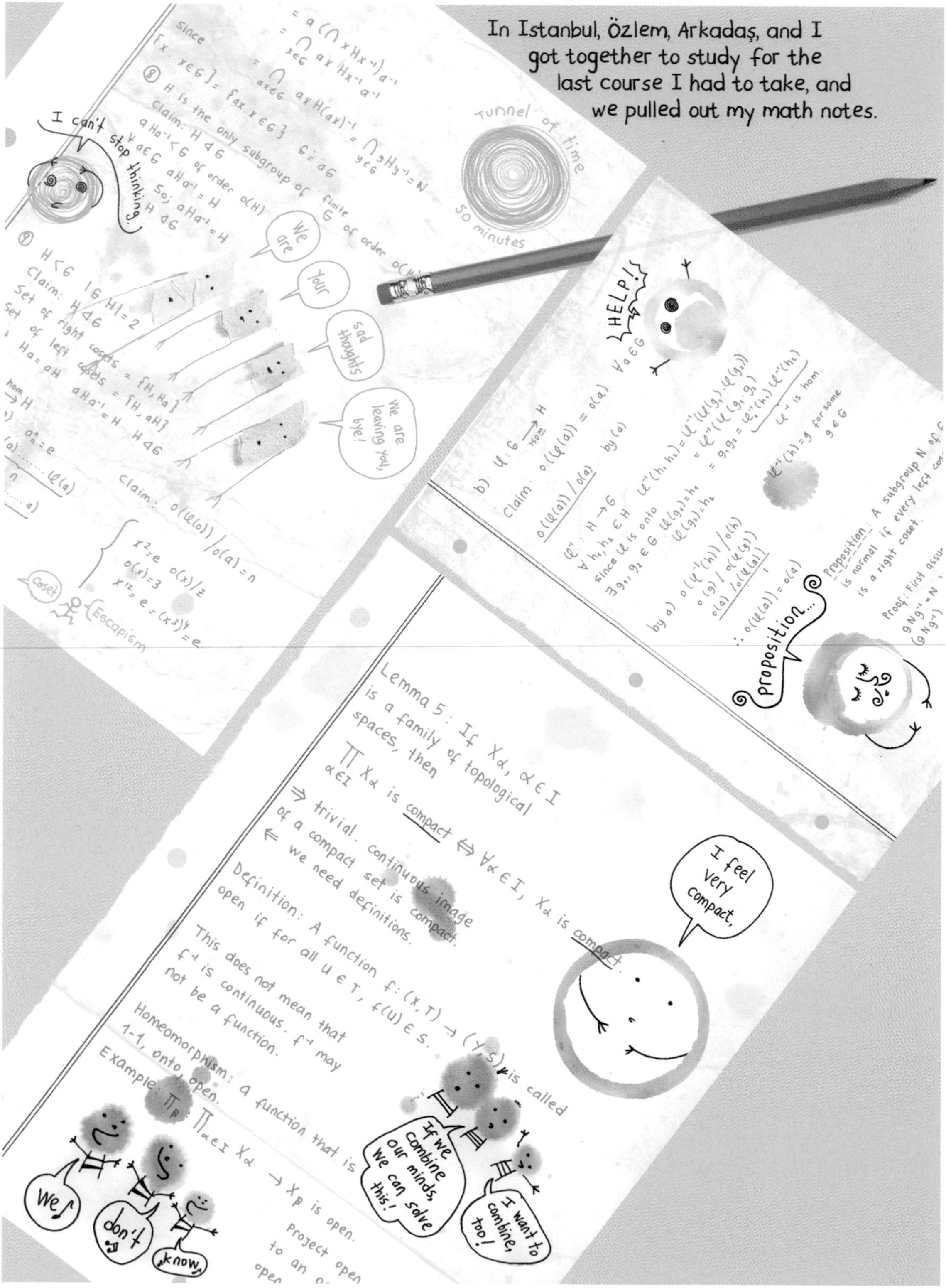

In Istanbul, Özlem, Arkadaş, and I got together to study for the last course I had to take, and we pulled out my math notes.
I can't stop thinking.
Tunnel of time
50 minutes
We are
your
sad thoughts
We are leaving you, bye!
HELP!
Coset
Escapism
Proposition...
I feel very compact.
If we combine our minds, we can solve this!
I want to combine, too!
We
don't
know.

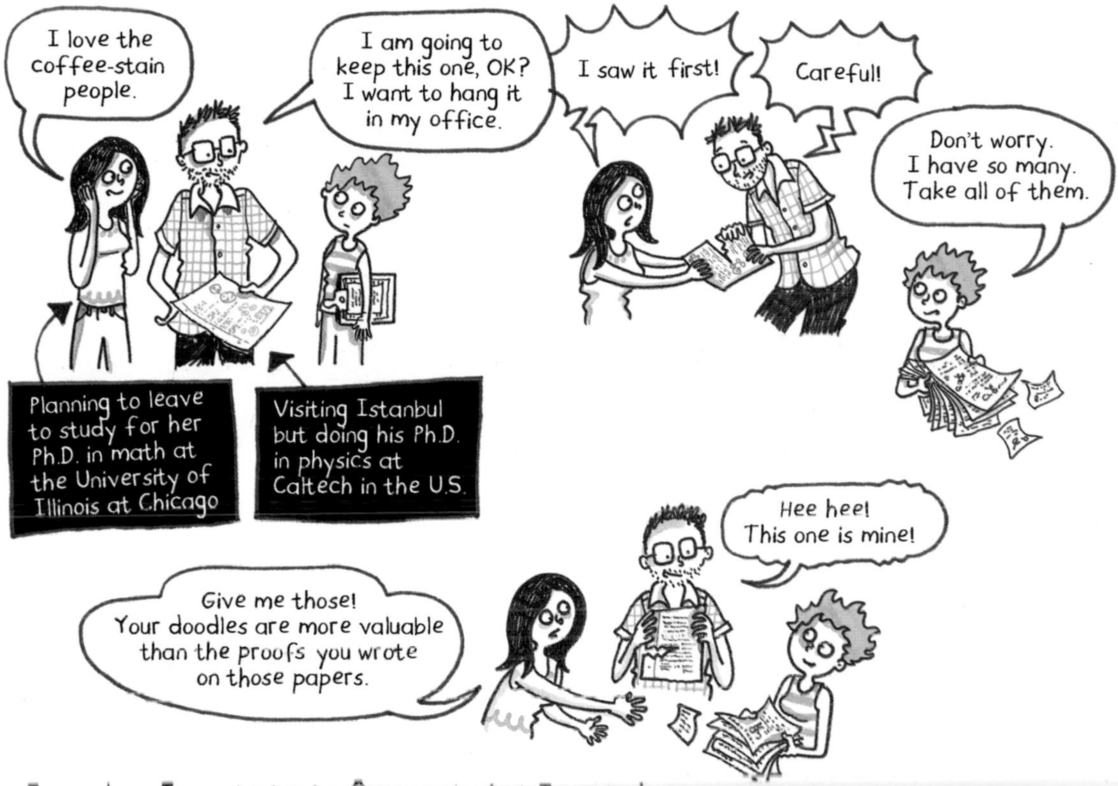
I love the coffee-stain people.
I am going to keep this one, OK? I want to hang it in my office.
Planning to leave to study for her Ph.D. in math at the University of Illinois at Chicago
Visiting Istanbul but doing his Ph.D. in physics at Caltech in the U.S.
I saw it first!
Careful!
Don't worry. I have so many. Take all of them.
Hee hee! This one is mine!
Give me those! Your doodles are more valuable than the proofs you wrote on those papers.

For so long I was trying to figure out what I wanted.

I have looked at the world with a purple and a red eye . . .

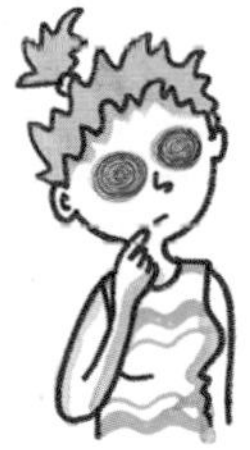

I have looked underwater . . .

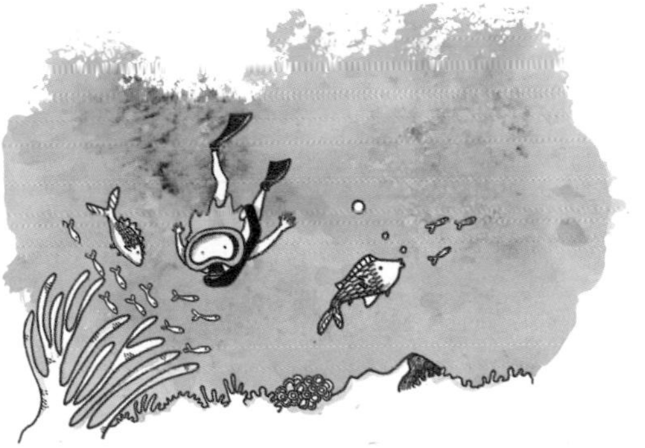

I have looked at the world of microorganisms . . .

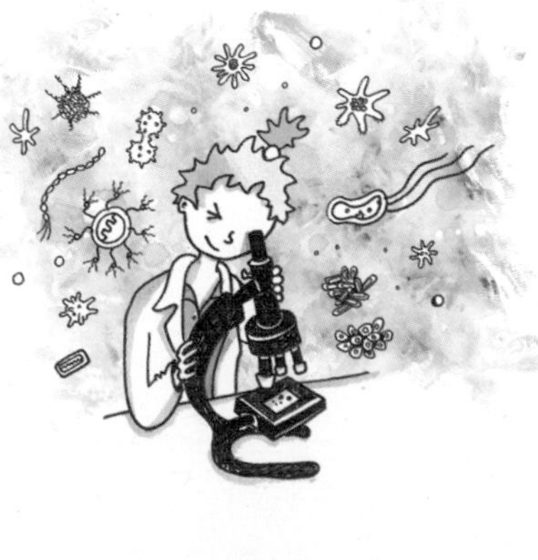

. . . and I have looked far, far away.

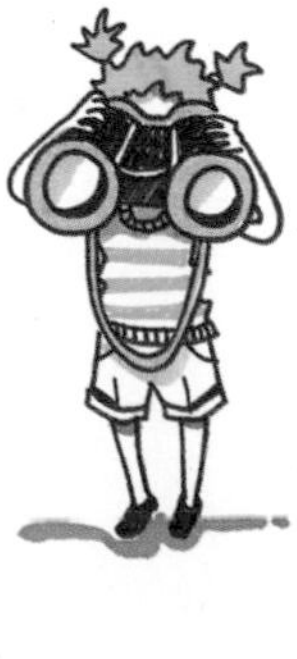

What I was looking for was right in front of me for many, many years.

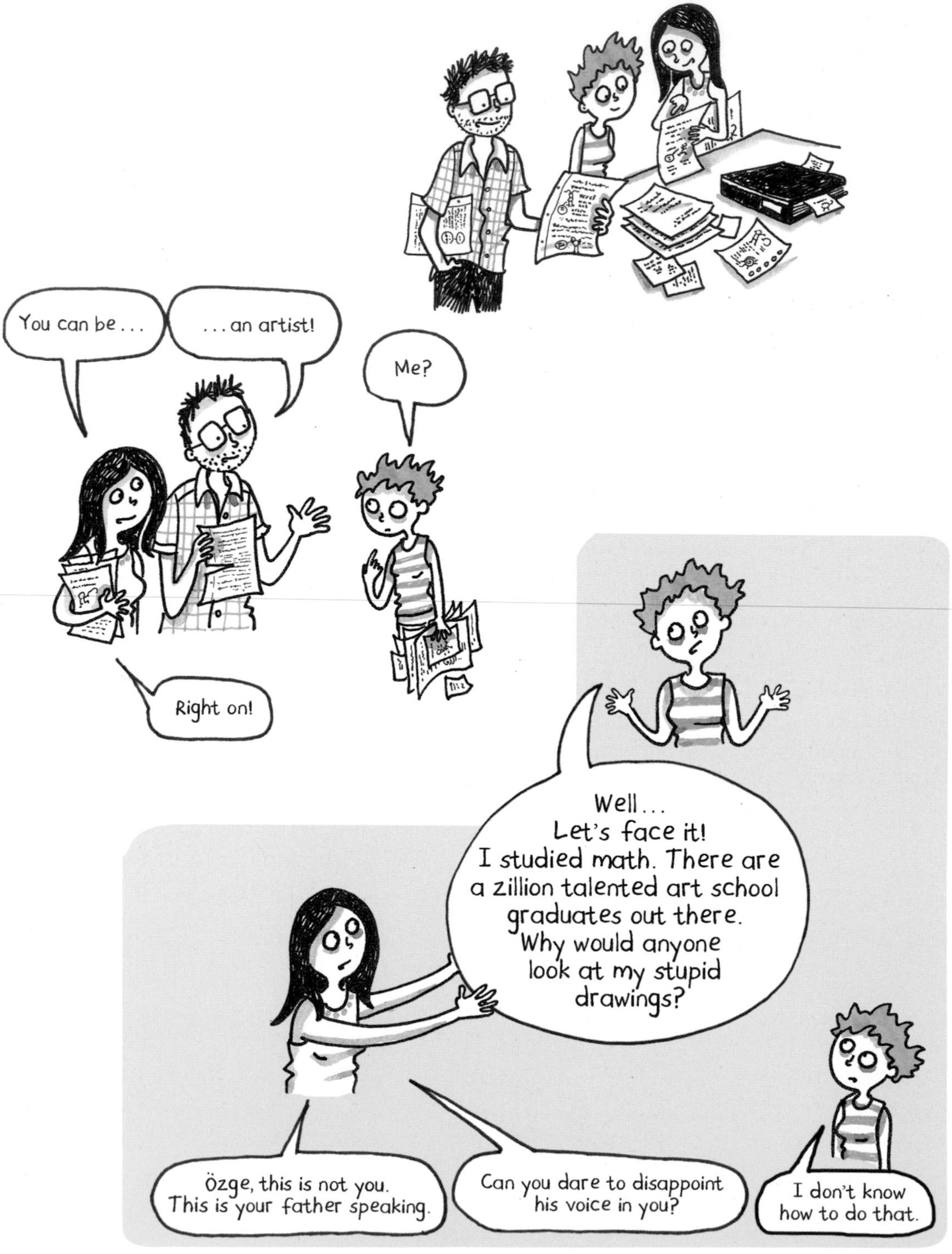
You can be . . .
. . . an artist!
Me?
Right on!
Well . . .
Let's face it!
I studied math. There are a zillion talented art school graduates out there.
Why would anyone look at my stupid drawings?
Özge, this is not you.
This is your father speaking.
Can you dare to disappoint his voice in you?
I don't know how to do that.

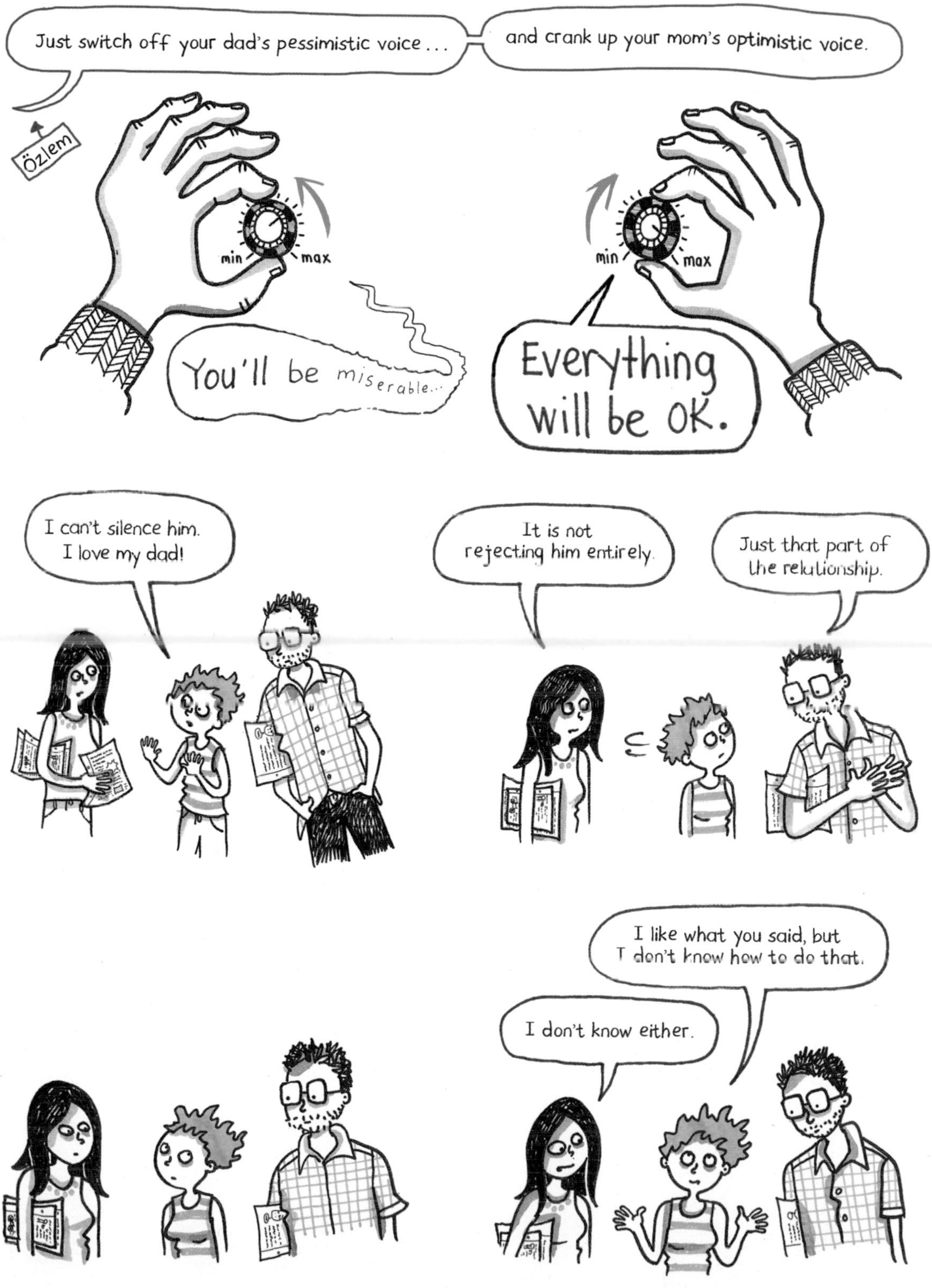
Just switch off your dad's pessimistic voice . . .
and crank up your mom's optimistic voice.
Özlem
min
max
You'll be miserable...
min
max
Everything will be OK.
I can't silence him. I love my dad!
It is not rejecting him entirely.
Just that part of the relationship.
I like what you said, but I don't know how to do that.
I don't know either.

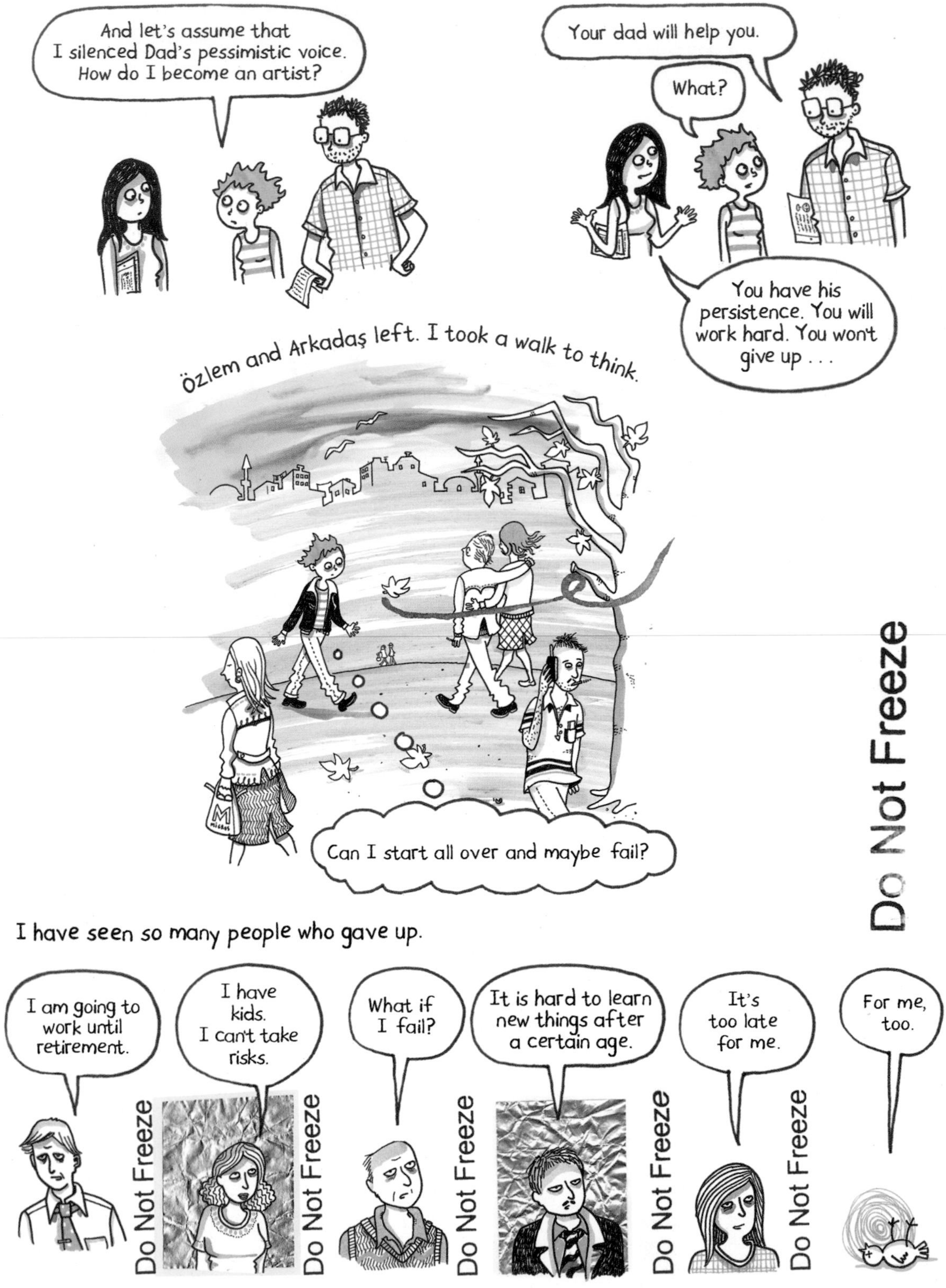
And let's assume that I silenced Dad's pessimistic voice. How do I become an artist?
Your dad will help you.
What?
You have his persistence. You will work hard. You won't give up . . .
Özlem and Arkadaş left. I took a walk to think.
Can I start all over and maybe fail?
Do Not Freeze
I have seen so many people who gave up.
I am going to work until retirement.
Do Not Freeze
I have kids. I can't take risks.
Do Not Freeze
What if I fail?
Do Not Freeze
It is hard to learn new things after a certain age.
Do Not Freeze
It's too late for me.
Do Not Freeze
For me, too.

Maybe Captain Cousteau was right. I had learned how to learn by studying mathematics.

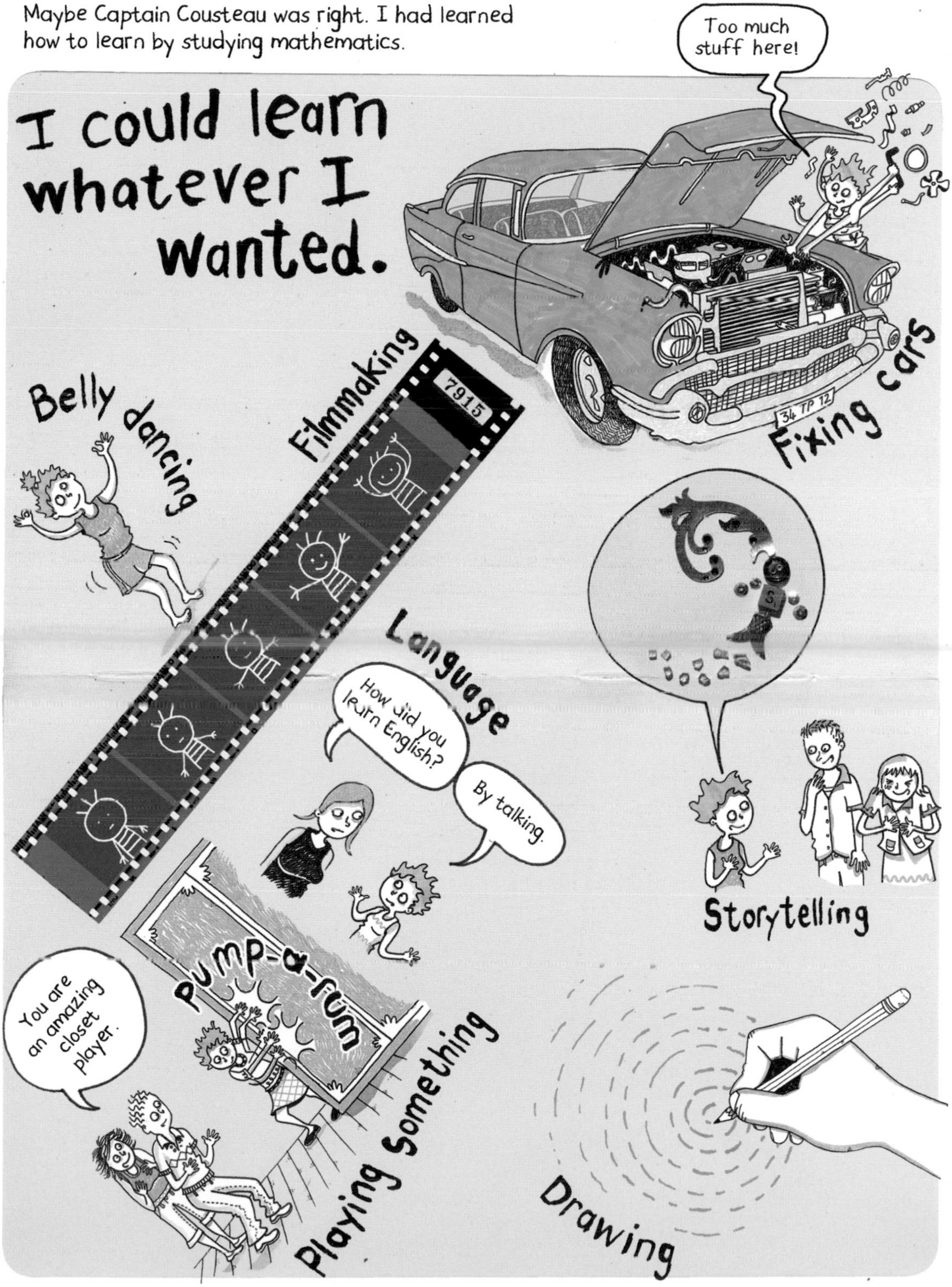

Too much stuff here!
I could learn whatever I wanted.
Fixing cars
34 TP 12
Belly dancing
Filmmaking
7915
Language
How did you learn English?
By talking.
Storytelling
Pump-a-rum
You are an amazing closet player.
Playing Something
Drawing

Even if I failed, life would keep bringing opportunities.

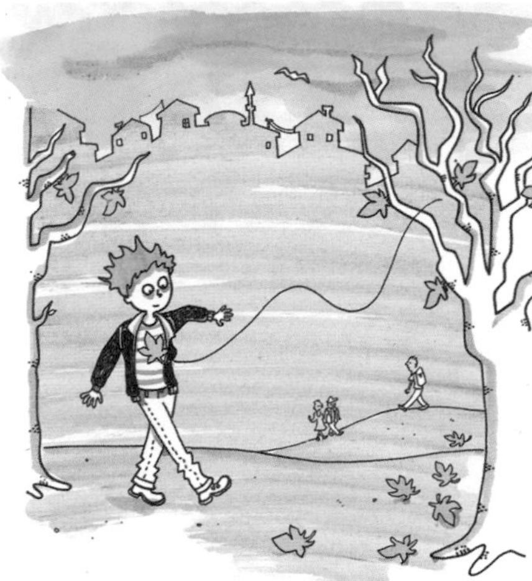

I knew well...

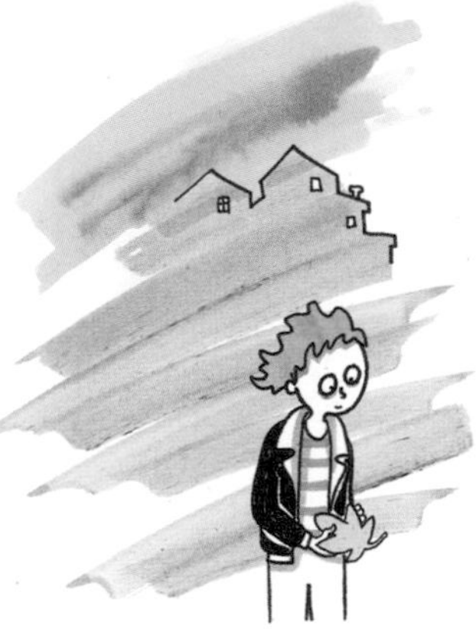

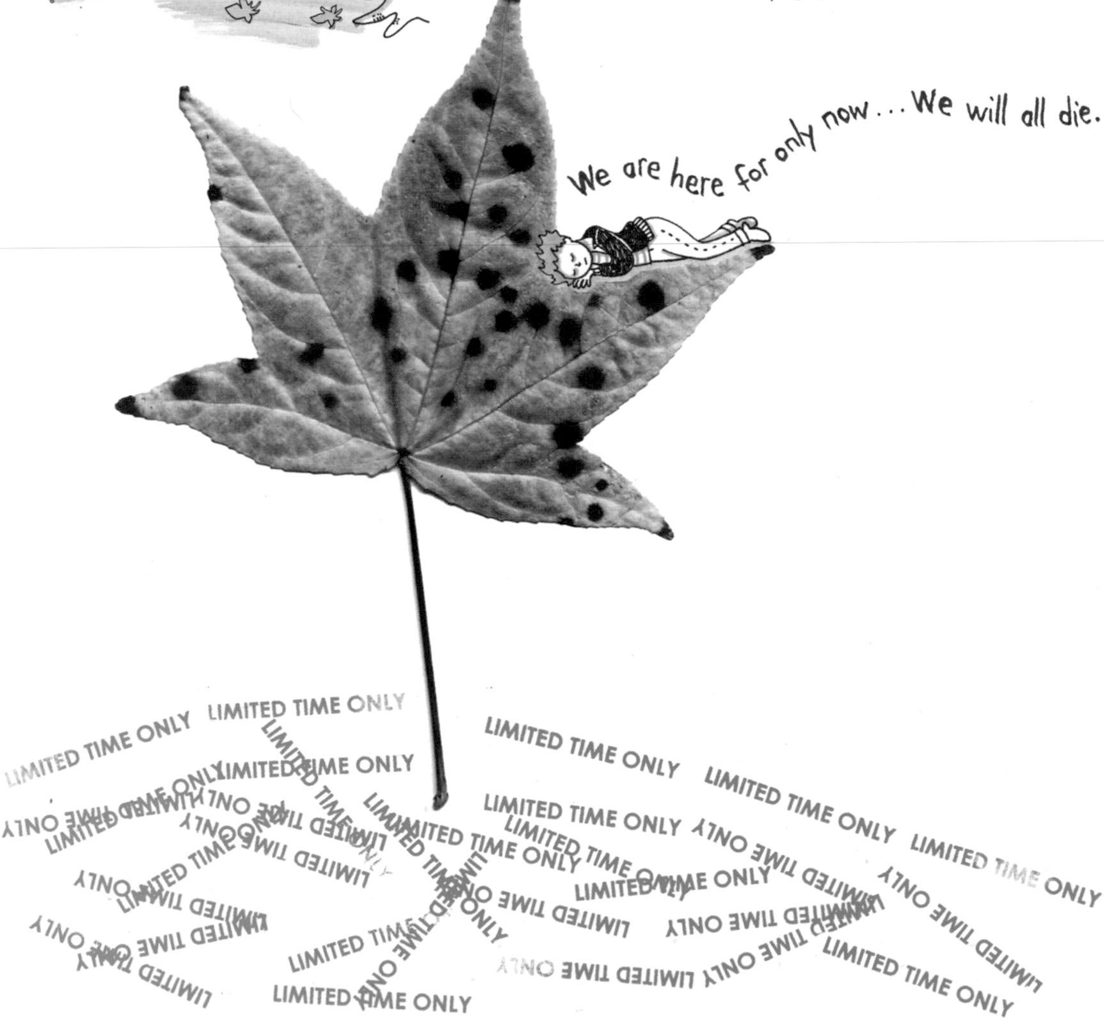
We are here for only now... We will all die.
LIMITED TIME ONLY

I had to do what I love to do, even if it was against the expectations of the people I love.

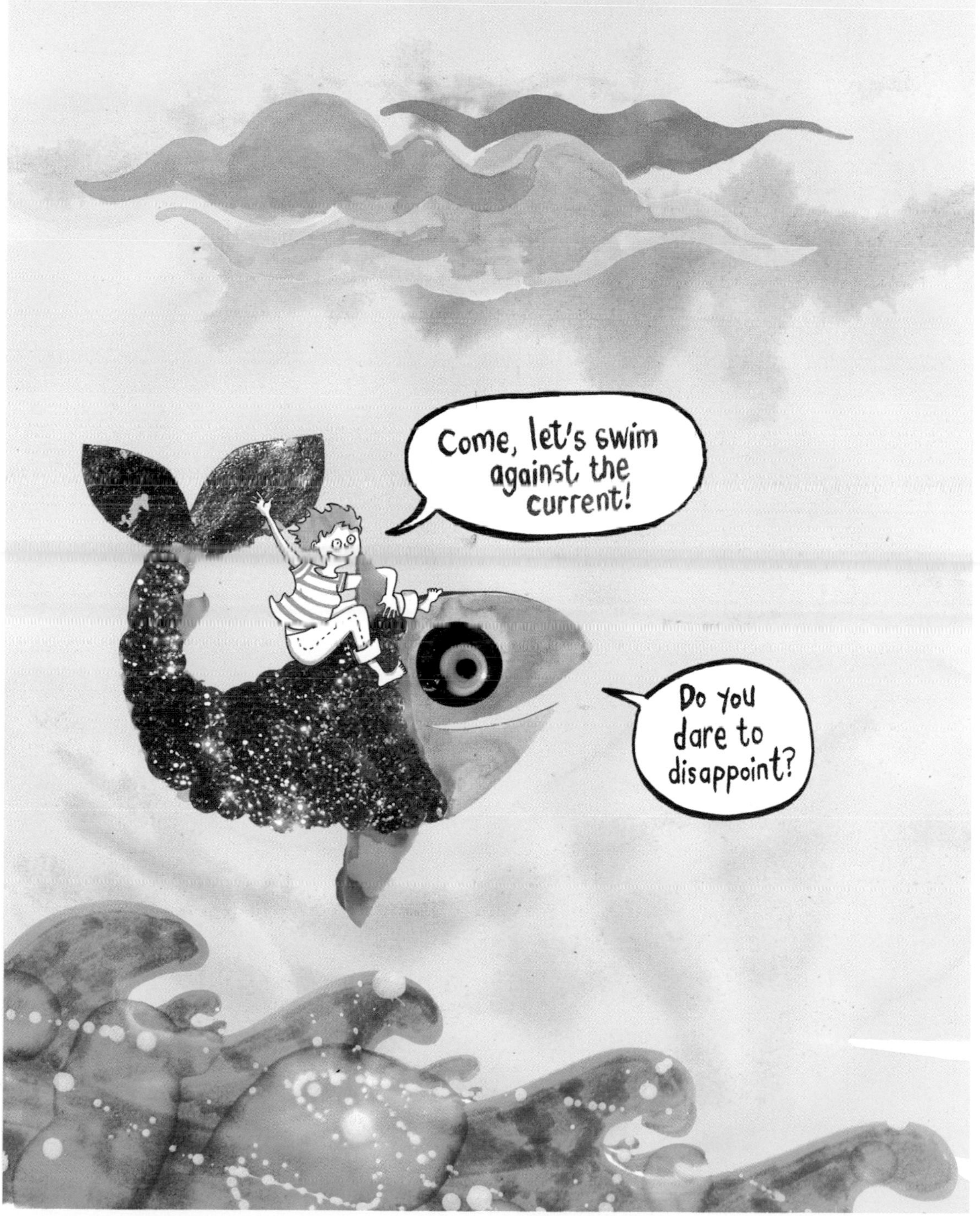
Come, let's swim against the current!
Do you dare to disappoint?

Special Thanks ♥♥

Shirley Adams, Margaret Ferguson, Jason Yarn, Jill Barber, Tuna Erdem, Lauren Berlant, Özlem Beyarslan, Arkadaş Özakın, Seda Ergül, Müsemma Sabancıoğlu, Jill Fantauzza, Meltem Gürle, Muhittin Mungan, Zeynep Dadak, Nihat Tüfenkçi, Derya Özkan, Feride Çiçekoğlu, Serazer Pekerman, Evren Savcı, Gözde Onaran